RESULTING TRUSTS

Resulting Trusts

ROBERT CHAMBERS

CLARENDON PRESS · OXFORD
1997

Oxford University Press, Walton Street, Oxford OX2 6DP
Oxford New York
Athens Auckland Bangkok Bogota Bombay
Buenos Aires Calcutta Cape Town Dar es Salaam
Delhi Florence Hong Kong Istanbul Karachi
Kuala Lumpur Madras Madrid Melbourne
Mexico City Nairobi Paris Singapore
Taipei Tokyo Toronto
and associated companies in
Berlin Ibadan

Oxford is a trade mark of Oxford University Press

Published in the United States by
Oxford University Press Inc., New York

British Library Cataloguing in Publication Data
Data available

Library of Congress Cataloging in Publication Data
Chambers, Robert, lecturer in law.
Resulting trusts / Robert Chambers.
p. cm.
Includes bibliographical references and index.
1. Resulting trusts—Great Britain. 2. Resulting trusts.
I. Title.
KD1485.C48 1997
346.4105'9—dc21 96–54803
ISBN 0–19–876444–8

1 3 5 7 9 10 8 6 4 2

Typeset by Graphicraft Typesetters Ltd., Hong Kong
Printed in Great Britain by
Biddles Ltd., Guildford and King's Lynn

Preface

This book grew out of an Oxford D.Phil. thesis researched and written from 1993 to 1995. It has been revised for publication twice. The first 'final' typescript was delivered to Oxford University Press in May 1996: two weeks before the House of Lords decided *Westdeutsche Landesbank Girozentrale* v. *Islington London Borough Council*. The unexpected overruling of *Sinclair* v. *Brougham* necessitated extensive revisions, which were completed in November 1996.

This book would not have been written but for my supervisor, Professor Peter Birks. I arrived in Oxford wanting to research the problems associated with trusts which provide restitution of unjust enrichment. Being Canadian, I assumed that this would centre on the constructive trust. Professor Birks' essay, 'Restitution and Resulting Trusts', proved to be an important turning point for me and the inspiration for this book. I owe an enormous debt of gratitude to Peter Birks for his kindness and wisdom.

Of course, there are many others who have contributed to the completion of this project. Chief among them are my dear wife, Carol, and our two sons, Tom and Nigel. It is no small task to leave family, friends, home and school and I will always be grateful for their sacrifice, patience and encouragement throughout. Our adventure was made a great deal easier thanks to the support from family and friends in Alberta and the kindness we met in Oxford. I am thankful to everyone who assisted us, but mostly to my parents, Tom and Lenore Chambers.

I would like to express my appreciation to some of the many people who provided help along the way. This book was written at a time when I leaned rather heavily on that support. Thank you to Dr. Michael Bryan, Dr. Steven and Janet Chambers, Joan Chambers, Dr. Andy and Debbie Dawson, Barbara Gardiner, Lawrence and Doris Guenette, Margaret Hatton, Dr. Huck-Ju Kwon and Hyeryung Ahn, Professor Moe Litman, Patrick Mealey, Dr. Ken and Libbie Mills, Claire Newman, Ken Oppel and Dr. Philippa Sheppard, Sir Francis Price Q.C. and Madam Justice Marguerite Trussler, David and Laura Riggs, Annette Ryan, Dr. Lionel Smith and Suzanne Gagnon, St. Peter's College and the University of Oxford.

Particular thanks are due to three Albertans whose advice and encouragement were instrumental to my going to Oxford: Dr. Mitchell McInnes, E. (Sonny) Mirth Q.C. and Professor Bruce Ziff. I would also like to thank Derek Davies and Simon Gardner for their helpful comments on my thesis proposal, my examiners, Professor Andrew Burrows and Jeffrey Hackney, for their kindness, and Richard Hart, Elissa Soave, Elizabeth Davison and everyone else at Oxford University Press who assisted with the production of this book.

I gratefully acknowledge the kind financial support from my parents, The Law Society of Alberta, the Committee of Vice-Chancellors and Principals of the United Kingdom, the Society of Public Teachers of Law and St. Peter's College.

Robert Chambers
27 January 1997

Contents

Table of Abbreviations

A.C. = Appeal Cases (Law Reports)
A.L.J.R. = Australian Law Journal Reports
A.L.R. = Australian Law Reports
A.R. = Alberta Reports (Canada)
Akron L.Rev. = Akron Law Review (USA)
All E.R. = All England Law Reports
All E.R.Rev. = All England Law Reports Annual Review
Alta.L.Rev. = Alberta Law Review (Canada)
App.Cas. = Appeal Cases (Law Reports)

B.C.L.C. = Butterworth Company Law Cases
Bank.&Fin.L.Rev. = Banking and Finance Law Review (Canada)
Bank.L.R. = Banking Law Reports

C.B.R. = Canadian Bar Review
C.L.J. = Cambridge Law Journal
C.L.P. = Current Legal Problems
C.L.R. = Commonwealth Law Reports (High Court of Australia)
Cal.L.Rev. = California Law Review (USA)
Can.Bus.L.J. = Canadian Business Law Journal
Ch. = Chancery (Law Reports)
Ch.App. = Chancery Appeal (Law Reports)
Ch.D. = Chancery Division (Law Reports)
Col.L.Rev. = Columbia Law Review (USA)
Conv. = Conveyancer and Property Lawyer
Cr.App.Rep. = Criminal Appeal Reports

D.L.R. = Dominion Law Reports (Canada)

E.G. = Estates Gazette
E.G.D. = Estates Gazette Digest of Land and Property Cases
E.R. = English Reports

F. = Federal Reporter (USA)
F.L.R. = Family Law Reports
F.Supp. = Federal Supplement (USA)
Fam.L.R. = Family Law Reports (Australia)

Gr. = Grant's Chancery Reports (Ontario, Canada)

H.L.R. = Housing Law Reports
Harv.L.Rev. = Harvard Law Review (USA)
Hastings L.J. = Hastings Law Journal (USA)

Int.Bank.L. = International Banking Law

J.B.L. = Journal of Business Law

K.B. = King's Bench (Law Reports)

Lectures L.S.U.C. = Special Lectures of the Law Society of Upper Canada

Leg.St. = Legal Studies
L.M.C.L.Q. = Lloyd's Maritime and Commerical Law Quarterly
L.Q.R. = Law Quarterly Review
L.R. = Law Reports
L.S.Gaz. = Law Society Gazette
L.T. = Law Times
Lloyd's L.R. = Lloyd's Law Reports

M.L.R. = Modern Law Review
McGill L.J. = McGill Law Journal (Canada)
Mel.U.L.Rev. = Melbourne University Law Review (Australia)

N.L.J. = New Law Journal
N.S.W.L.R. = New South Wales Law Reports (Australia)
N.Y. = New York Reporter (USA)
N.Z. Recent L. = New Zealand Recent Law
N.Z.L.R. = New Zealand Law Reports
N.Z.U.L.Rev. = New Zealand Universities Law Review

O.A.R. = Ontario Appeal Reports (Canada)
Ohio State L.J. = Ohio State Law Journal (USA)
O.J.L.S. = Oxford Journal of Legal Studies
O.R. = Ontario Reports (Canada)
O.W.N. = Ontario Weekly Notes (Canada)
O.W.R. = Ontario Weekly Reports (Canada)

P. = Probate, Divorce and Admiralty (Law Reports)
P.C. = Privy Council
Public L. = Public Law

Q.B. = Queen's Bench (Law Reports)
Q.B.D. = Queen's Bench Division (Law Reports)

R.L.R. = Restitution Law Review

S.A.S.R. = South Australia State Reports
S.C.R. = Supreme Court Reports (Supreme Court of Canada)
S.E. = Southeastern Reporter (USA)
S.W. = Southwestern Reporter (USA)
Sask.L.Rev. = Saskatchewan Law Review (Canada)
Sol.J. = Solicitors Journal
Syd.L.Rev. = Sydney Law Review (Australia)

T.L.Int. = Trust Law International

U.Ill.L.Rev. = University of Illinois Law Review (USA)
U.Qld.L.J. = University of Queensland Law Journal (Australia)
U.S. = United States Reports
U.T.Fac.L.Rev. = University of Toronto Faculty Law Review (Canada)
U.T.L.J. = University of Toronto Law Journal (Canada)
U.Tas.L.Rev. = University of Tasmania Law Review (Australia)
U.W.A.L.Rev. = University of Western Australia Law Review

V.L.R. = Victoria Law Reports (Australia)

W.L.R. = Weekly Law Reports
W.N. = Weekly Notes
W.W.R. = Western Weekly Reports (Canada)

Yale L.J. = Yale Law Journal (USA)

Table of Cases

Table of Statutes

A. UNITED KINGDOM

B. OTHER JURISIDICTIONS

1. Australia

(a) New South Wales

1. Canada

(a) Alberta

(b) Ontario

2. New Zealand

Introduction

'The law with regard to resulting trusts is not in doubt'.[1] This is commonly said of the resulting trust[2] and may explain why it has received so little attention in recent years, especially in comparison with the constructive trust. Most of the current academic writing about the resulting trust is found in the established textbooks on equity and trusts and these tend to provide little more than catalogues of the situations in which the resulting trust arises. However, these externalities mask a widespread uncertainty about the true nature of the resulting trust. There is no consensus on the principle by which the resulting trust operates, including the fundamental question whether it arises by operation of law or depends on the presumed intention to create a trust. This uncertainty interacts with another. Although it is widely believed that equity's weapon against unjust enrichment is the constructive trust, it is not clear why this work is not at least in part ascribed to the resulting trust. This book examines the true nature of the resulting trust and the question whether the trusts brought into being to reverse unjust enrichment should not include resulting trusts. It then considers whether the resulting trust, when properly understood, might not be equity's principal contribution to reversing unjust enrichment.

A. WHAT IS A RESULTING TRUST?

In *Hanbury and Martin's Modern Equity*, the resulting trust is described as 'a situation in which a transferee is required by equity to hold property on trust for the transferor; or for the person who provided the purchase money for the transfer'.[3] Professor Waters describes it in a similar fashion:[4] 'Broadly speaking, a resulting trust arises whenever legal or equitable title to property is in one party's name, but that party, because he is a fiduciary or gave no value for the property, is under an obligation to return it to the original title owner, or to the person who *did* give value for it'. Although both definitions are broad, they contain the 'essential characteristic'[5] of the resulting trust: 'the person in whose favour the trust arises is the person who provided the property or equitable interest vested in the person bound by the trust'.[6]

[1] *Vandervell* v. *I.R.C.* [1967] 2 A.C. 291, 307, per Lord Reid (dissenting).

[2] See *Dyer* v. *Dyer* (1788) 2 Cox 92, 93; *Sidmouth* v. *Sidmouth* (1840) 2 Beav. 447, 454; *Soar* v. *Foster* (1858) 4 K.&J. 152, 160–1; *In re Eykyn's Trusts* (1877) 6 Ch.D. 115, 118; *Bennet* v. *Bennet* (1879) 10 Ch.D. 474, 476; *Niles* v. *Lake* [1947] 2 D.L.R. 248, 254, S.C.C.; *Shephard* v. *Cartwright* [1955] A.C. 431, 445; *Napier* v. *Public Trustee (Western Australia)* (1980) 32 A.L.R. 153, 158, H.C.A.

[3] Martin (1993a), p. 233.

[4] Waters (1984), p. 300.

[5] Ibid. at p. 302.

[6] *Baird* v. *Columbia Trust Co.* (1915) 22 D.L.R. 150, 151, B.C.S.C., per Morrison J.

The resulting trust, like all true trusts, can only exist when certain requirements are met. As Mr. Gardner states, a trust is 'a situation in which property is vested in someone (a trustee), who is under an obligation to handle it in a certain way'.[7] The term 'constructive trustee' is sometimes used to describe someone who holds no property in trust, but has assisted a breach of trust and is under a personal liability to compensate the beneficiary for losses caused thereby.[8] 'Resulting trustee' is never used in this fashion. There must be identifiable assets vested in the resulting trustee capable of being the subject matter of a trust.[9] Although it is common to think of the subject matter as property, equity has taken a broad notion of property, so that choses in action (such as a creditor's rights against a debtor) may be held in trust.[10]

Most resulting trusts arise in one of two situations: (i) where there has been an apparent gift of property or (ii) where an express trust has failed to dispose of all of the trust property. In both cases, equity assumes that the owner was not intended to receive the benefit of the property and raises a resulting trust in favour of the provider of that property. In *Re Vandervell's Trusts (No. 2)*,[11] Megarry J. concluded that the resulting trust operated on different principles in each of these two situations. His lordship classified the resulting trust of an apparent gift as 'presumed' and the resulting trust on the failure of an express trust as 'automatic'. The presumed resulting trust was said to be based on the presumed intention of the provider of the property to create it and could be rebutted by evidence to the contrary. The automatic resulting trust arose independently of intention and was irrebuttable.

The distinction between presumed and automatic resulting trusts is explored and ultimately rejected in this book. One of the conclusions reached here is that all resulting trusts operate on precisely the same principle regardless of the situations in which they arise. They do not depend on an implied intention to create a trust, but neither do they arise completely independently of intention. All resulting trusts come into being because the provider of property did not intend to benefit the recipient. Another conclusion of this book is that the resulting trust is not limited to the two situations described above, but may be possible whenever the recipient of property was not intended to take it beneficially.

B. THE IMPORTANCE OF A PROPER CLASSIFICATION OF TRUSTS

Although we sometimes describe trusts according to their function (such as bare, discretionary or spendthrift trusts),[12] they are more usually classified by the

[7] Gardner (1990), p. 6. [8] See Harpum (1986); Harpum (1994).

[9] Hayton Youdan (1989) at p. 208.

[10] *Re Turcan* (1888) 40 Ch.D. 5; Maitland, p. 50; Hackney, pp. 54–5; Hovius and Youdan, p. 28; Sheridan, p. 18. [11] [1974] 1 Ch. 269.

[12] See Waters (1984), pp. 27–30; Gray, pp. 39–40.

manner of their origin as express, resulting, or constructive. It is generally agreed that the express trust is the product of intention, while the constructive trust is created by operation of law.[13] However, the current uncertainty over the basis on which the resulting trust arises has precluded an entirely satisfactory classification. Some have preferred to see the resulting trust as dependent on an implied intention to create a trust,[14] others as a trust arising by operation of law[15] and still others as a bit of both.[16] This has left the resulting trust in a limbo between express and constructive trusts.

The view put forward here is that resuting trusts arise by operation of law. It will be argued that when property has been transferred to another and the provider of that property did not intend to benefit the recipient, equity responds by imposing a resulting trust. The distinction between express and resulting trusts is that the former are created by an intention to create a trust, whereas the latter arise because of a lack of intention to benefit the recipient. This was Professor Scott's view,[17] but the purpose of this book is not to argue that we should adopt an American view of the resulting trust in place of our own. It will be shown that the English resulting trust already operates on this principle, although this is often overlooked or misunderstood.

It has been suggested that this distinction, between a positive intention to create a trust and an absence of intention to benefit the recipient, is unimportant.[18] However, the distinction can be crucial. Consider the cases where the provider of property lacks capacity to create a trust or is unaware of the transfer. If the resulting trust depended on the implied intention to create it, then it ought to be precluded in these cases, where the actual intention to create a trust is impossible. This should also be true where the intention to create a trust would be invalid unless made in writing. There is no reason why an implied intention to create a trust should be effective where the oral expression of that same intention would not be. However, if the resulting trust arises because equity responds to the absence of intention to give, rather than the positive intention to create a trust, it is possible in all these situations.

Recognizing that the resulting trust depends on the lack of intention to benefit the recipient should resolve the debate over whether it arises by operation of law or is created by the intention of the parties. As Professor Birks states:[19] 'There is a fine but important distinction between intent conceived as creative of rights, as in an express trust or a contract, and intent conceived as a fact which, along with others, calls for the creation of rights by operation of law'. The lack of

[13] Martin (1993a), p. 71; cf. Gardner (1990), p. 225.

[14] Costigan; Meagher and Gummow, *Jacobs' Law of Trusts*, p. 263; Riddall, p. 191; Gray, p. 373; Sheridan, pp. 189–90; Oakley (1994), pp. 27, 189; Swadling (1996).

[15] Maitland, pp. 77–80; Mowbray, *Lewin on Trusts*, p. 115; Scott and Fratcher, §404.1; Ford and Lee, §21000.

[16] Waters (1984), p. 301; Martin (1993a), p. 70.

[17] Scott and Fratcher, §404.1.

[18] *Allen* v. *Snyder* [1977] 2 N.S.W.L.R. 685, 698, C.A.

[19] Birks (1989a), p. 65.

intention to benefit the recipient is a fact which calls for the equitable response of resulting trust. We need to discard the belief that the resulting trust is created by the implied intention of the transferor. Not only has this theory interfered with the proper development and application of the resulting trust, it does not explain even the traditional categories of resulting trust, as the *Vandervell* litigation demonstrated.

Just as it is possible and important to discern the line between express and resulting trusts, the same is also true for resulting and constructive trusts. One might ask: if they both arise by operation of law, does it matter whether we call them resulting or constructive? Is a resulting trust not simply a constructive trust which happens to restore property to the person who provided it?[20] On this view, the resulting trust is a classification based on function rather than origin. As Birks states:[21]

> The term 'resulting trust' is capable of bearing two meanings. In the first it identifies a feature which has nothing to do with the trust's origin: the trust is resulting (from the Latin *resalire*, to jump back) if the interest arising under it is carried back to the settlor. This can happen however the trust originates, whether by expressed intention, implied intention, presumed intention, or irrespective of intention (constructive). In trusts created in all these ways the beneficial interest can 'jump back'. So the term 'resulting' in this wide sense cuts across other classifications.

Birks then wonders whether it is not possible to have a trust which is 'constructive in origin' and 'resulting in pattern'.[22] However, it will be argued that there are important reasons for distinguishing between resulting and constructive trusts on the basis of their origin, as well as their function.

The constructive trust has tended to be one of equity's more amorphous creations. It arises in various situations for a variety of reasons.[23] Attempts to create a unifying theory for the origin of the constructive trust have not been successful (outside the USA and possibly Canada). There is no defining characteristic of the constructive trust which necessarily excludes the resulting trust. On the other hand, the basis of the resulting trust (set out in this book) is well defined and clearly excludes the majority of constructive trusts. This leads naturally to the question whether those constructive trusts to which the definition of resulting trust does apply ought not to be re-classified as such. In other words, should they be recognized as resulting in origin as well as in pattern?

This question is not merely 'one of terminology and classification'.[24] The recognition of the principle of restitution in English law[25] and the growing use

[20] See Waters (1984), pp. 300–1, 374–5; Scane at 265; Youdan (1993).
[21] Birks (1989a), p. 60. [22] Birks (1989a) 62; cf. Birks (1992c) at pp. 363–4.
[23] Elias; Gardner (1990), pp. 225–46; Martin (1993a), pp. 291–330.
[24] Waters (1984), p. 20.
[25] *Lipkin Gorman* v. *Karpnale Ltd.* [1991] 2 A.C. 548; *Woolwich Equitable Building Society* v. *Inland Revenue Commissioners* [1993] 1 A.C. 70.

of the constructive trust as a restitutionary response[26] have led to a vexing problem: when should the right to restitution give rise to a personal obligation and when should the plaintiff be entitled to a proprietary interest in the defendant's assets? The distinction between obligation and ownership is becoming less certain.[27] The liberal use of the constructive trust as a restitutionary remedy in the USA and Canada has not solved the problem (or at least has not proved to be a trouble-free solution). They face the difficult task of finding limits to a remedy which is capable of riding roughshod over the legitimate interests of creditors and other third parties.[28]

The resulting trust may be the answer to these difficulties (at least in part). A trust which is resulting in both origin and pattern always operates to return specific property to its provider because he or she (i) provided that property and (ii) did not intend to benefit the recipient. Much of the law of restitution is concerned with the reversal of non-voluntary transfers. By its very nature, the resulting trust is capable of performing this task in accordance with certain principles, which are sorely needed in matters of proprietary restitution. The resulting trust necessarily identifies the property to be returned and the party to whom it should be returned, as well as providing the justification for so doing.[29] The constructive trust has no such inherent limitations.

It was a great merit of Elias' work on constructive trusts[30] that it sought to understand those trusts in terms not of one single idea, but of the principal ideas which, in other fields, we expect to explain legal consequences and responses. Thus he found that constructive trusts were sometimes aimed at perfecting promises or undertakings, sometimes designed to repair losses caused by wrongdoing and sometimes intended to effect restitution of unjust enrichment. It is essential, if trusts are not to be isolated from the rest of the law (a condition which inevitably involves both duplication of effort and danger of contradictory conclusions), that all trusts be related to these primary ideas or, more accurately, to the events which are the primary causes of legal responses.[31]

Much more useful than the conventional classification of trusts, as express, implied, resulting or constructive, would be a classfication distinguishing trusts as generated by consent, wrongs, unjust enrichment or other events. The advantage of this approach would be the greater ease of aligning the law of trusts with other areas of law responding to the same ideas. This book, travelling in the direction in which Elias pointed, suggests that, when trusts are classified in that way, the category of unjust enrichment trusts turns out to be filled in largest measure by resulting trusts, which is as much to say that resulting trusts are the chief contribution of equity to the law of restitution.

[26] e.g. *A.-G. Hong Kong* v. *Reid* [1994] 1 A.C. 324, P.C.
[27] Goode (1987) at 437; McKendrick (1994).
[28] Sherwin; Paciocco; Kull.
[29] Birks (1994c) at pp. 222–3.
[30] Elias.
[31] Birks (1994c) at p. 223.

C. RESULTING TRUSTS AND RESTITUTION

If the resulting trust has a greater role in the law of restitution than previously suspected, the interplay between these two subjects must be explored. Restitution has only recently been recognized as a distinctive part of the common law.[32] Having lain incognito for so long, many remarkably similar restitutionary problems have received oddly different solutions. The division between law and equity has added to the difficulty, but neither side of the divide has managed to achieve a uniform treatment of the subject on its own. This late recognition of the role of the resulting trust reveals even further inconsistencies.[33]

Consider, for example, the case of a plaintiff who is seeking to rescind a gift to the defendant because it was obtained by actual undue influence. If the plaintiff can prove that the defendant has exercised undue influence over the plaintiff and thereby obtained the gift,[34] it will be returned to the plaintiff. However, it has been said that the plaintiff has no equitable interest in the gift before it is rescinded, but only a 'mere equity'.[35] It is now recognized that rescission can be restitutionary: the gift in this case is returned to the plaintiff because his or her intention to benefit the defendant was imperfect, having been procured by undue influence.[36]

Now consider what happens if the same plaintiff claims instead the benefit of a resulting trust. Assuming the defendant is not the plaintiff's wife or child, equity will presume that a gift was not intended and, unless the defendant proves otherwise, the 'gift' will be held on a resulting trust for the plaintiff from the outset. Can the defendant meet this onus by proving that a gift was intended, even though that intention was the product of the defendant's undue influence? This example reveals a tension between rescission and the resulting trust, which needs to be reconciled. Although both are equitable responses to the plaintiff's imperfect intention to give, the onus of proof is different in each case, as are the facts which must be proven and the remedial outcome.

Other tensions can be revealed by an exploration of the resulting trust's potential. Many will be identified and discussed as this book considers the application of the resulting trust to transfers of property in a variety of circumstances, including those made by mistake, under duress, under undue influence, by persons lacking capacity, or for purposes incapable of fulfilment. These are all cases in which a transferor might seek restitution because of an imperfect intention to benefit the recipient. Each is governed by specific rules for recovery at law or in equity, which have developed quite independently of the resulting trust. If the resulting trust can also apply, latent conflicts are exposed. Most turn out to be more apparent than real, but any which remain will need to be resolved in one way or another.

[32] Seavey and Scott; Birks (1989a), pp. 1–6; Goff and Jones, pp. 5–15.

[33] Hazeltine at p. xv; Birks (1992c) at p. 338.

[34] *Barclays Bank p.l.c.* v. *O'Brien* [1994] 1 A.C. 180.

[35] *Phillips* v. *Phillips* (1862) 4 De G.F.&J. 208.

[36] Burrows (1993a), pp. 189–92.

The connexion between resulting trusts and the law of restitution is not a new idea. Professor Birks recognized it in *An Introduction to the Law of Restitution*[37] and developed it further in his essay 'Restitution and Resulting Trusts'.[38] Other commentators have supported it[39] and it has found expression in two recent cases.[40] Even in the USA and Canada, where the task of proprietary restitution has been almost wholly given over to the constructive trust, the restitutionary possibilities of the resulting trust have not gone unnoticed.[41] It is hoped that this book will advance the work that is already begun, by mapping out the place of the resulting trust in the English law of both trusts and restitution. That this should be occurring so late in the life of the resulting trust can be explained by reference to the long dispersal and only recent unification of the law of restitution itself.[42]

Birks said that *An Introduction to the Law of Restitution* was not intended to contradict Lord Diplock's statement that 'there is no general doctrine of unjust enrichment recognised in English law. What it does is to provide specific remedies in particular cases of what might be classified as unjust enrichment in a legal system that is based upon the civil law'.[43] The same is true of this book. The process of integrating resulting trusts with the law of restitution does not require the invention of new trust principles or even the alteration of old ones. It will be sufficient if we can obtain a better understanding of existing principles and a recognition of their full potential. In the words of Professor Birks:[44] 'What is proposed here is a scheme for better ordering the specific instances which Lord Diplock recognises. The generic conception of the event which triggers restitution adds nothing to the existing law and effects no change except what comes from better understanding of what is there already'.

The existing resulting trust is already capable of a far greater, and possibly central, role in proprietary restitution. We should not underestimate the change that will come from better understanding of it.

D. PLAN OF THE BOOK

This book is divided into two parts. The first (Chapters 1 to 3) looks at the situations in which resulting trusts arise. The second (Chapters 4 to 9) concerns the relationship between the resulting trust and the law of restitution.

[37] Birks (1989a), pp. 54–64.

[38] Birks (1992c) at p. 335. Also see Birks (1994c) at pp. 222–3.

[39] Millett (1991) at 76, 80; Millett (1993) at 13–14; Millett (1995) at 39; Norman at p. 102; Worthington.

[40] *El Ajou* v. *Dollar Land Holdings p.l.c.* [1993] 3 All E.R. 717, 734; rev'd on other grounds [1994] 2 All E.R. 685, C.A.; *Westdeutsche Landesbank Girozentrale* v. *Islington London B.C.* [1994] 4 All E.R. 890, 962, C.A.; varied [1996] 2 All E.R. 961, H.L.

[41] Scott and Fratcher, §440; Waters (1984), pp. 374–5; Litman at 469; Hovius and Youdan, p. 106; Scane at 265.

[42] See Birks (1989a), pp. 1–6.

[43] *Orakpo* v. *Manson Investments Ltd.* [1978] A.C. 95, 104; quoted in Birks (1989a), p. 26.

[44] Birks (1989a), p. 27.

In Part I, the nature of the resulting trust is revealed through an examination of the cases in which it has arisen. Chapters 1 (Apparent Gifts) and 2 (Trusts Which Fail) are about the traditional categories of resulting trust. The presumptions of resulting trust and advancement are discussed in Chapter 1 and the dichotomy of 'presumed' and 'automatic' resulting trusts in Chapter 2. Chapter 3 (Quistclose trusts) looks at resulting trusts which arise when property has been transferred to be used for certain purposes and those purposes become incapable of fulfilment.

In Part II, the relationship between the resulting trust and the law of restitution is examined. This is a continuation of the work begun in Part I. Having concluded that all resulting trusts operate on the same principle, it is argued in Chapter 4 that this principle is restitutionary: all resulting trusts operate to reverse unjust enrichment. The remaining chapters of Part II examine the place of the resulting trust in the law of restitution, by looking at (i) the types of unjust enrichment to which it responds, in Chapters 5 to 7, and (ii) how it responds, in Chapters 8 and 9.

A conclusion of Part I is that all resulting trusts arise because the provider of property did not intend to benefit the recipient. Chapters 5, 6, and 7 explore the extent to which this principle is commutative: do all non-voluntary transfers of property give rise to a resulting trust? In other words, what are the limits of the broader application of the resulting trust, when its true nature and restitutionary role are properly understood? The possibility of a broader role for the resulting trust leads to questions concerning the nature of its response to unjust enrichment. Chapter 8 considers whether resulting trustees are also personally liable to make restitution of the value received. In Chapter 9, the resulting trustee's fiduciary obligations are examined.

This book concludes by looking at three areas affected by the understanding of the resulting trust put forward in this book: (i) the classification of trusts, (ii) the availability of proprietary restitution and (iii) the application of defences to restitutionary claims.

I

The Situations in Which Resulting Trusts Arise

1

Apparent Gifts

This is the first of three chapters examining the situations in which resulting trusts arise. It concerns the traditional category of trusts which result in favour of persons who either gratuitously transfer property to others or provide the consideration for the transfer of property to others. This is the category most closely associated with the presumptions of resulting trust and advancement. Equity tends to be suspicious of gifts and often asks the recipient to prove that an apparent gift was intended as such. The failure to do so means that it will be held in trust for its provider. In short, there is a presumption of resulting trust.

There are situations where the presumption of resulting trust is not applied to an apparent gift. Traditionally, it did not apply to the provision of property by fathers to their children or husbands to their wives. It was said that the presumption of advancement applied instead, meaning that the recipient was beneficially entitled to the property unless it was proven not to be intended as a gift. Also, there is some doubt about whether gratuitous transfers of land attract the presumption of resulting trust. It may be that the presumption only applies to land in cases where some or all of the consideration for a transfer is provided by someone other than the transferor or the recipient.

The presumptions of resulting trust and advancement are presumptions of fact, that fact being the intention of the person who has provided property to another.[1] As Lord Diplock said in *Pettitt* v. *Pettitt*, the presumptions are instances of the courts' 'technique' of:[2]

> imputing an intention to a person whenever the intention with which an act is done affects its legal consequences and the evidence does not disclose what was the actual intention with which he did it . . . When the act is of a kind to which this technique has frequently to be applied by the courts the imputed intention may acquire the description of a 'presumption'—but presumptions of this type are not immutable. A presumption of fact is no more than a consensus of judicial opinion disclosed by reported cases as to the most likely inference of fact to be drawn in the absence of evidence to the contrary.

There are three tasks undertaken in this chapter. The first is to identify the facts which give rise to the presumptions of resulting trust or advancement, i.e. the primary facts which must exist before the court will infer certain secondary facts regarding intention. The second and more important task is to identify the secondary facts being inferred, i.e. what the court is presuming when either of

[1] The recipient's intention is discussed at pp. 35–8 below.

[2] [1970] A.C. 777, 823. See *Calverley* v. *Green* (1984) 155 C.L.R. 242, 264.

the two presumptions is applied. Thirdly (and no less important), is an examination of the principle of resulting trust, i.e. how the resulting trust responds to the facts proven and presumed.

A. PRESUMPTION OF RESULTING TRUST

1. Facts Giving Rise to the Presumption

The most frequently quoted statement of the presumption of resulting trust is found in *Dyer* v. *Dyer*, where Eyre C.B. said:[3]

> The clear result of all the cases, without a single exception, is that the trust of a legal estate, whether freehold, copyhold, or leasehold; whether taken in the names of the purchasers and others jointly, or in the names of others without that of the purchaser; whether in one name or several; whether jointly or successive—results to the man who advances the purchase-money. This is a general proposition, supported by all the cases, and there is nothing to contradict it; and it goes on a strict analogy to the rule of the common law, that where a feoffment is made without consideration, the use results to the feoffor. It is the established doctrine of a Court of equity, that this resulting trust may be rebutted by circumstances in evidence.

The plaintiff in that case claimed to be entitled to copyhold property which had been purchased for his brother by their father. If there had been a resulting trust for the father, the beneficial ownership of the property would have passed by his will to the plaintiff. Instead, the presumption of advancement applied in favour of the brother. Although the parties' relationship is a fact which is relevant to the application of the presumption of resulting trust, it will be discussed below in connexion with the presumption of advancement. All other facts essential to the presumption of resulting trust are examined here.

Dyer v. *Dyer* reveals the general principle that a presumption of resulting trust arises in favour of someone who pays the purchase-money for a transfer of property to another. It is not limited to legal estates, but applies to any form of property or asset capable of being held in trust, including personal property,[4] choses in action[5] and equitable interests.[6] The presumption of resulting trust is said to exist by analogy to the resulting use, which would arise upon a feoffment without consideration. The feature common to both these situations is the lack of consideration provided by the recipient. As Bagnall J. stated in *Cowcher* v. *Cowcher*, 'A resulting trust arises where a person acquires a legal estate but has not provided the consideration or the whole of the consideration for its acquisition,

[3] (1788) 2 Cox Eq. 92, 93.
[4] *The Venture* [1908] P. 218, C.A.; *Bateman Television Ltd.* v. *Bateman* [1970] N.Z.L.R. 453, C.A.
[5] *Shephard* v. *Cartwright* [1955] A.C. 431; *Niles* v. *Lake* [1947] 2 D.L.R. 248, 252, S.C.C.
[6] *In re Vandervell's Trusts (No. 2)* [1974] Ch. 269, 290.

unless a contrary intention is proved'.[7] Although this appears to be the essential fact which attracts the presumption of resulting trust, there is an important caveat. The application of the presumption to gratuitous transfers is not free from doubt and is therefore dealt with separately below.

Payment of the purchase price

Leaving gratuitous transfers aside for the moment, the principle set out in *Dyer* v. *Dyer* can be extended and refined. To begin with, the presumption of resulting trust is not restricted to cases involving the payment of purchase-money. Although this is the typical case, the presumption can apply in favour of the person who provides the consideration for the transfer, regardless of the nature of that consideration.[8] An interesting example is the American case of *Mumpower* v. *Castle*,[9] in which land was paid for with an assortment of farm animals. Some of the animals belonged to the purchaser's wife and there was a resulting trust of the land in her favour in proportion to her share of the value of the animals provided. In *Springette* v. *Defoe*,[10] a home purchased from a local council was held on resulting trust for the plaintiff based on her contribution to the purchase price, which included her entitlement, as a council tenant for 11 years, to a 41 per cent discount from the market value.

It is not necessary that the beneficiary of the resulting trust has provided all of the consideration for the transfer. Where two or more parties contribute to the payment of the purchase price, and the legal title to the property does not reflect those contributions, there is a presumption of resulting trust for the contributors in proportion with their contributions.[11] The presumption can arise where the recipient of the property has provided some, but not all, of the consideration for a transfer.[12] Where the instrument of transfer states that all of the consideration has been paid or is payable by the recipient, the presumption will not arise unless it is proven that the statement is false and that some of the consideration has been provided by the claimant.[13]

A contribution to a purchase can be made by accepting a liability to pay the purchase price, e.g. by way of mortgage. In this situation, the resulting trust is not necessarily affected if the loan is later repaid by other persons.[14] In *Calverley*

[7] [1972] 1 W.L.R. 425, 431.

[8] *Cowcher* v. *Cowcher* [1972] 1 W.L.R. 425; Scott and Fratcher, §455.

[9] (1920) 104 S.E. 706, Va.C.A.

[10] (1992) 24 H.L.R. 552, 555, C.A.

[11] *Wray* v. *Steele* (1814) 2 V.&B. 388; *Calverley* v. *Green* (1984) 155 C.L.R. 242; Mowbray, p. 132.

[12] *House* v. *Caffyn* [1922] V.L.R. 67, 78–80; *Napier* v. *Public Trustee (Western Austrlia)* (1980) 32 A.L.R. 153, 158, H.C.A.; *Reber* v. *Reber* (1988) 48 D.L.R. (4th) 376, 377, B.C.

[13] *Lench* v. *Lench* (1805) 10 Ves. 511; *Haigh* v. *Kaye* (1872) L.R. 7 Ch.App. 469; *Niles* v. *Lake* [1947] 2 D.L.R. 248, 253, 263; *Wirth* v. *Wirth* (1956) 98 C.L.R. 228, 237; *Neazor* v. *Hoyle* (1962) 32 D.L.R. (2d) 131, Alta.S.C.A.D.; *Mowbray, Lewin on Trusts*, p. 132; Baker and Langan, *Snell's Equity*, p. 178. Also see *Benger* v. *Drew* (1721) 1 P.Wms. 781.

[14] *Cowcher* v. *Cowcher* [1972] 1 W.L.R. 425; *Crisp* v. *Mullings* [1976] E.G.D. 730, C.A.

v. *Green*,[15] a house was purchased in the joint names of the plaintiff and defendant. One third of the purchase price was paid by the defendant as a deposit and the remainder was borrowed by way of a joint mortgage of the house. Even though the defendant had paid all of the mortgage instalments, the plaintiff was held to have contributed to the purchase price by undertaking the obligation to repay the loan. Mason and Brennann JJ. stated:[16] 'It is understandable but erroneous to regard the payment of mortgage instalments as payment of the purchase price of a home. The purchase price is what is paid in order to acquire the property; the mortgage instalments are paid to the lender from whom the money to pay some or all of the purchase price is borrowed.'

The defendant's payment of the mortgage did not alter the quantum of their beneficial interests under the resulting trust, but Mason and Brennann JJ. said that 'the defendant may be entitled to contribution from the plaintiff for her share of the payments and to an equitable charge to secure the making of her contribution'.[17] Although courts sometimes treat the contribution to the payment of another's mortgage debt as a contribution towards the acquisition of the mortgaged property,[18] this is usually for the purposes of establishing a constructive trust on the basis of detrimental reliance.[19]

It is often said that the consideration must have been provided 'in the character of purchaser'. However, as discussed below,[20] this does not mean that the contributor must have intended to purchase the property. The requirement is satisfied so long as the consideration was not intended to be a loan, gift, or payment for some other purpose.

Gratuitous transfers

Although the presumption of resulting trust is derived by analogy to the resulting use upon a feoffment made without consideration, there is some doubt about its application to gratuitous transfers. Other countries have reached different conclusions. It is accepted in Canada as 'trite law . . . that where a person transfers his property into another's name gratuitously a resulting trust in favour of the grantor is created and the transferee must prove, in order to retain title, that a gift was intended by the transferor'.[21] In the USA, it seems the opposite is true. Although a purchase in the name of another gives rise to the presumption of resulting trust, a direct transfer of real or personal property does not:[22]

[15] (1984) 155 C.L.R. 242. [16] Ibid. at 257. Cf. L.D. Smith (1995).

[17] *Calveley* v. *Green*, n. 15 above at 263; *Cowcher* v. *Cowcher* [1972] 1 W.L.R. 425; *Crisp* v. *Mullings* [1976] E.G.D. 730.

[18] *Gissing* v. *Gissing* [1971] A.C. 886, 907; Hayton (1990) at 383.

[19] See *Grant* v. *Edwards* [1986] Ch. 638, 655–6, C.A.; Matthews (1994); pp. 37–8, 228–9 below.

[20] At p. 27.

[21] *Goodfriend* v. *Goodfriend* [1972] S.C.R. 640, 22 D.L.R. (3d) 699, 702, per Spence J. See Waters (1984), pp. 301–10; *Niles* v. *Lake* [1947] 2 D.L.R. 248; *Reber* v. *Reber* (1988) 48 D.L.R. (4th) 376; *Re Dagle* (1990) 70 D.L.R. (4th) 201, P.E.I.S.C.A.D.

[22] *Restatement of Trusts*, §405. See Stone at 331–2; Scott and Fratcher, §405; Bogert and Bogert, §453; Fratcher. Several states have abolished the resulting trust by statute: see Scott and Fratcher, §440.2.

The common-law rule that a resulting use arises in favor of a person making a feoffment in fee simple to another where no consideration is paid for the feoffment and where no express use is declared by the feoffor, has not been applied in the modern law of trusts. Where a transfer of property is made without consideration, the inference is that the transferor intends to make a gift to the transferee, not that he intends that the transferee should hold the property for the benefit of the transferor. This is true even though it appears in the instrument of conveyance that no consideration is paid for the conveyance.

There is some doubt in Australia about the application of the presumption of resulting trust to gratuitous transfers. *Jacobs' Law of Trusts in Australia* states that, 'The question whether a resulting trust is presumed in the case of a voluntary transfer of land or personalty to a stranger alone is one which cannot be answered with any assurance'.[23] However, this doubt was not shared by Aickin J. in *Napier* v. *Public Trustee* (*Western Australia*):[24]

The law with respect to resulting trusts is not in doubt. Where property is transferred by one person into the name of another without consideration, and where a purchaser pays the vendor and directs him to transfer the property into the name of another person without consideration passing from that person, there is a presumption that the transferee holds the property upon trust for the transferor or the purchaser as the case may be.

The other members of the High Court of Australia, including Murphy J., were in general agreement with him, but the case involved the purchase of a house in the name of another and not a gratuitous transfer.

Four years later in *Calverley* v. *Green*,[25] Murphy J. had changed his mind and stated in his dissenting judgement that the presumption of resulting trust was 'inappropriate to our times'.[26] He was, however, in favour of the equal treatment of the purchase in the name of another and the gratuitous transfer to another:[27]

The position is said to be unclear where a voluntary transfer of land or personalty occurs (see *Jacobs' Law of Trusts in Australia* 4th ed., 1977, pp. 228–30). However there is no logical basis for distinguishing between a conveyance to another at the time of purchase and a voluntary transfer, so that a resulting trust will arise in one but not the other. It should not be presumed in either.

Calverley v. *Green* was also a case of trust resulting in favour of a contributor to the purchase price rather than the transferor.

House v. *Caffyn*[28] and *Wirth* v. *Wirth*[29] were cases involving gratuitous transfers of land. In the former, all three justices of the Supreme Court of Victoria thought the presumption of resulting trust applied, but the majority found it had been rebutted by the evidence.[30] In *Wirth* v. *Wirth*, Dixon C.J. and McTiernan J. were not sure whether the presumption of resulting trust applied, but decided that the transferor had intended to make a gift in any event.

In England, there is a presumption of resulting trust upon a gratuitous transfer

[23] Meagher and Gummow, *Jacobs' Law of Trusts*, p. 282. Also see Ford and Lee, §21080–§21100.
[24] (1980) 32 A.L.R. 153, 158.
[25] (1984) 155 C.L.R. 242.
[26] Ibid. at 264.
[27] Ibid. at 264–5.
[28] [1922] V.L.R. 67.
[29] (1956) 98 C.L.R. 228.
[30] See Ford and Lee, §21080.

of personal property,[31] but whether it also applies to a transfer of land is a 'debatable question'.[32] Ignoring for the moment the debate concerning land, the essential fact attracting the presumption is the same whether a person transfers his or her own property to another or purchases property for that other. Equity's suspicion is aroused by the lack of consideration provided by the recipient and not the form of the transaction.[33]

In *Drummer* v. *Pitcher*,[34] a husband had transferred some of his stock into joint names with his wife and later purchased more of the same stock in their joint names. Lord Brougham C. applied the presumption of advancement to both transactions, but assumed that 'the presumption of intention to give is considerably stronger'[35] for a gratuitous transfer. Professor Scott was of the same opinion.[36] However, it is not clear why this distinction should be drawn between two apparent gifts which are identical but for the manner in which they are given.[37]

Whether the presumption of resulting trust applies to a gratuitous transfer of land depends upon the effect of subsection 60(3) of the Law of Property Act 1925, which states: 'In a voluntary conveyance a resulting trust for the grantor shall not be implied merely by reason that the property is not expressed to be conveyed for the use or benefit of the grantee'.

The academic debate over this subsection has been recognised by the courts, but not resolved.[38] Although there is considerable support for the proposition that the presumption no longer applies in this situation,[39] it may be that subsection 60(3) was only consequential to the repeal of the Statute of Uses 1536 and not intended to change the law.[40] It is helpful to consider first the position under the Statute of Uses and then the effect of the Law of Property Act 1925.

Statute of Uses 1536

Prior to the enactment of the Statute of Uses in 1536, feoffments to the use of the feoffor were often made for the purposes of devising land by will and avoiding

[31] *Fowkes* v. *Pascoe* (1875) 10 Ch.App. 343; *Standing* v. *Bowring* (1885) 16 Ch.D. 282, C.A.; *Re Vinogradoff* [1935] W.N. 68; *Vandervell* v. *I.R.C.* [1967] 2 A.C. 291, 312–13; aff'g [1966] Ch. 261, 292, C.A.; *In re Figgis* [1969] 1 Ch. 123, 144; *Tinsley* v. *Milligan* [1994] 1 A.C. 340, 371; 48 *Halsbury's Laws* (4th edn., 1995 reissue) para. 607, pp. 320–1; Baker and Langan, *Snell's Equity*, p. 183; Riddall, pp. 204–5; Martin (1993a), p. 241; Pettit (1993), p. 131; Sheridan, pp. 212–13; Oakley (1994), pp. 200–1.

[32] *Hodgson* v. *Marks* [1971] 1 Ch. 892, 933, per Russell L.J.

[33] Gardner (1990), p. 55; Birks (1992c) at p. 345.

[34] (1833) 2 My.&K. 262.

[35] Ibid. at 273.

[36] Scott and Fratcher, §440.

[37] *Davies* v. *National Executors & Agency Co. of Australasia* [1912] V.L.R. 397, 401–2; *Calverley* v. *Green* (1984) 155 C.L.R. 242, 264–5; Birks (1992c) at p. 345.

[38] *Hodgson* v. *Marks* [1971] 1 Ch. 892, 933; *Tinsley* v. *Milligan* [1994] 1 A.C. 340, 371.

[39] Mowbray, *Lewin on Trusts*, p. 116; Megarry and Wade, p. 471; Hackney, pp. 148–9; Birks (1989a), p. 62; Baker and Langan, *Snell's Equity*, p. 183; Hayton (1991), p. 434; Riddall, p. 204; Pettit (1993), p. 130; Gray, p. 388.

[40] Maitland, p. 77 (but see p. 77, fn. 2, where his editors suggest the contrary); R.T. Oerton, *Underhill's Law Relating to Trusts and Trustees* 12th edn. (1970), p. 219; Martin (1993a) p. 249; Oakley (1994), p. 200. Cf. Hanbury, *Modern Equity*, p. 212.

the feudal incidents that might become payable on its descent to the heir.[41] The joint ownership of several feoffees to uses, and replacement of those who died, would ensure 'that the legal estate never passed by descent at all'.[42] The practice became so common in the fifteenth century that the doctrine of resulting use evolved, in which it would be presumed, 'where the feoffees gave no value to the feoffor, that the feoffees should hold to the use of the feoffor, unless the feoffee or feoffees could show a contrary intention'.[43]

The Statute of Uses was designed to restore lost feudal incidents by 'executing' the use, i.e. taking the legal estate away from the feoffee and vesting it in the *cestui que* use.[44] The presumption of resulting use continued to operate after 1536 and, to avoid the execution of the resulting use and the return of the legal estate to the feoffor, it became necessary to convey land unto and to the use of the feoffee.[45] The statute executed the use in favour of the feoffee and the legal estate would pass.[46]

Equity began to develop the concept of a trust which could exist independently of the use and avoid execution by the statute. A use upon a use was invalid at the time of the Statute of Uses,[47] but soon came to be enforceable as a trust upon a use.[48] It is permissible to prove a trust contrary to the use expressed in the conveyance[49] and, as Professor Scott points out, the expression of the use does not preclude the presumption of resulting trust in the case of a purchase in the name of another:[50] '[I]t is well settled that where one person pays the purchase price for land and takes title in the name of another, a resulting trust arises even though the instrument of transfer contains a recital of consideration paid by the grantee and even though the conveyance is expressly declared to be to the use of the grantee'.

There is no reason why the expression of the use should have any different effect in a gratuitous conveyance. The use operated, in conjunction with the Statute of Uses, to pass the legal estate to the recipient, but the equitable presumption of resulting trust would arise from the lack of consideration.[51] Although both Lord Hardwicke C.[52] and James L.J.[53] suggested *obiter* that the presumption of resulting trust did not apply to a gratuitous transfer of land, there are several cases to the contrary.[54]

[41] Megarry and Wade, p. 1165. [42] Simpson (1986), p. 183.
[43] Ibid. at p. 177. See Barton (1965) at 571–2.
[44] Simpson (1986), pp. 184–8; Megarry and Wade, pp. 1166–7. [45] Pettit (1993), p. 130.
[46] Maitland, p. 77; cf. Simpson (1986), pp. 204–5. [47] Simpson (1986), pp. 201–2.
[48] Baker (1990), p. 329; Barton (1966); *Duchess of Suffolk* v. *Herenden* (1560) in Baker (1977) at 36. Simpson states that an expressed trust upon a use was not fully enforceable until 1700: Simpson (1986), pp. 199–203. [49] *Fordyce* v. *Willis* (1792) 3 Bro.C.C. 577.
[50] Scott and Fratcher, §405. See Simpson (1986), p. 203. [51] Maitland, p. 77.
[52] *Lloyd* v. *Spillet* (1740) 2 Atk. 148; *Young* v. *Peachy* (1741) 2 Atk. 254.
[53] *Fowkes* v. *Pascoe* (1875) 10 Ch.App. 343, 348. See Baker and Langan, *Snell's Equity*, p. 182.
[54] *Lady Tyrell's Case* (1674) Freem.K.B. 304; *Elliot* v. *Elliot* (1677) 2 Ch.Cas. 231; *Duke of Norfolk* v. *Browne* (1697) Pr.Ch. 80; *R.* v. *Williams* (1735) Bunb. 342. Also see *Strong* v. *Bird*

Law of Property Act 1925

There has been much speculation about the effect of subsection 60(3) of the Law of Property Act 1925. As mentioned above,[55] the majority opinion seems to be that this section prevents the presumption of resulting trust from applying to gratuitous conveyances of land. The counter-argument is that, under the Statute of Uses, the expression of the use was needed solely to pass the legal estate and the presumption of resulting trust would apply independently of the expressed use. Therefore, by stating that 'a resulting trust for the grantor shall not be implied merely by reason that the property is not expressed to be conveyed for the use or benefit of the grantee', subsection 60(3) merely permits the expression of the use to be dropped without any significance being attributed to its absence, i.e. the vestiges of the use are removed without affecting modern trust principles in any way. This reading would have the advantage of ensuring that the presumption of resulting trust remains uniformly applicable to essentially similar apparent gifts, regardless of the nature of the property or form of the transaction.

Notwithstanding the immediate appeal of this interpretation, a plain reading of subsection 60(3) tends to favour the other view. Although the presumption of resulting trust is attracted by the lack of consideration provided by the recipient and not the expression of the use, the section only applies to 'a voluntary conveyance'. This suggests that some fact, in addition to the lack of consideration, is necessary before the presumption can arise.[56] If a sufficient additional fact is that the parties are strangers, i.e. not in a relationship giving rise to the presumption of advancement, then there is room for the presumption of resulting trust. If there must be 'some other reason for thinking that the grantor did not intend the grantee to take beneficially',[57] then the presumption is excluded. The presumption is no more than an 'inference of fact to be drawn in the absence of evidence to the contrary'[58] and, therefore, it no longer applies to gratuitous transfers of land if subsection 60(3) requires that evidence indicating the transferor's intention be given.

Either view of subsection 60(3) could reasonably be adopted by the courts, but two things should be kept in mind. First, there is no logical necessity that certain facts give rise to certain inferences of intention, but it is important that people in essentially similar situations are not treated differently without good cause. It is doubtful whether the differences between land and personalty and between methods of making apparent gifts provide meaningful bases for distinction. Secondly, a decision that the *presumption* of resulting trust no longer applies to gratuitous transfers of land will not make the resulting trust inapplicable. The presumption is only an inference of the provider's lack of intention to

(1874) L.R. 18 Eq. 315, 318; Maitland, p. 77; Mowbray, *Lewin on Trusts*, p. 116; Hackney, pp. 148–9; Birks (1989a), p. 62; Hayton (1991), p. 434; Pettit (1993), p. 130.

[55] At n. 39. [56] Mowbray, *Lewin on Trusts*, p. 116. [57] Ibid.

[58] *Pettitt* v. *Pettitt* [1970] A.C. 777, 823, per Lord Diplock.

benefit the recipient and it is permissible to prove that fact even where it is not presumed (except, perhaps, where the intention is illegal).[59] Although, as Deane J. stated in *Calverley* v. *Green*, the presumptions of resulting trust and advancement are 'too well entrenched as "land-marks" in the law of property . . . to be simply discarded by judicial decision',[60] they have weakened over time and readily give way to evidence to the contrary.[61]

2. The Fact Being Presumed

As discussed above, the existence of certain (primary) facts gives rise to an inference that another (secondary) fact exists. The primary facts are (subject to the Law of Property Act 1925 and the presumption of advancement) a transfer of property to someone who 'has not provided the consideration or the whole of the consideration for its acquisition'.[62] The secondary fact is the intention of the person who provided that property. That intention is identified in this section.

There are two main views on the intention being presumed. The first, and seemingly most popular, is that the provider of the property intended to create a trust for himself or herself.[63] The second and, it is respectfully suggested, better view is that the provider did not intend to give the benefit of that property to the recipient.[64] In *Allen* v. *Snyder*,[65] Samuels J.A. noted both views, but thought that it did not matter whether the presumption was of a positive intention to create a trust or the lack of an intention to benefit the recipient: 'Whether positive or negative, it is still a matter of intention'.[66] However, with respect, this distinction is crucial to our understanding of the resulting trust and of important practical consequences. This is discussed below.

Development of the presumption

It is probable that the presumption of resulting use was originally a presumption that the feoffor intended to create a use and become the *cestui que* use. Feoffments

[59] *Tinsley* v. *Milligan* [1994] 1 A.C. 340; *Tribe* v. *Tribe* [1995] 4 All E.R. 236, C.A.; *Nelson* v. *Nelson* (1995) 70 A.L.J.R. 47.

[60] (1984) 155 C.L.R. 242, 266.

[61] *Cole* v. *Cole* [1944] 1 D.L.R. 37, 39, B.C.C.A.; aff'd [1944] 2 D.L.R. 798, S.C.C.; *Pettitt* v. *Pettitt* [1970] A.C. 777, 813; *Gissing* v. *Gissing* [1971] A.C. 886, 907; *Calverley* v. *Green* (1984) 155 C.L.R. 242, 270; Pettit (1993), p. 122. Cf. *Charles Marshall Pty. Ltd.* v. *Grimsley* (1956) 95 C.L.R. 353, 365.

[62] *Cowcher* v. *Cowcher* [1972] 1 W.L.R. 425, 431, per Bagnall J.

[63] *Fowkes* v. *Pascoe* (1875) 10 Ch.App. 343, 348–9, 353; *In re Kerrigan* (1946) 47 S.R. (N.S.W.) 76, 81; *Gissing* v. *Gissing* [1971] A.C. 886, 902; *Dullow* v. *Dullow* (1985) 3 N.S.W.L.R. 531, 534, C.A.; *Westdeutsche Landesbank Girozentrale* v. *Islington L.B.C.* [1996] 2 All E.R. 961, 990–1, H.L.; Stone; Bogert and Bogert, §454, p. 249; Meagher and Gummow, *Jacobs' Law of Trusts*, p. 263; Riddall, p. 193; Sheridan, pp. 189–90; Martin (1993a), p. 257; Oakley (1994), p. 189; Swadling (1996).

[64] *Calverley* v. *Green* (1984) 155 C.L.R. 242, 246, 251–2; Mowbray, *Lewin on Trusts*, p. 115; *Restatement of Trusts*, vol. 2, p. 324; Scott and Fratcher, §404.1; Birks (1992c) at p. 346; Ford and Lee, §21060.

[65] [1977] 2 N.S.W.L.R. 685, C.A.

[66] Ibid. at 698.

were often made without declaring the use so that feoffors could have the freedom to dispose of or devise their property by a subsequent declaration of use. This widespread practice was probably the origin of the presumption that a feoffment without consideration or declaration of the use was for the use of the feoffor.[67] Although this presumption began as a natural assumption of what the feoffor actually intended, it evolved into a formal rule of law based on consideration.[68] Consideration was required to pass the use so that, without a reason for the feoffment, such as kinship or a bargain and sale, the use of the property remained with the feoffor. The presumption of resulting use meant that the feoffee bore the onus of proving the consideration for the feoffment. As Lord Nottingham C. stated in *Cook* v. *Fountain*:[69]

> [U]ses at common law were nothing else but secret confidences; but then it is observable that the law did not put the proof of trust upon him who claimed the secret confidence, but it put the proof upon him who claimed the estate, to show for what consideration he held it, else a use did arise to the donor.

The same concept of consideration was applied to the emerging resulting trust in the seventeenth century. In *Grey* v. *Grey*, Lord Nottingham C. described the presumptions of resulting trust and advancement as follows:[70] 'Generally and *prima facie*, as they say, a purchase in the name of a stranger is a trust, for want of consideration, but a purchase in the name of a son is no trust, for the consideration is apparent.'

The basis of the presumption of resulting trust evolved to become more dependent on intention than consideration. However, it should not be assumed that the relevant intention is an intention to create a trust. Although the resulting use first arose because feoffors commonly intended to create resulting uses, this had ceased to be the basis of the resulting use when it was made impossible by the Statute of Uses and was not the basis of the new resulting trust.[71] The ability to devise freehold property, provided by the Statute of Wills 1540 and Tenures Abolition Act 1660, had obviated the primary reasons for feoffments without consideration or a declaration of use.[72]

The essential fact

In many cases of resulting trust, providers intend to have the beneficial ownership of the property for themselves, i.e. they have an intention to create a trust, even if they do not recognize it as such. A good example of this is *Dullow* v. *Dullow*,[73] in which the plaintiff had purchased properties for her sons. Although she was 'lacking in any familiarity with the elementary concepts of property ownership' and 'did not have any clear view of what legal results flowed from

[67] Maitland, p. 33; Barton (1965) at 571–2; Simpson (1986), p. 177.
[68] Simpson (1986), p. 177.
[69] (1676) 3 Sanst. 585, 587; in Kiralfy, p. 270.
[70] (1677) 2 Swans. 594, 597.
[71] Cf. Swadling (1996) at 114–15.
[72] Simpson (1986), pp. 191–2; Baker (1990), pp. 293–4; see Megarry (1941). Barton suggested that a gap in the Statute of Wills encouraged the creation of trusts of freehold estates by purchase in the name of another: Barton (1966) at 223–4.
[73] (1985) 3 N.S.W.L.R. 531.

her intentions',[74] Hope J.A. concluded from the evidence 'that the plaintiff's intention was to reserve a beneficial interest in the properties for herself during her lifetime'.[75] This intention entitled her to a resulting trust of a life estate.

Cases of this sort support the view that the presumption of resulting trust is of an intention to create a trust. However, the other view can also explain every one of these cases, because the provider's intention to keep any portion of the beneficial interest necessarily means that he or she does not intend to pass that interest to the recipient. Most importantly, the converse is not true. Discussed below are many cases of resulting trust in which the provider did not intend to benefit the recipient and yet could not have intended to retain the beneficial interest, because the provider was unaware of the transfer, incapable of creating a trust, or mistaken. There are also cases where the intention to create a trust is unenforceable or simply improbable on the evidence. None of these can be satisfactorily explained by the theory of implied intention to create a trust.[76]

The essential fact of intention, common to all cases of resulting trust, is the provider's lack of intention to benefit the recipient. It should be noted that there is a difference between a presumption that the provider *did not intend* to benefit the recipient and a presumption that the provider *intended not* to benefit the recipient. Only the former can explain all of the cases of resulting trust, including those in which the provider did not form any relevant intention. The latter presumption, though preferable to the theory of presumed intention to create a trust, still requires a positive intention on the part of the provider.

Ignorance

This part is called 'ignorance' in the same sense that Professor Birks has used the term:[77] to describe cases where property has been transferred to another without the knowledge of the beneficial owner of that property. The earliest cases of resulting trust and ignorance involved the purchase of land using other people's money without their consent. This is a small, but logical, extension of the traditional resulting trust in favour of the person who advances the purchase-money.[78] In none of these cases can an intention to create a trust be inferred. The ignorance of the providers means that the only possible inference, capable of giving rise to a resulting trust, is that they did not intend to benefit the recipients of the property.

In *Ryall* v. *Ryall*,[79] the executor had received the assets from the estate and used them to purchase land in his own name. After his death, the testator's legatees brought a bill against the executor's heir at law to be paid their legacies out of the executor's real and personal estate. Their ignorance of the purchases did not prevent the application of the resulting trust. As Lord Hardwicke C. stated, 'the means of coming at this by way of resulting trust is excepted out of the statute of frauds; if the estate is purchased in the name of one, and the money

[74] Ibid. at 537, per Needham J.
[75] Ibid. at 541.
[76] Cf. Swadling (1996) at 131.
[77] Birks (1989a), pp. 140–1.
[78] *Dyer* v. *Dyer* (1788) 2 Cox Eq. 92.
[79] (1739) 1 Atk. 59.

paid by another, it is a trust notwithstanding there is no declaration in writing by the nominal purchaser'.[80]

In *Lane* v. *Dighton*,[81] a husband had persuaded the trustees of the marriage settlement to let him have half of the trust assets, which he used to purchase land in his own name. Under the trust, he was only entitled to the interest on the assets for life, the remainder belonging to his wife and their children. Despite their ignorance of the transaction,[82] they recovered the property on the principle that, 'if *A*. buys land in the name of *B*., *A*. may prove that he paid the consideration, and there will be a resulting trust for him'.[83]

In *Williams* v. *Williams*,[84] a father purchased lands and, without his knowledge, the conveyance was taken in his son's name. The son and the solicitor had honestly, but mistakenly, believed this to be in accordance with the father's wishes. If the father had directed the conveyance into the name of his son and said nothing more, the presumption of advancement would have applied. However, his ignorance of the conveyance to his son negated the possibility that he intended to benefit him, thereby rebutting the presumption of advancement and giving rise to a resulting trust. The outcome should have been reversed if the presumption of resulting trust was either that the father intended to create a trust or that he positively intended not to benefit his son.

There are three Canadian cases of resulting trust and ignorance. In *Merchants Express Co.* v. *Morton*,[85] a hotel in Toronto was purchased with the proceeds from a train robbery in the USA. The victims obtained an injunction, restraining the robbers from disposing of the hotel, on the basis of 'the principle of resulting trust arising from the purchase of property by one with the moneys of another, and upon the principle of the Court following moneys or other property; and fastening upon them in favour of the true owner'.[86] This was followed in *Re Kolari*,[87] where assets purchased by a bank teller, with money stolen from her former employer, were recovered by the employer on the basis that a 'resulting trust arises where property is obtained by fraud or theft'.[88] In *Sharp* v. *McNeil*,[89] a partner secretly used partnership money to purchase land in the name of his sister. The partners became insolvent and the curator of their estate recovered the land. Townshend C.J. stated:[90] 'The law is not so helpless as to leave the party wronged without a remedy, and it holds the person to whom such a conveyance has been made as a trustee for the rightful owner. In other words a resulting trust follows.'

El Ajou v. *Dollar Land Holdings p.l.c.*[91] is a recent case which may herald a

[80] Ibid. at 59–60. [81] (1762) Amb. 409.
[82] See Grant M.R.'s comments on *Lane* v. *Dighton* in *Lench* v. *Lench* (1805) 10 Ves. 511, 517.
[83] *Lane* v. *Dighton* (1762) Amb. 409, 411, per Clarke M.R. [84] (1863) 32 Beav. 370.
[85] (1868) 15 Gr. 274. [86] Ibid. at 278, per Spragge V.C. [87] (1981) 36 O.R. (2d) 473.
[88] Ibid. at 478, per Stortini D.C.J.
[89] (1913) 15 D.L.R. 73 (N.S.S.C.A.D.); aff'd (1915) 70 D.L.R. 740, S.C.C.
[90] Ibid. at 75. [91] [1993] 3 All E.R. 717; rev'd [1994] 2 All E.R. 685.

revival of the application of the resulting trust to these situations. The plaintiff's agent was bribed to invest over 13 million dollars of the plaintiff's money in worthless shares. The money was passed through several accounts in different countries before some of it was invested in land owned by the defendant. Millett J. considered the question of the plaintiff's right to trace the money in equity and was of the opinion that the misappropriation of his money gave rise to 'an old-fashioned institutional resulting trust'.[92]

Incapacity

In cases of ignorance, the plaintiff has no intention to benefit the recipient because he or she is unaware of the transfer. There is a similar absence of intention to benefit the recipient when the provider lacks the legal or mental capacity to consent to the transfer. In *Goodfellow* v. *Robertson*, property was transferred while the owner may have been suffering from an 'unsoundness of mind'.[93] Spragge C. relied on *Ryall* v. *Ryall*, in which the providers were unaware of the transfer,[94] to conclude that a resulting trust could apply where the provider lacked capacity, because, in both cases, there was no 'assenting mind'.[95] The evidence of incapacity does not rebut the presumption of resulting trust, but confirms it. One would expect the opposite to be true if the presumption was of an intention to create a trust.

Mistake

There are many cases in which property has been transferred by mistake and the court has declared the recipient to be a trustee for the transferor.[96] However, the courts have rarely classified the trust in this situation. In two cases, the trust was expressly identified as resulting: *El Ajou* v. *Dollar Land Holdings*[97] and *Clelland* v. *Clelland*.[98]

As discussed above, *El Ajou* v. *Dollar Land Holdings* is a case of ignorance in which the plaintiff's agent had been bribed to purchase worthless shares. Millett J. also considered the plight of other victims of the defendant's fraud, who had themselves paid their money under a fraudulently induced mistake and could not rely on an agent's breach of fiduciary duty. His lordship stated *obiter*:[99]

> It would, of course, be an intolerable reproach to our system of jurisprudence if the plaintiff were the only victim who could trace and recover his money. Neither party before me suggested that this is the case; and I agree with them. But if the other victims of the fraud can trace their money in equity it must be because, having been induced to

[92] Ibid. at 734. [93] (1871) 18 Gr. 572, 574, per Spragge C. [94] Above, p. 21.

[95] (1871) 18 Gr. 572, 575, per Spragge C. Also see *Lench* v. *Lench* (1805) 10 Ves. 511, where a wife's incapacity as *feme covert* made her consent irrelevant.

[96] e.g. *Leuty* v. *Hillas* (1858) 2 De G.&J. 110; *Craddock Brothers* v. *Hunt* [1923] 2 Ch. 136, C.A.; *Chase Manhattan Bank N.A.* v. *Israel-British Bank (London) Ltd.* [1981] Ch. 105; *Blacklocks* v. *J.B. Developments (Godalming) Ltd.* [1982] Ch. 183. [97] [1993] 3 All E.R. 717.

[98] [1945] 3 D.L.R. 664, B.C.C.A.; aff'g [1944] 4 D.L.R. 703.

[99] [1993] 3 All E.R. 717, 734.

purchase the shares by false and fraudulent misrepresentations, they are entitled to rescind the transaction and revest the equitable title to the purchase money in themselves, at least to the extent necessary to support an equitable tracing claim . . . But, if this is correct, as I think it is, then the trust which is operating in these cases is not some new model remedial constructive trust, but an old-fashioned institutional resulting trust.

The other victims' mistake, like the plaintiff's ignorance, proved the lack of intention to benefit the recipients necessary for the resulting trust.

In the Canadian case of *Clelland* v. *Clelland*, the plaintiff and defendant went through an invalid ceremony of marriage. While the plaintiff was in England during the Second World War and the parties believed they were legally married to each other, he transferred practically all of his assets to the defendant or into their joint names. His reason for doing so was to provide for his wife in the event of his death. Upon the breakdown of their relationship, the plaintiff obtained a declaration that the defendant held her interest in the transferred assets in trust for the plaintiff.

The British Columbia Court of Appeal held that there was a presumption of resulting trust, which was affirmed by evidence that the plaintiff intended to give only a right of survivorship and no 'present beneficial interest at all'.[100] The difficulty with this approach is that proof of the intention to give a right of survivorship should partially rebut the presumption of resulting trust to the extent of that right of survivorship.[101]

The trial judge had also concluded there was a resulting trust, but by a somewhat different route:[102]

The parties agree that there is no presumption of advancement in respect of transfers made by a man to a woman who is not his wife with one qualification. Counsel for the defendant submits that the presumption of advancement rests on intention, and while it is true that no presumption of advancement arises in respect of such a transfer, yet if the transferor thought the transferee to be his wife, then his intention governs the construction of his act, and the presumption is the same as if she were his wife. I do not think this is so. I think the law is that if he is so mistaken, then the mistake excludes intention . . . The mistake here was, as I see it, fundamental or basic. I find that all the plaintiff did, he did on the underlying assumption that the defendant was his wife and she was not.

The trial judge's reasoning supports the declaration of resulting trust of the defendant's entire interest in the property. The intention to grant of a right of survivorship, which would otherwise partially rebut the presumption of resulting trust, is vitiated by proof of the plaintiff's mistake.[103] Although the mistake

[100] [1945] 3 D.L.R. 664, 666, per Robertson J.A.

[101] *Fowkes* v. *Pascoe* (1875) 10 Ch.App. 343, 351; *Napier* v. *Public Trustee* (1980) 32 A.L.R. 153, 158; Meagher and Gummow, *Jacobs' Law of Trusts*, p. 277; Ford and Lee, §21140. See *Davies* v. *National Executors* [1912] V.L.R. 397, 406.

[102] [1944] 4 D.L.R. 703, 706–7, per Macfarlane J.

[103] Cf. Bogert and Bogert, §459, pp. 332–3; *Street* v. *Hallett* (1874) 21 Gr. 255, 259–60, where a woman's claim for a resulting trust failed in spite of the finding that she would not have advanced the purchase money to the defendant had she known her marriage to him was invalid due to his bigamy.

cannot support an inference that the plaintiff intended to create a trust of that right, it does prove a lack of intention to benefit the defendant.

Unenforceable intention

Hodgson v. *Marks*[104] is a case in which an intention to create a trust was unenforceable. The plaintiff had transferred her house to her lodger and intended that he should hold the house in trust for herself. The express trust was ineffective because it was not made in writing as required by subsection 53(1) of the Law of Property Act 1925. The Court of Appeal held that the plaintiff was the beneficiary of a resulting trust:[105]

> [T]he evidence is clear that the transfer was not intended to operate as a gift, and, in those circumstances, I do not see why there was not a resulting trust of the beneficial interest to the plaintiff, which would not, of course, be affected by section 53(1). It was argued that a resulting trust is based upon implied intention, and that where there is an express trust for the transferor intended and declared—albeit ineffectively—there is no room for such an implication. I do not accept that. If an attempted express trust fails, that seems to me just the occasion for implication of a resulting trust, whether the failure be due to uncertainty, or perpetuity, or lack of form. It would be a strange outcome if the plaintiff were to lose her beneficial interest because her evidence had not been confined to negativing a gift but had additionally moved into the field forbidden by section 53(1) for lack of writing.

This was not a case concerning the presumption of resulting trust, because there was proof of the transferor's intention. Her intention to create a trust was significant because it proved the lack of intention to transfer the beneficial interest. The court had evidence of the transferor's intention to create a trust for herself and identified the absence of intention to benefit the recipient as the essential element which gave rise to the resulting trust.[106] The presumption of resulting trust cannot be of a different intention than that which, when proven, gives rise to the resulting trust.

Improbable intention

There are other cases where the construction of an intention to create a trust is possible, but not probable, thereby making it difficult to infer an intention to create a trust. This problem is easily avoided by the realization that the relevant question is not whether the provider intended to create a trust, but whether he or she intended to benefit the recipient.

In *Re Vinogradoff*[107] and *Re Muller*,[108] the intention to create a trust was highly improbable because the recipients were less than 7 years old at the time. It was argued in *Re Vinogradoff* that the provider must have known about

[104] [1971] 1 Ch. 892. [105] Ibid. at 933, per Russell L.J.

[106] This simple explanation of the case renders redundant the more complex explanation in Birks (1989a), pp. 61–2; as Birks later recognized in Birks (1992c) at pp. 363–4.

[107] [1935] W.N. 68. [108] [1953] N.Z.L.R. 879.

section 20 of the Law of Property Act 1925 (which makes void the appointment of infants as trustees) and therefore could not have intended to create a trust. Farwell J. rejected this argument and held that the section 'did not operate to make any difference to the presumption'.[109] This was followed in *Re Muller*, where Northcroft J. held that 'a benefit to the children has not been shown to have been intended, and they must be regarded as trustees'.[110]

In *Lattimer* v. *Lattimer*,[111] a mother purchased real property in the joint names of herself and her son. Although the mother had instructed her solicitor to obtain title this way and she and her son had executed a mortgage of the property, she did not understand what joint ownership meant. Grange J. stated, 'Having observed both mother and son giving evidence I am satisfied that both could have signed the mortgage without knowing how title was taken'.[112] The son failed to rebut the presumption of resulting trust. He was unable to show that his mother had intended a gift, but the outcome might well have been different if the issue was whether his mother intended to create a trust.

Brown v. *Brown*[113] is very similar. A mother contributed to the purchase of a house in the name of her sons (and may not have been aware that legal title was taken in their names only). The evidence showed that the parties had not 'thought through the consequences of their transaction, or made any agreement about title to the land that was being purchased'.[114] The court concluded that the mother 'did not have any intention concerning the potential ownership of the' property.[115] Although the presumption of advancement was applied in favour of the sons, the majority held it was rebutted by the fact that the mother 'did not intend to make a gift (or a loan) to her sons'.[116]

In these cases, the courts focused on the essential element of the resulting trust: the lack of the provider's intention to benefit the recipient of the property. There was no need to impute a possibly fictional intention to create a trust to people who had failed to appreciate the relationships created by their transactions.

It is of interest that Kirby P. dissented in *Brown* v. *Brown* because the presumption of advancement had not been adequately rebutted, there being no evidence 'that the mother positively intended *not* to make a gift to her sons'.[117] This vividly demonstrates the importance of stating the presumption of resulting trust in negative, rather than positive terms (i.e. 'not intended' instead of 'intended not').[118] The finding of 'no intention to give' is a fact, which displaces the inferences arising in the absence of evidence regarding intention. This fact is sufficient to both confirm the presumption of resulting trust and rebut the presumption of advancement.[119]

[109] [1935] W.N. 68. [110] [1953] N.Z.L.R. 879, 883.
[111] (1978) 82 D.L.R. (3d) 587 (Ont.). [112] Ibid. at 589.
[113] (1993) 31 N.S.W.L.R. 582, C.A. [114] Ibid. at 586, per Gleeson C.J.
[115] Ibid. at 587, per Gleeson C.J. [116] Ibid. at 591, per Gleeson C.J.
[117] Ibid. at 601, per Kirby P. [118] Cf. *Allen* v. *Snyder* [1977] 2 N.S.W.L.R. 685, 698.
[119] Hovius and Youdan, p. 102; Youdan (1993) at 172.

Intention to purchase

It is often said that a resulting trust will not arise in favour of a contributor to the purchase price unless he or she made the contribution 'in the character of a purchaser'.[120] This does not mean that the contributor must have intended to purchase the property in question. As established in *Ryall* v. *Ryall* and many of the other cases discussed above, the resulting trust can arise in favour of the contributor even though he or she was unaware of the contribution having been made.[121] The expression really means that the presumption of resulting trust will not apply if the contribution was intended to be a gift, loan[122] or payment for some other purpose.

This issue was examined in *Goodfellow* v. *Robertson*, where the intention to purchase may have been impossible because of the contributor's mental incapacity. Spragge C. thought that the resulting trust could still apply:[123]

> It could scarcely lie in the mouth of a person so appropriating his money to deny it in a case where the application of the rule would be for the benefit of the owner of the money; it is a trust resulting by operation of law, and it does not seem to be necessary to prove that the money was advanced by its owner in order to its application in the purchase of the land. If such proof were necessary, an assenting mind on his part would necessarily have to be shewn; and in the case of the money of a lunatic, the rule could not apply. In nearly all the cases certainly the money was advanced by the nominal purchaser for the purpose of making the purchase; but there are some cases in which this was not the case; *Ryall* v. *Ryall* was one of these.

B. PRESUMPTION OF ADVANCEMENT

1. Facts Giving Rise to the Presumption

Where facts exist which normally give rise to the presumption of resulting trust, the presumption will not apply if the parties are in a relationship which gives rise to the presumption of advancement. The existence of certain relationships (traditionally, where the provider was the recipient's father or husband) creates an inference that the provider intended to make a gift to the recipient. The application of the presumption of advancement has evolved over time and been modified by statute in many jurisdictions.

[120] *Bateman TV* v. *Bateman* [1970] N.Z.L.R. 453, 460, per Turner J. See *Aveling* v. *Knipe* (1815) 19 Ves. 441; *Davies* v. *National Executors* [1912] V. L.R. 397; *Clark* v. *MacInnis* [1953] O.W.N. 551; *Hussey* v. *Palmer* [1972] 1 W.L.R. 1286, 1293, C.A.; *Calverley* v. *Green* (1984) 155 C.L.R. 242, 246; Mowbray, *Lewin on Trusts*, p. 130; Waters, p. 305; Gray, p. 390; Ford and Lee, §21110.

[121] Also see *Scott* v. *Scott* (1963) 109 C.L.R. 649, 663–4. Cf. Bogert and Bogert, §455, §458.

[122] *In re Sharpe* [1980] 1 W.L.R. 219; *Calverley* v. *Green* (1984) 155 C.L.R. 242, 246; Mowbray, *Lewin on Trusts*, p. 130; Meagher and Gummow, *Jacobs' Law of Trusts*, p. 270; Oakley (1994), p. 190. Cf. *Hussey* v. *Palmer* [1972] 1 W.L.R. 1286, 1291–2.

[123] (1871) 18 Gr. 572, 575.

Fathers and persons in *loco parentis*

It is well settled that a father's provision of property to his child gives rise to a presumption of advancement.[124] This has been extended to include property provided by someone standing *in loco parentis* to the recipient.[125] The reason for this treatment of the relationship between father and child may originally have been explained by the early doctrine of consideration. Consideration was needed to pass the use, and the kinship of the feoffee, like a bargain and sale, provided a reason for the feoffment which would cause the use to pass.[126] This was rejected as a basis for the presumption of advancement by Eyre C.B. in *Dyer* v. *Dyer* (albeit reluctantly) and it was thought that the relationship of the parties was evidence which made it more likely that a gift was intended.

The presumption of advancement was attributed to the father's duty to make some provision for his children which would 'advance' them in the world and, therefore, would not apply if the provision had already been made.[127] Jessel M.R. described the father's duty as a 'moral legal obligation',[128] which appears to have meant a duty which was not enforceable, but recognized by a court of equity as the source of the presumption. This provided the reason for extending the presumption of advancement to those standing *in loco parentis*, who were under 'the duty of a father of a child to make a provision for that child',[129] and not extending it to mothers,[130] who were not under the same duty.

Mothers

Although the presumption of advancement clearly applies to fathers, it was not established with the same degree of certainty that it did not apply to mothers.[131] In *Garrett* v. *Wilkinson*, Knight Bruce V.C. thought that the presumption of advancement 'probably' applied to mothers.[132] In *Sayre* v. *Hughes*, Stuart V.C. stated:[133]

> It has been argued that a mother is not a person bound to make an advancement to her child, and that a widowed mother is not a person standing in such a relation to her child as to raise a presumption that in a transaction of this kind a benefit was intended for the

[124] *Dyer* v. *Dyer* (1788) 2 Cox Eq. 92, 93–4; *Charles Marshall Pty. Ltd.* v. *Grimsley* (1956) 95 C.L.R. 353, 363–4. See Waters (1984), p. 315; Martin (1993a), p. 245.

[125] *Ebrand* v. *Dancer* (1680) 2 Ch. Cas. 26; *Currant* v. *Jago* (1844) 1 Coll. 261; *Bennet* v. *Bennet* (1879) 10 Ch.D. 474, 476–7; *Charles Marshall Pty. Ltd.* v. *Grimsley* (1956) 95 C.L.R. 353, 364; *Re Paradise Motor Co. Ltd.* [1968] 2 All E.R. 625, 629, C.A.

[126] *Grey* v. *Grey* (1677) 2 Swans. 594; *Soar* v. *Foster* (1858) 4 K.&J. 152; *Wirth* v. *Wirth* (1956) 98 C.L.R. 228, 237; *Calverley* v. *Green* (1984) 155 C.L.R. 242, 249.

[127] *Elliot* v. *Elliot* (1677) 2 Ch.Cas. 231; *Grey* v. *Grey* (1677) 2 Swans. 594, 600. See *Ward* v. *Lant* (1701) Pr.Ch. 182; Mowbray, *Lewin on Trusts*, pp. 134–5.

[128] *Bennet* v. *Bennet* (1879) 10 Ch.D. 474, 478.

[129] Ibid. at 477, per Jessel M.R.

[130] Ibid. at 478; *Scott* v. *Pauly* (1917) 24 C.L.R. 274, 281–2; *Pickens* v. *Metcalf* [1932] N.Z.L.R. 1278, 1282–3; *Lattimer* v. *Lattimer* (1978) 82 D.L.R. (3d) 587, 590.

[131] Mowbray, *Lewin on Trusts*, p. 139; Hovius and Youdan, pp. 60–2; Gray, p. 408; Oakley (1994), p. 194.

[132] (1848) 2 De G.&Sm. 244, 246.

[133] (1856) L.R. 5 Eq. 376, 381.

child. But the case of a stranger who stands in loco parentis seems not so strong as that of a mother . . . maternal affection, as a motive of bounty, is, perhaps, the strongest of all, although the duty is not so strong as in the case of a father, inasmuch as it is the duty of a father to advance his child. That, however, is a moral obligation, and not a legal one.

In *Bennett* v. *Bennett*, Jessel M.R. expressly rejected the reasoning in *Sayre* v. *Hughes* on the basis that mothers were not under an obligation to provide for their children and 'equity does not presume an obligation which does not exist'.[134] His lordship did think that, 'in the case of a mother very little evidence beyond the relationship is wanted, there being very little additional motive required to induce a mother to make a gift to her child'.[135] Jessel M.R.'s opinion appears to have prevailed and the presumption of resulting trust was applied to a purchase by a mother for her daughter as recently as 1989 in *Sekhon* v. *Alissa*.[136]

The presumption of advancement is applied to the mother–child relationship in the USA on the basis that 'an intention to make a gift to a child is as natural in the case of a mother as in the case of a father'.[137] It has also been applied to mothers in several Australian and Canadian cases,[138] sometimes with the justification that there is now 'an obligation upon a mother to support her children'.[139] However, the duty being referred to is statutory and, unlike the father's traditional obligation of advancement, it only lasts through the child's minority or further dependency.

Although the statutory duty of care does not itself provide a convincing reason for extending the presumption of advancement to mothers, the fact remains that there is today no difference between the duties fathers and mothers owe their children nor any reason to suppose that one parent is more likely to intend a gift than the other.[140] One can only assume that the equal treatment of mothers and fathers will become the order of the day.[141] However, it should be considered whether the presumption of advancement ought to apply in all cases. Substantial gifts from elderly parents to children on whom they depend might well be circumstances of which equity should be suspicious. The way forward might be to look back to the 1848 case of *Garrett* v. *Wilkinson*,[142] where Knight Bruce V.C. assumed that the presumption of advancement applied to mothers as well as fathers, but refused to apply the presumption in favour of a son who was a solicitor looking after his mother's financial affairs. The Vice-Chancellor

[134] (1879) 10 Ch.D. 474, 478. [135] Ibid. at 480. [136] [1989] 2 F.L.R. 94.

[137] Scott and Fratcher, §442; also see *Restatement of Trusts*, §442; Bogert and Bogert, §460.

[138] *Rupar* v. *Rupar* (1964) 46 D.L.R. (2d) 553 (B.C.); *Cohen* v. *Cohen* (1985) 60 A.R. 234; *Re Dagle* (1990) 70 D.L.R. (4th) 201, 208 (P.E.I.); *Brown* v. *Brown* (1993) 31 N.S.W.L.R. 582, C.A.; *Dreger* v. *Dreger* [1994] 10 W.W.R. 293, 301–2, Man. C.A.; *Nelson* v. *Nelson* (1995) 70 A.L.J.R. 47.

[139] *Re Dagle* (1990) 70 D.L.R. (4th) 201, 208. Also see *Cohen* v. *Cohen* (1985) 60 A.R. 234, 237; *Brown* v. *Brown* (1993) 31 N.S.W.L.R. 582, 599.

[140] *Brown* v. *Brown* (1993) 31 N.S.W.L.R. 582. [141] Cf. Sarmas (1994b).

[142] (1848) 2 De G.&Sm. 244.

said, 'the very particular position in which the son stood towards his mother neutralises or prevents the application of the general rule, in my judgment'.[143]

Spouses

It was at one time settled that there was a presumption of advancement on a transfer from husband to wife,[144] but not from wife to husband.[145] This may have been based on a husband's duty to provide for his wife or on a judicial desire to protect the interests of economically dependent wives.[146] It was implied in *Soar* v. *Foster*[147] that the presumption of advancement from husband to wife could not rest on the husband's moral obligation to provide for his wife. In that case, a man had married his deceased wife's sister 5 years after such marriages were prohibited by statute.[148] Page Wood V.C. refused to apply the presumption of advancement to the void marriage, even though, 'Any moralist would say that a man was bound to make provision for the woman with whom he had so cohabited'.[149] If the presumption of advancement rested on the husband's duty, it must have been his legal duty to provide for his wife.[150]

The presumption of advancement has been applied to a transfer from a man to a woman made in contemplation of their marriage.[151] The courts have consistently refused to apply the presumption of advancement to transfers between '*de facto* spouses'.[152] However, in *Calverley* v. *Green*, Gibbs C.J. would have extended the presumption of advancement to this situation on the basis that:[153] 'The presumption should be held to be raised when the relationship between the parties is such that it is more probable than not that a beneficial interest was intended to be conferred, whether or not the purchaser owed the other a legal or moral duty of support'. Murphy J. wanted to abandon the presumption of resulting trust altogether,[154] but he and Gibbs C.J. were in the minority on these issues.

The utility of the presumption of advancement from husband to wife has been called into question[155] and, in many jurisdictions, has been amended by legislation.[156] There is clearly no longer any possible justification for applying different presumptions to men and women. There has also been criticism of the different treatment of spouses and *de facto* spouses,[157] but it should be remembered that *de facto* spouses are not treated as exceptions to the rule. The presumption of

[143] Ibid. at 246. [144] *In re Eykyn's Trusts* (1877) 6 Ch.D. 115, 118.
[145] *Re Curtis* (1885) 52 L.T. 244, 245. [146] *Pettitt* v. *Pettitt* [1970] A.C. 777, 793.
[147] (1858) 4 K.&J. 152. [148] Lord Lyndhurst's Act 1835, 5&7 Will. 4, c. 54.
[149] (1858) 4 K.&J. 152, 161. [150] Maxton (1986) at 82–4.
[151] *Moate* v. *Moate* (1948) 2 All E.R. 486; *Wirth* v. *Wirth* (1956) 98 C.L.R. 228, 237. See Lowe.
[152] *Napier* v. *Public Trustee* (1980) 32 A.L.R. 153; *Calverley* v. *Green* (1984) 155 C.L.R. 242.
[153] (1984) 155 C.L.R. 242, 250. [154] Above, p. 15.
[155] *Pettitt* v. *Pettitt* [1970] A.C. 777, 793, 811; *Rathwell* v. *Rathwell* (1978) 83 D.L.R. (3d) 289, 304, S.C.C.; *Re Dagle* (1990) 70 D.L.R. (4th) 201, 207; Gray, p. 408.
[156] See Waters (1984), pp. 313–14, 361–3; Hovius and Youdan, p. 64 ff; Ford and Lee, §21220.
[157] *Calverley* v. *Green* (1984) 155 C.L.R. 242, 250–1, 264–5; Maxton (1986).

resulting trust applies to them as it does to most people, including married women, unless modified by statute. In equity, only husbands and parents are not protected by the presumption.

2. The Fact Being Presumed

The presumption of advancement has been described as nothing more than a situation to which the presumption of resulting trust does not apply.[158] Another view is that the presumption of advancement operates because the relationship between the parties 'is no more than a circumstance of evidence which may rebut the presumption of resulting trust'.[159] It is undoubtedly true that the relationship is an additional fact nullifying the inference that the provider did not intend to benefit the recipient. However, it also raises an inference that the provider intended to make a gift.[160] As Spence J. stated in *Goodfriend* v. *Goodfriend*:[161] 'when, however, the relationship between the transferor and transferee is husband and wife, or father and child, there is a presumption of advancement, that is, that the transferor intended to make a gift of the subject-matter of the transfer to the transferee'.

The presumptions of resulting trust and advancement are not exactly converse inferences. The former is that the recipient was not intended to have the beneficial ownership of the property; the latter that it was intended as a gift. There is at least one other possibility: the creditor–debtor relationship, in which the beneficial ownership was intended to pass, but was to be paid for.[162] Evidence of the intention to create a debt rebuts both the presumption of resulting trust[163] and the presumption of advancement,[164] by showing both that the recipient was intended to enjoy the benefit of the property and that no gift was intended.

Seldon v. *Davidson*[165] demonstrates the independent nature of the presumption of advancement. The plaintiff pleaded that she had made a loan to the defendant, her chauffeur-handyman at that time. The defendant acknowledged receiving the money, but alleged it was a gift. The Court of Appeal, on an interlocutory motion, decided that the burden of proof was on the defendant, who must therefore begin the case:[166]

[158] *Martin* v. *Martin* (1959) 110 C.L.R. 297, 303–4; *Calverley* v. *Green* (1984) 155 C.L.R. 242.

[159] *Pettitt* v. *Pettitt* [1970] A.C. 777, 814, per Lord Upjohn. See *Dyer* v. *Dyer* (1788) 2 Cox Eq. 92, 93–4; *Scott* v. *Pauly* (1917) 24 C.L.R. 274, 281–2.

[160] *Re Eykyn's Trusts* (1877) 6 Ch.D. 115, 118; *Sidmouth* v. *Sidmouth* (1840) 2 Beav. 447, 454; *Soar* v. *Foster* (1858) 4 K.&J. 152, 160–1; *Bennet* v. *Bennet* (1879) 10 Ch.D. 474, 476–7; *Davies* v. *National Executors* [1912] V.L.R. 397; *Charles Marshall* v. *Grimsley* (1956) 95 C.L.R. 353, 364; Maitland, p. 78; Lowe at 141–2; Waters (1984), p. 313; Hackney, p. 150; Gardner (1990), p. 57; Sheridan, p. 198; Pettit (1993), pp. 132–3.

[161] [1972] S.C.R. 640, 22 D.L.R. (3d) 699, 703.

[162] Riddall, p. 206; see *Sekhon* v. *Alissa* [1989] 2 F.L.R. 94, 99.

[163] *Hussey* v. *Palmer* [1972] 1 W.L.R. 1286, 1292 (Cairns L.J., dissenting); *Re Sharpe* [1980] 1 W.L.R. 219, 223; Meagher and Gummow, *Jacobs' Law of Trusts*, p. 275; Gray, p. 404; Sheridan, p. 197.

[164] *Re Whitehouse* (1888) 37 Ch.D. 683; Mowbray, *Lewin on Trusts*, p. 138.

[165] [1968] 2 All E.R. 755, C.A.

[166] Ibid. at 757, per Willmer L.J. Cf. Ford and Lee, §21100.

Payment of the money having been admitted, prima facie that payment imported an obligation to repay in the absence of any circumstances tending to show anything in the nature of the presumption of advancement. This is not a case of father and child, or husband or wife, or any other such blood relationship which could give rise to a presumption of advancement.

This shows how the presumption of advancement, being an inference that a gift was intended, can be applied to cases having nothing to do with the resulting trust.[167]

C. PRINCIPLE OF RESULTING TRUST

There is an important distinction between the presumption of resulting trust and the resulting trust itself. This distinction was clearly drawn in *Hodgson* v. *Marks*, where the Court of Appeal was 'not concerned with the debatable question whether on a voluntary transfer of land by A to stranger B there is a presumption of a resulting trust'.[168] The resulting trust arose independently of the presumption because it was proven that the transfer 'was not intended as a gift'.[169]

The presumption is an inference of a fact drawn from the existence of other facts, whereas the resulting trust is the equitable response to those facts, proven or presumed.[170] The facts which give rise to the presumption of resulting trust are (i) a transfer of property to another, (ii) for which the recipient does not provide the whole of the consideration. The facts which give rise to the resulting trust itself are (i) a transfer of property to another, (ii) in circumstances in which the provider does not intend to benefit the recipient. It should be noted that the first fact (a transfer of property) is the same in both cases, but the second is not.

There are two things to note about this difference. First, the lack of consideration required for the presumption is not a requirement for the resulting trust.[171] Secondly, the lack of intention to benefit the recipient required for the resulting trust is precisely the fact being inferred when the presumption is applied. In other words, the resulting trust always requires (i) that property has been transferred to another[172] and (ii) that the provider did not intend to benefit the recipient, but the existence of the second fact may be inferred where the recipient did not provide the whole consideration for the transfer.

It should also be noted that the presumptions of resulting trust and advancement do not apply if the question whether the provider intended to benefit the

[167] Cf. Meagher and Gummow, *Jacobs's Law of Trusts*, p. 270; and see *Black* v. *S. Freedman & Co.* (1910) 12 C.L.R. 105, 109, where a man paid stolen money to his wife and Griffith C.J. used the presumption of advancement to infer that she had not given value for the payment.

[168] [1971] 1 Ch. 892, 933, per Russell L.J.

[169] Ibid., per Russell L.J.

[170] Ford and Lee, §21060.

[171] See, e.g., *Barclays Bank Ltd.* v. *Quistclose Investments Ltd.* [1970] A.C. 567; discussed in Chapter 3, below.

[172] *Vandervell (No. 2)* [1974] Ch. 269, 294.

recipient can be answered from the evidence.[173] Lord Upjohn said that the 'presumption of a resulting trust is no more than a long stop to provide the answer when the relevant facts and circumstances fail to yield a solution'.[174] As Lamm J. stated, 'Presumptions may be looked on as the bats of the law, flitting in the twilight but disappearing in the sunshine of actual facts'.[175]

This is sometimes overlooked. For example, in *Brown* v. *Brown*, where the presumption of advancement was rebutted by evidence that the mother did not intend to make a gift or loan to her sons, Gleeson C.J. concluded: 'Since there was no operative presumption of advancement, the basic presumption of resulting trust applied'.[176] However, proof of the provider's intention leaves nothing to presume. Care should be taken to keep the presumption of resulting trust separate from the trust itself. Their confusion tends to obscure the nature of each and the fact that the resulting trust can apply even though the presumption does not (e.g. where it is precluded by statute,[177] the recipient has given consideration for the transfer, or the presumption of advancement applies).

1. The Role of Intention

It has long been accepted that resulting trusts arise by operation of law.[178] However, there are many who pay only lip service to this concept and really conceive of the resulting trust as a case where the intention to create a trust is presumed.[179] Professor Waters asks, 'The nature of the resulting trust is still the subject of some discussion, however; is it a trust which is concerned with the intent of the transferor of the property, or does it describe a trust obligation imposed by law?'[180] These two options are not contradictory and the resulting trust is really both, because it is dependent on the provider's intention, but not the intention to create a trust. Where the provider does not intend to benefit the recipient, the resulting trust arises by operation of law.[181] It is equity's response to the receipt of property by someone who was not intended to have the benefit of that property.[182]

[173] *Pettit* v. *Pettit* [1970] A.C. 777, 823; *Scott* v. *Pauly* (1917) 24 C.L.R. 274; *Muschinski* v. *Dodds* (1985) A.L.J.R. 52, 64; Gray, p. 402.

[174] *Vandervell* v. *I.R.C.* [1967] 2 A.C. 291, 313.

[175] *Mackowik* v. *Kansas City* (1906) 94 S.W. 256, 262; quoted in Gray, p. 402.

[176] (1993) 31 N.S.W.L.R. 582, 591.

[177] e.g. Law of Property Act 1925, s. 60(3); Alberta Matrimonial Property Act, R.S.A. 1980, c. M-9, s. 36(2): 'the fact that property is placed or taken in the name of both spouses as joint owners is prima facie proof that a joint ownership of the beneficial interest in the property is intended'; see Hovius and Youdan, p. 64 ff.

[178] *Willis* v. *Willis* (1740) 2 Atk. 71; *Withers* v. *Withers* (1752) Amb. 151; *Lane* v. *Dighton* (1762) Amb. 409, 411; *Barton* v. *Muir* (1874) L.R. 6 P.C. 134, 145; *Davies* v. *National Executors* [1912] V.L.R. 397, 401; *Martin* v. *Martin* (1959) 110 C.L.R. 297, 304–5; Waters (1984), p. 300.

[179] e.g. Meagher and Gummow, *Jacobs' Law of Trusts*, p. 263; Gray, p. 386.

[180] Waters (1984), p. 18. Also see *Allen* v. *Snyder* [1977] 2 N.S.W.L.R. 685, 698.

[181] *Davies* v. *National Executors* [1912] V.L.R. 397, 401.

[182] See *Cooke* v. *Smith* (1890) 45 Ch.D. 38, 41–2 (Kekewich J.); aff'd [1891] A.C. 297; *Niles* v. *Lake* [1947] 2 D.L.R. 248, 256.

It is essential that this principle be properly understood. Mr. Swadling has suggested 'that the trust which arises in the case of a transfer made without consideration does so because of a presumption that this is what the parties actually intended'.[183] Although this theory found favour with Lord Browne-Wilkinson in *Westdeutsche Landesbank Girozentrale* v. *Islington L.B.C.*,[184] it cannot explain many of the cases of resulting trust discussed above. However, there is another important objection: why should the presumed intention to create a trust be effective to do so? It would contradict the well established requirement of certainty of intention to create a trust. As du Parq L.J. stated in *Re Schebsman*, unless an intention to create a trust is clearly to be collected from the language used and the circumstances of the case, I think that the court ought not to be astute to discover indications of such an intention'.[185] Additionally, there are situations in which an intention to create a trust, even when proved, will not be effective unless made in accordance with certain formalities (e.g. trusts of land and testamentary trusts).

In *Hodgson* v. *Marks*,[186] the plaintiff's expressed intention to create a trust of land for herself was ineffective because it was not made in writing as required by section 53(1) of the Law of Property Act 1925. Section 53(2) exempts resulting trusts from that requirement, not because an express trust for oneself need not be in writing, but because the resulting trust arises by operation of law in response to facts other than an intention to create a trust. Suppose that Mrs. Hodgson had orally expressed an intention to create a trust for a third person. This would rebut a presumption that she intended to create a trust for herself and yet the consequence would be the same: a resulting trust for herself. It has been suggested that these two situations are entirely different,[187] but it will be shown in the next chapter that this is not so. In both cases, the resulting trust arises as an equitable response to the same facts. The intention to create a trust, though ineffective for that purpose, proves that the transfer 'was not intended as a gift'.[188]

The way in which the resulting trust responds to the (presumed or proven) intention of a person who provides property to another illustrates the 'fine but important distinction between intent conceived as creative of rights, as in an express trust or a contract, and intent conceived as a fact which, along with others, calls for the creation of rights by operation of law'.[189] If the resulting trust was created by the presumed intention that it should exist, it could not properly be applied whenever that intention was impossible, improbable, or unenforceable. The court would then be forced to either resort to the presumption of a fictional intention or deny the appropriate relief. The problem created by this misunderstanding would be similar to the vexation caused by treating

[183] Swadling (1996) at 115. [184] [1996] 2 All E.R. 961, 990–1.
[185] [1944] Ch. 83, 104. [186] [1971] 1 Ch. 892; see p. 25 above.
[187] *Re Vandervell's Trusts (No. 2)* [1974] 1 Ch. 269, 288–96 (per Megarry J.).
[188] *Hodgson* v. *Marks* [1971] 1 Ch. 892, 933, per Russell L.J. [189] Birks (1989a), p. 65.

quasi-contractual obligations as implied contracts.[190] It is a problem which is entirely avoidable by a proper understanding of the resulting trust.

2. The Recipient's Intention

In most cases of resulting trust, the only relevant intention is that of the provider.[191] The presumptions of resulting trust and advancement are inferences of the provider's intention and it is the lack of his or her intention to benefit the recipient which attracts the resulting trust itself. The recipient's intentions are usually irrelevant and the presumptions and resulting trust can apply even though he or she is unaware of the receipt of the property in question.[192] There are, however, three situations in which the recipient's intention or knowledge can affect the application of the resulting trust.

Bona fide purchase

The first and most important situation in which the recipient's knowledge is relevant is where the legal ownership of the property subject to the resulting trust is acquired for value by a *bona fide* purchaser. So long as the recipient has acted in good faith and without notice of the trust or the circumstances giving rise to that trust,[193] his or her claim will prevail over that of the resulting trust beneficiaries.

Contract

The second situation is much like the first. The defence of *bona fide* purchase is normally reserved for cases involving at least three parties: where the legal owner of property, which is subject to an equitable interest in favour of the plaintiff, transfers the legal ownership to the defendant. A related principle can apply in two-party situations. As becomes apparent in Chapter 3, resulting trusts can arise even though the property was transferred pursuant to a valid contract. Like the recipient in a three-party situation, the recipient directly from the resulting trust claimant is not affected by that trust if he or she acquired the property for value in good faith and without notice. In the USA, the defence of *bona fide* purchase applies in both situations.[194] Although the English position is not free from doubt, it may be that the recipient in the two-party situation is protected

[190] See Birks (1989a), pp. 34–9.

[191] *Cowcher* v. *Cowcher* [1972] 1 W.L.R. 425, 431; *Calverley* v. *Green* (1984) 155 C.L.R. 242, 251; *Muschinski* v. *Dodds* (1985) A.L.J.R. 52, 54; Hovius and Youdan, pp. 71–2; Gray, p. 402.

[192] *Birch* v. *Blagrave* (1755) Amb. 264; *Childers* v. *Childers* (1857) 1 De G.&J. 482; *Standing* v. *Bowring* (1885) 16 Ch.D. 282; *Re Vinogradoff* [1935] W.N. 68; *Re Muller* [1953] N.Z.L.R. 879; *Tattersfield* v. *Leo Tattersfield Ltd.* (1980) 7 N.Z. Recent L. 79. See *Restatement of Trusts*, §440, comment f; Waters (1984), p. 299, fn. 2.

[193] See *Barclays Bank* v. *Quistclose Investments* [1970] A.C. 567.

[194] See *Restatement of Restitution*, §172; Scott and Fratcher, §474.

through the law of contract, rather than the defence of *bona fide* purchase.[195] This is considered further below,[196] but, either way, the recipient's knowledge will be important where he or she gave value for the property in question.[197]

Common intention

The recipient's intention can also be relevant where more than one person has contributed to the purchase. This is often encountered in cases involving the division of property on the breakdown of a marriage or similar relationship. The assets acquired during the relationship may be held in trust for the parties based on their 'common intention' regarding the beneficial ownership of those assets. Although their intentions may give rise to an express trust, the typical case involves real property, in which any express trust would be invalid for want of writing.[198] However, their common intentions may give rise to either a resulting or constructive trust.

Resulting trusts

Where their common intention gives rise to a resulting trust, it is because both parties provided the consideration for the acquisition of the property and their intentions are relevant as providers. As Gibbs C.J. stated in *Calverley* v. *Green*:[199]

> Where one person alone has provided the purchase money it is his or her intention alone that has to be ascertained . . . Where there are two purchasers, who have contributed unequal proportions, but have taken the purchase in their joint names, the intentions of both are material. Even if the parties had no common intention, the intentions of each may have to be proved, for the purpose of proving or negating that one intended to make a gift to the other.

However, as with parties to a contract, where there are two (or more) contributors to the acquisition of property, it may be that the relevant intentions are not their secret wishes, but those which have been manifested to the others. In *Gissing* v. *Gissing*, Lord Diplock stated:[200]

> As in so many branches of English law in which legal rights and obligations depend upon the intentions of the parties to a transaction, the relevant intention of each party is the intention which was reasonably understood by the other party to be manifested by that party's words or conduct notwithstanding that he did not consciously formulate that intention in his own mind or even acted with some different intention which he did not communicate to the other party.

[195] Burrows (1993a), pp. 472–4; Barker (1995a) at p. 191.

[196] At pp. 132, 168–9, 180–1, 237–8.

[197] See *Re Australian Elizabethan Theatre Trust* (1991) 102 A.L.R. 681, 693.

[198] *Gissing* v. *Gissing* [1971] A.C. 886, 905; *Cowcher* v. *Cowcher* [1972] 1 W.L.R. 425, 431.

[199] (1984) 155 C.L.R. 242, 251. See *Cowcher* v. *Cowcher* [1972] 1 W.L.R. 425, 431; *Muschinski* v. *Dodds* (1985) A.L.J.R. 52, 54; Hovius and Youdan, p. 105; Youdan (1992) at p. 546; Gray, p. 402.

[200] [1971] A.C. 886, 906.

As Mason and Brennan JJ. said in *Calverley* v. *Green*, 'When a common intention is in issue, it is not ordinarily to be found in an uncommunicated state of mind; it is to be inferred from what the parties do or say'.[201]

In *Cowcher* v. *Cowcher*, Bagnall J. suggested that the parties could agree that their contributions were being made in proportions other than they actually were. This would then give rise to a resulting trust by operation of law in accordance with their notional contributions.[202] This approach has been rightly criticized.[203] However, Bagnall J. also said that such an agreement was easiest to infer where the purchase price had been paid out of a common fund.[204] Although fictional contributions cannot give rise to a resulting trust, the parties' agreement regarding the ownership of a common fund can, on normal resulting trust principles, affect the ownership of property purchased with that fund. For example, where the sole contributor to a joint fund intends to give a joint interest to the other party, both parties are contributors to purchases made with that fund and a resulting trust may arise accordingly.[205]

In *Westdeutsche Landesbank Girozentrale* v. *Islington L.B.C.*, Lord Browne-Wilkinson suggested *obiter* that resulting trusts are 'traditionally regarded as examples of trusts giving effect to the common intention of the parties'.[206] This is surprising since it is clear that a common intention is not a requirement for a resulting trust, which can arise even though one of the parties is unaware of the transfer.[207] Lord Browne-Wilkinson's speech in *Tinsley* v. *Milligan*[208] indicates that he is mixing the requirements for resulting trusts with those for constructive trusts in the context of family home ownership. That case involved a resulting trust based on the common intention of the parties. Both parties had contributed to the purchase of a house and their intentions were relevant as providers. However, his lordship did not distinguish between the resulting trust based on their contributions and the constructive trust based 'on a common intention acted upon by the parties to their detriment'.[209]

Constructive trusts

A common intention regarding the ownership of property can also support a trust in favour of a party who has not provided any consideration for the purchase or has provided a smaller proportion of the consideration than his or her

[201] (1984) 155 C.L.R. 242, 261. Also see *Springette* v. *Defoe* (1992) 24 H.L.R. 552, C.A.

[202] [1972] 1 W.L.R. 425, 431–2.

[203] *Re Densham* [1975] 1 W.L.R. 1519, 1525; *Allen* v. *Snyder* [1977] 2 N.S.W.L.R. 685, 691–2; Hovius and Youdan, p. 103.

[204] [1972] 1 W.L.R. 425, 437.

[205] *Jones* v. *Maynard* [1951] Ch. 572. See *Milroy* v. *Lord* (1862) 4 De G.F.&J. 264; *Gage* v. *King* [1961] 1 Q.B. 188; *In re Bishop* [1965] Ch. 450; Meagher and Gummow, *Jacobs' Law of Trusts*, pp. 280–1.

[206] [1996] 2 All E.R. 961, 990, H.L.

[207] *Ryall* v. *Ryall* (1739) 1 Atk. 59; *Birch* v. *Blagrave* (1755) Amb. 264; *Lane* v. *Dighton* (1762) Amb. 409; *Childers* v. *Childers* (1857) 1 De G.&J. 482; *Williams* v. *Williams* (1863) 32 Beav. 370; *Re Vinogradoff* [1935] W.N. 68; *In re Muller* [1953] N.Z.L.R. 879.

[208] [1994] 1 A.C. 340.

[209] Ibid. 371.

share under the trust. There was at one time some confusion over the proper classification of such trusts, occasioned by the variety of speeches in *Pettitt* v. *Pettitt* and *Gissing* v. *Gissing* (and Lord Diplock's statement that it was unnecessary to distinguish between resulting, implied, and constructive trusts because they were all excepted from the writing requirement of section 53 of the Law of Property Act 1925).[210] Although this confusion has led to the classification of these trusts as resulting in Canada,[211] it is now accepted that they are constructive.[212] Lord Browne-Wilkinson has twice overlooked this distinction.[213] This is unfortunate because our understanding of constructive and resulting trusts depends on our ability to identify and distinguish between the various events to which they respond. The proper classification of trusts is discussed further in the concluding chapter.[214]

D. SUMMARY

The presumption of resulting trust is that the provider of property to another did not intend to benefit the recipient. It is an inference of fact arising when property has been transferred to someone who has not provided the entire consideration for the transfer. Subsection 60(3) of the Law of Property Act 1925 may prevent the presumption from applying to gratuitous transfers of land, but this is not settled. If it does, then the presumption only applies to land where some or all of the consideration for the transfer has been provided by someone other than the transferor or recipient.

The presumption of resulting trust does not apply where the provider is the husband or father of, or stands *in loco parentis* to, the recipient. It might not apply where the provider is the recipient's mother. Instead, the existence of the relationship gives rise to the presumption of advancement, which is an inference that the provider intended to make a gift to the recipient. Neither presumption applies if the question whether the provider intended to benefit the recipient can be answered from the evidence.

There is an important distinction between the presumption of resulting trust and the resulting trust itself. The resulting trust arises by operation of law when (i) property has been transferred to another and (ii) the provider did not intend to benefit the recipient. The presumption is merely an inference that this latter fact

[210] *Gissing* v. *Gissing* [1971] A.C. 886, 905.

[211] *Pettkus* v. *Becker* (1980) 117 D.L.R. (3d) 257, S.C.C.; see Waters (1984), p. 360; Waters (1992) at p. 488.

[212] *Grant* v. *Edwards* [1986] Ch. 638, 646–7, 654, C.A.; *Lloyds Bank p.l.c.* v. *Rosset* [1991] 1 A.C. 107, 132–3; Tory, at 60–1; Hayton, in Youdan (1989a) p. 205, at p. 228; Hovius and Youdan, p. 100; Youdan (1992) at p. 539; Gardner (1993); Eekelaar.

[213] *Tinsley* v. *Milligan* [1994] 1 A.C. 340, 371; *Westdeutsche Landesbank Girozentrale* v. *Islington L.B.C.* [1996] 2 All E.R. 961, 990, H.L.

[214] Below, pp. 220–30.

exists, which is drawn because the recipient did not provide all of the consideration for the transfer, whereas the resulting trust is an equitable response to the existence of that fact, whether presumed or proven.

Standing back from the necessarily complex detail, the simplest summary of the ideas operating in this field is that equity approaches some apparent gifts with suspicion. Within certain relationships, where 'advancement' is to be expected, it is not suspicious. In other cases, it presumes that a beneficial gift was not intended and, unless shown otherwise, acts on that presumption by imposing a trust to return the property to its provider. It will be seen in Part II of this book that this fact being presumed and acted upon (that a beneficial transfer was not intended) creates a crucial link with a larger category of causes of action for restitution of unjust enrichment.

2
Trusts Which Fail

The previous chapter was about resulting trusts of apparent gifts. This one concerns the resulting trust which arises when an express trust fails to dispose of all the property conveyed to the trustees. Together, they describe the two most common situations in which resulting trusts arise. Megarry J. drew a marked distinction between them in *Re Vandervell's Trusts (No. 2)*,[1] with his classifications of 'presumed' and 'automatic' resulting trusts. The division depends on whether the transfer of property to the recipient was made in trust: the resulting trust is 'presumed' where there is a transfer which 'is not made on any trust' and 'automatic' where a transfer 'is made on trusts which leave some or all of the beneficial interest undisposed of'.[2]

These two categories have long been recognized as the main situations in which resulting trusts arise,[3] but Megarry J. was the first to define and contrast presumed and automatic resulting trusts for the purpose of demonstrating that 'they operate in different ways'.[4] Where a transfer from A to B is not made in trust:[5] '[F]rom the absence of consideration and any presumption of advancement B is presumed not only to hold the entire interest on trust, but also to hold the beneficial interest for A absolutely. The presumption thus establishes both that B is to take on trust and also what that trust is'.

Different rules are said to apply where the transfer is made on trusts which fail to completely dispose of the property:[6] 'The resulting trust here does not depend on any intentions or presumptions, but is the automatic consequence of A's failure to dispose of what is vested in him. Since ex hypothesi the transfer is on trust, the resulting trust does not establish the trust but merely carries back to A the beneficial interest that has not been disposed of'.

In Megarry J.'s scheme, the presumed resulting trust depends on the provider's presumed intention to make the recipient a trustee of the property for the provider. The automatic resulting trust, on the other hand, is merely the automatic re-direction of the failed express trust to return any remaining trust property to the provider. As discussed below, this classification was created for the purpose of explaining the speeches of Lord Upjohn and Lord Wilberforce in *Vandervell* v. *Inland Revenue Commissioners*.[7] It has been adopted, in whole

[1] [1974] 1 Ch. 269, 288–96. [2] Ibid. at 294, per Megarry J.
[3] *Lloyd* v. *Spillet* (1740) 2 Atk. 148, 150.
[4] *Vandervell (No. 2)* [1974] 1 Ch. 269, 289, per Megarry J.
[5] Ibid. at 294, per Megarry J. [6] Ibid., per Megarry J. [7] [1967] 2 A.C. 291.

or in part, by many academics in recent years,[8] but there are some who criticize the division[9] or note it without acceptance.[10]

It is suggested with great respect that the categories of presumed and automatic resulting trusts should be abandoned because there is no real distinction between the two. In both situations, the resulting trust arises by operation of law because the provider of the property did not intend to benefit the recipient. The classification made in *Vandervell (No. 2)* tends to obscure the true nature of the resulting trust and divert our attention from the essential issues involved.

It is argued in this chapter that: (i) the distinction between presumed and automatic resulting trusts is not adequately supported by *Vandervell* v. *I.R.C.*; (ii) the intention to create an express trust is not a satisfactory basis for distinguishing between the two categories of resulting trust; (iii) resulting trusts in both categories are dependent on whether the provider intended to benefit the recipient; and (iv) the resulting trust on the failure of an express trust is not merely the failure to dispose of the surplus, but an active response to the fact that the settlor did not intend to benefit the trustee. This chapter continues with a brief look at the reception of Megarry J.'s classification in Australia, Canada and the USA and concludes with a discussion of three other possible responses to the failure of an express trust: the rule in *Hancock* v. *Watson, cy près* and *bona vacantia*.

A. INTERPRETING *VANDERVELL* V. *I.R.C.*

Vandervell (No. 2) was the third round of litigation concerning Mr. Vandervell's tax liability for dividends paid on shares in Vandervell Products Ltd. The 1958–60 dividends were the subject of *Vandervell* v. *I.R.C.* and the 1961–65 dividends where the subject of *Re Vandervell's Trusts*[11] and *Vandervell (No. 2)*. In *Vandervell* v. *I.R.C.*, the House of Lords decided that an option to purchase the shares was held on resulting trust for Mr. Vandervell, making him liable to pay surtax on the dividends.

In *Vandervell (No. 2)*, Megarry J. created the categories of presumed and automatic resulting trusts as a means of understanding *Vandervell* v. *I.R.C.* The law lords did not make this classification themselves. It was Megarry J.'s explanation of their decision to declare a resulting trust without applying the presumption

[8] Maxton (1986) at 80; Hackney, pp. 153–4; Gardner (1990), pp. 3–4, 55–7; Oosterhoff and Gillese, pp. 273–4; Hayton (1993), p. 16; Martin (1993a), p. 70; Pettit (1993), pp. 59, 149–50; Swadling (1996) at 113.

[9] Riddall, pp. 191–207; Oakley (1994), pp. 30–1; Ford and Lee, §21060, fn. 2; *Westdeutsche Landesbank Girozentrale* v. *Islington L.B.C.* [1996] 2 All E.R. 961, 991.

[10] Waters (1984), pp. 19, 301; Sheridan, pp. 210–14.

[11] *In re Vandervell's Trusts* [1971] A.C. 912 (deciding that the Inland Revenue Commissioners could not be joined as defendants).

of resulting trust.[12] Although Megarry J. was reversed by the Court of Appeal,[13] it is commonly accepted that they did not upset his classification of the resulting trust.[14] However, it should be noted that the Court of Appeal offered no support for this classification.

1. The Facts

Mr. Vandervell wanted to give money to the Royal College of Surgeons. In 1958, he transferred shares in Vandervell Products Ltd. to the College, which then granted an option to purchase those shares to Vandervell Trustee Ltd. (a trustee of several trusts, including a settlement in favour of Mr. Vandervell's children). From 1958 to 1960, Vandervell Products declared dividends on the College's shares, In 1961, the trust company exercised the option and, using money from the children's settlement, purchased the shares from the College. Over the next 4 years, dividends were declared and paid to the trust company.

Vandervell v. *I.R.C.* decided that Mr. Vandervell was liable to pay surtax on the dividends paid to the College because the trust company held the option to purchase on resulting trust for him during that period. As that litigation progressed, Mr. Vandervell became worried about possible surtax liability with respect to the dividends being paid to the trust company and, in 1965, executed a deed releasing any interest he might have in the shares to the trust company in trust for the children's settlement.

Mr. Vandervell died in 1967 and his estate was assessed for surtax on the dividends paid to the trust company before his deed of release was executed. His executors brought an action against the trust company to recover those dividends. In *Vandervell (No. 2)*, Megarry J. held that the trust company had acquired the shares on trust and, because no effective trusts had been declared, held them on resulting trust for Mr. Vandervell. The Court of Appeal agreed with Megarry J. that the trust company had acquired the shares on trust, but allowed the appeal on the basis that there was a valid trust in favour of the children's settlement.[15]

2. Megarry J.'s Interpretation

In *Vandervell* v. *I.R.C.*, the House of Lords decided that Mr. Vandervell was the beneficiary of a resulting trust, even though he had wanted to rid himself of his interest in the trust property. That decision was reached without applying the presumption of resulting trust. For Megarry J., these conclusions were irreconcilable with the presumed resulting trust and could only be explained by the existence of another type of resulting trust operating on different principles.

[12] [1974] 1 Ch. 269, 293, 295. See *Vandervell* v. *I.R.C.* [1967] 2 A.C. 291, 312–13, 317, 329.

[13] [1974] 1 Ch. 269.

[14] Megarry and Wade, p. 469, fn. 1; Waters (1984), p. 301, fn. 11; Meagher and Gummow, *Jacobs' Law of Trusts*, p. 263, fn. 1.

[15] [1974] 1 Ch. 269, 319–20, 325.

It is respectfully suggested that Megarry J.'s interpretation of the speeches in *Vandervell* v. *I.R.C.* was based on two common misconceptions of the nature of the resulting trust. The first is the belief that the resulting trust of an apparent gift is based on the provider's presumed intention to create that trust. It was clear that Mr. Vandervell did not have this intention. However, his intention that the trust company should hold the option in trust for beneficiaries to be chosen later meant that he did not intend to benefit the trust company. As discussed in the previous chapter, this absence of intention to benefit the recipient is the true basis of the resulting trust of an apparent gift.

The second misconception is the confusion of the presumption of resulting trust with the resulting trust itself. Lord Upjohn doubted whether the presumption applied to an option to purchase, but found it unnecessary to decide that point because there was sufficient evidence of the actual intention of the parties:[16] 'As I think the facts and circumstances are sufficient for this purpose without resort to this long stop presumption, it is unnecessary finally to decide whether the doctrine of resulting trust does apply to an option'.

Megarry J. recognized that Lord Upjohn was using the terms 'presumption' and 'doctrine' interchangeably,[17] but did not consider that he might be distinguishing between the presumption which gives rise to the resulting trust and the resulting trust itself:[18] 'I do not then see how the application of the doctrine or presumption of resulting trusts to options can have been left undecided if it was decided that it was that doctrine or presumption that carried the beneficial interest in the option to Mr. Vandervell'.

As discussed in the previous chapter, the resulting trust arises because the provider did not intend to benefit the recipient. There is no need to resort to a presumption of the provider's intention where it has been proved. This confusion of presumption and principle led Megarry J. to believe that Lord Upjohn had rejected one category of resulting trust in favour of another.

Megarry J. reached the same conclusion regarding Lord Wilberforce's statement that:[19] 'The transaction has been investigated on the evidence of the settlor and his agent and the facts have been found. There is no need, or room, as I see it, to invoke a presumption'. Megarry J. said:[20] 'Now it seems to me this passage shows Lord Wilberforce as rejecting the application of what I have called the 'presumption' class of resulting trust and accepting that the case falls into what I have called the 'automatic' class'.

However, Lord Wilberforce did not reject that class of resulting trust. The Court of Appeal had applied the presumption of resulting trust.[21] Lord Wilberforce agreed with their judgments,[22] but preferred 'a slightly different and simpler approach'.[23] The same principle of resulting trust was applied, but based on Mr. Vandervell's actual, rather than presumed, intention.

[16] [1967] 2 A.C. 291, 315. [17] [1974] 1 Ch. 269, 293. [18] Ibid., per Megarry J.
[19] [1967] 2 A.C. 291, 329. [20] [1974] 1 Ch. 269, 295.
[21] *Vandervell* v. *I.R.C.* [1966] Ch. 261, 292, C.A. [22] [1967] 2 A.C. 291, 324.
[23] Ibid. at 329.

B. INTENTION TO CREATE AN EXPRESS TRUST

For Megarry J., the essential fact separating presumed and automatic resulting trusts was whether the transfer was made on trust. Discussed in this section are three reasons why this is not an adequate basis for distinguishing between different categories of resulting trusts: (i) there is no clear distinction between the two situations, (ii) where an express trust fails, there is no trust capable of being re-directed to the settlor, and (iii) the transfer on trust creates no more than a presumption that the recipient was not intended to have the surplus for his or her own benefit.

1. No Clear Distinction

It can be difficult to tell whether a transfer is or is not made on trust. *Vandervell* v. *I.R.C.* was itself a borderline case. There had been no declaration of trust with respect to the option granted to the trust company and there was nothing about the transaction itself that indicated a trust. It was the evidence of Mr. Vandervell's financial advisors which revealed that the trust company was intended to be a trustee of the option for unidentified beneficiaries. This intention was not effective to create a trust because it was either an intention to create a trust in the future or an attempt to create a trust which failed for lack of certainty of objects.[24] In either case, there was no express trust, but merely proof that the trust company was not intended to receive the benefit of the option.[25] This is not a sufficient basis for making a fundamental distinction between this and other gratuitous transfers where there is an absence of intention to benefit the recipient. The fact that proof of the absence of intention arises in the context of an intended, but non-existent, trust does not justify the application of an entirely different set of principles.[26]

Acceptance of the distinction between presumed and automatic resulting trusts would force the law into one of two untenable positions: (i) that a presumed resulting trust of an apparent gift arises because of a presumed intention to create that trust, but if the presumed intention is proven to exist (as in *Hodgson* v. *Marks*) then an entirely different set of principles applies to produce an automatic resulting trust on the failure of an express trust; or (ii) that an ineffective intention to create a trust for oneself (*Hodgson* v. *Marks*) and an ineffective intention to create a trust for someone else (*Vandervell* v. *I.R.C.*) produce resulting trusts operating on entirely different principles. Fortunately, the law is not driven to these extremes. In both situations, the resulting trust operates on the same principles as a response to the lack of intention to benefit the recipient.

[24] [1974] 1 Ch. 269, 319, C.A.; Martin (1993a), pp. 94, 99; Waters (1984), p. 107: 'the trust fails to come into existence or, to put it differently, is void'.

[25] See *Hodgson* v. *Marks* [1971] 1 Ch. 892, 933, C.A.; discussed above, pp. 25, 34.

[26] Ibid.

2. No Express Trust Exists

Megarry J. said that the automatic 'resulting trust does not establish the trust but merely carries back . . . the beneficial interest that has not been disposed of'.[27] As mentioned above, Mr. Vandervell's intention was insufficient to create an express trust. It is therefore impossible for the resulting trust to merely re-direct a trust that he established.

Where, as in *Vandervell* v. *I.R.C.*, there is an unsuccessful attempt to create a trust, the settlor has not created any obligations which bind the trustee with respect to the property and the resulting trust is created entirely by operation of law.[28] Maitland reveals the proper approach to this situation:[29]

> I convey land unto and to the use of A and his heirs upon trust, but I declare no trust. Here the use does not result, for a use is declared in favour of A and therefore A gets the legal estate. But I have by the words 'upon trust' declared my intention that A is not to enjoy the land for his own behoof—on the other hand I have not saddled him with any particular trust. Here a trust results for me.

The words, 'upon trust', do not create a trust. The obligation to hold the property for the benefit of the settlor is imposed by equity because those words make it clear that the recipient was not intended to enjoy the benefit of the property.[30]

The same principle applies when the settlor has created a valid trust which does not exhaust the trust property. Where a trust is completely executed or fails in part, the equitable obligations created by the settlor no longer bind the property remaining in the trustee's hands. The obligation to hold the remainder for the benefit of the settlor is created entirely by operation of law.[31]

3. Presumption of Resulting Trust

Where trusts do not exhaust the trust property, there is not necessarily a resulting trust of the remainder, but only a presumption that the trustees were not intended to retain it for their own benefit.[32] The role of intention is discussed in the next section. The point here is that the same rule applies regardless of the existence of the express trust obligation. Although the presumption of resulting trust is much stronger where a transfer is made on trust, this is a difference of degree, not kind.

In *Re West*,[33] the residue of an estate had been granted to four persons on trusts which did not exhaust the property. Kekewich J. stated:[34]

[27] *Vandervell (No. 2)* [1974] 1 Ch. 269, 294.
[28] See *Morice* v. *Bishop of Durhum* (1805) 10 Ves. 522, 536–7.
[29] Maitland, p. 76.
[30] Mowbray, *Lewin on Trusts*, pp. 115, 121.
[31] See *Bishop of Cloyne* v. *Young* (1750) 2 Ves.Sen. 91, 96.
[32] 48 *Halsbury's Laws* (4th edn., 1995 reissue) para. 601, p. 316.
[33] [1900] 1 Ch. 84.
[34] Ibid. at 87.

It is impossible to say that because property is given to persons as trustees they therefore take no beneficial interest. That is contrary to all experience of the construction of wills, there being many instances of trustees taking beneficially. Nevertheless, there is a presumption that a gift in trust is not a beneficial gift. It is, however, not uncommon to find a gift of a fund charged with certain payments, or coupled with a condition that a certain amount be paid to a third person. Whether the charge takes effect by way of trust or condition, it is not intended to do more than give a certain amount out of the fund to another person.

The transfer on trust did 'not settle the question', because it was still possible that 'the trustees were intended to take beneficially'.[35] In *Re West*, the fact that the testatrix created a trust for sale, indemnified the trustees, and reimbursed them for their services indicated that they were not intended to take beneficially and, therefore, there was a resulting trust for the heirs and next of kin.

It has been doubted whether there is in fact such a presumption, some cases treating it instead as a rule of construction of the document.[36] Either way, where there is no evidence of intention beyond the granting of property in trust, the court will assume that the trustee was not intended to enjoy the benefit of the remainder. However, slight indications of an intention to give can sometimes be sufficient to prove the contrary.[37]

The presumption of resulting trust applies to executors in much the same way it applies to express trustees. Under the Administration of Estates Act 1925, the personal representative of a testator is a trustee, for those who take on intestacy, 'of the part of the estate not expressly disposed of unless it appears by the will that the personal representative is intended to take such part beneficially'.[38] This is essentially a statutory presumption of resulting trust in favour of those persons designated by the Act as the recipients of the residue of the estate on an intestacy.

At one time, the executor was entitled to keep the residue of any personal property undisposed of by the will, except where the testator intended otherwise,[39] in which case it went to the next of kin. The Executors Act 1830 shifted the onus to the executor to prove that he or she was intended to receive the benefit of the personal property.[40] Before 1926, real property was treated differently. There was once a strong presumption against disinheriting the heir, which meant that if the beneficial interest in any real property was not clearly disposed of, there was a resulting trust for the heir.[41]

[35] Ibid. at 89, per Kekewich J.

[36] *Barrs* v. *Fewkes* (1864) 2 H.&M. 60, 66; *In re Rees* [1950] Ch. 204, 207, C.A.; *Moffit* v. *Moffit* [1954] 2 D.L.R. 841, 846–7, B.C.

[37] *Croome* v. *Croome* (1888) 59 L.T. 582, C.A.; aff'd (1889) 61 L.T. 814; *In re Foord* [1922] 2 Ch. 519.

[38] Administration of Estates Act 1925, s. 49(b).

[39] *Blinkhorn* v. *Feast* (1750) 2 Ves.Sen. 27; *Bishop of Cloyne* v. *Young* (1750) 2 Ves.Sen. 91; *Walton* v. *Walton* (1807) 14 Ves. 318, 321; *Langham* v. *Sanford* (1816) 19 Ves. 642, 646; *Ellcock* v. *Mapp* (1851) 3 H.L.C. 492, 507; *Williams* v. *Arkle* (1875) L.R. 7 H.L. 606, 615.

[40] *Ellcock* v. *Mapp* (1851) 3 H.L.C. 492; *Williams* v. *Arkle* (1875) L.R. 7 H.L. 606, 615, 630; Oakley (1994), p. 208.

[41] *Ackroyd* v. *Smithson* (1780) 1 Bro.C.C. 503, 506; *Nash* v. *Smith* (1810) 17 Ves. 29, 33; *Kellett* v. *Kellett* (1815) 3 Dow. 248, 254.

C. INTENTION TO BENEFIT THE TRUSTEE

Megarry J. stated that the automatic resulting trust 'does not depend on any intentions or presumptions, but is the automatic consequence of' the failure of the express trust to dispose of the trust property.[42] This is the central characteristic of the automatic resulting trust and that to which the most important objections are raised. It is true that a resulting trust cannot arise in this situation unless the express trust fails to dispose of all the trust property. However, the resulting trust arises precisely because the settlor did not intend to benefit the trustee with that surplus. This is the same principle which applies to apparent gifts. The importance of the settlor's intention is discussed next, followed by a look at why it has been obscured in many cases.

1. The Importance of Intention

Although intention is supposed to be irrelevant to the automatic resulting trust, the question whether Mr. Vandervell intended to benefit the trust company was the central issue which divided the House of Lords in *Vandervell* v. *I.R.C.* and caused Lord Upjohn 'so much difficulty'.[43] Megarry J. treated this question whether the option was granted on trust as a preliminary matter of categorization. This approach may have a tendency to obscure the essential issue in this type of case.

Where there is an express trust which fails to exhaust the trust property, the resulting trust is not the automatic consequence of that failure, but is dependent on the intention of the settlor. Where it can be proven by admissible evidence that the trustee was intended to enjoy the benefit of the remainder, there will be no resulting trust. This has been established by a long line of authority which has come to be forgotten in the wake of *Vandervell (No. 2)*.

In *Cook* v. *Hutchinson*,[44] a father transferred property to his son on trusts which did not exhaust the property. Lord Langdale M.R. held that there was no resulting trust of the remainder:[45]

> [A]fter having carefully looked through the whole of this deed, I have come to the conclusion, considering the relation between the parties, and the object and purport of the instrument, that the father intended to part with all beneficial interest in the property, and that he meant his son to have the benefit of that part of the property of which the trusts are not expressly declared.

His lordship relied on the authority of *King* v. *Denison*[46] and *Hill* v. *Bishop of London*[47] to reach this conclusion:[48]

[42] *Vandervell (No. 2)* [1974] 1 Ch. 269, 294. [43] [1967] 2 A.C. 291, 316.
[44] (1836) 1 Keen 42. [45] Ibid. at 51. [46] (1813) 1 V.&B. 260.
[47] (1738) 1 Atk. 618.
[48] (1836) 1 Keen 42, 50, per Langdale M.R. The admissibility of evidence to rebut the resulting trust is discussed below, pp. 50–1.

In general, where an estate or fund is given in trust for a particular purpose, the remainder, after that purpose is satisfied, will result to the grantor; but that resulting trust may be rebutted even by parol evidence, and certainly cannot take effect where a contrary intention, to be collected from the whole instrument, is indicated by the grantor . . . the question whether there is or is not a resulting trust must depend upon the intention of the grantor.

King v. *Denison* concerned the difference between a devise charged with the payment of debts and a devise on trust to pay debts. However, the principle set out by Lord Eldon C., that there will be no resulting trust where the recipient was intended to retain the surplus,[49] is not restricted to charges, but also applies to express trusts. In *Cook* v. *Hutchinson*, the father had created a trust and not merely a charge, but this did not prevent the son from being beneficially entitled to the remainder. The question whether there is a resulting trust does not depend on whether a trust or a charge has been created, but, as Lord Langdale M.R. stated, 'upon the intention of the grantor'.[50]

The same principle was applied in *Croome* v. *Croome*,[51] where a barrister had devised all his real estate to his brother on trusts which did not exhaust the whole. The Court of Appeal, following Lord Eldon in *King* v. *Denison*, held that the brother was entitled to the surplus. The language of the will showed 'that it was not a devise for a particular purpose, or particular purposes and nothing more, but that the intention was that the brother should be something more than a mere trustee, and have a beneficial interest in it'.[52]

The principle was also applied in *Re Foord*,[53] where a testator gave the residue of his estate to his sister in trust to pay his wife an annuity. Sargant J. held that there was no resulting trust of the surplus. The question addressed by the court was not whether the testator had created a trust or a charge, but whether he had intended a gift of the residue to his sister:[54]

While a gift to A. upon trust for the provision of a certain interest for B., without more, must, I think, be construed as a gift to A. merely to fulfil the beneficial interest of B. and must not be construed as a gift to A. of all that is not required to satisfy B.'s interest, yet looking at the case of *Croome* v. *Croome*, which I employ for the purpose of seeing the general spirit in which the Court deals with cases of this character, I find that the Court is prepared to hold that there is a beneficial gift to the first taker on slight expressions and indications of intention.

The testator wrote in his will, 'All of my effects . . . I leave absolutely to my sister Margaret Juliet on trust to pay to my wife'[55] so much per annum. The factors which led Sargant J. to conclude that a gift of the residue had been intended were (i) the use of the word 'absolutely' by a non-lawyer in a non-technical will, (ii) the description of the trustee as 'my sister', (iii) the use of her first names

[49] *King* v. *Denison* (1813) 1 V.&B. 260, 272–3. [50] (1836) 1 Keen 42, 50.
[51] (1888) 59 L.T. 582. [52] Ibid. at 585, per Bowen L.J. [53] [1922] 2 Ch. 519.
[54] Ibid. at 521–2, per Sargant J. [55] Ibid. at 519.

and (iv) the inclusion of non-income producing properties in the bequest. This approach shows that it is not a question of merely defining the extent of the express trust so that anything left over automatically results to the settlor. In *Re Foord*, as in *Croome* v. *Croome*, the extent of the express trust was clear and the question was whether a gift of the remainder had been intended.

Before *Vandervell (No. 2)*, it was recognized that the resulting trust on the failure of an express trust was dependent on the intention of the settlor.[56] Notwithstanding *Vandervell (No. 2)*, several authors continue to believe that intention has a role to play.[57] Even among those who accept the concept of the automatic resulting trust, there are some who recognize the possibility of the trustee's entitlement to the undisposed-of surplus.[58]

2. The Role of Intention Obscured

It may be useful to consider what has obscured the role of intention in resulting trusts arising on the failure of an express trust. Four factors can readily be suggested as having contributed to this problem: in many cases (i) the courts resolve the issue by deciding that no trust was intended, (ii) other issues are more important, (iii) the settlor's intention to benefit third persons is ineffective, or (iv) evidence of the settlor's intention is inadmissible.

Whether trust intended

The issue whether the settlor intended the trustee to retain the surplus is often confused with the issue whether the settlor intended to create a trust at all. For example, in *Re Rees*,[59] Evershed M.R. approved of Sargant J.'s judgment in *Re Foord*,[60] but in the following terms:[61] 'It is right to say that, as Sargant J. observed, the cases show that slight indications may well suffice to persuade the court that the intention of the testator was not to create a trust estate in the devisee but to give him a conditional gift'. However, as discussed above, the issue in *Re Foord* was not whether the testator had created a trust, but whether his sister was intended to retain the benefit of the surplus. Professor Waters has very usefully described the problem of failing to distinguish between the two issues:[62]

> It is always open to a settlor to confer a beneficial interest upon the person who is also to be a trustee. Often, then, two questions present themselves: is the obligated person a trustee, and if he is a trustee for the purposes of carrying out the obligation concerning the property, is he also to take a beneficial interest in any excess? The apposition has been put in this way: 'it is rather a gift upon condition than a gift upon trust', but this

[56] Maitland, pp. 75–6; Mowbray, *Lewin on Trusts*, p. 115.
[57] Riddall, p. 191; Sheridan, p. 211; Oakley (1994), pp. 30–1, 202, 206.
[58] Megarry and Wade, p. 470; Gardner (1990), p. 4, fn. 5; Martin (1993a), pp. 53–4.
[59] [1950] Ch. 204. [60] [1922] 2 Ch. 519. [61] [1950] Ch. 204, 208.
[62] Waters (1984), p. 86.

is somewhat misleading. Certainly one who is found to be a trustee is often found to have been excluded from any beneficial enjoyment, no doubt because the testator did not wish to expose his trustee to any conflict of interest and duty, but such a finding is not automatic. It is not even a presumption; it is simply a matter of construction. The question is what did the testator intend should happen to moneys left over when the trust purposes have been fulfilled.

Other issues

The second factor obscuring the role of intention in this context is that, in the vast majority of cases, the issue to be resolved is not whether the settlor intended to give the residue to the trustee. It is usually clear from the outset that the trustee was not intended to enjoy any benefit and the real dispute is over whether the prior express trust has failed to dispose of the whole trust property. This does not change the fact that the resulting trust arises precisely because the trustee was not intended to receive the benefit of the property. The acceptance or admission of that fact does not make it irrelevant.

Ineffective intention

This factor is related to the preceding one. In many resulting trust cases, the settlor intended to create a trust for a third party, but failed to do so. As discussed above, the focus on whether the intended trust is effective can create the false impression that the resulting trust is merely the automatic consequence of that failure. This is made worse by the fact that the resulting trust can appear to be directly contrary to the settlor's wishes, as it was in *Vandervell* v. *I.R.C. Re Boyes*[63] provides another example. The testator tried to create a secret trust, but did not communicate the objects of the trust before his death. The objects were set out in letters found in the testator's possession and the trustee wished to carry out those trusts. The trusts were invalid and there was a resulting trust for the testator's next of kin.

Where the settlor's wishes are clear but ineffective, the resulting trust appears to arise in spite of them. However, the resulting trust does not strip the beneficial ownership from the intended beneficiaries. In the absence of a valid trust in their favour, the contest is between the settlor and the trustee. The intention to benefit the third party shows that the settlor did not intend to benefit the trustee, which is the fact giving rise to the resulting trust by operation of law.

Admissibility of evidence

Limits on the admissibility of evidence of the settlor's intention have also tended to obscure the role of intention for the resulting trust. Where a trust is set out in writing, the parol evidence rule means that extrinsic evidence is not admissible to contradict the trust document and the court must construe the settlor's

[63] (1884) 26 Ch.D. 531.

intention from the document itself.[64] Where the trust is testamentary, the court is restricted to testamentary documents which have been admitted to probate.[65] However, where an *inter vivos* trust has been created without writing, parol evidence of the settlor's intention to benefit the trustee is admissible.[66] These restrictions on the ability to prove the intention of the settlor may lead to the belief that intention is not relevant in those contexts, but this is certainly not the case. Although the court is often restricted to looking at a document, it does so for the very purpose of ascertaining the settlor's intention[67] and, where it can be discovered from the document that the trustee was intended to enjoy the benefit of the remainder of the trust property, there will be no resulting trust.

At one time, parol evidence was admissible to rebut the presumption of resulting trust arising in a will, provided it did not contradict the express language of the will.[68] This was because the resulting trust was treated as an equitable presumption and parol evidence was admissible to rebut such presumptions.[69] This was doubted[70] and eventually overruled.[71] The presumption of resulting trust in this context arises from the construction of the will and extrinsic evidence is not admissible to contradict that construction of the testator's intention.[72]

D. PROPRIETARY ARITHMETIC

There is one further objection to the concept of the automatic resulting trust. This is the notion that the settlor merely retains property that he or she has not parted with. It is what Mr. Hackney calls 'proprietary arithmetic' and describes as follows:[73]

> This manifestation of the resulting trust seems to be an application of ordinary principles of property law. If I give land to trustees on trust for A for life, plainly I keep the rest of the interest which endures after A's death. Nothing springs back to me; what I have, never left me . . . This is called a resulting trust, though again it does not spring back in any theoretical sense. This rule does not depend on a presumption of intention, but on a simple process of proprietary arithmetic; what I once had and have not granted away,

64 Maitland, p. 77; Mowbray, *Lewin on Trusts*, p. 115.

65 *Re Rees* [1950] Ch. 204, 210–11; *In re Pugh's Will Trusts* [1967] 1 W.L.R. 1262, 1264; Clark and Ross Martyn, *Theobald on Wills*, p. 109.

66 *In re Tyler* [1967] 1 W.L.R. 1269, 1275; Scott and Fratcher, §4, §164.1.

67 *Perrin* v. *Morgan* [1943] A.C. 399, 406; Clark and Ross Martyn, *Theobald on Wills*, pp. 199, 226–8. The Administration of Justice Act 1982, s. 21, allows extrinsic evidence of the testator's intention to be admitted in certain circumstances; see *Theobald on Wills*, pp. 233–4.

68 *Brown* v. *Selwin* (1734) Cas.t. Talbot 240, 242; *Bishop of Cloyne* v. *Young* (1750) 2 Ves.Sen. 91; *Walton* v. *Walton* (1807) 14 Ves. 318, 321–2; *Langham* v. *Sanford* (1816) 19 Ves. 642; *Gladding* v. *Yapp* (1820) 5 Madd. 56, 58–9; *Cook* v. *Hutchinson* (1836) 1 Keen 42, 50.

69 *Moffit* v. *Moffit* [1954] 2 D.L.R. 841, 846–7.

70 *Mallabar* v. *Mallabar* (1735) Cas.t.Talbot 78, 80; *Blinkhorn* v. *Feast* (1750) 2 Ves.Sen. 27, 28.

71 *Re Rees* [1950] Ch. 204, 210.

72 *Moffit* v. *Moffit* [1954] 2 D.L.R. 841, 847.

73 Hackney, pp. 153–4.

I keep. It will not matter that I intended to grant it away or that I wished I had; if I have not effectively alienated, I keep what I had. My intention is relevant only as a component in interpreting what I have in fact done. This simple truth received judicial recognition by Megarry J. in *Re Vandervell's Trusts No. 2* (1974).

Some support for this view can be gleaned from the speeches of Lord Upjohn and Lord Wilberforce in *Vandervell* v. *I.R.C.*, as well as Megarry J.'s interpretation of Lord Upjohn's speech.[74] Lord Upjohn stated:[75]

If A intends to give away all his beneficial interest in a piece of property and thinks he has done so but, by some mistake or accident or failure to comply with the requirements of the law, he has failed to do so, either wholly or partially, there will, by operation of law, be a resulting trust for him of the beneficial interest of which he had failed effectually to dispose. If the beneficial interest was in A and he fails to give it away effectively to another or others or on charitable trusts it must remain in him.

Lord Wiberforce seemed to be applying the same concept:[76]

The conclusion, on the facts found, is simply that the option was vested in the trustee company as a trustee on trusts, not defined at the time, possibly to be defined later. But the equitable, or beneficial interest, cannot remain in the air: the consequence in law must be that it remains in the settlor.

The concept of proprietary arithmetic is useful for determining the extent of the various beneficial interests involved or for describing the end result of the transactions from which a resulting trust arises. However, it does not accurately describe the steps leading to that end, nor does it describe the true nature of the resulting trust itself. The interest which the settlor has at the end of the story, as the beneficiary of a resulting trust, is an equitable interest which is different from the legal ownership he or she had at the beginning. This fact is glossed over by the common use of the phrase, 'beneficial interest', which can describe both legal and equitable ownership.

Except as restricted by equity or statute, the legal owner has the full beneficial enjoyment of the property at common law and does not have an equitable interest in his or her own property. As Mr. Hackney explains:[77]

Ownership at common law is a beneficial interest giving its owner economic advantages. The beneficial owner at common law has no equitable interest. The Chancellor has nothing to do with him; the common law gives him all the protection he requires. But if a jurisdiction-generating fact (fraud, acceptance of the role of trustee etc.) occurs, an equitable interest will be created, and the common law title will be stripped of its economic value and cease to be ownership . . . Equity only operates when the common law result is unacceptable. It does not operate over the whole area and for the most part leaves the common law to get on with it.

[74] *Vandervell (No. 2)* [1974] 1 Ch. 269, 291. [75] [1967] 2 A.C. 291, 313.
[76] Ibid. at 329.
[77] Hackney, p. 25. Also see *Pilcher* v. *Rawlins* (1872) L.R. 7 Ch.App. 259, 268–9; Birks (1989a), p. 71.

At one time, a person may have been able to hold property for his or her own use, so that a transfer with no consideration and no declaration of use would leave the use behind,[78] but this is not true of the trust. A person cannot be a trustee solely for his or her own benefit.[79] The legal owner does not have an equitable interest in the property and, therefore, cannot retain an equitable interest on a transfer of the property. As Lord Browne-Wilkinson stated in *Westdeutsche Landesbank Girozentrale* v. *Islington L.B.C.*: 'A person solely entitled to the full beneficial ownership of money or property, both at law and in equity, does not enjoy an equitable interest in that property. The legal title carries with it all rights. Unless and until there is a separation of the legal and equitable estates, there is no separate equitable title'.[79A]

D.K.L.R. Holding Co. (No. 2) Pty. Ltd. v. *Commissioner of Stamp Duties*[80] provides a wonderful example of this principle. A property management corporation, called 29 Macquarie, transferred land to D.K.L.R. Holding Co., which immediately executed a declaration of trust of its entire interest in favour of 29 Macquarie. The case went to the High Court of Australia over 50 dollars of stamp duty, which had been assessed on the full value of the property. D.K.L.R. argued that the stamp duty should be nominal because only bare legal title had been transferred. Aickin J. stated:[81]

> In my opinion this argument is based upon a fundamental misconception as to the nature of legal and equitable interests in land or other property. If one person has both the legal estate and the entire beneficial interest in the land he holds an entire and unqualified legal interest and not two separate interests, one legal and the other equitable . . . It is a fundamental principle of both the common law and of equity that the holder of an estate in fee simple cannot be a trustee of that fee simple estate for himself for what he holds is a single estate, being the largest estate in land known to the law.

Brennan J. stated:[82]

> [T]he interest which 29 Macquarie had after the transfer was not the same as it had before. Before the transfer it did not hold legal and equitable estates in the property: it held the legal estate alone. There was no equitable estate, for a person cannot be a trustee for himself alone . . . A transferee does not become a trustee by failing to acquire an interest in the property transferred; a trustee holds on trust only such interest as he acquires. An equitable interest is not carved out of a legal estate but impressed upon it. It may be convenient to say that DKLR took only the bare legal estate, but that is merely to say elliptically that 29 Macquarie transferred to DKLR the property in respect of which DKLR had declared that it would be a trustee.

[78] *Burgess* v. *Wheate* (1759) 1 Black. 123, 185.

[79] *Goodright* v. *Wells* (1781) 2 Dougl. 771, 778; *In re Douglas* (1884) 28 Ch.D. 327, 331; *In re Selous* [1901] 1 Ch. 921, 922; *In re Cook* [1948] Ch. 212, 214–15; *Re Heberley* [1971] N.Z.L.R. 325, 333, C.A.; Scott and Fratcher, §99, §410.

[79A] [1996] 2 All E.R. 961, 989.

[80] (1982) 40 A.L.R. 1, H.C.A.; aff'g in part [1980] 1 N.S.W.L.R. 510, C.A.

[81] Ibid. at 26.

[82] Ibid. at 35.

These principles apply to all trusts, including resulting trusts. Where the owner of property transfers it to trustees on trusts which fail to exhaust the beneficial interest, the trustees acquire the entire ownership which belonged to the settlor. At the same time, the equitable obligation to hold that property for the benefit of the trust beneficiaries is created by the settlor. Because the beneficial interest has not been completely disposed of and the trustees were not intended to enjoy the benefit of the legal ownership for themselves, the resulting trust arises, either at the time of transfer or possibly later upon the failure of the express trust. The settlor's interest as a beneficiary of the resulting trust is a new interest which did not exist before the transfer of property to the trustees. As Aickin J. said, 'It is of the nature of a resulting trust that it arises when the entire interest is vested in the transferee and at the very moment it becomes so vested'.[83]

D.K.L.R. Holding is not necessarily inconsistent with *Vandervell* v. *I.R.C.*, even though Lord Upjohn spoke of the beneficial interest remaining in the settlor. The use of the generic term, 'beneficial', is consistent with a description of the net effect of the transaction and should not be taken as an assertion that Mr. Vandervell had retained the identical equitable interest throughout. Lord Wilberforce's reference to an 'equitable, or beneficial interest',[84] remaining in the settlor is somewhat harder to reconcile; however, it is not out of place in Mr. Vandervell's case.

When the story began, the shares in Vandervell Products Ltd. were owned by a bank as trustee for Mr. Vandervell. At his direction, the bank transferred the legal and beneficial ownership of the shares to the College, which then granted the option to purchase to the trust company. The option was a new chose in action against the College, which was held on a resulting trust for Mr. Vandervell. Mr. Vandervell began as the equitable owner of the shares and finished as the equitable owner of an option to purchase those shares. It is therefore unlikely that Lord Wilberforce was expressing the opinion that Mr. Vandervell merely retained the same equitable interest he had at the beginning.

In any event, the issue in *Vandervell* v. *I.R.C.* was whether Mr. Vandervell had any interest in the shares and not whether it was an interest that had been retained from the outset. The true nature of legal and equitable ownership was the central issue in *D.K.L.R. Holding* and the concept of proprietary arithmetic was clearly rejected by the High Court of Australia. The High Court relied on English authority[85] and it is not suggested that the law is any different in England. *Northern* v. *Carnegie*[86] does appear to be a contrary authority, in which the settlor had transferred an incorporeal hereditament to trustees on trusts which did not exhaust the entire beneficial interest. Kindersley V.C. stated:[87]

[83] Ibid. at 27. [84] *Vandervell* v. *I.R.C.* [1967] 2 A.C. 291, 329.
[85] *Harmood* v. *Oglander* (1803) 8 Ves. 106, 127, and the cases cited in n. 79, above.
[86] (1859) 4 Drew 587. Also see *In re Llanover Settled Estates* [1926] Ch. 626, 637.
[87] *Northern* v. *Carnegie* (n. 86 above) at 593.

[S]o far as [the settlor] had not parted with the beneficial interest, it remained in him as a resulting trust. It was not a new estate, but merely so much *remaining* in him as he has not parted with . . . In this case, therefore, though [the settlor] parted with the whole *legal* interest, yet so much of the *beneficial* interest as he has not parted with remains his estate.

The Vice Chancellor spoke of 'the beneficial interest', which is capable of describing both legal and equitable interests, and his assertion that the interest 'was not a new estate' should not be construed to conflict with the principles set out in *D.K.L.R. Holding*. Nothing in *Northern* v. *Carnegie* turned on whether the settlor had retained the identical interest. The settlor started with a beneficial interest at law and ended with a new equitable interest under a resulting trust. It 'was not a new estate' in the sense that it was the beneficial ownership of the same incorporeal hereditament, but the beneficial ownership at law had been replaced by the beneficial ownership in equity.

E. AUTOMATIC RESULTING TRUSTS ABROAD

1. Australia

The automatic resulting trust has received a mixed reception in Australia. Ford and Lee appear to accept that it arises independently of the settlor's intention,[88] but reject the distinction between presumed and automatic resulting trusts, on the basis that both are the automatic consequence of a failure to dispose of the beneficial interest in the property.[89] In *Jacob's Law of Trusts in Australia*, the Vandervell cases are discussed and *Vandervell* v. *I.R.C.* is identified as 'an example of an "automatic" resulting trust'.[90] However, this is never reconciled with the book's categorization of all resulting trusts as implied trusts which arise because 'the law presumes that the settlor or purchaser, as the case may be, intended to retain the beneficial interest which he has not disposed of'.[91]

2. Canada

The automatic resulting trust has fared no better in Canada. Although Hovius and Youdan[92] and Oosterhoff and Gillese[93] support the concept, Waters refers to it without acceptance[94] and Ziff makes no reference to *Vandervell*.[95] There do not appear to be any Canadian cases adopting Megarry J.'s classification, but there are several which are inconsistent with it because they recognize that the

[88] Ford and Lee, §21010 (cf. §21030). [89] Ibid. at §21060.
[90] Meagher and Gummow, *Jacob's Law of Trusts*, p. 263. [91] Ibid.
[92] Hovius and Youdan, pp. 32–3; Youdan (1993). [93] Oosterhoff and Gillese, pp. 273–4.
[94] Waters (1984), p. 301, fn. 11. [95] Ziff.

resulting trust upon failure of an express trust is dependent on the settlor's intention.[96]

3. USA

It would appear that the automatic resulting trust has no place in American law. The *Restatement of the Law of Trusts, Second* sets out the following general rule applicable to all resulting trusts:[97]

> A resulting trust arises where a person makes or causes to be made a disposition of property under circumstances which raise an inference that he does not intend that the person taking or holding the property should have the beneficial interest therein, unless the inference is rebutted or the beneficial interest is otherwise effectively disposed of.

Where an express trust fails or is performed without exhausting the trust property, there will be no resulting trust if the settlor 'properly manifested an intention that no resulting trust should arise' in that event.[98] This includes a manifestation of intention that the trustee may keep the surplus on the failure or performance of the express trust.[99] In the USA, the resulting trust upon the failure of an express trust arises for precisely the same reason as the resulting trust on a purchase in the name of another: the absence of intention to benefit the recipient of the legal title.

F. OTHER RESPONSES

Where an express trust fails, the remainder does not always either result to the settlor or stay with the trustee. There are other possible responses: (i) the rule in *Hancock* v. *Watson*, (ii) *cy près* or (iii) *bona vacantia*. The first two give effect to other dispositions in accordance with the settlor's wishes (at least in theory) and therefore do not conflict with the resulting trust. The transfer of property to the Crown as *bona vacantia* is an unintended disposition which does not always sit well with resulting trust principles. It is therefore discussed at greater length.

1. *Hancock* v. *Watson*

The failure of an *inter vivos* or testamentary trust will not give rise to a resulting trust if the rule in *Hancock* v. *Watson* applies, which Lord Davey described as follows:[100]

[96] *Fraser* v. *Fraser* [1937] 1 W.W.R. 91 (Alta.); *Re MacPherson* [1953] O.W.N. 663; *Moffit* v. *Moffit* [1954] 2 D.L.R. 841; *Re Walker* (1970) 13 D.L.R. (3d) 688 (Ont.).

[97] *Restatement of Trusts*, §404. Cf. Bogert and Bogert, §§468–9.

[98] Ibid. §412, §431. See Scott and Fratcher, §412.

[99] Ibid.

[100] *Hancock* v. *Watson* [1902] A.C. 14, 22.

[I]t is settled law that if you find an absolute gift to a legatee in the first instance, and trusts are engrafted or imposed on that absolute interest which fail, either from lapse or invalidity or any other reason, then the absolute gift takes effect so far as the trusts have failed to the exclusion of the residuary legatee or next of kin as the case may be.

The rule is well discussed elsewhere[101] and, as those authors point out, the difficulty is not understanding the rule, but applying it. In *Hancock* v. *Watson* itself, the testator gave the residue of his estate to trustees in trust to be divided among four persons. He then declared that one of the recipients should take only a life interest in her portion, the remainder going on trusts which turned out to be invalid. It was construed as an absolute gift from which the remainder was carved, rather than a life estate. Therefore, the recipient took her portion free of the invalid trust and there was no resulting trust.

The rule does not conflict with or limit the operation of the resulting trust. The application of the rule means that another valid disposition of the trust property is effective and, therefore, the trustees do not retain the trust property for their own benefit.

2. Cy Près

The doctrine of *cy près*, meaning 'as near as practicable',[102] is often applied when a trust for a charitable purpose becomes impossible or impractical to carry out. Rather than letting the trust fail and returning the undisposed-of trust property to the settlor by way of a resulting trust, the court can approve of a scheme for amending the trust to use the property for another charitable purpose which is as near as possible to the one chosen by the settlor. In England, the *cy près* doctrine has been modified by statute. *Cy près* is no longer limited to situations where the original trusts are impossible or impractical,[103] the Charity Commissioners have scheme-making powers,[104] and trustees of small charitable trusts have some power to modify the trust objects.[105]

The application of the *cy près* doctrine depends on whether the charitable trust fails initially or subsequently. Where the particular charitable purpose fails at the outset, the trust property cannot be applied *cy près* unless the settlor had a general charitable intention (but anonymous donors who cannot be identified are deemed to have that intention).[106] As Waters said, 'a general charitable intent might be better described as a requirement of a paramount or overriding intention to give for the charitable purpose of which the particular object set out by the trust . . . is merely one mode of furtherance'.[107] This requirement means that

[101] Mowbray, *Lewin on Trusts*, pp. 122–4; Waters (1984), pp. 372–4; Ford and Lee, §21030.

[102] J.A. Simpson and E.S.C. Weiner, *The Oxford English Dictionary* 2nd ed., (1989) vol. 4, p. 198.

[103] Charities Act 1993, s. 13.

[104] Ibid. s 16.

[105] Ibid. s. 74 (applies to trusts with not more than £5,000 annual income).

[106] Ibid. s. 14; see Oakley (1994), pp. 348–9.

[107] Waters (1984), p. 624. See Scott and Fratcher, §399.

(in theory) the property is only applied *cy près* when that would accord with the settlor's wishes.[108]

Cy Près is more readily available where the charitable purpose becomes impossible or impractical after the property is already vested in trust for that purpose. The only requirement for the application of the surplus *cy près* on a subsequent failure is that the property has been given wholly to charity, in the sense that no other persons have an interest in it.[109] Although this can result in the application of the trust property contrary to the settlor's wishes,[110] this is justifiable in light of the special treatment accorded to charitable trusts. As Professor Scott points out, they are exempted from the rule against perpetuities because they further public interests. However:[111] 'The public interest is not promoted by the creation of a charity which by the lapse of time ceases to be useful. The founder of a charity should understand therefore that he cannot create a charity which shall be forever exempt from modification'.

Much has been written about *cy près* and charitable trusts.[112] The doctrine is but one of many designed to further charitable purposes.[113] The application of trust property *cy près* affects the resulting trust in the same manner as the rule in *Hancock* v. *Watson*: another effective disposition of the trust property is substituted for the failed trust. The existing trust is modified so that the trustees continue to hold the property in trust for charitable purposes. Therefore, the resulting trust is not required to prevent the trustees from obtaining the unintended benefit of the trust property.

3. Bona Vacantia

Lawrence L.J. provided this useful description of *bona vacantia* in *Re Wells*:[114]

> Bona Vacantia (the Crown's right to which is not in dispute) are defined in Blackstone's Commentaries, vol. i., p. 298, as 'goods in which no one else can claim a property'. The expression 'goods' in this definition has admittedly a larger significance than goods properly so called, and has long since been construed and accepted by the Courts as extending to personal property of every kind, both corporeal and incorporeal (including equitable interests in personalty).

The general principle is that ownerless personal property belongs to the Crown,[115] but this is not a universal principle. As Bell states, 'only certain fish

[108] *In re Ulverston and District New Hospital Building Trusts* [1956] Ch. 622, 634, C.A.

[109] *In re Wright* [1954] Ch. 347, 362–3, C.A.; *Re Ulverston* [1956] Ch. 622, 635–6; Waters (1984), p. 629; Gardner (1990), p. 98; Martin (1993a), pp. 446–7. Cf. Scott and Fratcher, §399.3.

[110] *In re Peel's Release* [1921] 2 Ch. 218, 223.

[111] Scott and Fratcher, §399.4. See *Canada Trust Co.* v. *Ontario Human Rights Commission* (1990) 74 O.R. (2d) 481, C.A..

[112] See Waters (1984); Scott and Fratcher; Baker and Langan, *Snell's Equity*; Martin (1993a); Oakley (1994).

[113] See Gardner (1990), pp. 90–112.

[114] [1933] Ch. 29, 49.

[115] Ibid. at 55.

and wild birds belong to the Crown, but the rest belong to no-one'.[116] It is also possible for personal property to be abandoned, in which case it does not pass to the Crown as *bona vacantia*, but is available to the first taker or possibly the occupier of the land it is abandoned on.[117] The Crown's right to *bona vacantia* is not a general right to all ownerless personal property, but 'is determined by common law and statute'.[118] Real property did not become *bona vacantia* at common law.[119] On the death of the owner in fee simple, without heirs, his or her estate would come to an end and the property would escheat to the lord from whom the owner held tenure.[120]

Bona vacantia normally arises when an individual dies, without heirs or next of kin, having failed to dispose of all of his or her property by will. A similar, but less common situation is the dissolution of a corporation which has failed to distribute all of its property. In both situations, the property has become ownerless because the owner has ceased to exist without disposing of it. These are now dealt with by statute.

Under the Administration of Estates Act 1925, the undisposed-of real and personal property of a deceased individual goes to those entitled under the act and, if no one else is entitled, 'shall belong to the Crown or to the Duchy of Lancaster or to the Duke of Cornwall for the time being, as the case may be, as bona vacantia, and in lieu of any right to escheat'.[121]

Under the Companies Act 1985, the property owned by a company immediately before its dissolution is 'deemed to be bona vacantia'.[122] There are other statutes which can also affect the ownership of the surplus property of companies and other organisations.[123] One important situation not covered by statute is property held in trust for defunct unincorporated associations. This is discussed below.

Trust property

That trust property should become *bona vacantia* is interesting because it does not become ownerless on the death of the trust beneficiary, without next of kin, but remains vested in the trustees. As Romer L.J. stated in *Re Wells*:[124]

> The extension of the doctrine to equitable interests was not, however, accomplished without some difficulty. Where there was an owner at law, such as a trustee, the common law doctrine would be inapplicable. The property was not without any other owner. The doctrine could therefore only be applied by analogy. But a formidable obstacle in the way of doing this was thought to have been occasioned by the case of *Burgess* v. *Wheate*.

[116] Bell at p. 405.
[117] Ibid.; Hudson (1993) at pp. 431–2; *Waverley B.C.* v. *Fletcher*, [1995] 4 All E.R. 756, C.A.
[118] Bell at p. 406.
[119] *Henchman* v. *Attorney-General* (1834) 3 My.&K. 485, 492–4.
[120] Hardman, at 323.
[121] Administration of Estates Act 1925, s. 46(vi).
[122] Companies Act 1985, s. 654.
[123] See Bell at pp. 415–18, 421–2.
[124] [1933] Ch. 29, 56–7.

The issue in *Burgess* v. *Wheate*[125] was whether real property would escheat to the Crown in equity when the trust beneficiary had died without heirs[126] and without disposing of her interest in the property. The trustee was entitled to keep the property even though it was clear that he had obtained the legal estate only as a trustee and not for his own benefit. The majority of the court decided that the Crown had no equity with which to affect the trustee's title to the property.[127] They did not think it unconscionable for the trustee to retain the benefit of the property in the circumstances. As Scott said of *Burgess* v. *Wheate*, 'There was a windfall to the trustee, but at no one's expense'.[128] Lord Mansfield C.J. dissented:[129]

> I can find no clear and certain rule to go by; and yet I think equity should follow the law throughout. Yet I am satisfied it must shock common sense, that the heirs of an attorney or the trustee should take the estate from the family of the owner, the King, and every body else. The least analogy to any legal right ought to be preferred to the trustee, who is the mere form and instrument of conveyance . . . The exclusion of the trustee from all benefit was surely in the contemplation of the parties.

It was decided 24 years later, in *Middleton* v. *Spicer*,[130] that the principle in *Burgess* v. *Wheate* did not apply to a trust of personal property. In that case, a testator had directed that his leasehold property be sold and the proceeds be paid to the Gospel Society. This bequest was void under the Statute of Mortmain and his three executors claimed the undisposed-of residue for their own benefit. They had been given legacies and Lord Thurlow C. decided that they were not intended to receive the benefit of the property:[131] 'The executors being excluded, and no relations to be found, I consider the executors as much trustees for the crown, as they would have been for any of the next of kin, if these could have been discovered'.

Lord Thurlow C. distinguished *Burgess* v. *Wheate* as a case of escheat and refused to let the executors retain the property. It appears that his lordship thought it would be unconscionable for the executors to retain the benefit of the personal property they had received, which is opposite to the conclusion of the majority in *Burgess* v. *Wheate* with respect to real property.

Burgess v. *Wheate* was consistently followed with respect to real property[132] until the Intestates Estates Act 1884 made the law of escheat applicable to equitable estates in land.[133] That statute was repealed by the Administration of Estates Act 1925, which abolished escheat and made it possible for real property

[125] (1759) 1 Black. 123.
[126] The trust beneficiary had an heir at law, *ex parte materna*, but it was decided that the trust property could only dscend to paternal heirs. [127] (1759) 1 Black. 123, 176, 184.
[128] Scott and Fratcher, §411.4. [129] (1759) 1 Black. 123, 170–1.
[130] (1783) 1 Bro.C.C. 201. [131] Ibid. at 205.
[132] *Taylor* v. *Haygarth* (1844) 14 Sim. 8; *Henchman* v. *A.-G.* (1834) 3 My.&K. 485.
[133] Intestates Estates Act 1884, s. 4.

to pass to the Crown as *bona vacantia*. *Middleton* v. *Spicer* has been consistently followed with respect to trusts of personal property.[134]

Resulting trusts

In most cases of *bona vacantia* upon the failure of an express trust, the Crown's claim to the trust property as *bona vacantia* is not in competition with a settlor's claim to a resulting trust. Typically, a testator has died without next of kin and has failed to dispose of his or her entire estate. The executors or trustees would normally hold the residue on a resulting trust for the testator's next of kin, but none exist and the beneficial interest created by the resulting trust passes to the Crown as *bona vacantia*. The Crown does not claim in competition with the resulting trust, but as the beneficiary of the resulting trust which arises because the executors or trustees were not intended to enjoy the benefit of the residue of the estate. This was the outcome in *Middleton* v. *Spicer*, where Lord Thurlow C. granted a declaration that there 'was a resulting trust in the executors for the benefit of the crown'.[135]

It is interesting to compare *Middleton* v. *Spicer* with *Henchman* v. *Attorney-General*,[136] where an executor was entitled to retain a copyhold estate on the death of a testator without heirs. There could be no escheat while the executor had legal title and no resulting trust in the absence of an heir:[137] 'As, therefore, the lord cannot take; as, beyond all question, the Crown cannot take; and as there is here no heir of the testator, the devisee alone can take. He takes from necessity, indeed, and because there is none other to take, the resulting trust failing for want of a *cestui que trust*'.

In *Middleton* v. *Spicer*, there was a resulting trust of personalty, which went to the Crown in the absence of next of kin, while, in *Henchman* v. *Attorney-General*, the resulting trust of realty failed in the absence of an heir. Although it is difficult to reconcile this different treatment of real and personal property, it does reveal an absence of conflict between the Crown's claim to *bona vacantia* and the resulting trust: they operated together over personalty and both failed in connexion with realty.

It has been suggested that there will not be a resulting trust where the beneficiary of an express trust is absolutely entitled to the trust property and dies without next of kin.[138] Unfortunately, the only cases given in support of this proposition are those in which the settlor has died without heirs or next of kin and there is a resulting trust for the Crown.[139] This seems to be a sensible suggestion nonetheless. If the beneficiary of an express trust was absolutely entitled to the trust property, the trust would not come to an end upon his or her

[134] *In re Higginson & Dean* [1899] 1 Q.B. 325, 329; *Taylor* v. *Haygarth* (1844) 14 Sim. 8; *Re Wells* [1933] Ch. 29, 50–1.

[135] (1783) 1 Bro.C.C. 201, 205.

[136] (1834) 3 My.&K. 485.

[137] Ibid. at 494, per Brougham L.C.

[138] Baker and Langan, *Snell's Equity*, p. 177; Sheridan, p. 213; Oakley (1994), p. 208.

[139] *Middleton* v. *Spicer* (1783) 1 Bro.C.C. 201; *In re Bond* [1901] 1 Ch. 15.

death and the beneficial interest would pass to those entitled under the beneficiary's will or on intestacy. In this situation, there is no reason why there should be a resulting trust for the settlor if the beneficiary should die without leaving any successors. The express trust has not failed to dispose of the trust property, but the beneficiary's interest has become ownerless and, as *bona vacantia*, should pass to the Crown, who takes the place of the beneficiary of the express trust.[140]

Unincorporated associations

In the situations discussed above, the Crown's claim to trust property as *bona vacantia* is not in competition with the settlor's claim under a resulting trust: the Crown takes as the beneficiary of either a resulting trust (in the absence of a settlor) or an express trust (in the absence of benficiaries). There does appear to be a competition, however, in several cases dealing with property held in trust for defunct unincorporated associations. In this situation, the surplus assets can pass to the Crown as *bona vacantia* even though there are existing contributors (or their successors) who are claiming a resulting trust. The reasons given for this are that the contributions either (i) were not made in trust, but as contractual payments or gifts, or (ii) have been abandoned. As discussed below, neither explanation is satisfactory.

Contractual payments and gifts

In *Cunnack* v. *Edwards*, Chitty J. decided that the surplus property of a defunct friendly society was held on resulting trust for the estates of the deceased members in proportion to their contributions.[141] This was reversed on appeal, where it was decided that the Crown was entitled to the surplus as *bona vacantia*.[142] However, the difference of opinion was not over two possible responses to a failed express trust, but whether a trust had been created at all. The members made regular contributions to the society for the purpose of providing annuities for their widows and over £1,200 remained after all the members and annuitants had died. No resulting trust arose because the contributing members were not settlors, but had contracted with the society for the purchase of rights for their widows.

Cunnack v. *Edwards* was followed in *Braithwaite* v. *Attorney-General*[143] and *Re West Sussex Constabulary's Widows, Children and Benevolent (1930) Fund Trusts*.[144] In the latter case, the undisposed-of assets of a defunct society had several sources: members' subscriptions, entertainments, sweepstakes, donations, legacies and collecting boxes. The members and ticket purchasers had paid on the basis of contract, in exchange for valuable consideration, and those who had donated money through collecting boxes had made absolute gifts to the society.

[140] See *Re Higginson & Dean* [1899] 1 Q.B. 325, where a corporation's beneficial interest under a statutory trust become *bona vacantia* following the dissolution of the corporation.

[141] [1895] 1 Ch. 489, 498.

[142] [1896] 2 Ch. 679, C.A.

[143] [1909] 1 Ch. 510.

[144] [1971] 1 Ch. 1.

These funds went to the Crown as *bona vacantia*, subject to any contractual claims of former members.

There was a resulting trust of the portion derived from donations and legacies for the donors or their estates. Goff J. drew a distinction between these donors and those who had given anonymously through collecting boxes, following *Re Ulverston and District New Hospital Building Trusts*, where Jenkins L.J. said:[145] 'Prima facie, the subscriber who gives his name intends to subscribe for the particular and exclusive purpose for which his subscription has been solicited and none other, and there will be a resulting trust in his favour if that purpose fails'.

A finding that contributions were either contractual payments or gifts can explain why there is no resulting trust (although, as discussed in Chapters 3 and 6, a contractual payment or gift to be used for a specific purpose can give rise to a resulting trust if that purpose fails). However, it does not explain why those contributions should become *bona vacantia*. In *Cunnack* v. *Edwards*, it was admitted that the surplus did 'not belong to the society, for its objects have come to an end',[146] but the Court of Appeal did not address the question of who owned the fund prior to dissolution or how it became ownerless afterwards. Neither did Goff J. in the *West Sussex* case. This is a stumbling block. The payments, having been made for valuable consideration or as gifts, should have become the beneficial property of the recipients.

A better approach was taken in *Re Bucks Constabulary Widows' and Orphans' Fund Friendly Society*,[147] where the surplus was neither held on resulting trust for the contributors nor *bona vacantia*. As Walton J. stated, subject to any declaration of trust, mortgage or other valid disposition of the society's assets, 'the persons, and the only persons, interested therein are the members'.[148] Someone normally holds the assets in trust for the members where the society is unincorporated, but this method of ownership does not mean that the contributors are settlors.[149] The generally preferred view is that the assets are received and held by the members beneficially, subject to the contract between them in the rules of the society.[150] Their beneficial ownership is not lost on the dissolution of the society. Accordingly, the surplus assets of the society are divided among the members existing at the date of dissolution.

Walton J. pointed out that the outcome of both *Cunnack* v. *Edwards* and *Braithwaite* v. *Attorney-General* can be explained by the combined effect of the rules of those societies and the Friendly Societies Acts.[151] It was unlawful to

[145] [1956] Ch. 622, 634. Goff J. chose not to follow *In re Gillingham Bus Disaster Fund* [1958] Ch. 300, 314.

[146] [1896] 2 Ch. 679, 684, per Smith L.J.

[147] [1979] 1 All E.R. 623.

[148] Ibid. at 626.

[149] Gardner (1992) at 42–8.

[150] *Neville Estates Ltd.* v. *Madden* [1962] Ch. 832; *Re St. Andrew's Allotment Association* [1969] 1 W.L.R. 229; *In re Recher's Will Trusts* [1972] Ch. 526; Martin (1993a), pp. 239–45. Cf. Warburton (1985); Hackney, pp. 75–82.

[151] Friendly Societies Act 1793, s. 14; Friendly Societies Act 1829, s. 26. Cf. Gardner (1992) at 47–8.

distribute the assets of the society among the members other than in accordance with the rules, which failed to provide for the distribution of the assets on the termination of the society. As each member died, his or her interest in the fund ceased and, when the last member had died without an amendment of the rules of the society, the fund had become ownerless. This is nothing other than the usual case of *bona vacantia* in which the owners of property have ceased to exist without disposing of it.[152] This cannot, however, explain the result in the *West Sussex* case and Walton J. expressly declined to follow it.

Abandonment

Cunnack v. *Edwards* was decided on the basis that the payments had been made pursuant to contract and not on trust. However, A.L. Smith L.J. also commented on why payments made in trust give rise to a resulting trust and not *bona vacantia*:[153] '[T]he implication in such a case would be that the settlor intended that when the trust came to an end the fund should revert to his representatives, he not having provided to whom it should then go. In such a case there would be no abandonment of the fund as in the present case'.

This suggests (i) that the resulting trust depends upon the implied intention of the settlor to have the surplus property returned and (ii) that a settlor can abandon his or her interest in a resulting trust, thereby leaving the property ownerless. Both of these notions are clearly contrary to the principles laid down by the House of Lords in *Vandervell* v. *I.R.C.*, but they have popped up from time to time in several potential resulting trust cases.

For example, in *Re Hillier's Trusts*,[154] money was collected for the construction of a hospital in Slough, but the project was made redundant by the Ministry of Health's decision to build one there. Upjohn J. held that there could be no resulting trust for people donating to collecting boxes because 'the circumstances in which the money was given, negative the idea that the donor ever intended that he should receive any of that money back'.[155] His lordship thought it was 'an open matter as to whether the true result is that there is a general charitable intention, or the gifts become bona vacantia'.[156] The Court of Appeal held that the donors' intention 'to part, out-and-out, with their money in any event' proved their general charitable intention.[157]

Cy près was also the issue in *Re Ulverston and District New Hospital Building Trusts*,[158] which involved facts similar to those in *Re Hillier's Trusts*. Jenkins L.J. stated *obiter* that an anonymous contributor, who had formed no intention regarding the plight of his contribution on the failure of the trust, might be

[152] Gardner (1992) at 43. [153] [1896] 2 Ch. 679, 684.
[154] [1954] 1 W.L.R. 9; rev'd in part [1954] 1 W.L.R. 700, C.A.
[155] Ibid. at 22; following *In re Welsh Hospital (Netley) Fund* [1921] 1 Ch. 655.
[156] Ibid. [157] [1954] 1 W.L.R. 700, 711, per Evershed M.R.
[158] [1956] Ch. 622.

treated as having 'simply abandoned his contribution so that it became bona vacantia on the failure of the purpose for which it was contributed'.[159]

In one Australian case, the settlors were treated as having abandoned their contributions. *Re Producers' Defence Fund*[160] concerned an association formed for the purpose of promoting the interests of rural agricultural producers. The members voted to disband the association and made a declaration of trust of the surplus, which was for non-charitable purposes and therefore invalid. Smith J. stated:[161]

> [T]he disposition of the fund . . . was intended to be a final disposition, reserving no interest to the members whether by way of resulting trust or otherwise. I think, further, that it is clear that it was not intended that the trustees should in any circumstances take any beneficial interest in the fund. And it follows, in my opinion, that the beneficial interest in the said fund passed to the Crown as *bona vacantia.*

There are four reasons why abandonment does not provide a satisfactory explanation of how resulting trust property becomes *bona vacantia*. First, abandonment requires a positive intention by the owner to abandon the property.[162] This is not found in cases where the failure of the society or trust was unforeseen and the contributors had not considered the plight of their contributions in those circumstances (Jenkins L.J.'s example in *Re Ulverston*, above). Although their absence of intention shows a lack of intention to benefit the trustees capable of giving rise to a resulting trust, it is inconsistent with abandonment.

Secondly, the desire to exclude others from the property is sufficient to prevent abandonment from occurring.[163] The positive intention not to benefit the trustees, found in *Re Producers' Defence Fund*, was consistent with resulting trust, but not abandonment.

Thirdly, the intention to give property to another is also inconsistent with the intention to abandon it. A failed attempt to give or create a trust does not dispose of the property. As Plowman J. stated in *Vandervell* v. *I.R.C.*:[164] '[A] man does not cease to own property simply by saying "I don't want it." If he tries to give it away the question must always be, has he succeeded in doing so or not? If he has not succeeded in giving it away, it still belongs to him, even if he does not want it'.

Finally, it is not clear that abandoned trust property would become *bona vacantia*. Abandoned goods do not, but are instead available to the first taker.[165] If the contributors were settlors who had abandoned their entitlement to a resulting trust, it may be that the trustees, who already have legal ownership, would

[159] Ibid. at 633–4. [160] [1954] V.L.R. 246. [161] Ibid. at 256.

[162] Hudson (1993) at p. 441; *Moorhouse* v. *Angus & Robertson Pty. Ltd.* [1981] 1 N.S.W.L.R. 700, C.A.

[163] Hudson (1993) at p. 432; *R.* v. *Edwards* (1877) 13 Cox C.C. 384, 36 L.T. 30; *Williams* v. *Phillips* (1957) 41 Cr.App.Rep. 5.

[164] [1966] Ch. 261, 275–6; quoted with approval by Lord Upjohn: [1967] 2 A.C. 291, 314.

[165] Bell at p. 405; Hudson (1993) at pp. 431–2.

be entitled to retain the property for their own benefit. The doctrine of *bona vacantia* was extended to equitable interests in *Middleton* v. *Spicer*,[166] because Lord Thurlow C. thought it would be unconscionable for the property to be retained by the trustees who were not intended to receive it for their own the benefit. That rationale is missing if the settlor has abandoned the property.

The abandonment of resulting trust property is highly improbable, if not impossible. There should be only two possibilities: either the contributors did not intend the recipients to enjoy the benefit of the property, in which case there is a resulting trust regardless of their wishes in connexion with any undisposed-of surplus, or the contributions were given absolutely, in which case the recipients are entitled to retain them. *Vandervell* v. *I.R.C.* clearly established that resulting trusts (i) do not depend on the actual or implied intention of the settlor to have the property returned and (ii) arise even though the settlors do not want their property back. As long as the recipient was not intended to enjoy the benefit of the property and the settlor has failed to make any other disposition of the property, a resulting trust arises by operation of law.

As an isolated case, *Re Producers' Defence Fund* could be ignored as having been implicitly over-ruled by *Vandervell* v. *I.R.C.* However, the same ideas reappeared in three English cases concerning defunct pension plans and in a recent *obiter dictum* of Lord Browne-Wilkinson.[167] In each of the pension plan cases, the resulting trust was excluded by the contributors' intention that it should not apply and the surplus went to the Crown as *bona vacantia*. It is difficult to understand how this conclusion is possible after *Vandervell* v. *I.R.C.* The settlors' intentions are relevant to whether they intended to benefit the trustees or (where *Hancock* v. *Watson* applies) made another disposition of the property or (where *cy près* applies) had a general charitable intention. However, the mere desire not to have the property returned, in the absence of some other effective disposition, cannot prevent the resulting trust from arising by operation of law.

G. SUMMARY

There is no valid distinction between 'presumed' and 'automatic' resulting trusts. In both situations, the resulting trust arises by operation of law because the provider of the trust property did not intend to benefit the recipient. Where a transfer is made on trust, there is a presumption that the trustee was not intended to enjoy the benefit of the property. This can be rebutted by admissible evidence showing that the settlor intended the trustee to retain the benefit of any surplus.

[166] (1783) 1 Bro.C.C. 201; see pp. 60–1, above.

[167] *In re ABC Television Pension Scheme* (unreported) 22 May 1973; *Jones* v. *Williams* (unreported) 15 March 1988; *Davis* v. *Richards & Wallington Industries Ltd.* [1990] 1 W.L.R. 1511. The two unreported cases are quoted in the *Davis* case. Per Lord Browne-Wilkinson, [1996] 2 All E.R. 961, 991.

The settlor does not retain the equitable ownership of the trust property which is not disposed of by the express trust, nor does the resulting trust merely redirect the equitable interests created by the express trust. The resulting trust is the creation of a new equitable interest for the settlor.

The surplus of a failed express trust is not always returned to the settlor under a resulting trust. Where the rule in *Hancock* v. *Watson* or the *cy près* doctrine applies, the surplus is effectively given to other persons or charitable purposes. A beneficial interest under a resulting trust can become ownerless and pass to the Crown as *bona vacantia* if the settlor has died without successors. The beneficial interest under an express trust may also become *bona vacantia* if the beneficiary is absolutely entitled to all the trust property and dies without successors. In several cases, the surplus assets of defunct unincorporated associations and pension plans were held to be *bona vacantia*, but without a satisfactory explanation of how those assets became ownerless.

3
Quistclose Trusts

This chapter concerns resulting trusts which arise when property has been transferred for specific purposes which fail. The *Quistclose* trust takes its name from *Barclays Bank Ltd.* v. *Quistclose Investments Ltd.*,[1] in which money loaned to be used for a specific purpose was held in trust for the lender when the purpose became impossible to fulfil. It lies outside the traditional categories of resulting trust. The transfer need not be an apparent gift and the purpose need not be an express trust (although this latter point is not free from controversy). This extension of the resulting trust beyond the traditional categories is not an innovation. The principle behind the *Quistclose* trust dates back almost two centuries,[2] but only recently has it been identified as a resulting trust.

Quistclose was decided by the House of Lords over 25 years ago and yet the *Quistclose* trust is still the subject of academic debate.[3] Its nature and effect have remained elusive even though the principle is simple to describe: money which is loaned for the purpose of paying other creditors of the borrower does not form part of the borrower's general assets; if the purpose cannot be fulfilled, the money is held in trust for the lender. There is disagreement about whether this trust is express or implied and what becomes of the beneficial interest in the money as events take their course. Perhaps this is why the principle has not found a more comfortable place within the accepted classification of trusts, but is still known only as the *Quistclose* trust.

Three propositions are advanced in this chapter. First, the loan of money to be used for a specific purpose does not create a trust for the benefit of the intended recipients of the money; nor does the lender retain full equitable ownership of it. The borrower receives the entire beneficial ownership of the money, subject only to the lender's right to prevent it being used for any other purpose. Secondly, upon failure of that purpose, there is a resulting trust in favour of the lender, which arises because the lender did not intend the borrower to keep the beneficial ownership of the money for any other purpose. Thirdly, the *Quistclose* trust is not restricted to loans for the purposes of paying other creditors of the borrower. It applies whenever money is paid to another to be used for a specific purpose, even where that purpose does not redound to the benefit of an identifiable class of beneficiaries and is therefore 'abstract'.

[1] [1970] A.C. 567; aff'g [1968] 1 Ch. 540, C.A.; rev'g [1967] 1 Ch. 910.
[2] *Hassall* v. *Smithers* (1806) 12 Ves. 119.
[3] See pp. 70–1 below.

A. *BARCLAYS BANK* V. *QUISTCLOSE INVESTMENTS*

'In the spring of 1964 Rolls Razor was in Queer Street'.[4] The company had an overdraft with Barclays Bank of almost double its agreed limit of £250,000. At a general meeting on 2 July 1964, a dividend of £209,719 8s 6d was approved to be paid on 24 July. The company arranged to borrow the money to pay the dividend from Quistclose Investments and, on 15 July, sent Barclays a cheque from Quistclose and a letter which stated:[5]

> Confirming our telephone conversation of today's date, will you please open a No. 4 ordinary dividend share account. I enclose herewith a cheque valued £209,719 8s. 6d. being the total amount of the dividend due on July 24, 1964. Will you please credit this to the above mentioned account. We would like to confirm the agreement reached with you this morning that this account will only be used to meet the dividend due on July 24, 1964.

However, on 17 July, the directors of Rolls Razor resolved that the company should petition for winding up and, on 27 August, the company went into liquidation. The dividend was never paid and, on 28 August, the bank set off the sum in the No. 4 dividend share account against other indebtedness of Rolls Razor.

Quistclose brought an action against Rolls Razor and Barclays, claiming a declaration that it was beneficially entitled to the money in the share dividend account. Plowman J. concluded that Rolls Razor received the money subject to a trust, but when the dividend could not be paid, the relationship between Quistclose and Rolls Razor became that of creditor and debtor. However, the Court of Appeal and House of Lords were both unanimous in holding that there was a trust in favour of Quistclose when the payment of the dividend became impossible and that Barclays had notice of the trust and could not use the account to set off against other indebtedness of Rolls Razor. Lord Wilberforce gave a short judgment, with which the other law lords agreed, and concluded that 'the decision of the Court of Appeal was correct on all points and the appeal should be dismissed'.[6]

Lord Wilberforce found that the loan was made solely for the purpose of paying the dividend and that it was therefore an implied term of the loan 'that if, for any reason, the dividend could not be paid, the money was to be returned to'[7] Quistclose Investments. His lordship then stated:[8]

> That arrangements of this character for the payment of a person's creditors by a third person, give rise to a relationship of a fiduciary character or trust, in favour, as a primary trust, of the creditors, and secondarily, if the primary trust fails, of the third person, has been recognised in a series of cases over some 150 years.

[4] *Quistclose* [1968] 1 Ch. 540, 548, per Harman L.J. [5] Ibid. at 550.
[6] [1970] A.C. 567, 582. [7] Ibid. at 580. [8] Ibid.

Lord Wilberforce was referring to a series of bankruptcy cases beginning with *Toovey* v. *Milne*.[9] In each, a person had committed an act of bankruptcy and borrowed money to pay his creditors. The money had either been paid to those creditors or refunded to the lender before the commencement of the bankruptcy and the assignee in bankruptcy was trying to recover the money as a fraudulent preference over the other creditors. The claims failed because money received for a specific purpose could not be used by the assignee for distribution among the general creditors. As Abbott C.J. stated in *Toovey* v. *Milne*:[10]

> [T]he fair inference from the facts proved was that this money was advanced for a special purpose, and that being so clothed with a specific trust, no property in it passed to the assignee of the bankrupt. Then the purpose having failed, there is an implied stipulation, that the money shall be repaid. That has been done in the present case; and I am of the opinion that that repayment was lawful.

In Quistclose, Lord Wilberforce stated:[11] 'In the present case the intention to create a secondary trust for the benefit of the lender, to arise if the primary trust, to pay the dividend, could not be carried out, is clear and I can find no reason why the law should not give effect to it'.

B. COMPETING VIEWS

The statements quoted above, taken in isolation, support the view that (i) a loan for the purpose of paying creditors creates a trust of which those creditors are the beneficiaries and (ii) on the failure of that purpose, there is an express trust in favour of the lender.[12] However, as discussed below, this view does not provide a satisfactory explanation of the cases leading up to *Quistclose* or *Quistclose* itself.[13] Although it is possible that a lender will intend to create a trust on these terms, there are compelling reasons why loans for special purposes should not be construed as express trusts unless that intention is made clear.

There is considerable support for the view that there is (or at least can be) a resulting trust for the lender on the failure of the purpose.[14] However, there are others who prefer to see it as more of a constructive trust arising because it would be unconscionable for the borrower to use the property for other purposes.[15] Mr.

[9] (1819) 2 B.&Ald. 683. [10] Ibid. at 684. [11] [1970] A.C. 567, 582.

[12] *Re Australian Elizabethan Theatre Trust* (1991) 102 A.L.R. 681, 691; Goodhart and Jones at 493; Priestly at p. 217; Martin (1993a), p. 234; Swadling (1996) at 124.

[13] Hackney, p. 51; Oditah at 474.

[14] *Quistclose* [1968] 1 Ch. 540, 566–7; *Re EVTR* [1987] B.C.L.C. 646, C.A.; *Re Australian Elizabethan Theatre Trust* (1991) 102 A.L.R. 681, 691; Meagher and Gummow, *Jacobs' Law of Trusts*, p. 17; Rickett (1991); Martin (1993a), p. 234.

[15] *Carreras Rothmans Ltd.* v. *Freeman Mathews Treasure Ltd.* [1985] 1 Ch. 207, 222; Hardcastle; Arora at 226–30. Cf. Rickett (1993) at p. 351.

Hackney described it as 'a new creature . . . invented to protect from risk of failure a secret commercial venture for profit by two parties at the ultimate expense of general creditors'.[16]

There is more controversy over whether a loan to pay the borrower's other creditors creates a trust for those creditors. Sir Peter Millett (now Lord Justice Millett) has forcefully argued against this proposition in his essay, 'The Quistclose Trust: Who Can Enforce It?'.[17] He suggested instead that the lender is, from the outset, the sole beneficiary of the *Quistclose* trust.[18] Although this was an important contribution to our understanding of the *Quistclose* trust, it is suggested below with great respect that it does not adequately explain the interests of the lender, borrower, and creditors in the *Quistclose* trust. Another view is that the loan gives rise to a non-charitable purpose trust, which leaves the beneficial interest in suspense,[19] but this suffers from the same inadequacies.

The view put forward here (that the specific purpose need not be an express trust and that a resulting trust arises on the failure of that purpose) is presented (i) in the belief that it explains existing *Quistclose* cases, using established legal principles, and (ii) with the hope that it will permit both the better integration of the *Quistclose* trust in the law of trusts and its broader application to logically similar situations. It will be convenient to examine the nature of the relationships created by the receipt of funds for a special purpose, before looking at the trust for the lender upon failure of that purpose.

C. EFFECT OF THE PURPOSE

1. The Essential Element

In *Quistclose*, Lord Wilberforce referred to the 'primary trust' as a trust in favour of the creditors and a trust to pay the dividend,[20] but never discussed the creditors' interest in the money. The decision depended instead on the lender's interest: 'when the money is advanced, the lender acquires an equitable right to see that it is applied for the primary designated purpose (see *In re Rogers*, . . . where both Lindley L.J. and Kay L.J. recognised this)'.[21] The lender's right to prevent the unauthorized use of the money is the backbone of the *Quistclose* trust. As Lindley L.J. stated in *Re Rogers*:[22]

[16] Hackney, p. 51; see Bridge; Klinck 45; Swadling (1996) at 120–4.

[17] Millett (1985).

[18] This view was also taken by P.D. Finn (see Priestley at p. 237) and in *General Communications Ltd.* v. *Development Finance Corp. of New Zealand Ltd.* [1990] 3 N.Z.L.R. 406, C.A. Also see *Re Australian Elizabethan Theatre Trust* (1991) 102 A.L.R. 681, 693–4; Bridge; Klinck.

[19] *In re Northern Developments (Holdings) Ltd.* (unreported) 6 October 1978, Ch.D., Megarry V.C.; *Carreras Rothmans* [1985] 1 Ch. 207; Rickett (1991).

[20] [1970] A.C. 567, 580, 582.

[21] Ibid. at 581, per Lord Wilberforce.

[22] (1891) 8 Morrell 243, 248.

The trustee is endeavouring to affirm the transaction in part and to repudiate it in part. He wants to claim the money as the bankrupt's because it came into his hands and at the same time to reject the terms and conditions on which alone the bankrupt procured it. This is manifestly unjust and contrary to principle . . . I entertain no doubt that [the lender] could have obtained an injunction to restrain the bankrupt from using that money for any purpose except that of paying his pressing creditors. If this be so, the money never was the bankrupt's in any proper sense so as to vest in his trustee as part of his general assets.

Although it might be said that the proceeds of such a loan are not available to the general creditors because they are held in trust, this would be stating the principle too broadly. The trustee in bankruptcy takes the property of the bankrupt 'subject to the equities', i.e. has no greater rights to the property than did the bankrupt.[23] The property is not available for distribution if the bankrupt could have been restrained from using the property for that purpose. The bankrupt need not be a trustee with only bare legal title.

The restriction on the borrower's freedom to deal with the property has, on several occasions, been affirmed as the basis for what is now known as the *Quistclose* trust. In *Edwards* v. *Glyn*, Crompton J. stated:[24]

The advance being, to use the expression of Abbott C.J. in *Toovey* v. *Milne,* clothed with a specific trust, the bankrupts, though they might have a legal, had not an equitable right to use the money for any other purpose; and equity would, I think, have interfered to prevent them from doing so. Therefore, on the principle that the assignees of a bankrupt take only the property to which the bankrupt has both a legal and equitable right, the plaintiffs have no ground of action.

In *Re Drucker*,[25] the bankrupt paid £300 of the £1,000 he owed to his bank, which was accepted on the understanding that the money had been loaned to the bankrupt for that purpose. The trustee in bankruptcy could not recover the payment as a fraudulent preference because, as Romer L.J. stated, 'there was never a moment of time at which this money could have been used for any other purpose than that of paying the bank'.[26] In that case, the trial judge, Wright J., had stated:[27]

I cannot help thinking that this money was never free, and never became part of the general assets of the debtor at all. He never had any right to receive it, or use it, or apply it to any purpose except this one particular purpose. Under these circumstances it seems to me it was impressed with a trust—not in the strict sense of the word—but in substance with a quasi-trust that it should be applied . . . for the discharge pro tanto of the claim of the bank.

[23] *Taylor* v. *Wheeler* (1706) 2 Ver. 564; *Ex parte Dumas* (1754) 2 Ves.Sen. 582, 585, per Hardwicke L.C.: 'the assignees under the commission take the estate of the bankrupt and any legal interest of the bankrupt subject to all the same equities as it stood in the bankrupt at the time of the bankruptcy'.

[24] (1859) 2 El.&El. 29, 50–1.

[25] [1902] 2 K.B. 237, C.A.; aff'g [1902] 2 K.B. 55.

[26] Ibid. at 238–9.

[27] [1902] 2 K.B. 55, 57.

In *Re Watson*,[28] a theatre manager advanced money to the bankrupt, Watson, for the purpose of obtaining the release of scenery and costumes seized from Watson by the sheriff. Cozens-Hardy M.R. stated:[29]

> The money was advanced solely for the purpose of releasing the goods which were not the property of the bankrupt. If Watson had attempted to intercept the money and apply it to his own purposes, it would have been a breach of faith, and the theatre manager might have restrained him by injunction.

In the Divisional Court, Phillimore J. (like Wright J. in *Re Drucker*, above) spoke of a 'quasi-trust':[30] 'Somebody may lend the bankrupt or give the bankrupt a sum of money to enable him to pay off a particular pressing creditor, and may say to him, "You must use it for that purpose and for no other". There upon the money is impressed with a quasi-trust'. Although the term 'quasi-trust' was not used by the Court of Appeal in either case, it more accurately describes the nature of the arrangement between the lender and the bankrupt. The contract between them, like a trust, has the effect of preventing the trustee in bankruptcy from distributing the proceeds of the loan among the general creditors of the bankrupt. But, unlike a conventional trust, the interests of the three parties involved (lender, borrower, and creditors) do not correspond to those of a settlor, trustee, or beneficiary. It will be useful to examine each of their interests separately.

2. The Lender's Interest

Right to prevent misuse

As Sir Peter Millett stated, 'it is elementary that a settlor who retains no beneficial interest cannot enforce the trust which he has created'.[31] This is true of both trusts for persons[32] and trusts for purposes.[33] The fact that the lender can, in equity, restrain the borrower's use of a loan made for a specific purpose means that the lender's interest differs from that of a mere settlor. There are two possibilities: either, as Millett believed, the lender 'can enforce the primary trust *because he is the beneficiary*'[34] or there is no trust in the strict sense of the word. Millett argued that the *Quistclose* trust:[35]

> is simply an example of what is sometimes called an 'illusory trust'. The best known example of such a trust is a disposition of property by a debtor to trustees for the benefit of his creditors . . . the apparent beneficiaries take no beneficial interest at all, the trustees holding the property transferred to them in trust for the debtor exclusively . . .
>
> In such a case, the only trust which is created is a trust to comply with A [the settlor]'s

[28] (1912) 107 L.T. 783, C.A.; aff'g (1912) 107 L.T. 96.
[29] Ibid. at 783.
[30] (1912) 107 L.T. 96, 98.
[31] Millett (1985) at 287. Also see Maitland, p. 31; *Restatement of Trusts*, §200; Waters (1984), p. 291; Hayton (1993), p. 126.
[32] *Mallott* v. *Wilson* [1903] 2 Ch. 494.
[33] *In re Astor's Settlement Trusts* [1952] Ch. 534.
[34] Millett (1985) at 288.
[35] Ibid. at 288–9.

directions. The trust itself is not revocable, but prima facie A's directions are, so that A is free to change his mind, revoke the directions he has given, and either substitute new directions, allow B [the trustee] to retain the money beneficially, or require repayment to himself.

This excellent suggestion, that the lender has a beneficial interest in the fund, has cleared away a lot of the fog surrounding the *Quistclose* trust and has been expressly adopted by the New Zealand Court of Appeal.[36] However, it is suggested with great respect that the *Quistclose* trust is not an illusory trust because the lender does not have the full equitable ownership of the money. Unlike the settlor of an illusory trust, who can revoke the instructions given to the trustee, the *Quistclose* lender cannot revoke the loan.[37] Within the confines of the special purpose for which the loan was made, the borrower has the right to use the money and the lender has no right to interfere.

If Rolls Razor had complied with the conditions of the loan, Quistclose could not have prevented the payment of the dividend when due. The lender's sole interest in the fund is the right to restrain the borrower from misapplying it. The lender, like the borrower, is bound by the contract of loan between them and the terms of that contract are not revocable by the lender. The special purpose is revocable in one sense only: the lender can waive the restriction on the use of the money, this being a term of the contract solely for the lender's benefit. The lender cannot, however, unilaterally alter that term and require the borrower to apply the money for some other purpose.

This is illustrated by *Re Schebsman*,[38] where employers had contracted with an employee (on the termination of his employment) to make payments to his wife and daughter after his death. The employee became bankrupt and died and the trustee-in-bankruptcy unsuccessfully attempted to recover the amounts due to his widow. Although the parties to the contract could have agreed to vary its terms and thereby re-direct the payments, neither the employee nor his successors had the right to unilaterally interfere with the employers' obligation to pay the widow. As du Parq L.J. stated, 'in the case of such a contract there cannot be a variation at the will of one of the parties any more than a condition introduced into a contract for the benefit of both parties can be waived by only one of them'.[39]

Right to compel payment

It is also suggested that Quistclose, unlike the settlor of an illusory trust, could not have compelled Rolls Razor to pay the dividend. The loan was made on the

[36] *General Communications* v. *D.F.C.N.Z.* [1990] 3 N.Z.L.R. 406, 432–3.

[37] Even if a loan is made on a demand basis, the lender's decision to call the loan would make the debt payable, but should not give rise to a trust in favour of the lender as long as the purpose is otherwise capable of fulfilment and the borrower is willing to carry out that purpose.

[38] [1944] Ch. 83, C.A.

[39] Ibid. at 102.

condition that it would 'only be used to meet the dividend',[40] not that it *must* be used to meet the dividend. Rolls Razor was under no contractual duty to Quistclose to make that payment and, therefore, Quistclose's only interest in the fund was to prevent it from being used for other purposes. Although Lord Wilberforce said that, 'when the money is advanced, the lender acquires an equitable right to see that it is applied for the primary designated purpose',[41] it must be remembered that his lordship relied on *Re Rogers*[42] as authority for this principle. In that case, the money had already been paid over to the creditor and the Court of Appeal decided that the lender could have prevented the borrower's misuse of the money, not that he could have compelled the payment. Lord Wilberforce's statement should be construed in keeping with *Re Rogers* and not as authority that a lender for a special purpose has the right to compel the fulfilment of that purpose.

There are two cases in which the provider of a fund for the purpose of paying the recipient's creditors was able to compel the recipient to pay those creditors.[43] In both, the provider was not a lender, but the party for whose benefit the creditors were to be paid. The recipient of the money had incurred liabilities to the creditors at the provider's request and owed a duty to the provider to pay those creditors.

It should not be assumed that the presence of a contractual obligation to apply money for a specific purpose will necessarily give the provider an equitable right to compel the payment. As Lord Wrenbury stated in *Palmer* v. *Carey*, 'An agreement for valuable consideration that a fund shall be applied in a particular way may found an injunction to restrain its application in another way',[44] but something more is required before the obligation will be specifically enforceable.[45] This is consistent with the court's greater willingness to grant an injunction enforcing a negative obligation than to specifically enforce a positive one.[46] The specific performance of contracts to pay money is exceptional.[47]

Fiduciary relationship

Lord Wilberforce said that the arrangements between the lender and borrower 'give rise to a relationship of a fiduciary character or trust'.[48] Millett suggested that this is best understood, 'as an indication that the arrangements may or may not constitute a trust, depending on the circumstances of the particular case'.[49]

[40] [1968] 1 Ch. 540, 550, C.A. [41] [1970] A.C. 567, 581.
[42] (1891) 8 Morrell 243.
[43] *Hassall* v. *Smithers* (1806) 12 Ves. 119; *Carreras Rothmans* [1985] 1 Ch. 207. They are discussed below, pp. 78–80.
[44] [1926] A.C. 703, 706 P.C.; quoted with approval by Lord Wilberforce in *Swiss Bank Corporation* v. *Lloyds Bank Ltd.* [1982] A.C. 584, 613.
[45] See, e.g., *Beswick* v. *Beswick* [1968] A.C. 58.
[46] *Doherty* v. *Allman* (1878) 3 App.Cas. 709, 719. [47] Martin (1993a), pp. 685–6.
[48] *Quistclose* [1970] A.C. 567, 580. [49] Millett (1985) at 275.

This may be the best interpretation if the choice is limited to a fiduciary relationship, on one hand, and a trust in favour of the creditors, on the other. However, it may be that Lord Wilberforce was describing the relationship which Phillimore and Wright JJ. called a 'quasi-trust'.[50] In a broad sense, the arrangement is a trust, either because someone other than the owner has equitable rights in the property or because the recipient has been trusted to use the money in a certain way. Perhaps Russell L.J. said it best when he stated:[51] 'Granted that the arrangement . . . imposed upon Rolls Razor the character of a trustee of the money advanced, the trust that was reposed in Rolls Razor was that Rolls Razor would not use the money for any purpose of Rolls Razor other than payment of the dividend'.

One difficulty in understanding the *Quistclose* trust arises simply from the use of the word 'trust'. Although it is natural to assume that the borrower has only bare legal title to the money under a conventional trust, the word 'trust' is capable of describing a broader range of equitable relationships and duties. As Gummow J. stated in *Re Australian Elizabethan Theatre Trust*, it 'is important to appreciate both the flexibility of the institution of the express trust and the range of equitable institutions which fall short of but have some characteristics of the trust'.[52] As discussed below, equitable rights can amount to full beneficial ownership or something much less and more specific. This is perhaps what Abbott C.J. meant in *Toovey* v. *Milne* when he said the money was 'clothed with a specific trust'.[53]

Further difficulties may stem from the modern tendency to talk about legal and equitable ownership of property as if both are always in existence at any given time. This has led to a search for the location of the equitable interest as a key to understanding the *Quistclose* trust. In *Carreras Rothmans Ltd.* v. *Freeman Mathews Treasure Ltd.* (discussed below), Gibson J. concluded that the lender could not have retained a beneficial interest in the proceeds of the loan and, therefore, 'the beneficial interest is in suspense until the payment is made' to the creditors.[54] With respect, these difficulties can be avoided if the jurisdictional basis of equity is remembered. When money is borrowed without restriction on its use, the beneficial interest is not in suspense, but neither has the borrower received the equitable ownership of the money. Equity has nothing to do with it. The borrower has the full benefit of the money at common law and there is no reason for equity to interfere.[55]

When a loan is made for a special purpose, equity will interfere to prevent the borrower from using that money for any other purpose. Although the lender's right to enforce the restriction can be regarded as a trust, the use of the word 'trust' does not enlarge the lender's interest in the fund. The borrower is completely

[50] Above, n. 27 and n. 30.
[51] *Quistclose* [1968] 1 Ch. 540, 557.
[52] (1991) 102 A.L.R. 681, 693.
[53] (1819) 2 B.&Ald. 683.
[54] [1985] 1 Ch. 207, 223.
[55] See pp. 52–3 above.

entitled to the beneficial use of the money, subject only to the lender's right to prevent its misuse. There is no need to either talk about the beneficial interest as being in suspense or look for it elsewhere.

3. The Borrower's Interest

As suggested above, as long as the purpose is capable of being carried out, the borrower has the full benefit of the proceeds of the loan at common law, subject only to the lenders' ability to restrict the borrower's use of the property. Although this is a form of trust, it would not be accurate to say that the entire beneficial ownership of the property is held in trust. The lender has the only equitable interest. The fact that the loan proceeds are not divisible among the general creditors of the borrower has led to the assumption that the borrower has no more than 'a dry legal interest'.[56] However, the lender's limited equitable interest in the fund is, by itself, sufficient to prevent its use for that purpose.

Lord Wilberforce said of *Re Rogers* that the money 'was impressed with a trust for the purpose and never became the property of the bankrupt'.[57] Although this suggests that the borrower received no beneficial interest, it must be remembered that, in *Re Rogers*, Lindley L.J. said that 'the money never was the bankrupt's *in any proper sense so as to vest in his trustee as part of the general assets*'.[58] In *Quistclose*, Russell L.J. stated that 'Rolls Razor was not at liberty to treat the money advanced as the beneficial property of Rolls Razor *except for the limited activity of paying a particular class of its creditors*'.[59] Sachs L.J. stated that:[60]

> [T]he beneficial property in the sums in Dividend Account No. 4 never at any material time vested in Rolls Razor Ltd. or the liquidator *in any sense which could entitle the bank to use it . . . for a purpose which was entirely contrary to the terms on which they knew it had been paid into that account.*

Although Lord Wilberforce said that Barclays had notice that the loan 'was trust money and not the assets of Rolls Razor',[61] it was not necessary that Rolls Razor be a bare trustee in order to prevent Barclays from combining the accounts. Barclays' knowledge that the fund was subject to an equitable interest was sufficient to prevent it from acquiring legal title free of that interest as a *bona fide* purchaser.[62]

None of the *Quistclose* trust cases depended on the borrower having only a dry legal interest in the proceeds of the loan. In *Gibert* v. *Gonard*, where money had been borrowed for the purpose of purchasing a manufactory of condensed

[56] *Re Australian Elizabethan Theatre Trust* (1991) 102 A.L.R. 681, 692, per Gummow J.
[57] *Quistclose* [1970] A.C. 567, 580.
[58] (1891) 8 Morrell 243, 248 (emphasis added).
[59] [1968] 1 Ch. 540, 557 (emphasis added).
[60] Ibid. at 567 (emphasis added).
[61] [1970] A.C. 567, 582.
[62] *Quistclose* [1968] 1 Ch. 540, 561; *Barclays Bank p.l.c.* v. *O'Brien* [1994] 1 A.C. 180.

milk, North J. stated that the duty to use the money for that purpose created a 'fiduciary relation'.[63] In *Carreras Rothmans Ltd.* v. *Freeman Mathews Treasure Ltd.*, Gibson J. stated:[64]

> I doubt if it is helpful to analyse the *Quistclose* type of case in terms of the constituent parts of a conventional settlement, though it may of course be crucial to ascertain in whose favour the secondary trust operates (as in the *Quistclose* case itself) and who has an enforceable right. In my judgment the principle in all these cases is that equity fastens on the conscience of the person who receives from another property transferred for a specific purpose only and not therefore for the recipient's own purposes, so that such person will not be permitted to treat the property as his own or to use it for other than the stated purpose.

It is suggested that the best conclusion to be drawn from the cases is that a loan of money to be used for a specific purpose places the borrower under a fiduciary obligation not to misuse that money. This is the extent of the 'trust' and the borrower is the beneficial owner of the money, subject to that obligation.

4. The Creditors' Interest

Until *Re Northern Developments (Holdings) Ltd.*,[65] it had not been necessary to decide if the creditors had an interest in the fund while it remained in the hands of the borrower. In every case but one, the lender was trying to recover the fund or it had already been paid to the lender or creditors. The exception was *Hassall* v. *Smithers.*[66] Although the creditors in that case were able to recover the money from the recipient's estate, the question of their right to call for the fund was expressly avoided, because the provider of the fund had joined them in their petition.

In *Hassall* v. *Smithers*, the fund has been provided by Mr. Illingworth for the purpose of answering his acceptances of certain bills drawn on the recipient. After the recipient died intestate, Illingworth and the bill holders brought a petition to compel his representatives to use the fund for that purpose. Grant M.R. stated:[67]

> Clearly the intestate was bound so to apply that remittance; if it had got into his hands. He had no option, even if he had been a creditor at the time upon other accounts, to apply that fund to any other demand; for Illingworth had a right to prescribe in the first instance, in what manner, and to what account, the remittance should be applied. If the intestate had been a bankrupt, property in his hands under such circumstances would not have passed to his assignees; but would have been applicable to the bills, to answer which it was specifically remitted. The representatives cannot be in any better plight than the intestate himself would have been in. They have no election to consider this remittance,

[63] (1884) 54 L.J. Ch. 439, 440. [64] [1985] 1 Ch. 207, 222.
[65] Unreported, 6 October 1978, Ch.D., Megarry V.C. [66] (1806) 12 Ves. 119.
[67] Ibid. at 121–2.

> not as a fund applicable to the bills outstanding, but as part of the general assets. They are bound to apply it for Illingworth. Then the bill-holders desire, with the assent of Illingworth, to have it applied in discharge of these bills; and he joins them in that request; and that avoids the question upon the strength of their own claim to insist upon the application: for there can be no doubt, that there is in them, and him, joining them, a complete right to insist upon the application, that he originally prescribed; and, if it were otherwise, the grossest injustice would be the consequence; for that would be the application of Illingworth's money, not in executing the purpose, for which he made the remittance, but to pay other debts of the intestate.

Although the question of the creditors' interest in the fund was left unanswered, it seems clear that Illingworth, as the provider of the fund, has the power to compel the payment to the creditors.

There are three cases since *Quistclose* in which the courts decided that the creditors had the right to enforce payment to themselves: *Re Northern Developments (Holdings) Ltd.*,[68] *Carreras Rothmans Ltd.* v. *Freeman Mathews Treasure Ltd.*[69] and *General Communications Ltd.* v. *Development Finance Corporation of New Zealand Ltd.*[70] In the first of these, Megarry V.C. found that the creditors had enforceable rights against the holder of the fund, rather than an interest in the fund itself:[71]

> There is perhaps some parallel in the position of a beneficiary entitled to a share of residue under a will. What he has is not a beneficial interest in any asset forming part of residue, but a right to compel the executor to administer the assets of the deceased properly. It seems to me that it is that sort of right which the creditors . . . had.

This was followed in *Carreras Rothmans*, concerning a fund the plaintiff had provided to an advertising agency for the purpose of paying the agency's debts to trade creditors in connexion with the plaintiff's advertisements. When the agency became insolvent without paying the creditors, the plaintiff paid them directly, took assignments of their claims against the agency and brought an action to recover the fund. The situation was similar to *Hassall* v. *Smithers* because the plaintiff came to court both as the provider of the fund and in the shoes of the creditors. Gibson J. stated:[72]

> I cannot accept the joint submission that the third party creditors for the payment of whose debts the plaintiff had paid the moneys into the special account had no enforceable rights. In any event I do not comprehend how a trust, which on no footing could the plaintiff revoke unilaterally, and which was still capable of performance, could nevertheless leave the beneficial interest in the plaintiff which had parted with the moneys. On Sir Robert Megarry V.C.'s analysis the beneficial interest is in suspense until the payment is made.

[68] Unreported, 6 October 1978, Ch.D., Megarry V.C.
[69] [1985] 1 Ch. 207.
[70] [1990] 3 N.Z.L.R. 406.
[71] Megarry V.C.; quoted by Gibson J. in *Carreras Rothmans* [1985] 1 Ch. 207, 223.
[72] *Carreras Rothmans* [1985] 1 Ch. 207, 223.

This is confusing because the basis of the judgment was that 'the plaintiff as the provider of the moneys has an equitable right to an order for the carrying out by the defendant of the trust'.[73] With respect, there was no irrevocable trust, just an irrevocable payment to the agency, because those funds were provided as payment of the plaintiff's debts to the agency. This does not mean that the plaintiff was prevented from waiving the restriction concerning the use of those funds. The finding that the creditors had enforceable rights to the fund was unnecessary.

Why does the purpose fail?

If a loan for a specific purpose gives the creditors an interest in the fund, it is difficult to understand why, in most cases, the lender recovers and not the creditors. It has been pointed out that the purpose would not have failed in *Quistclose* if the shareholders had acquired a beneficial interest.[74] The Companies Act 1948 prevented the payment of the dividend once the liquidator was appointed on 27 August, but the proceeds of the loan were in Rolls Razor's account when the dividend came due on 24 July. If the shareholders had a beneficial interest in the fund at that time, 'there is no good reason why their right to the money should be affected by the subsequent liquidation of' Rolls Razor.[75]

In *Toovey* v. *Milne*,[76] the borrower had obtained a loan for the purpose of settling with his creditors and voluntarily returned the money after his bankruptcy. There was nothing to prevent him from paying his creditors. As Millett rightly stated:[77]

> There are only two possible explanations. Either the arrangements created a power but not a trust for the payment of B [the borrower]'s creditors, and B elected not to exercise it, or the purpose for which A [the lender] lent the money was taken to be, not to enable C [the creditors] to be paid, but to save B from bankruptcy.

In *Gibert* v. *Gonard*[78] and *Re Vautin*,[79] the purpose of the loan was not fulfilled solely because the borrower chose not to use the money for that purpose. In the former case, the lender was able to recover the balance of the loan from the borrower and, in the latter, the borrower returned the money unrequested. The decisions in all four cases are difficult to explain if it is assumed that the creditors had acquired a beneficial interest in the proceeds of the loan.

Presumption against trust

In cases like *Carreras Rothmans*, where the borrower is, by contract with the lender, obliged to pay the creditors, this duty and the lender's corresponding

[73] Ibid. at 224, per Gibson J.
[74] Goodhart and Jones at 494, fn. 28; Millett (1985) at 275–6; Meagher and Gummow, *Jacobs' Law of Trusts*, p. 17; Oditah at 475.
[75] Millett (1985) at 276. Under the Insolvency Act 1986, s. 86, the winding-up is deemed to commence at the time the resolution for winding-up is passed.
[76] (1819) 2 B.&Ald. 683.
[77] Millett (1985) at 271.
[78] (1884) 54 L.J. Ch. 439.
[79] [1900] 2 Q.B. 325.

right to enforce it do not give the creditors a beneficial interest in the fund. Although the arrangement appears to be very much like a trust for the creditors, it should be presumed that there is no such trust. The lender would normally be free to waive the borrower's obligation to use the money in a certain way, this being a term of the contract solely for the benefit of the lender. A trust in favour of the creditors would mean that the lender's rights are lost and the creditors have acquired a beneficial interest. The creditors have not given value for the payment to the borrower and cannot enforce the contract between the lender and the borrower.[80] It would be wrong to assume that the lender intended to dispose gratuitously of an interest in the property in favour of the creditors and the presumption should be the other way.[81] As du Parq L.J. stated in *Re Schebsman*:[82]

> It is true that, by the use possibly of unguarded language, a person may create a trust, as Monsieur Jourdain talked prose, without knowing it, but unless an intention to create a trust is clearly to be collected from the language used and the circumstances of the case, I think that the court ought not to be astute to discover indications of such an intention. I have little doubt that in the present case both parties . . . intended to keep alive their common law right to vary consensually the terms of the obligation undertaken by the company, and if circumstances had changed . . . injustice might have been done by holding a trust had been created and that those terms were accordingly unalterable.

In the cases of illusory trusts, deeds of express trusts for the payment of creditors have been construed to be trusts in favour of the settlors.[83] In *Smith* v. *Hurst*,[84] a debtor transferred his property to a trustee in trust for his creditors. Turner V.C. decided this was a settlement for the debtor's own convenience and, therefore, did not transfer any beneficial interest to the creditors:[85]

> [I]n cases of deeds purporting to be executed for the benefit of creditors, and to which no creditor is a party, the motive of the party executing the deed may have been either to benefit his creditors or to promote his own convenience; and the Court there has to examine into the circumstances, for the purpose of ascertaining what was the true purpose of the deed.

These reasons for invalidating an express deed of trust for the benefit of one's own creditors apply *a fortiori* to a loan made for the purpose of paying another's creditors. There is no reason to infer that the lender intended to create a trust for the benefit of the borrower's creditors.

Subsequent conduct

Re Northern Developments and *General Communications Ltd.* v. *Development Finance Corp.*[86] were cases where the creditors were able to enforce payment to

[80] *Re Schebsman* [1944] Ch. 83; *Beswick* v. *Beswick* [1968] A.C. 58.
[81] Goodhart and Jones at 489; Rickett (1993) at p. 332; Meagher and Gummow, *Jacobs' Law of Trusts*, p. 57; Swadling (1996) at 121; cf. Gardner, p. 54; Goddard at 24.
[82] [1944] Ch. 83, 104.
[83] See Millett (1985) at 288–9, for a discussion of the illusory trust.
[84] (1852) 10 Hare 30.
[85] Ibid. at 47.
[86] [1990] 3 N.Z.L.R. 406.

themselves. In each case, this conclusion was necessary to the result and correct, but not on the basis that the arrangement between the lender and the borrower gave a beneficial interest to the creditors. The creditors' interests arose because of the subsequent conduct of the parties. As Turner V.C. stated in *Smith* v. *Hurst* (continuing the previous quotation regarding illusory trusts):[87]

> [T]he Court there has to examine into the circumstances, for the purpose of ascertaining what was the true purpose of the deed; and this examination does not stop with the deed itself, but must be carried on to what has subsequently occurred, because the party who has created the trust may, by his own conduct, or by obligations which he has permitted his trustee to contract, have created an equity against himself.

In *Re Northern Developments*, pressing creditors were told of the existence of the fund to obtain their forbearance. Although Megarry V.C. did not rely on this aspect of the case, Millett thought that it 'ought to be decisive; for on well-settled principles communication of the arrangements to C [the creditors], followed by forbearance by C, raises an equity against A [the settlor] which prevents him from revoking the arrangements or otherwise intercepting payment to C'.[88] Millett reached this conclusion because, 'communication to C perfects an assignment of A's equitable interest to C, and converts A's revocable mandate into an irrevocable trust for C'.[89] With respect, this explanation does not function satisfactorily in the context of the *Quistclose* trust. The lender has the right to prevent the misapplication of the fund. The creditors who have relied on the arrangement have the right to compel payment to themselves. Not only is their interest different from the lender's, there is nothing which indicates that the lender has lost or assigned the right to prevent misuse of the fund. In other words, the lender's equitable interest continues unchanged and the creditors have acquired a new interest. The borrower's enjoyment of the fund at common law is now subject to two equitable interests: one in favour of the lender and another in favour of the creditors.

In *General Communications* v. *Development Finance Corp.*,[90] money was loaned for the purpose of buying video equipment. The lender paid the money to the borrower's solicitors in reliance on their written undertaking to hold it in their trust account and pay it directly to the supplier after the borrower received the equipment. The supplier provided the equipment on 90-days credit. This was supposed to be secured by a letter of credit, but the supplier accepted instead a letter from the borrower's solicitors confirming they would be making the payment on receipt of the money from the lender. The lender and the supplier were unaware of each other's arrangements with the borrower's solicitors. After the equipment was delivered, but before the 90 days had passed, the borrower became insolvent and the borrower's solicitors returned the money to the lender. The supplier successfully recovered the money from the lender.

[87] (1852) 10 Hare 30, 47. [88] Millett (1985) at 278. [89] Ibid. at 289.
[90] [1990] 3 N.Z.L.R. 406.

The New Zealand Court of Appeal concluded that, although 'there was no forbearance or detrimental act by the suppliers in response to the creation of the fund',[91] the lender had created an equity against itself by communicating to the supplier that payment would be made through the borrower's solicitors and that this was sufficient to enable the borrower to enforce the trust. The court also concluded that the lender must have intended to create an irrevocable trust in favour of the supplier.

This case was difficult because of the separate communications by the borrower's solicitors to the lender and supplier. It was made worse by the court's assumption that the borrower would be a bare trustee of the fund for the lender, unless the lender had somehow transferred its beneficial interest to the supplier. The lender's equitable interest in the fund was the right to prevent its misuse and this right was not lost. The lender could not interfere with the payment to the supplier, because this was not a misuse of the fund, but the fulfilment of the purpose for which it was loaned. The borrower had the full benefit of the fund at common law, subject only to the lender's interest, and had created an additional equity against itself through its solicitors. Although the supplier did not detrimentally rely on the terms by which the lender created the fund, it certainly relied on the anticipated existence of the fund and the borrower's solicitors' promise to pay upon receipt of the money.

D. THE TRUST UPON FAILURE OF THE PURPOSE

It is clear that, upon the failure of the purpose of the loan, the borrower becomes a bare trustee of the money for the lender. There is some disagreement, however, on the proper classification of that trust. Despite assertions that there is an express trust for the lender, it is suggested that the *Quistclose* trust is a resulting trust (or at least need not be an express trust) and that its improper classification obscures its true nature and may impede its proper application in the future.

The cases up until *Quistclose* did not specify the nature of the trust and *Quistclose* itself left the classification in doubt. Harman L.J. stated:[92] 'I do not see why this needs to be called a resulting trust; the bankruptcy cases never so suggest. It is a trust always attaching to the money involved in the conditions of the loan . . . the second trust did not arise on failure of the first; it was present throughout'. Sachs L.J. was content to find that there was either 'a further trust in favour of'[93] Quistclose or a resulting trust.

According to Lord Wilberforce, there was an 'intention to create a secondary trust for the benefit of the lender',[94] which could be implied from an implied term of the agreement that the money would be returned if the dividend could

[91] Ibid. at 434, per Hardie Boys J. [92] [1968] 1 Ch. 540, 554. [93] Ibid. at 566.
[94] [1970] A.C. 567, 582.

not be paid.[95] Although it is possible for a lender to create an express trust on these terms, the court should not be overly astute to discover one based on two layers of implication, for the *Quistclose* trust does not depend on it.[96] This is illustrated by the difference between a trust 'to A for life, remainder to the settlor' and a trust which is simply 'to A for life'. In the first case, the settlor has become a beneficiary under an express trust. In the second, there is a resulting trust, which arises because the settlor did not intend the trustee (or anyone else) to receive a beneficial interest in the remainder. In the same way, the lender for a special purpose does not intend the borrower to receive the beneficial ownership of the money, except to use in accordance with the special purpose. If that purpose cannot be fulfilled, the beneficial ownership of the money results back to the lender.

It is not essential that there be an express trust, nor even that the parties address their minds to the possibility of failure of the purpose. This was important in *Re EVTR*,[97] where the lender provided £60,000 to the borrower for the purpose of buying video equipment. The money was paid over to the supplier and temporary equipment was delivered. The supplier held the money as a deposit until the new equipment was delivered, but the borrower was put into receivership before that could happen. The supplier returned the deposit to the receiver (less an agreed amount for the supplier's damages) and the lender was able to recover this money from the receiver by virtue of a *Quistclose* trust. Dillon L.J. stated:[98]

> [N]obody gave a conscious thought to any possibility that, after the documents had all been signed up and the £60,000 had been paid to . . . [the supplier], the purchase of the Encore System might yet fall through and the £60,000, or a large part of it, might be repaid. That however is not conclusive against the appellant, since a resulting or constructive trust normally arises by implication of law when circumstances happen to which the parties has not addressed their minds.

Both Dillon and Bingham L.JJ. found that the trust in favour of the lender was a resulting trust (Dillon L.J. also thought that *Quistclose* itself was a case of resulting trust).[99]

In *Gibert* v. *Gonard*, the lender was allowed to recover upon failure of the purpose, even though, as North J. stated, 'the money was lent by way of a loan, and was to be repaid, and was a sum not intended to go back in specie in any way to the person who lent it'.[100] The resulting trust arises not because the lender intended such a trust, but because the lender did not intend the borrower to retain the money in the events which have occurred. This is the connexion between *Quistclose* trusts and the traditional categories of resulting trust. In all cases, the resulting trust arises in response to the lack of intention to benefit the recipient. It should be noted, however, that the *Quistclose* trust is not a subset of either of

[95] Ibid. at 580. [96] Cf. Swadling (1996) at 121, 124. [97] [1987] B.C.L.C. 646, C.A.
[98] Ibid. at 650. [99] Ibid. at 649, 650, 652. [100] (1884) 54 L.J. Ch. 439, 440.

the traditional categories. There is no apparent gift in most *Quistclose* cases, since the payment is usually made in exchange for valuable consideration, and there is no failure of an express trust. When a resulting trust arises in a *Quistclose* case, the purpose has failed, but the primary trust has not. The lender's equitable interest, being the ability to prevent the borrower's misuse of the fund, continues in full force, becoming merged in the greater equitable ownership under the resulting trust.

E. NATURE OF THE PURPOSE

So far, this chapter has examined the effect of a payment to be used for a specific purpose and the consequences of the failure of that purpose. The nature of the purpose capable of giving rise to a *Quistclose* trust is considered in this section. The *Quistclose* cases tend to involve loans made for the purpose of paying other creditors of the borrower. It is suggested here that the *Quistclose* trust is not limited to that situation, but is possible whenever money is paid to another on the condition that it be used for a specific purpose. The purpose need not be the payment of creditors, but can be anything which creates an enforceable restriction on the recipient's use of the money.

1. Types of Purposes

In *Re Miles*, Pincus J. stated that 'it would not be right to apply the *Quistclose* principle beyond the field defined by the House of Lords—i.e. actual payment of money, by the party claiming to be the beneficiary of a resulting trust, for the purpose of discharge of debts by the payee, that purpose having failed'.[101] However, with respect, it is difficult to understand why the principle should not apply whenever money has been paid to be used for a particular purpose.[102] The payment of money for the purpose of purchasing equipment has been held to create a *Quistclose* trust.[103] In Canada, the same principle has been applied to a payment for the purpose of meeting a dishonoured cheque given to charity,[104] a sale of shares for the purpose of raising money to purchase other shares,[105] and levies by municipal governments for the purpose of making local improvements.[106] So long as the purpose restricts the recipient's use of the money and

[101] (1989) 85 A.L.R. 216, 221. Also see Swadling (1996) at 122.
[102] See Rickett (1991) at 618, 628.
[103] *Gibert* v. *Gonard* (1884) 54 L.J. Ch. 439; *Re EVTR* [1987] B.C.L.C. 646, C.A.; *General Communications Ltd.* v. *Development Finance Corp. of New Zealand Ltd.* [1990] 3 N.Z.L.R. 406, C.A.
[104] *Gamble* v. *Lee* (1878) 25 Gr. 326.
[105] *Anderson, Greene & Co. Ltd.* v. *Kickley* [1934] 3 D.L.R. 787, S.C.C.
[106] *Smith* v. *Township of Raleigh* (1882) 3 O.R. 405, 411; *Ferguson* v. *City of Toronto* [1944] 3 D.L.R. 317, Ont. C.A.

is sufficiently certain to be enforceable, there is no reason not to give effect to it.

2. Abstract Purposes

Professor Rickett has raised an important question concerning the broader application of the *Quistclose* trust:[107] 'It is interesting to speculate on whether the *Quistclose* analysis could apply where the stated purpose would not involve in its fulfilment any factual benefit to ascertainable "beneficiaries"; where, for instance, the purpose might be characterised as "abstract or impersonal".' It is suggested here that it can and does. As discussed above, a payment for the purpose of paying other creditors of the recipient does not (or at least need not) create an express trust. Indeed, many *Quistclose* cases cannot be satisfactorily explained if a trust existed before the failure of the purpose.[108] The *Quistclose* trust depends on the restriction of the recipient's right to use the property, rather than the existence of an express trust. Therefore, the nature of the purpose in a *Quistclose* case need not meet the requirements for a valid trust. It need only create an enforceable restriction on the recipient's use of the money.

In a few *Quistclose* cases, where money was provided to pay identifiable creditors, it appears that the real purpose which failed was something other than the payment of those creditors and therefore abstract. In *Moore* v. *Barthrop*,[109] a father and son in business together had borrowed £200 for the purpose of reducing their overdraft at the bank. They each committed an act of bankruptcy and decided to return the money to the lender. As Millett L.J. noted extra-judicially:[110] 'If the purpose of the arrangements failed, it can only be because that purpose was not simply to achieve a reduction in the partnership's overdraft, but to facilitate the obtaining of further credit with which to carry on the partnership business'.

In *Re Vautin,* Wright J. said that the purpose of the loan in question was 'for clearing off the liabilities of the borrower and making him a free man, and for that purpose only'.[111] In *Re Groom*,[112] money was provided by the bankrupt's husband for payment to her creditors. The stated purpose of the loan was the annulment of the bankruptcy and Riley J. held that this was sufficient to attract the *Quistclose* trust.[113]

Although it is possible to view these as cases involving abstract purposes, they are equivocal because they also involve payments to identifiable creditors. In *Edwards* v. *Glyn*, the purpose of the loan was 'to meet a run upon the bankrupts' bank on a particular day'.[114] On receipt of the loan, it became apparent that the loan would be insufficient to meet the run and the money was returned

[107] Rickett (1991) at 617.
[108] See p. 80 above.
[109] (1822) 1 B.&C. 5.
[110] Millett (1985) at 271–2.
[111] [1900] 2 Q.B. 325, 327; see p. 80 above.
[112] (1977) 16 A.L.R. 278.
[113] Ibid. at 282.
[114] (1859) 2 El.&El. 29, 48, per Erle J.

unused. Although it might be possible to describe any depositors who happened to call on the bank that day as an ascertainable class of beneficiaries, the case is inexplicable on that basis. There was nothing to prevent the payment to depositors, if that was the purpose, yet all four members of the court held that the purpose of the loan had failed.

Conservative and Unionist Central Office v. *Burrell*[115] was not a *Quistclose* case, but it shows that a payment for an abstract purpose can create an enforceable restriction on the recipient's use of the funds. The issue was whether the central office was an unincorporated association for taxation purposes and the Crown argued that it could not otherwise hold funds. The Court of Appeal disagreed. It was clear that the recipients could not be 'trustees since the law does not recognise trusts for non-charitable purposes'.[116] However, the court thought that contributions could be made subject to the contributor's mandate to use the funds only for the purposes of the party. Brightman L.J. stated:[117]

> [T]he contributor has no right to demand his contribution back, once it has been mixed with other money under the authority of the contributor . . . This does not mean, however, that all contributors lose all rights once their cheques are cashed, with the absurd result that the treasurer or other officers can run off with the mixed fund with impunity. I have no doubt that any contributor has a remedy against the recipient (i.e. the treasurer, or the officials at whose direction the treasurer acts) to restrain or make good a misapplication of the mixed fund except so far as it may appear on ordinary accounting principles that the plaintiff's own contribution was spent before the threatened or actual misapplication.

Although this case has been criticized (for failing to reflect the true intentions of contributors or explain how testamentary contributions are received),[118] it does show that someone who has provided money to be used for purely abstract purposes can restrain its misuse by the recipient. This restriction should be a sufficient foundation for a *Quistclose* trust if the purpose ever became incapable of fulfilment. The application of *Quistclose* principles in this situation should not engender fears of unexpected priorities in insolvency. The *Quistclose* trust would not protect the funds from the creditors of the party, because the payment of party debts would fall within the purpose of the contribution. It should, however, protect the funds from the recipients' personal creditors.

3. Non-Charitable Purpose Trusts

The application of the *Quistclose* trust to payments for abstract purposes raises two questions: (i) why is a *Quistclose* trust for an abstract purpose not caught by the rule against non-charitable purpose trusts and (ii) why do non-charitable purpose trusts fail if a *Quistclose* trust for the same purpose would be valid?

A charitable purpose trust is enforceable by the Attorney-General, but a trust

[115] [1982] 2 All E.R. 1. [116] Ibid. at 6, per Lawton L.J. [117] Ibid. at 7.
[118] Hackney, pp. 80–2.

for a non-charitable purpose is, with few exceptions, invalid because there are no beneficiaries to enforce it.[119] This problem should not affect the *Quistclose* trust because the provider maintains the equitable right to prevent the misuse of the fund until the purposes are fulfilled. It is clear that the *Quistclose* arrangement is valid where the purpose involves payments to identifiable third parties and yet that arrangement does not normally give those third parties any right to enforce the purpose.[120] The presence of an identifiable class of intended payees is irrelevant to the validity of the *Quistclose* trust, which depends only on the provider's right to prevent the misuse of the fund. Although an abstract purpose would not create an enforceable restriction on the use of money if it was too uncertain or offended a rule of public policy, there is no logical reason why the abstract nature of the purpose should itself have any effect. As Birks said:[121]

> If I advance money for a purpose, my remedial position should not depend, or should not without absolute necessity be made to depend, on the fortuitous difference between a purpose which is abstract and a purpose which can be construed as redounding to the benefit of an ascertained class of beneficiaries.

It may seem odd to uphold a transfer for a non-charitable purpose on *Quistclose* principles and yet strike down a trust for that same purpose. Although these dispositions are alike, they are differently constituted: the *Quistclose* trust exists because of the equitable rights of the provider, whereas a conventional trust depends on the interest of the intended beneficiaries: with no identifiable beneficiaries and no possibility of enforcement by the settlor,[122] the non-charitable purpose trust fails. Distinctions of this kind may seem overly technical, but equity has been willing to draw them. For example, discretionary trusts and powers of appointment (often called trust powers and mere powers) are two, almost indistinguishable means of holding property and yet they rest on entirely different footings. The beneficiaries of a trust power can compel its exercise, whereas the potential donees of a mere power have no rights to enforce it.[123] Instead, those entitled in default of the appointment are able to restrain its improper exercise.[124]

Why is a non-charitable purpose trust ineffective when the *Quistclose* purpose takes effect as an enforceable restriction on the recipient's use of the money? The short answer is that a court will not save an ineffective trust by construing it to be some other valid disposition.[125] Equity has not been willing to take the extra step of saying that a similar disposition might be better than no disposition at all.[126] The court gives effect, if possible, to the intentions of the transferor, but

[119] *Morice* v. *Bishop of Durham* (1804) 9 Ves. 399, 404–5; *Re Diplock* [1941] Ch. 253, 259, C.A.; *Re Astor's Settlement Trusts* [1952] Ch. 534, 541–2; *Leahy* v. *A.-G. N.S.W.* [1959] A.C. 457, 478–9, P.C.; *Re Endacott* [1960] Ch. 232, 246, 250, C.A.; *Re Recher's Will Trusts* [1972] Ch. 526, 538.
[120] Above, pp. 78–81. [121] Birks (1992c) at p. 352.
[122] Above, p. 73. [123] *In re Baden's Deed Trusts* [1971] A.C. 424, 445.
[124] *In re Gulbenkian's Settlements* [1970] A.C. 508, 525.
[125] *I.R.C.* v. *Broadway Cottages Trust* [1955] Ch. 20, 36; *Re Shaw* [1957] 1 W.L.R. 729, 746.
[126] In the USA, a non-charitable purpose trust does not fail entirely, but is treated as a power of

does not amend those intentions.[127] The settlor of a non-charitable purpose trust intends to dispose of the entire beneficial ownership of the property and, therefore, does not retain the power to prevent its misuse. The *Quistclose* trust is not a questionable attempt to avoid the rule against non-charitable purpose trusts, because the provider intended to create a different relationship and the courts have been willing to give effect to that intention.

F. SUMMARY

When money is loaned to be used for a specific purpose, the lender acquires an equitable right to prevent the use of those funds for any other purpose. This right derives from the express or implied term of the contract between the lender and the borrower restricting the borrower's use of the money. If the contract requires the borrower to apply the money for a purpose beneficial to the lender, the lender may also acquire the equitable right to compel the fulfilment of that purpose. Although this arrangement can be described as a trust, the borrower acquires more than just bare legal title and has the full beneficial use of the money at common law, subject only to the equitable rights of the lender. The creditors do not have any beneficial interest in the money, unless they acquire some equitable rights over the borrower's interest as a result of some arrangement with the borrower or detrimental reliance on the actions of the borrower. Even if the creditors acquire a beneficial interest in the fund, the lender's equitable rights are not thereby extinguished.

If the purpose of the loan fails, either because it becomes impossible to fulfil or the borrower chooses not to fulfil it, the money is held by the borrower on resulting trust for the lender. This resulting trust does not depend on the failure of a prior express trust, but arises because the lender did not intend that the borrower should retain the benefit of the money, other than for use in accordance with the purpose for which it was obtained.

The *Quistclose* trust is not limited to situations in which money is loaned to be used for the payment of creditors. It should apply whenever money is paid to another on condition that it be used for a particular purpose. The purpose can be anything which creates an enforceable restriction on the recipient's use of the money, even if that purpose does not redound to the benefit of an identifiable class of persons and is therefore 'abstract'. The possible application of the resulting trust to cases where money is paid for purposes unrelated to the recipient's use of the money is the subject of Chapter 6.

appointment or something equivalent to an illusory trust: Scott and Fratcher, §§418–19. In Alberta, non-charitable purpose trusts are converted into powers of appointment which are valid for 21 years: Perpetuities Act, R.S.A. 1980, c. P-4, s. 20(1).

[127] See *Milroy* v. *Lord* (1862) 4 De G.F.&J. 264, 274–5; Maitland, p. 72; Hovius and Youdan, pp. 38–41.

II
Resulting Trusts and Restitution

4
Restitution

The circumstances in which resulting trusts arise were explored in Part I and it was concluded that resulting trusts operate on the same principle regardless of their situation. The facts giving rise to a resulting trust are: (i) a transfer of property, (ii) in circumstances in which the provider of that property did not intend to benefit the recipient. The property may be any sort of property interest or asset capable of being the subject of a trust. The provider may be the previous owner of the property or one who has provided consideration for the transfer. The provider's intention may be presumed or proven.

This chapter has two purposes. The first is to show that all resulting trusts effect restitution to the provider of what would otherwise be the unjust enrichment of the recipient. Restitution is the label given to a variety of legal and equitable responses to unjust enrichment gained at the expense of another, which cause that enrichment to be given up to that other. As this chapter demonstrates, the resulting trust is one of those responses. Its second purpose is to begin the important task (continued in the next five chapters) of identifying the place of the resulting trust in the law of restitution, i.e. the nature and extent of the resulting trust's response to unjust enrichment.

These tasks are undertaken with the aid of the taxonomy of the law of restitution developed by Professor Birks in *An Introduction to the Law of Restitution*. Although there are other means of segregating restitution from other subjects and of organizing the law of restitution itself, Birks' taxonomy is the most widely accepted in the common law world (outside the USA). Even those with quite different views on the subject acknowledge the importance of his contribution.[1] As discussed below, some aspects of Birks' definition have been criticized as overly inclusive, but these are not involved in its application to the resulting trust. In areas relevant to this book, his views on the scope of the law of restitution are at least as restrictive as those of most other commentators.

A. BIRKS' DEFINITION OF RESTITUTION

Birks defines restitution as '*the response which consists in causing one person to give up to another an enrichment received at his expense or its value in*

[1] See Moriarty (1986); Gummow; Beatson (1991), p. 22; McCamus at p. 136 (see pp. 131–41); McBride and McGrath at 36, 49.

money'.[2] A closer look at each component of this definition will show that it fits the resulting trust. They are: (i) causing one person to give up to another (ii) an enrichment (iii) received at his expense (iv) or its value in money. Before the examination of these four elements begins, it is important to note that it will not be sufficient merely to prove that they apply to the resulting trust. As Birks points out, this definition is capable of describing responses other than restitution unless two exclusions are made: (i) obligations or property rights created by consent[3] and (ii) the preservation of the owner's pre-existing title.[4] Therefore, to show that resulting trusts are restitutionary, it is necessary to prove both that Birks' definition applies to all resulting trusts and that these two excluded categories do not.

Birks' definition of restitution speaks of enrichment, but not *unjust* enrichment. This is not an oversight, but the avoidance of a redundancy: in Birks' taxonomy, restitution is always and necessarily a response to unjust enrichment:[5]

> In the phrase 'unjust enrichment' the word 'unjust' might, with a different throw of the dice, have been 'disapproved' or, more neutrally, 'reversible' . . . The essential point is that, whatever adjective was chosen to qualify 'enrichment', its role was only to identify in a general way those factors which, according to the cases themselves, called for an enrichment to be undone. No enrichment can be regarded as unjust, disapproved or reversible unless it happens in circumstances in which the law provides for restitution.

The proof that resulting trusts are restitutionary makes it unnecessary to ask whether they respond to unjust enrichment. If they reverse enrichments, those enrichments are unjust.

1. Giving Up to Another

All resulting trusts cause one person to give something up to another. They are usually bare trusts, meaning that the trustee's primary duty is to convey the trust property to (or at the direction of) the beneficiary.[6] Like all trusts, they can only exist when there is some separation of legal and equitable ownership. A sole trustee cannot also be the sole beneficiary, because that person would hold his or her beneficial interest in the property free of the trust.[7] Several persons can be trustees for themselves, but only if there is some difference between their interests as trustees and their interests as beneficiaries.[8] This difference means that resulting trustees are, in all cases, giving up some proprietary interest or asset to another.

Lake v. *Craddock*[9] falls near the line. Five people contributed equally to the

[2] Birks (1989a), p. 13; also see Beatson (1991), p. 1. [3] Birks (1989a), pp. 44–5, 51, 54.
[4] Ibid. at p. 15. [5] Ibid. at p. 19 (see pp. 16–18). Cf. Beatson (1991), pp. 24–5.
[6] *Herdegen* v. *Federal Commissioner of Taxation* (1988) 84 A.L.R. 271, 281; Scott and Fratcher, §410, §411.2; Ford and Lee, §21180. [7] See p. 53 above.
[8] *In re Selous* [1901] 1 Ch. 921; *In re Cook* [1948] Ch. 212. [9] (1733) 3 P. Wms. 158.

purchase of land as joint tenants in fee and one of them died. Jekyll M.R. 'decreed, that the survivorship should not take place; for that the payment of money created a trust for the parties advancing the same'.[10] Although the tenancies in common arising under the resulting trust were almost identical to the joint interests they had expressly created, the difference between joint and common ownership meant that the resulting trust could take effect to cause the survivors to give up the benefit of their rights of survivorship.

2. Enrichment

What counts as an enrichment in the law of restitution is a contentious issue. The *Restatement of the Law of Restitution* states that a 'person is enriched if he has received a benefit' and defines 'benefit' broadly as 'any form of advantage'.[11] The subject matter of a resulting trust is always some form of property interest or asset, which is expressly included in the *Restatement's* concept of enrichment: 'A person confers a benefit upon another if he gives to the other possession of or some other interest in money, land, chattels, or choses in action'.[12]

The receipt of money is always an enrichment, but the same cannot be said for other types of property.[13] There is a great deal of controversy surrounding the provision of goods or services which produce no lasting benefit. It has been argued they are not enriching unless they leave a marketable residuum or save a necessary expense.[14] There is also the issue of 'subjective devaluation', which Birks explains as follows:[15]

> [M]oney is the very measure of enrichment. By contrast benefits in kind are less unequivocally enriching because they are susceptible to an argument which for convenience can be called 'subjective devaluation'. It is an argument based on the premiss that benefits in kind have value to a particular individual only so far as he chooses to give them value. What matters is his choice. The fact that there is a market in the good which is in question . . . is irrelevant to the case of any one particular individual.

Happily, neither of these difficulties affect the resulting trust. The subject matter of the trust, being a property interest or asset, is necessarily some form of residuum in the recipient's hands. It is usually the very thing received, in which case its value (either in the market place or to the recipient) is irrelevant. As Professor Burrows explains:[16]

> Where the plaintiff seeks restitution of property retained by the defendant, establishing the latter's benefit is straightforward. There is no valuation involved. The benefit is established simply by showing that the defendant has the particular property claimed: the

[10] Ibid. at 159. [11] *Restatement of Restitution*. §1, p. 12.
[12] Ibid. [13] Goff and Jones, pp. 17–22, 26–8; Birks (1989a), pp. 109–14.
[14] Stoljar (1987b); Burrows (1988); Beatson (1991), pp. 31–4; McBride and McGrath. Cf. Jones (1990) at pp. 1, 3–7; Birks (1991a); Chambers. [15] Birks (1989a), p. 109.
[16] Burrows (1993a), p. 7; also see Birks (1989a), p. 130.

defendant cannot validly refuse to give up the property on the ground that it is of no value to him.

The recipient of property is not being asked to pay for it and, therefore, cannot resort to the argument of subjective devaluation to defeat the provider's claim to a resulting trust of that property.

A resulting trust can attach to the substitute of the original property transferred to the recipient, as it did in *Lane* v. *Dighton*,[17] where the plaintiff's husband received annuities (belonging in equity to the plaintiff) and sold them to pay for land purchased in his own name. In these cases, both the original property and its substitute are an enrichment to the resulting trustee: they cannot be subjectively devalued, regardless of their nature. A sale or exchange of the original property realizes its value. When sold for money, the original property has been objectively valued and the resulting trustee has derived an incontrovertible benefit from it.[18] When exchanged for other property, the original property has been valued (at least subjectively) as equivalent to the property acquired in exchange. The exchange product has been chosen by the resulting trustee and, therefore, cannot be subjectively devalued[19] unless he or she mistakenly believed himself or herself to be beneficially entitled to the original property.[20] In any event, there can be no objection to a resulting trust over the exchange product on the basis that it is of no value.

3. At the Expense of

There are two senses in which an enrichment might be at the expense of another: (i) by being subtracted from or provided by that other, or (ii) because it was acquired by doing a wrong to that other.[21] We are concerned, at present, only with the former sense. Where there is a transfer of property from P to D, and D holds that property on resulting trust for P, it is clear that the resulting trust is returning an enrichment received by D at P's expense. The subject of the trust had been subtracted from P's wealth and added to D's.

The story is only slightly more complex where the resulting trust arises, not in favour of the transferor, but in favour of a contributor to the purchase price. Where P pays X to transfer property to D, D is enriched at the expense of P, not X. The subtraction from X's wealth is in exchange for a corresponding addition provided by P. X is neutral in the story and the real cause of D's enrichment is the subtraction from P's wealth. This accords with our intuitive sense that there is no real difference between a direct transfer and a purchase in the name of

[17] (1762) Amb. 409. [18] Birks (1989a), p. 121; Burrows (1993a), p. 10.

[19] See Birks (1991a) at p. 129; Burrows (1993a), pp. 11–14.

[20] Birks (1992a), p. 138.

[21] Birks (1989a), pp. 23–4, 40–4; Burrows (1993a), pp. 16–21; Goff and Jones, p. 38. Cf. McCamus at p. 139; McBride and McGrath at 44–5.

another. They are merely different means of conferring the same enrichment. Although the *presumption* of resulting trust may apply differently in each situation, this difference is not caused by any difficulty identifying the provider of the enrichment. It derives from statute[22] or, possibly, different indications of the provider's intention to benefit the recipient.[23]

The unjust enrichment is still at the expense of the contributor to the purchase price even where the value of the property purchased exceeds the price paid for it.[24] If P pays £100 to X to transfer £200 worth of property to D, D's enrichment is still at P's expense, provided the purchase from X was *bona fide* and there is no basis on which X might impeach the transaction. P has obtained a good bargain and, if the property had been transferred to P instead of D, P would not be unjustly enriched. Although P may be enriched at X's expense, the enrichment is not unjust and P is entitled to retain it. The transfer to D instead of P has no effect on the expense to X. The advantage of the bargain was P's and the enrichment of D was entirely at P's expense. The matter would be different if the transaction was impeachable by X. So, for example, if P pays X to transfer property to D and, by mistake, X transfers more property than intended to D, some of D's enrichment is at P's expense and some at X's. In that case, there should be a resulting trust in favour of both P and X in proportion to their contributions.

It has been suggested that, in cases of unjust enrichment by subtraction, the measure of restitution is restricted to the lesser of the defendant's enrichment and the plaintiff's loss.[25] In many cases, the plaintiff has transferred money or other property directly to the defendant and the two measures are the same. However, this suggestion does not properly account for those cases where the plaintiff is seeking restitution of the value of goods (*quantum valebat*) or services (*quantum meruit*). So long as the defendant is unable to subjectively devalue, the measure of his or her enrichment is the cost of obtaining the same goods or services from someone else in the plaintiff's position.[26] It is never measured by the cost to the plaintiff to provide them. The defendant's enrichment will fortuitously match the plaintiff's loss where, because of market demand, the plaintiff would have provided the same goods or services to another paying customer if the defendant had not received them.[27] However, restitution is always the giving up of an enrichment and never compensation for loss.[28]

The better view is that there is no requirement in the law of restitution that the recipient's enrichment must equal the provider's loss. The phrase 'by subtraction

[22] Law of Property Act 1925, s. 60(3). See pp. 18–19 above.
[23] *Drummer* v. *Pitcher* (1833) 2 My.&K. 262. See p. 16 above.
[24] Goode (1991) at p. 233.
[25] Burrows (1993a), pp. 19, 38–9; L.D. Smith (1992) at 696–7; Stevens (1989) at 286, 294, 345; McInnes (1996b) at p. 33.
[26] *Lodder* v. *Slowey* [1904] A.C. 442, 444, 453, P.C.; *Deglman* v. *Guaranty Trust Co. of Canada* [1954] 3 D.L.R. 785, S.C.C.; Goff and Jones, pp. 28–30.
[27] Cf. Beatson (1991), p. 34.
[28] Birks (1989a), p. 11.

from the plaintiff' indicates the source of the enrichment and not the measure of the plaintiff's loss. The subject matter of the resulting trust is always received at the expense of the resulting trust beneficiary because it was provided by that beneficiary. Its cost to that beneficiary is irrelevant. In any event, the resulting trust meets the 'at the expense of' requirement even for those who wish to restrict the measure of restitution to the plaintiff's loss. In the example above, where P paid £100 to X to transfer £200 of property to D, the loss to P is £200. P, as purchaser, could have obtained the property from X and has therefore lost that property, not just the value of the consideration paid for it.[29]

Professor Burrows might not agree with this last proposition. He is a leading proponent of the theory that restitution is restricted to the plaintiff's loss and, using the division of family property as an example, doubts whether resulting (or constructive) trusts are restitutionary:[30]

> If P contributes £10,000 (in money or money's worth) to the purchase or improvement of D's home, in which they are both living, D's unjust enrichment at P's expense (at least in the absence of wrongdoing e.g. a breach of promise by D) requires a correlation between P's loss and D's gain and is therefore confined to £10,000 (plus interest). Yet no restriction to the true restitutionary measure has been imposed in the cases.

He correctly points out that, in many of these cases, courts are not ordering restitution, but fulfilling expectations or social policy.[31] However, as discussed above and below,[32] the trusts in these cases are not resulting and tell us nothing about the true nature of the resulting trust. There are cases in which a resulting trust of the family home is based on the proportional contribution to its acquisition.[33] These are restitutionary even though they are not limited to the value of the original contribution, plus interest. Where P has contributed to the acquisition of D's home, in such a way that P has provided a portion of that home to D, the restitutionary measure is a corresponding interest in that home. It is no different than cases where P is the sole purchaser of a home in D's name or P has transferred a home to D. In each situation, P has provided property to D and the restitutionary measure is the value of that property, not its original cost plus interest.

4. Value in Money

The last part of Birks' definition ('or its value in money') is normally irrelevant to the resulting trust, which attaches to the actual enrichment in the hands of the recipient. Although there may be co-existing remedies, the resulting trust itself does not usually include either the obligation or the option to pay for the value

[29] See Birks (1989a), pp. 133–9; cf. L.D. Smith (1991). [30] Burrows (1993a), p. 38.
[31] Ibid. [32] At pp. 37–8, 228–9.
[33] e.g. *Cowcher* v. *Cowcher* [1972] 1 W.L.R. 425; *Crisp* v. *Mullings* [1976] E.G.D. 730, C.A.; *Calverley* v. *Green* (1984) 155 C.L.R. 242; *Springette* v. *Defoe* (1992) 24 H.L.R. 552, C.A.

of the property subject to the trust. Where the trust property has been sold pending litigation and the proceeds paid into court, those proceeds are (or stand in the place of) the subject of the resulting trust. The court's direction to pay that money differs from an order that a party must pay a certain sum as money had and received, *quantum meruit* or *quantum valebat*, which is a personal obligation independent of the continued existence of the enrichment received.[34]

Recently, in *Westdeutsche Landesbank Girozentrale* v. *Islington London Borough Council*,[35] the Court of Appeal decided that a resulting trustee was personally liable to the provider of the trust property to pay for the value of that property. The House of Lords overturned the finding that the recipient was a resulting trustee, without discussing this type of liability. This case is examined in more detail in Chapter 6 and the personal liability of resulting trustees is the subject of Chapters 8 and 9. It is sufficient for present purposes to note that an order to pay for the value of resulting trust property received would fall within Birks' definition of restitution under the fourth component ('or its value in money').

B. EXCEPTIONS TO BIRKS' DEFINITION

The application of Birks' definition of restitution to resulting trusts has turned out to be relatively straightforward: they always cause 'one person to give up to another an enrichment received at his expense'.[36] Although the discussion has touched on matters of contention among restitution scholars concerning the nature and measure of enrichment, the resulting trust is little affected by this lack of consensus. Applying the exceptions to Birks' definition, however, may prove to be somewhat more contentious, but only because the true nature of the resulting trust has often been misunderstood or overlooked.

1. Obligations and Property Interests Created by Consent

Birks states that 'restitutionary rights are always created by the operation of law as opposed to the consent of the party enriched'.[37] Contractual obligations can superficially appear to be restitutionary: promises to pay for goods or services received are often equal to the *quantum valebat* or *quantum meruit* by which restitutionary obligations are measured. However, a contractual obligation is never restitutionary, because it is created and measured by the consent of the party undertaking it and not his or her unjust enrichment at the expense of the other party.[38] This exclusion of consensually undertaken obligations from the law of restitution does not affect resulting trusts, for it is clear that they are never

34 Birks (1989a), pp. 77–8.
35 [1994] 4 All E.R. 890; varied [1996] 2 All E.R. 961, H.L.
36 Birks (1989a), p. 13.
37 Ibid. at p. 44.
38 Ibid. at p. 46; cf. Beatson (1991), p. 38.

created by the consent of the party enriched. A person can be a resulting trustee even though he or she is a very young child,[39] incapable of being an express trustee,[40] or unaware of the transfer.[41] Prior to *Westdeutsche* v. *Islington*, it had not been suggested, in the way it had with 'quasi-contract', that the resulting trust arises from the recipient's implied promise to restore the property. In that case, Lord Browne-Wilkinson suggested *obiter* that '[a] resulting trust is not imposed by law against the intentions of the trustee (as is a constructive trust) but gives effect to his presumed intention'.[42] As discussed in Chapters 1 and 2,[43] this statement cannot be reconciled with those cases in which the resulting trustee was unaware of the facts giving rise to the resulting trust or with *Vandervell* v. *I.R.C.*,[44] where the resulting trust was imposed against the wishes of everyone concerned (except the Inland Revenue).

In any event, however, a modification is needed if this exception is to be applied properly to the law of trusts: we are concerned not so much with the consent of the party enriched as with the intention of the party who provided the enrichment. Although a person must ordinarily consent to be an express trustee,[45] the primary focus is whether the provider of the trust property intended to create a trust, either expressly or by implication. If the trust obligation is created by his or her intention, it is not restitutionary. As Birks states:[46]

> [E]xpress trusts never create restitutionary beneficial interests. Suppose I transfer shares to you on trust for myself. My new equitable interest carries back your enrichment at my expense, leaving you with bare legal title. But again the restitutionary pattern is without meaning, because I could have carved out any interests at all or none. Equity responds to my intent, not to the enrichment of the trustee.

It was established in Part I that the source of the resulting trust is not the implied intention to create it, but the lack of intention to benefit the recipient. This is why it can arise even though the provider of property was legally or mentally incapable of creating a trust,[47] was unaware of the transfer,[48] or clearly did not want to create a resulting trust.[49] Although the resulting trust depends on whether the provider intended to benefit the recipient, it arises as an equitable response to that intention as a fact. As Birks states, 'There is a fine but important distinction between intent conceived as creative of rights, as in an express trust

[39] *Re Vinogradoff* [1935] W.N. 68; *In re Muller* [1953] N.Z.L.R. 879.

[40] Ibid.; Ford and Lee, §21060.

[41] *Birch* v. *Blagrave* (1755) Amb. 264; *Childers* v. *Childers* (1857) 1 De G.&J. 482; *Standing* v. *Bowring* (1885) 16 Ch.D. 282, C.A.; *Dreger* v. *Dreger* [1994] 10 W.W.R. 293, Man.C.A.

[42] [1996] 2 All E.R. 961, 990–1.

[43] Above, pp. 37, 66.

[44] [1967] 2 A.C. 291.

[45] Waters (1984), pp. 672–4; Gardner (1990), p. 13.

[46] Birks (1989a), p. 54. See Gardner (1990), p. 11.

[47] *Lench* v. *Lench* (1805) 10 Ves. 511; *Goodfellow* v. *Robertson* (1871) 18 Gr. 572.

[48] *Ryall* v. *Ryall* (1739) 1 Atk. 59; *Lane* v. *Dighton* (1762) Amb. 409; *El Ajou* v. *Dollar Land Holdings p.l.c.* [1993] 3 All E.R. 717; see pp. 21–3 above.

[49] *Vandervell* v. *I.R.C.* [1967] 2 A.C. 291.

or a contract, and intent conceived as a fact which, along with others, calls for the creation of rights by operation of law'.[50]

Hodgson v. *Marks*[51] provides an excellent example of the role of intention in the creation of the resulting trust. The plaintiff transferred her house to her lodger and it was agreed that he would hold the house in trust for her. The lodger sold the house to the defendant and the plaintiff claimed an overriding interest. The plaintiff's agreement with her lodger was not in writing and therefore ineffective to create an express trust of the land.[52] However, it gave rise to a resulting trust because it proved 'that the transfer was not intended to operate as a gift'.[53] As Russell L.J. stated:[54]

> It was argued that a resulting trust is based upon implied intention, and that where there is an express trust for the transferor intended and declared—albeit ineffectively—there is no room for such an implication. I do not accept that . . . It would be a strange outcome if the plaintiff were to lose her beneficial interest because her evidence had not been confined to negativing a gift but had additionally moved into the field forbidden by section 53(1) for lack of writing.

It is clear that the resulting trust was a response not to Ms. Hodgson's intention to create a trust, but to her lack of intention to make a gift to her lodger. The ineffective intention to create a trust was not given effect under the guise of resulting trust; it merely provided proof of the absence of intention to benefit the recipient.[55] Although the resulting trust in this case had the same content as the ineffective express trust, that was merely fortuitous. If Ms. Hodgson had orally intended to create a different trust, say for a third party, the resulting trust would still have arisen in her favour for the same reason (the absence of her intention to benefit the transferee).[56]

The extent of the resulting trust might have been different if Ms. Hodgson had orally intended to create a trust for herself and her lodger, but this is not an exception to the principle set out above. The difference in the resulting trust would not be the direct product of her intention to create a trust on those terms, but a response to her partial intention to benefit her lodger. If, for example, she had intended to create a trust for the two of them in equal shares, this would prove that she intended her lodger to have only half the benefit of the property. Having received the entire legal ownership, he should then hold one half on resulting trust for Ms. Hodgson.

Napier v. *Public Trustee (Western Australia)*[57] provides another example of a partial intention to give. A man purchased a house in the name of the woman with whom he lived. She died and it was clearly proved that he 'did not intend,

[50] Birks (1989a), p. 65. [51] [1971] 1 Ch. 892, C.A.; see pp. 25, 34 above.
[52] Law of Property Act 1925, s. 53. [53] [1971] 1 Ch. 892, 933, per Russell L.J.
[54] Ibid. [55] Birks (1989a), p. 59; Birks (1992c) at pp. 363–4.
[56] e.g. *In re Boyes* (1884) 26 Ch.D. 531. Cf. Bogert and Bogert, §462.
[57] (1980) 32 A.L.R. 153, H.C.A.

at the time when he made the purchase, that [she] should take any beneficial interest other than a life interest in the house'.[58] He was therefore entitled to a resulting trust of the remainder, for, as Aickin J. stated, 'a resulting trust need not necessarily relate to the entire interest in the property'.[59] If the oral arrangement had been reduced to writing, it would have had the same effect as the resulting trust. Notwithstanding this similarity, the resulting trust is still an equitable response to a partial absence of intention to benefit the recipient and not the product of consent.

Although resulting trusts arise in response to the intentions of persons who have provided property to others, they are not excluded from the law of restitution as obligations or property interests created by consent. This is because they are not the product of an intention to create a trust, but equity's reaction to the lack of intention to benefit the recipients. As Birks states, the 'negative role played by intent is compatible with a characterisation of these interests as restitutionary'.[60]

2. Preservation of Title

The second qualification on Birks' definition of restitution removes those cases where plaintiffs are able to recover property in the possession of others because their pre-existing title to that property continues: 'The principle is that passive preservation of existing title is not restitution but that active creation of interests to reverse enrichment is'.[61] Goff and Jones also exclude the 'pure proprietary claim where the plaintiff asserts that the property which he has identified in the defendant's hands belongs, and has always belonged, to him'.[62] Burrows, on the other hand, takes a wider view of the scope of restitution as including cases where the defendant retains the plaintiff's property without his or her consent.[63] Although it has been suggested that all proprietary claims ought to be excluded from the law of restitution,[64] the consensus of opinion on this issue defines restitution at least as broadly as Birks.[65] If the resulting trust satisfies his definition of restitution, it will do so for most others.

Whether resulting trusts are excluded from Birks' definition of restitution depends on whether they create new equitable interests for the providers of property or merely preserve their pre-existing equitable ownership. The answer to this question depends on the nature of beneficial ownership: does the legal owner of property, to which no one else is entitled, also have an equitable interest in that property? If so, then, as Birks says,[66] 'the transferor's interest under the resulting trust might also be said to exemplify anticipation rather than

[58] Ibid. at 154, per Gibbs A.C.J. [59] Ibid. at 158.
[60] Birks (1989a), p. 63. [61] Birks (1989a), p. 70.
[62] Goff and Jones, p. 68 (also see pp. 26, 73–4). [63] Burrows (1993a), p. 362 ff.
[64] See Matthews (1995) (quoted at p. 243 below); cf. Stoljar (1987b).
[65] See Maddaugh and McCamus, p. 37; *Restatement of Restitution,* §4, §128, §160; Moriarty (1986) at 130–1. [66] Birks (1989a), pp. 70–1.

reversal of enrichment. For it could be argued that before the transfer the transferor had both legal and equitable title, that the legal title passed and the equitable title passively stayed behind'.

In *Re Vandervell's Trusts (No. 2)*,[67] Megarry V.C. suggested that the resulting trust upon the failure of an express trust merely preserved the settlor's pre-existing beneficial ownership. This view is accepted by Mr. Hackney:[68] 'This is called a resulting trust, though again it does not spring back in any theoretical sense. This rule does not depend on a presumption of intention, but a simple process of proprietary arithmetic; what I once hand and have not granted away, I keep'. Burrows treats all resulting trusts this way (but he might consider this restitutionary).[69]

The view put forward here has been set out in Chapter 2.[70] Absolute legal ownership of property is full beneficial ownership at law. Equity has nothing to do with it. This is a view shared by Ford and Lee,[71] Birks[72] and Hackney, who states (somewhat surprisingly in light of his concept of proprietary arithmetic):[73] 'Ownership at common law is a beneficial interest giving its over economic advantages. The beneficial owner at common law has no equitable interest'.

This view is consistent with the historical development of equitable interests, although, as Birks acknowledges, that alone does not justify its continuation:[74]

> [I]t can reasonably be said that history should not be decisive in such a matter and, further, that the boundaries of the law of restitution should not be fixed on the basis of assertions which, once deprived of their historical support, are not more than metaphysical speculations. Someone who prefers the passive analysis of the . . . resulting trust . . . is not likely to fall into deep error in relation to any practical question. But he will be driven to adopt a narrower view of the content of the law of restitution.

Most commentators tend not to express an opinion on this issue, being content to talk of *beneficial* interests when speaking about the resulting trust. Although it will rarely have practical effect, it is nonetheless important to remember that beneficial ownership can be legal or equitable. The resulting trust is commonly explained as a 'failure to dispose of the beneficial interest',[75] but this is only a shorthand description of an event in which a legal beneficial interest is replaced with a new equitable beneficial interest in the same property.[76]

There are a few cases, like *D.K.L.R. Holding Co. (No. 2) Pty. Ltd.* v. *Commissioner for Stamp Duties* (discussed in Chapter 2),[77] where the outcome depends

[67] [1974] Ch. 269. [68] Hackney, p. 153.
[69] Burrows (1993a), pp. 38–9 (cf. pp. 366–9). [70] Above, pp. 51–5.
[71] Ford and Lee, §21070.
[72] Birks (1989a), pp. 59, 70–2; Birks (1992c) at pp. 360–1.
[73] Hackney, p. 25. [74] Birks (1989a), p. 71.
[75] See, e.g. Waters (1984), p. 364; Meagher and Gummow, *Jacobs' Law of Trusts*, p. 264; Riddall, p. 192.
[76] *D.K.L.R. Holding Co. (No. 2)* v. *Comm'r for Stamp Duties* (1982) 40 A.L.R. 1, 35, H.C.A.
[77] Ibid.; see pp. 53–5 above.

on a proper understanding of legal and equitable ownership. Possibly more important is the largely unnoticed, adverse effect the other view has had on our understanding of the resulting trust. For example, it is easier to believe that the 'automatic' resulting trust has nothing to do with intention if it is merely the inertia of the settlor's pre-existing equitable ownership. Our recognition that resulting trusts always create new equitable interests makes us more likely to ask why equity has responded in this fashion.

As Birks states, the concept of the resulting trust as the passive preservation of title would drive us 'to adopt a narrower view of the content of the law of restitution'.[78] This would mean that, notwithstanding our recognition that resulting trusts arise by operation of law to cause persons to give up to others enrichments received at their expense, we maintain the division between resulting trusts and the law of restitution. The failure to treat like cases alike is thus perpetuated, but without justification.

There are few proponents of the passive concept of the resulting trust. This concept, so far as it can be said to have been approved at all, is the product of the (normally harmless) failure to differentiate between legal and equitable beneficial interests. It found favour in *Re Vandervell's Trusts (No. 2)*, but only because the 'automatic' resulting trust was needed to cope with another error: that 'presumed' resulting trusts depended upon an implied intention to create a trust.[79] The passive resulting trust turns out to serve no useful purpose and requires a view of equitable ownership which is contrary to history and precedent. The theory of passive preservation of equitable ownership should be discarded.

C. ROLE OF THE RESULTING TRUST

This chapter began with the proposition, established in Part I, that all resulting trusts operate on the same principle: when property has been transferred and the provider of that property did not intend to benefit the recipient, the resulting trust arises to restore that property to its provider. An examination of this principle has shown that it is restitutionary: resulting trusts reverse unjust enrichments. This conclusion adds nothing to the principle of resulting trust. It merely restates that principle, using general terms taken from the language of restitution. However, this restatement is nonetheless valuable, for it alerts us to possible connexions between the resulting trust and other legal and equitable responses that can be described in the same way.

It has been suggested that resulting trusts have no place outside the traditional categories of apparent gifts and trusts which fail.[80] This opinion is based on the

[78] Birks (1989a), p. 71. [79] See pp. 42–3 above.
[80] Swadling, (1996); *Westdeutsche Landesbank Girozentrale* v. *Islington L.B.C.* [1996] 2 All E.R. 961, 990–2.

incorrect assumption that resulting trusts depend upon an intention to create a trust. Without that assumption, it is extremely difficult to maintain a rational division between the traditional categories and other situations in which the provider of property to another can point to to lack of intention to benefit the recipient.[81] There are several cases in which a misappropriation of property has given rise to a resulting trust.[82] Is there any reason why a resulting trust should not apply whenever title to property is obtained through theft or fraud? What about case of mistake, duress, or undue influence? These questions are explored in the next chapter.

The recognition that resulting trusts reverse unjust enrichment does not change their nature or function. They are already restitutionary whether they are confined to their traditional categories or allowed to operate more freely outside those categories, in situations which have come to be associated with the law of restitution. The connexion between resulting trusts and restitution will not cause the resulting trust to leave its home in the law of trusts to join the rank of restitutionary remedies (as the American constructive trust did when it appeared in the *Restatement of Restitution* but not the *Restatement of Trusts*). A greater or even central role in proprietary restitution will not change the resulting trust, which will continue to operate on the same principles.

Having recognized that resulting trusts have a place in the modern law of restitution, it is important now to move on and identify that place. Restitution is always a response to unjust enrichment and the role of the resulting trust within the law of restitution can be identified by asking (i) how it responds to unjust enrichment and (ii) what type of unjust enrichment it responds to.

D. NATURE OF THE RESPONSE

Birks states that:[83]

> The most important division in the subject called 'restitution' is between two different measures in which the plaintiff may recover. The first or normal measure is 'value received'. What the defendant received can be and is determined without reference to whether he still retains it or anything represented by it. The second or exceptional measure is 'value surviving'.

First-measure claims to the value received are necessarily personal,[84] whereas second-measure claims to the value surviving are usually, but not necessarily, proprietary.[85] Although recovery in the first measure is 'normal' and the second measure is 'exceptional' in the law of restitution as a whole, a resulting trust typically effects restitution in that exceptional measure.

[81] Birks (1996b) at 16–17. [82] See pp. 21–3 above. [83] Birks (1989a), p. 6.
[84] Ibid. at p. 77. [85] Ibid. at p. 85.

1. First-Measure and Other Personal Claims

An important issue addressed in this book is the nature and extent of the resulting trustee's personal liability (if any) to the beneficiaries of the resulting trust. Two potential sources of personal liability are considered: the receipt of property belonging in equity to another is discussed in Chapter 8 (First-Measure Liability) and breach of trust in Chapter 9 (Fiduciary Obligations). They are discussed separately because liability for breach of a resulting trust is not confined to restitution in the first measure. A first-measure claim based on receipt is (arguably) distinct from a claim based on breach of trust.

2. The Second Measure

The resulting trust itself always effects restitution in the second measure (of the value surviving), because it can arise 'only in respect of something identified as existing in the defendant's hands'.[86] Like all trusts, it cannot exist unless it is 'possible to identify clearly the property which is subject to the trust'.[87] The subject matter is sufficiently certain if, at the time the trust arises,[88] it is ascertained or would at least be ascertainable by the court.[89] There are situations where value still survives in the hands of the recipient, but the subject matter has become insufficiently certain to maintain the resulting trust. Although the resulting trust was possible at the moment of receipt, the subsequent loss of certainty may reduce the provider's claim from a trust to a charge[90] or wholly defeat the claim *in rem*.

This book is not concerned with the process of tracing to identify value surviving in mixtures, substitutions, or the hands of third persons.[91] However, it should be noted that none of these three events will necessarily prevent or destroy a resulting trust. Where resulting trust property is transferred to a third person, the trust will continue to exist unless the transferee is a *bona fide* purchaser of the legal estate for value without notice.[92] Where resulting trust property is used to acquire other property, a resulting trust should arise over the substitute in accordance with the ordinary principle that it arises in favour of a

[86] Birks (1989a), p. 85.

[87] Waters (1984), p. 117 (also see p. 368). See p. 2 above; Baker and Langan, *Snell's Equity*, pp. 115, 117; *Cowcher* v. *Cowcher* [1972] 1 W.L.R. 425, 430.

[88] *Re Beardmore Trusts* [1952] 1 D.L.R. 41; *Re Goldcorp Exchange Ltd.* [1995] 1 A.C. 74, 91, 96–7, P.C.

[89] *Re Golay's Will Trusts* [1965] 1 W.L.R. 969. See *Hunter* v. *Moss* [1994] 1 W.L.R. 452, C.A.; noted by Hayton (1994); Scott and Fratcher, §76.

[90] See *Re Hallett's Estate* (1880) 13 Ch.D 696, C.A.; *Sinclair* v. *Brougham* [1914] A.C. 398, 421; *Westdeutshe Landesbank Girozentrale* v. *Islington London B.C.* [1994] 1 W.L.R. 938, C.A.

[91] Those issues are examined by L.D. Smith in his Oxford D.Phil. thesis, *Tracing, Property and Restitution* (1994) to be published by Oxford University Press as *The Law of Tracing*. See Birks (1989a), pp. 358–75; Burrows (1993a), pp. 57–76; Goff and Jones, pp. 75–93.

[92] *Hodgson* v. *Marks* [1971] 1 Ch. 892, C.A.

contributor to the purchase price.[93] Where there are multiple contributors to a fund or to the purchase of property, the resulting trust is not defeated by the inability to determine which part was supplied by each contributor, but arises over the whole fund or property in favour of the contributors in proportion to their contributions.[94] It should not matter whether the contributions from several persons are mingled before or after the resulting trust arises.[95] If a fund held on resulting trust for several contributors was mixed with money belonging to others, a resulting trust ought to arise over the new mixture in favour of both groups in proportion to their contributions.

E. UNJUST ENRICHMENT

This chapter so far has been about the resulting trust's response to unjust enrichment. It now turns to consider the unjust enrichments to which the resulting trust responds. Unjust enrichments can be analysed in two ways, depending on (i) the type of enrichment or (ii) why the enrichment is unjust. The question of enrichment is straightforward, so far as resulting trusts are concerned. As discussed above, all resulting trusts effect restitution of assets capable of being the subject matter of a trust. Due to the possibility of mixtures or substitutions by the recipients, the assets subject to the resulting trust need not be those which were originally received at the expense of the provider.[96] Nevertheless, in every case of resulting trust, the original enrichment is always some form of property or asset capable of being the subject of a trust.[97]

The question why enrichments are unjust is far more complex. In the language of restitution, the word 'unjust' performs two closely related functions. Not only does it qualify the word 'enrichment' to denote those which are reversible, but commentators often refer to the 'unjust factor' when discussing why enrichments are reversible.[98] Unjust enrichments can be, and have been, classified according to their 'unjust factors'. For example, some enrichments are reversible because the provider was mistaken; others because they were provided under duress or undue influence or for a consideration which has failed. These unjust factors can be analysed and organized at greater levels of generality. This analysis makes it possible to identify the unjust enrichments to which the resulting trust does and should respond.

[93] *Lane* v. *Dighton* (1762) Amb. 409.

[94] *Wray* v. *Steele* (1814) 2 V.&B. 338; *Re British Red Cross Balkan Fund* [1914] 2 Ch. 419; *Calverley* v. *Green* (1984) 155 C.L.R. 242; Waters (1984), pp. 306–7; Martin (1993a), p. 258; Sheridan, pp. 190–1; Ford and Lee, §21020.

[95] *In re Diplock* [1948] Ch. 465, 536–7, C.A.

[96] See p. 22 above.

[97] This was somewhat obscured by the 'common intention' family property cases, which failed to distinguish between constructive and resulting trusts; see pp. 37–8 above; pp. 228–9 below.

[98] Burrows (1988); Birks (1992a), p. 89; Burrows (1993a), p. 21.

1. Expense to the Provider

If, as Birks suggests,[99] the most important division in the law of restitution is between the two measures of recovery, then the second is between 'autonomous unjust enrichment' and 'restitution for wrongs'.[100] This division is hidden in the phrase 'unjust enrichment at the expense of another'.[101] An enrichment may be at another's expense either (i) because it was subtracted from or provided by that person or (ii) because it was acquired by doing a wrong to that person.[102] The resulting trust always operates in the former sense, by restoring property (or the substitute of property) that has been subtracted from or provided by another. In some resulting trust cases, the recipient has done the provider a wrong, but this is merely incidental to the resulting trust. The facts upon which the resulting trust arises, whether or not they are capable of being characterized as a wrong, are (i) a transfer of property, (ii) in circumstances in which the provider of that property did not intend to benefit the recipient.[103]

For example, in *El Ajou* v. *Dollar Land Holdings p.l.c.*,[104] the plaintiff's agent had been bribed to invest the plaintiff's property in worthless shares. Millett J. thought that the vendor would be a resulting trustee of the purchase-money for the plaintiff.[105] The fraud was a wrong done to the plaintiff, but he could also point to a subtraction from him which was non-voluntary and therefore unjust regardless of the wrong. *Attorney-General for Hong Kong* v. *Reid*[106] provides a useful contrast. The plaintiff's Director of Public Prosecutions was convicted of accepting bribes and was declared to be a trustee of those bribes for the plaintiff. That trust cannot be resulting because the bribe money had not been provided by the plaintiff. It was a case of restitution for wrongs, in which the alternative analysis of enrichment by subtraction was not available.[107]

2. Unjust Factors

The cases of unjust enrichment by subtraction can be further organized on the basis of why the enrichment is unjust. This process is not free from controversy. The most important category is non-voluntary transfer, but there may be others such as unconscientious receipt and public policy.[108] Resulting trusts arise because the provider of property did not intend to benefit the recipient and, *prima facie*, they belong in the category of non-voluntary transfer, in which 'the

[99] Birks (1989a), p. 6; cf. Birks (1992a), p. 1.
[100] Burrows (1993a), pp. 21–3; 376; Birks and Chambers, p. vi.
[101] Birks (1989a), p. 23.
[102] Ibid. at pp. 23–5, 40–4; Birks (1992c) at pp. 364–5; Burrows (1993a), pp. 16–18; *Commissioner of State Revenue* v. *Royal Insurance Australia Ltd.* (1994) 182 C.L.R. 51, 73.
[103] Birks (1992c) at p. 365.
[104] [1993] 3 All E.R. 717; rev'd [1994] 2 All E.R. 685. [105] Ibid. at 734.
[106] [1994] 1 A.C. 324, P.C. [107] Birks (1992c) at pp. 365, 367.
[108] Birks (1993c) at 206; Birks and Chambers, p. vii; modifying Birks (1989a), p. 99.

explanation of the response is always reducible in the simplest terms to the statement that the plaintiff did not mean the defendant to have the money in question or the other enrichment, whatever it might be'.[109] The main issue explored in Chapters 5, 6, and 7 is the extent to which the resulting trust corresponds with the category of non-voluntary transfer. Whether resulting trusts can (or should) respond to any other unjust factors is an interesting question, which is considered briefly near the end of the book.[110]

Birks gives this 'warning' regarding the concept of non-voluntary transfer:[111]

> The notions of voluntariness and non-voluntariness in parting with wealth are controlled by the cases. You cannot conclude in favour of restitution just by looking at the story of a transfer from P to D and deciding, as though it were only a question of fact, that P did not mean D to have the given item of his wealth. The issue is too difficult, too metaphysical, and there are always complex sub-issues. Hence even if as a matter of impression it looks as though the transfer was not voluntary, you have to go down to the cases to see if it was non-voluntary in the way in which the law counts as calling for restitution.

This warning must be taken in connexion with the present task. Whether a transfer is sufficiently non-voluntary to allow for restitution is a question controlled by the cases. Whether it will also attract the principle of resulting trust can only be answered in the same way. In many situations, the cases do not yet provide an answer. However, they do point the way and it will be argued that, whenever a plaintiff is entitled to restitution of property on the basis of non-voluntary transfer, the resulting trust will apply, provided the defendant does not obtain the unfettered beneficial ownership of that property before the right to restitution arises.

The issues relating to non-voluntariness are explored in the three chapters which follow: Chapter 5, Vitiated Intention, Chapter 6, Qualified Intention, and Chapter 7, Mere Equities. This division of the subject of non-voluntary transfer is derived from Birks, who states:[112]

> There are two sub-divisions, according to the nature of the reason why we say that the plaintiff did not mean the transfer to happen. In the one his judgement in forming the intent to transfer was vitiated (using 'vitiated' in the widest sense so as to include 'nullified' and even not exercised'). In the other there was no vitiating factor: in making or allowing the transfer he exercised his judgement freely but he qualified his intention by specifying the event in which, or basis on which, he wanted the defendant to have the benefit. Here the reason why we ultimately say the transfer was non-voluntary is that the specified event or basis failed to materialise: in the events which have occurred he did not want the defendant to have the benefit.

The additional chapter on mere equities concerns an issue which primarily affects the category of vitiated intention. Two of the more traditional remedies

[109] Birks (1989), p. 100. [110] At pp. 229–30
[111] Birks (1989), p. 100. See Birks (1993b) at 167. [112] Birks (1989a), p. 101.

for the recovery of property in these circumstances are rectification (correcting mistakes in written instruments) and rescission (setting a side transactions for mistake, undue influence, etc.). It is commonly believed that these responses are of a lesser nature: not a trust entailing a beneficial proprietary interest from the outset, but a 'mere equity' to recover property at the end of the day. An important question is whether the provider is restricted to this mere equity or ought to be entitled to the benefit of a resulting trust as well. This is examined in Chapter 7, where it is concluded that everyone who is entitled to rectify or rescind a transaction, and thereby recover property, has an equitable beneficial interest in the recoverable property which should be recognized as a resulting trust.

F. SUMMARY

Resulting trusts are restitutionary because they arise by operation of law to cause a person who has received an enrichment at the expense of another to give that enrichment up to that other. The resulting trust is created neither by the consent of the party enriched nor because the party who provided the enrichment intended to create a trust. It is an equitable response to the provider's lack of intention to benefit the recipient. Resulting trusts actively reverse unjust enrichments. They do not exemplify the preservation of the provider's pre-existing property interest through an interruption of possession. Resulting trustees are normally liable in the second measure to restore the trust property still surviving in their hands. First-measure and other personal claims are the subject of Chapters 8 and 9.

The only type of enrichment which will give rise to a resulting trust is the receipt of property capable of being the subject of a trust. An enrichment held on resulting trust is always obtained at the expense of the resulting trust beneficiary because it is (or is the substitute of) property that was subtracted from or provided by that beneficiary. Whether the resulting trustee has engaged in wrongful conduct, which would also justify equity's intervention, is normally irrelevant to the resulting trust. The largest category of unjust enrichment by subtraction is non-voluntary transfer. All resulting trusts arise because the provider of property did not intend to benefit the recipient and, *prima facie*, they respond to that category. The extent of that response is discussed in the next three chapters.

5
Vitiated Intention

This chapter is the first of three which explore the extent of the resulting trust's response to enrichments which are unjust on the basis of non-voluntary transfer. The focus of these chapters is not on the nature of the enrichment, but on the unjust factors to which the resulting trust does or should respond. It is argued that, whenever property is transferred to another and the provider is entitled to restitution on the basis of non-voluntary transfer, the resulting trust should apply unless the recipient obtains the unfettered beneficial ownership of that property before the right to restitution arises.

The law in this area is complex, even confused. One reason is that the language of resulting trust, and the attendant reliance on presumptions, has concealed the close relationship between the central examples of resulting trust and other restitutionary responses to non-voluntary transfer. In consequence, equity has allowed itself to respond in different ways to different examples of non-voluntary transfer. The usual remedies for the recovery of property in these circumstances are rectification and rescission. Whether the resulting trust also applies is a question which necessarily involves the relationship between the resulting trust and these more-familiar remedies. That relationship is the subject of Chapter 7 (Mere Equities).

This chapter concerns those cases in which the provider's intention to benefit the recipient is absent or vitiated. The next chapter (Qualified Intention) concerns the cases in which the provider intended to benefit the recipient, but only in circumstances other than those which have occurred. The division between vitiated and qualified intention is not always clear (in practice). For example, in *Rover International Ltd.* v. *Cannon Film Sales Ltd.*,[1] the Court of Appeal held that the provider of property under a void contract had both a vitiated intention (caused by a mistaken belief in the validity of the contract) and a qualified intention (to benefit the recipient only in exchange for reciprocal benefits under the purported contract).

Conversely, the two bases for restitution discussed in this chapter (absent and vitiated intention) might have been separated. Providers in the former category do not intend to benefit the recipients at all, e.g. where their money has been stolen. Providers in the latter category intended to benefit the recipients, but some factor (such as mistake, fraud, duress, or undue influence) vitiated their intentions to the extent that each of them could say, in a legally relevant way,

[1] [1989] 1 W.L.R. 912. See Evans, S., at 402.

'I did not mean it'. The line separating absence and vitiation of intention to benefit the recipient is not all that distinct.[2] For example, a vendor may be unaware that the transfer of land he or she is signing contains a misdescription, thereby transferring more property than intended.[3] Also, it may be difficult to say whether a person suffering from an incapacity, due to mental infirmity, minority, or *ultra vires*, has an absent or merely vitiated intention to benefit the recipient.

There is no magic in the division between absent and vitiated intention, except perhaps for this: in the traditional categories of resulting trust, providers usually have no intention to benefit the recipients and, therefore, there may some hesitation about crossing the divide into situations where providers did intend to benefit the recipients but, because of some impairment of judgement, their intentions were sufficiently vitiated to allow for restitution. There is a sliding scale of defective intention giving rise to rights of restitution, ranging from cases in which the provider is ignorant of the transfer[4] down to cases like *Louth* v. *Diprose*,[5] where the provider had intentionally made a gift to the recipient, but was nonetheless entitled to rescind it because of the unconscionable manner in which the recipient had caused him to form the intention to give. One possibility is that the resulting trust applies at one end of the scale, but not the other. If this is true, then, at some point on the scale, the intention to benefit the recipient, though defective, is being treated as sufficient to prevent the resulting trust from arising. However, a more coherent position is that any vitiation of intention which gives rise to the right of restitution must also suffice for the resulting trust.

An additional complicating factor is the difference between void and voidable transactions at law and in equity. For example, a transaction induced by fraud may be void at law[6] or in equity[7] or voidable at law[8] or in equity,[9] depending on the nature or severity of the fraud and the nature of the property involved. It is suggested that the resulting trust should apply in all cases where the avoidance allows for the recovery of property, except where the transaction is void and the plaintiff has thereby retained either the beneficial legal ownership of the property (in which case the question of trust does not arise) or a pre-existing equitable interest (which continues intact without the aid of a resulting trust). The plaintiff's position is weakest where the transaction is merely voidable in equity and the arguments made below are directed primarily to this situation on the understanding that they should apply *a fortiori* to cases where the transaction is void or is voidable at law.

The remainder of this chapter is organized according to the unjust factors which motivate restitution on the basis of either an absent or vitiated intention

[2] Goff and Jones, p. 108.
[3] e.g. *Blacklocks* v. *J.B. Developments (Godalming) Ltd.* [1982] Ch. 183.
[4] See pp. 21–3 above.
[5] (1992) 175 C.L.R. 621; discussed below, pp. 137–8, 141–2.
[6] *Ingram* v. *Little* [1961] 1 Q.B. 31, C.A.
[7] *Cloutte* v. *Storey* [1911] 1 Ch. 18, C.A.
[8] *Babcock* v. *Lawson* (1880) 5 Q.B.D. 284, C.A.
[9] *Stump* v. *Gaby* (1852) 2 De G.M.&G. 623.

to benefit the recipient. They are set out in an order which roughly corresponds to a 'sliding scale' of defective intention: ignorance, incapacity, mistake, duress, undue influence, and unconscionable conduct. Before the discussion of that list begins, the traditional categories of resulting trust are considered to identify the unjust factors to which they respond.

A. TRADITIONAL CATEGORIES OF RESULTING TRUST

The traditional categories of resulting trust have received little attention in writings on the law of restitution. Most of that effort has been spent on the question whether resulting trusts are restitutionary, rather than on identifying where, within the law of restitution, the traditional categories belong. The treatment of the subject by Birks, Burrows, and Goff and Jones suggests that, to the extent that resulting trusts do come within the law of restitution, they are cases of non-voluntary transfer.[10] The question addressed here is whether the unjust factor operating in the traditional categories of resulting trust can be more specifically identified within the group of unjust factors described 'at a rather high level of generality' as 'non-beneficial transfer'.[11] This is not intended to suggest that resulting trusts cannot respond to all the unjust factors in this group. Indeed, a central argument of this book is that they can and should respond in every case in which the provider is entitled to restitution on the basis of non-voluntary transfer, so long as (i) the enrichment consists of assets capable of being the subject of a trust and (ii) the recipient does not obtain the unfettered beneficial ownership of those assets before the right to restitution arises. The sole task of this section is to see if the traditional categories of resulting trust can be matched up more specifically to unjust factors within the group of non-voluntary transfer.

1. Apparent Gifts

For most restitutionary claims based on non-voluntary transfer, the provider of the property must establish affirmatively that, as a result of ignorance, mistake, failure of consideration, etc., he or she did not intend to enrich the recipient. These claims can be categorized at various levels of generality. Consider the example of a bank making the same payment twice due to a clerical error.[12] This can be classified as mistake or, with increasing generality, as vitiated intention or non-voluntary transfer. It is also possible to move in the other direction to categories based on finer distinctions, such as spontaneous (vs. induced) mistake, or mistake of fact (vs. law). The presumption of resulting trust is not as

[10] See Birks (1989a), pp. 57–65, 156, 158–9, 378–84; Birks (1992c); Burrows (1993a), pp. 35–40; Goff and Jones, pp. 564–8; Birks (1994c) at pp. 222–3.

[11] Birks (1992c) at p. 371.

[12] *Chase Manhattan Bank N.A.* v. *Israel-British Bank (London) Ltd.* [1981] Ch. 105.

amenable to this type of analysis (although this may simply be because it has not received the same scrutiny as other restitutionary responses). Birks states that, 'Presumptions of resulting trust . . . cynically imply that a gratuitous donor must have been decisively mistaken . . .'[13] However, there does not appear to be any judicial indication that the presumption is of any particular unjust factor more specific than non-voluntary transfer (apart from the view, argued against in Chapter 1, that the presumption is of an intention to create a trust and therefore not restitutionary). No specific reason for the presumption, such as a suspected impairment of the decision-making process, has been spelled out by the courts and it is made perhaps for no other reason than equity's natural suspicion of gifts.[14]

Where the resulting trust arises from the proof, rather than presumption, of the provider's lack of intention to benefit the recipient, the evidence often reveals an intention to retain the beneficial ownership, rather than an impairment of the intention to part with it. This creates an apparent, but irrelevant, distinction between some of the central examples of resulting trust and other cases of non-voluntary transfer. *Hodgson* v. *Marks* illustrates this point.[15] The plaintiff had transferred her house to her lodger to prevent her nephew from evicting him. The plaintiff was elderly and 'lacked even the most elementary knowledge of legal and financial matters',[16] while the lodger was an ingratiating rogue who had used his influence over her to his own advantage. However, the resulting trust was not a response to the failure of the purpose of the transfer, the plaintiff's mistake, or the lodger's fraud or undue influence. It arose because the plaintiff had intended to keep the beneficial interest for herself, which proved affirmatively 'that the transfer was not intended to operate as a gift'.[17] There was no discussion of these other potential unjust factors because her intention to retain the beneficial ownership proved the non-voluntary transfer *a fortiori*. As discussed below, this should not be taken as an indication that these other unjust factors are different in kind than those which ordinarily give rise to resulting trusts.

The recognition that all resulting trusts are restitutionary both allows and requires a more coherent integration of those two subjects. There are many cases, like *Hodgson* v. *Marks*, in which the lack of intention to benefit the recipient is proven by the provider's intention to retain the beneficial ownership. These are cases where the provider has no intention to benefit the recipient and, therefore, belong with 'ignorance' on the spectrum of absent and vitiated intention. However, the intention to retain an interest is not a requirement for the resulting trust[18] and there is no compelling reason why vitiating factors, located further down the scale, cannot prove a lack of intention sufficient to raise a resulting trust. This is discussed below.

[13] Birks (1989a), p. 156. [14] Gray, p. 386; see p. 39 above.
[15] [1971] 1 Ch. 892, C.A.; see pp. 25, 32 above. [16] Ibid. at 900, per Ungoed-Thomas J.
[17] Ibid. at 933, per Russell L.J. [18] Above, p. 19 ff.

The proper integration of resulting trusts and restitution also requires that care is taken not to misunderstand the presumption of resulting trust. The presumption reverses the usual burden of proof found elsewhere in the law of restitution (except in cases of presumed undue influence) by requiring the recipient to prove the provider's intention to transfer the benefit of the property. It arises not from a suspicion of any particular unjust factor, such as mistake or duress, but in response to the lack of consideration provided by the recipient. These qualities should not lead to the conclusion that an absence of consideration is a sufficient unjust factor. As discussed in Chapters 1 and 6,[19] the lack of consideration merely raises an inference of non-voluntary transfer, i.e. that an unjust factor of that genus exists, but without specifying the factor. Proof of such a factor should confirm the presumption of resulting trust (or rebut the presumption of advancement). Even where there is no evidence of the provider's intention, the presumption of resulting trust leads to restitution on the basis of non-voluntary transfer.

2. Trusts Which Fail

Goff and Jones place the resulting trust which arises on the failure of an express trust in a category with ineffective contracts, thereby suggesting that the resulting trust is responding to the failure of the purpose of the transfer (sometimes referred to as a failure of consideration). Birks takes a similar approach: 'a transfer on a trust which proves ineffective . . . produces a resulting trust because from the beginning the transferor's intent was conditional and the condition has never been purified'.[20] It is suggested with respect that, in most of these cases, the proper analysis is that the provider had no intention to benefit the recipient, rather than a qualified intention. The confusion over this issue is caused by the failure to precisely identify the function of the resulting trust in this situation.

Where an express trust fails, for whatever reason, that failure removes the equitable ownership of the trust property from the trust beneficiaries (or from its commitment to charitable purposes) without the aid of the resulting trust. Where the resulting trust applies, it effects restitution of the surplus trust property not from the beneficiaries, but from the trustees. Although the failure of the express trust explains why the trustees have a surplus, it does not explain why they are not allowed to retain it. As discussed in Chapter 2,[21] that depends on whether the settlor intended to benefit the trustees, which is a separate question.

It is usually true that settlors give property to trustees only because they want that property held in trust for certain persons or purposes. This makes the resulting trust on the failure of an express trust look superficially like restitution upon

[19] At pp. 32, 163–6. [20] Birks (1994c) at p. 223. [21] Above, pp. 47–9

a failure of consideration. However, unlike failures of consideration, where the providers intended to benefit the recipients, but only in other circumstances, settlors usually have no intention to benefit the trustees whatsoever. The circumstance which brings about the failure of the express trust, whether it is a failure to meet the requirements for a valid trust, a supervening event (such as the death of the beneficiary) or simply the fulfilment of all the settlor's purposes, is not a relevant fact to which the resulting trust responds. The resulting trust arises when the express trust fails because the trustees have property they were not intended to enjoy. However, the failure does not affect the settlors' intention to benefit the trustees. The absence of intention to benefit the trustees exists from the outset, regardless of the circumstances which have caused the express trust to fail.

There is a closely related situation in which resulting trusts do respond to the failure of the purpose of a transfer. In some cases, the settlor recovers the surplus trust property where there is no failure of the trust, but rather a failure of the purpose for which it was created. The most notable of these is *Re Ames' Settlement*,[22] in which the balance of a marriage settlement was returned to the settlor after the marriage had been annulled. The failure of consideration did not cause the express trust to fail, but meant that the trust beneficiaries were not intended to enjoy the benefit of the property in the circumstances.

The resulting trust in this situation is responding to the lack of intention to benefit the trust beneficiaries (brought about by the failure of the purpose for which the trust was created), as well as the lack of intention to benefit the trustees (which continues throughout). Although Goff and Jones cite *Re Ames' Settlement* when making the link between failure of consideration and the resulting trust upon the failure of an express trust,[23] the two situations are distinguishable. As discussed in Chapter 6, *Re Ames' Settlement* is a case of failure of consideration, in which the benefit happened to be conferred by way of a trust settlement. It has more in common with the *Quistclose* trust than with the traditional category of resulting trusts upon the failure of an express trust.

B. IGNORANCE

As discussed above,[24] the word 'ignorance' is used here not in a pejorative sense, but to describe those cases in which 'wealth is transferred to the defendant wholly without the knowledge of the plaintiff'.[25] The resulting trust should apply whenever someone obtains title to another's property in these circumstances. In many cases, the provider will retain the legal ownership of the property taken

[22] [1946] Ch. 217. [23] Goff and Jones, p. 565. [24] At p. 21.
[25] Birks (1989a), p. 140.

without consent, but there will be many others in which title does pass, e.g. where stolen money is used as currency or deposited in a bank account. The resulting trust ought to arise from the moment title to the provider's property, or its exchange product, passes to the recipient. *Re Kolari*[26] provides a good example. A bank teller stole money from her employer and used it to purchase a car. The title to the stolen funds passed to the vendor (who received them in good faith) and title to the car passed to the thief. A resulting trust arose when the thief obtained the car and her employer was entitled to it *in specie*.

There are two misconceptions about the resulting trust which have tended to inhibit its application to cases of ignorance. The first is the belief that resulting trusts depend on the implied intention to create them. The second is the belief that, where the provider's money is used by the recipient to acquire other property, the provider must have intended to purchase that property.[27] The realization that the resulting trust depends not on any positive intention, but on the lack of intention to benefit the recipient, clears away these impediments.

It has been wondered whether thieves, who are not otherwise fiduciaries for their victims, can become trustees for them. The possibility that the absence of a pre-existing fiduciary relationship would prevent the innocent victim from using equity's (supposedly more generous) tracing rules and from obtaining equitable proprietary relief has been rightly criticized.[28] Naturally, no question of trust arises so long as the victim retains legal title to the stolen property in the thief's possession, but if the stolen property is used to purchase other assets, the newly acquired assets should be held on resulting trust for the victim on the traditional basis that he or she is the provider of the purchase price.

Where the stolen property is money, the victim's legal ownership will be lost once the money is passed to a *bona fide* purchaser.[29] Where other types of stolen property have been sold or exchanged, the victim should be entitled to either follow his or her legal title into the hands of a third person or claim a resulting trust over the proceeds in the hands of the thief (or possibly both, subject to limits preventing double recovery).[30] The thief will always be a resulting trustee of the proceeds, either for the original victim or the third person, depending on the outcome of the victim's claim to the stolen property in the hands of the third person.

As discussed above,[31] the application of the resulting trust to cases of ignorance has a long history, which had been largely overlooked until *El Ajou* v. *Dollar Land Holdings*, where Millett J. recognized the operation of 'an old-fashioned institutional resulting trust' in similar circumstances.[32] In 1981 in *Re*

[26] (1981) 36 O.R. (2d) 473. [27] See p. 27 above.

[28] Maudsley; McKendrick (1991a); Jones (1992) at p. 394; Burrows (1993a), p. 70; Goff and Jones, pp. 83–6; Oakley (1995) at 384, 428; see Goode (1991) at p. 229; pp. 22–3, 104–5 above.

[29] *Clarke* v. *Shee* (1774) 1 Cowp. 197, 200; *Sinclair* v. *Brougham* [1914] A.C. 398, 418–19.

[30] Cf. Birks (1989a), pp. 91–2; Goode (1991) at pp. 233–4. [31] At pp. 21–3.

[32] [1993] 3 All E.R. 717, 734; rev'd on other grounds [1994] 2 All E.R. 685.

Kolari, a Canadian judge was able to say with confidence that a 'resulting trust arises where property is obtained by fraud or theft',[33] but that case and the line of authority on which it is based have received little attention in the wake of *Pettkus* v. *Becker* and the ensuing Canadian fascination with the constructive trust.[34] Similarly, in *Black* v. *S. Freedman & Co.*, O'Connor J. stated in the High Court of Australia that, 'Where money has been stolen, it is trust money in the hands of the thief'.[35] That judgment's pedigree has more to do with resulting than constructive trusts and yet the application of the resulting trust in cases of ignorance has been even less common in Australia than in England or Canada.

C. INCAPACITY

The law concerning the recovery of property on the basis of incapacity is complex, perhaps unnecessarily so. The purpose of this section is not to attempt a resolution of the conflicts and tensions in this branch of the law, but to see how far the principle of resulting trust can be reconciled with existing rules governing the recovery of property on the basis of incapacity. Nevertheless, it is worth noting at the outset three factors which have tended to complicate this subject. First, it often happens that assets, which a provider seeks to recover on the basis of incapacity, have been transferred pursuant to a contract. Attention is thereby focused on issues concerning the validity of the contract and failure of consideration, sometimes obscuring the role of incapacity as a factor vitiating the provider's intention to confer the assets in question. Secondly, the role of incapacity as an unjust factor which motivates restitution is sometimes confused with its role as a defence to restitutionary claims. Thirdly, insufficient attention has been paid to the similarities between the three main types of incapacity (mental infirmity, minority and *ultra vires*), thereby leading to independent rules for recovery in each sub-category.

As discussed above,[36] resulting trusts can respond to incapacity. In the Canadian case of *Goodfellow* v. *Robertson*,[37] proceeds from the sale of property, belonging to a person who may have been suffering from a mental infirmity, were used as part payment for lands purchased in the name of his father-in-law. Spragge C. ordered an inquiry into the provider's 'mental capacity to assent to the application of this money towards the purchase'.[38] If he lacked capacity at the time, then a resulting trust was possible on the authority of *Ryall* v. *Ryall*,[39] in which Lord Hardwicke applied a resulting trust in favour of providers who were ignorant of the fact that their assets had been used to purchase the lands

[33] (1981) 36 O.R. (2d) 473, 478, per Stortini D.C.J.
[34] [1980] 2 S.C.R. 834, 117 D.L.R. (3d) 257; see Maddaugh and McCamus, pp. 129–41.
[35] (1910) 12 C.L.R. 105, 110. [36] At pp. 23, 27. [37] (1871) 18 Gr. 572.
[38] Ibid. at 579. [39] (1739) 1 Atk. 59; discussed at pp. 21–2 above.

in question. The cases were similar in that none of the providers had 'an assenting mind'.[40]

Capacity is often based on status and treated as an all or nothing commodity (e.g. everyone is either a minor or an adult, according to a readily ascertainable fact). However, the question whether a person has capacity can be difficult, especially in cases of mental infirmity, where the facts can be difficult to prove and there is often no clear line dividing capacity and incapacity. The resulting trust should not be limited to cases in which the provider's incapacity has produced a total absence of consent to the transfer of property. Any degree of incapacity which will support a claim for restitution of property ought to produce a sufficient lack of intention to benefit the recipient for the purposes of resulting trust.

1. Mental Infirmity

Mental Health Act 1983

There are normally two main variables affecting the question whether someone has sufficient mental capacity to provide property to another: (i) the provider's level of understanding and (ii) the level of understanding required for the particular transaction.[41] These variables are not relevant, however, when the provider's property had been placed under the control of a Court of Protection under the Mental Health Act 1983.[42] As the High Court of Australia stated in *Gibbons* v. *Wright*:[43]

> Such a person is held incompetent to dispose of his property, not because of any lack of understanding (indeed he remains incompetent even in a lucid interval), but because the control, custody and power of disposition of his property has passed to the Crown to the exclusion of himself. Accordingly his disposition is completely void: *Re Walker*.

In *Re Walker*,[44] the Court of Appeal held that a person found to be a lunatic under the Lunacy Act 1890 could make a will, if found to have sufficient testamentary capacity at the time, but had no power to make an *inter vivos* disposition of his or her property. This was because the Crown had control of that property and it would create a conflict if the owner could also dispose of it. The incapacity in this situation is not directly caused by the owner's lack of understanding, but is a legal status derived from the court's previous finding of that fact. The owner cannot dispose of his or her property because it is *ultra vires* someone of that status. The inability to consent to the disposition of property, means that there is necessarily a lack of intention to benefit the recipient, which

[40] *Goodfellow* v. *Robertson* (1871) 18 Gr. 572, 575, per Spragge C.

[41] *Gibbons* v. *Wright* (1954) 91 C.L.R. 423, 437; *In re Beaney* [1978] 1 W.L.R. 770, 774.

[42] Mental Health Act 1983, s. 94. See Hudson (1986) at 182; Burrows (1993a), p. 326.

[43] (1954) 91 C.L.R. 423, 439–40.

[44] [1905] 1 Ch. 160.

should give rise to a resulting trust in every case where legal title to the property has passed.

Powers of attorney

In *McLaughlin* v. *Daily Telegraph Newspaper Co. Ltd.*,[45] a husband 'of unsound mind' signed a power of attorney in favour of his wife, who then sold his shares in the defendant and another company. She was aware of his incapacity and the power of attorney was absolutely void. Although the power was invalidated by the husband's inability to understand it, rather than his status (because control of his property had not yet been removed by the court), his incapacity did not directly invalidate the sale of his shares. Instead, those sales were invalid because his wife was not his agent and had no power to dispose of his property. In cases like this, where property is transferred by someone without authority, there is a complete absence of intention to benefit the recipient, which should attract the resulting trust (if legal title passes).

The recipient's knowledge

In the cases discussed above, the validity of the transfer depended on the transferor's status and, therefore, they are related to the group of cases, discussed below under the heading 'Ultra Vires', in which the primary issue is the transferor's authority, rather than his or her comprehension. Where someone suffers from a mental infirmity, but has control of his or her own property, the question of his or her capacity to provide property to another is undeniably complex. As mentioned above, it depends on a comparison of the provider's level of understanding with the level required for the particular transaction. Additionally, a finding of incapacity is an insufficient basis for recovery of property which has been transferred by contract to a recipient who has given value. In such a case, restitution is only possible if the recipient was (or ought to have been) aware of the provider's incapacity.[46]

This additional requirement (that the recipient has knowledge of the provider's incapacity) does not mean that bad faith is an element of the cause of action or that the unjust factor is 'defendant-sided' in any way;[47] nor does it create any tensions or inconsistencies between the rules governing recovery for mental infirmity and the principle of resulting trust. The knowledge requirement is simply an element of the defence of good faith exchange (and therefore inapplicable to gifts).[48] This was made clear in *Elliot* v. *Ince*, where Lord Cranworth C. stated:[49]

[45] (1904) 1 C.L.R. 243; leave to appeal refused, [1904] A.C. 776.
[46] *Imperial Loan Co.* v. *Stone* [1892] 1 Q.B. 599, C.A.; *Hart* v. *O'Connor* [1985] A.C. 1000.
[47] Birks (1992a) pp. 51–2; see Birks (1989a), p. 265.
[48] *In re Beaney* [1978] 1 W.L.R. 770; Burrows (1993a), p. 328.
[49] (1857) 7 De G.M.&G. 475, 487.

> [A]n executed contract, where parties have been dealing fairly and in ignorance of the lunacy, shall not afterwards be set aside . . . a contrary doctrine would render all ordinary dealings between man and man unsafe . . . But it is obvious that no such question can arise when there is no contract for value—when in fact there has been merely a dealing by the lunatic with his own property without any consideration passing from others.

The knowledge requirement has been criticized as an undue restriction on restitution in this area.[50] In *Gibbons* v. *Wright*, the High Court of Australia hinted that it might have been better to allow restitution regardless of the recipient's knowledge on the basis that: 'a contract requires the assent of both parties; a person of unsound mind is incapable of assenting; therefore no contract can come into existence between parties of whom one is of unsound mind'.[51] However, the court accepted that the law had committed itself to giving priority to good faith exchange over the right to restitution for this type of incapacity. Although there are valid arguments for either approach, the knowledge requirement not only protects those who deal in good faith with people of apparent capacity, but, as Birks points out, is necessary 'to preserve the dignity and autonomy of all elderly people', who otherwise 'would not be able to deal with their property in an adult, independent and unsupervised manner'.[52]

Good faith exchange should also be a defence to the resulting trust or, more accurately, prevent the trust from arising even though the provider has a lack of intention to benefit the recipient which would otherwise give rise to it. This defence is discussed further below,[53] but it is sufficient for present purposes to note that there is no conflict between resulting trusts and other means of restitution on the basis of mental incapacity. The trust should apply from the outset whenever legal ownership of property is transferred and otherwise recoverable on that basis. Although there are various degrees of mental incapacity, any level which allows for restitution ought to prove the lack of intention to benefit the recipient needed for a resulting trust.

2. Minority

The policies behind the law's treatment of minority appear to be similar to the policies which motivate and govern restitution on the basis of mental incapacity. As Lord Mansfield stated in *Zouch* v. *Parsons*:[54]

> [M]iserable must the condition of minors be, excluded from the society and commerce of the world; deprived of necessaries, education, employment, and many advantages; if they could do no binding acts. Great inconvenience must arise to others, if they were bound by no act. The law, therefore, at the same time that it protects their imbecility and indiscretion from injury through their own imprudence, enables them to do binding acts, for their own benefit; and, without prejudice to themselves, for the benefit of others.

[50] *Archer* v. *Cutler* [1980] 1 N.Z.L.R. 386, 401; Hudson (1984b) and (1986).
[51] (1954) 91 C.L.R. 423, 441.
[52] Birks, (1992a) p. 52.
[53] At pp. 132, 168–9, 237–8.
[54] (1765) 3 Burr. 1794, 1801.

However, the law's methods of implementing those policies with respect to minority are remarkably different from those chosen for mental infirmity.

Minority is a status to which certain protective rules apply. The rules operate regardless of the minor's level of maturity and, conversely, an adult cannot appeal to them even if he or she is especially immature. This status-based approach is mitigated somewhat by equity's willingness to provide relief to young adults from unconscionable bargains and undue influence.[55] Also, a child who is too young to understand a transaction would probably be entitled to restitution on the basis of mental incapacity, as well as minority.[56]

Minors are bound by fair contracts for necessary goods or services,[57] but have a right to repudiate other contracts within a short time after reaching the age of majority.[58] This right exists even if the other party was unaware of the minority; i.e. there is no defence of good faith exchange.[59] However, there are two other major restrictions on the minor's right to restitution after repudiation of a contract. The first, affirmed by the Court of Appeal in *Steinberg* v. *Scala (Leeds) Ltd.*, is 'that, although the contract may be rescinded the money paid cannot be recovered back unless there has been an entire failure of the consideration for which the money has been paid'.[60] In that case, a minor agreed to purchase shares in the defendant and, after paying half of the purchase price, repudiated the agreement. She was released from the contract, but unable to recover the money already paid because she had enjoyed the benefit of the shares for over a year.

The second restriction on the infant's right of recovery was set out by the Court of Appeal in *Chaplin* v. *Leslie Frewin (Publishers) Ltd.*, where Dankwerts L.J. stated that 'the transfers of property made by the plaintiff remain effective against him, even if the contract is otherwise revocable'.[61] In that case, the minor had sold the copyright in his autobiography to the defendant and wanted to restrain its publication. A majority of the Court of Appeal (with Lord Denning M.R. dissenting) held that it was a reasonable contract for necessaries and therefore binding on the minor, but, even if the contract was revocable, the transfer of copyright was not.

Both restrictions have been criticized.[62] Burrows states that, 'The policy justification for allowing minors out of contracts—protecting the young against foolishness and poor judgment—should surely be fully carried over to restitution'.[63] As the law stands, a minor's incapacity does not seem to provide an

[55] *Smith* v. *Kay* (1859) 7 H.L.C. 750, 780; *Earl of Aylesford* v. *Morris* (1873) L.R. 8 Ch. App. 484; *In re Pauling's Settlement Trusts* [1964] Ch. 303, 337, C.A.; *Smyth* v. *Szep* [1992] 2 W.W.R. 673, B.C.C.A.; Burrows (1993a), pp. 199–203; Goff and Jones, pp. 287–8.

[56] See *Edwards* v. *Carter* [1893] A.C. 360, 367; Goff and Jones, p. 524.

[57] *Chaplin* v. *Leslie Frewin (Publishers) Ltd.* [1966] Ch. 71, C.A.; Goff and Jones, pp. 525–6.

[58] *Edwards* v. *Carter* [1893] A.C. 360.

[59] Birks (1992a) pp. 51–2.

[60] [1923] 2 Ch. 452, 458, per Lord Sterndale M.R.

[61] [1966] Ch. 71, 94.

[62] Goff and Jones, pp. 528, 530.

[63] Burrows (1993a), p. 325.

independent basis for the restitution of property transferred pursuant to contract. Birks points out that it does give the minor one advantage over the adult: 'The minor can get rid of the contract on the ground of his minority without pointing to any breach'.[64] This right then leads to restitution on the basis of failure of consideration, presumably in an otherwise ordinary fashion.

Whether the resulting trust can respond to cases of minority depends on the role of minority in a restitutionary claim by the minor. If, as suggested above, it merely allows a minor to repudiate a contract without breach, thereby triggering restitution on the basis of failure of consideration, then the resulting trust may be possible on the basis of the minor's qualified intention to benefit the recipient, so long as other requirements for that trust are met. The discussion of those requirements is left for the next chapter, but one observation is offered at this stage: the restriction on the recovery of property set out in *Chaplin* v. *Leslie Frewin* ought not to leave the minor in a worse position than an adult in similar circumstances.

Birks suggests the possibility 'that there is such a thing as a restitutionary claim based on the inexperience of the minor but that it is easily lost'.[65] This may provide an alternative view of the nature of the minor's claim to restitution as one which is based on the minor's incapacity, but defeasible upon his or her receipt of benefits from the other party to the contract. On this scheme, the resulting trust might arise at the moment of transfer (as a response to the vitiation of intention) and be quickly defeated, but this does not seem to be a satisfactory explanation. It is unlikely to have any practical effect and it would certainly be anomalous if the resulting trust could be determined by counter-performance which does not amount to good faith exchange or *bona fide* purchase.

3. Ultra Vires

This form of incapacity usually gives rise to restitution where a supposed contract is *ultra vires* one of the parties and therefore void. Because restitution is normally available on the basis of failure of consideration, the role of the party's incapacity as an independent unjust factor is rarely considered. *Brougham* v. *Dwyer*[66] provides a good example. It concerned a banking business which had been *ultra vires* its operator, the Birkbeck Permanent Benefit Building Society, which was also the subject of the better known *Sinclair* v. *Brougham*.[67] The liquidator of the society was trying to recover, as money had and received, £35 which had been loaned to a customer by way of an overdraft. The trial judge held that the society's incapacity was a defence to the claim, but Ridley and Lush JJ. quite rightly rejected this defence and allowed the liquidator's appeal. Lush J. stated:[68]

[64] Birks (1989a), p. 217. [65] Birks (1989a), p. 217. [66] (1913) 108 L.T. 504.
[67] [1914] A.C. 398; discussed in the next chapter. [68] (1913) 108 L.T. 504, 505.

It turned out that in point of law the building society were incompetent to make such a contract, and it followed that the contract which the directors thought they were making was not a contract at all, but was simply a transaction which in point of law did not exist . . . The case appears to me to be on all fours with one in which money had been advanced on something which was thought to be a contract, but as to which it turns out that there was a total failure of consideration.

The society's lack of capacity invalidated the contract, leading to recovery on the basis of failure of consideration. However, that incapacity also created a lack of intention to benefit the recipient, which could have provided an additional, independent ground for restitution. In other words, the liquidator could point to both a vitiated and a qualified intention to benefit the recipient. However, as recovery will usually be available on the latter basis, the former is often safely ignored, as it was in *Brougham* v. *Dwyer*.

In *Auckland Harbour Board* v. *The King*,[69] incapacity due to *ultra vires* was used as an independent unjust factor. The Government of New Zealand had been authorized by statute to pay £7,500 to the appellant in consideration for the appellant granting a lease to a third party. The money was paid even though the lease was not granted and the Government later deducted that amount from other payments due to the appellant. The appellant brought a petition to obtain the money withheld, but failed because the Government was entitled to set off its claim to restitution of the £7,500. Although the condition for the payment had not been fulfilled, the basis of the right to restitution was not the failure of consideration, but lack of capacity. As Viscount Haldane stated, 'Any payment out of the consolidated Fund made without Parliamentary authority is simply illegal and ultra vires, and may be recovered by the Government if it can, as here, be traced'.[70]

There does not appear to be any authority determining whether incapacity due to *ultra vires* can give rise to a resulting trust, but in principle it should: the lack of authority for the payment produces a complete absence of intention to benefit the recipient. In *Woolwich Equitable Building Society* v. *I.R.C.*, Lord Goff said that the claim in *Auckland Harbour Board* v. *The King* was 'proprietary in nature',[71] possibly because of Viscount Haldane's reference to tracing. However, that claim was for set-off against other debts and, as Burrows and Goff and Jones note[72] and Newton J. observed in *Commonwealth of Australia* v. *Burns*,[73] Viscount Haldane was probably referring to the need to identify the recipient of the payment, rather than the nature of the Government's claim. Nevertheless, the resulting trust should arise at the outset and continue, subject to defences, for as long as the subject matter remains identifiable.

[69] [1924] A.C. 318. See Burrows (1993a), pp. 300–2; Burrows (1995) at 19.
[70] Ibid. at 326–7.
[71] [1993] 1 A.C. 70, 177.
[72] Burrows (1993a), p. 331; Goff and Jones, pp. 160–1, fn. 36.
[73] [1971] V.R. 825, 828.

In *El Ajou* v. *Dollar Land Holdings p.l.c.*,[74] the plaintiff's agent had been bribed to invest the plaintiff's money in worthless shares. As discussed above,[75] Millett J. was of the opinion that the vendor would be a resulting trustee of the purchase money for the plaintiff. This was treated earlier as a case of ignorance, because the plaintiff was unaware of his loss, but it could well be viewed as a case of incapacity: the agent exceeded his authority, thereby disposing of the plaintiff's property without consent. Millett J. indicated that the resulting trust arose once the plaintiff rescinded the purchase 'for the bribery of his agent',[76] but did not indicate whether this could be classified as ignorance or incapacity. Either approach demonstrates that the plaintiff had no intention to benefit the recipient.

Agents' *ultra vires* actions can sometimes bind their principals, e.g. where an agent has ostensible authority[77] or a statute validates a disposition by a mercantile agent[78] or corporate officer.[79] This restricts the principal's right to restitution in a manner which is equivalent or similar to good faith exchange. A recipient who is aware that an agent is acting *ultra vires* cannot rely on his or her ostensible authority[80] and statutory protection requires that the recipient has acted in good faith.[81] The resulting trust should be excluded whenever a principal is otherwise bound by an agent's disposition of his or her property. Even where the agent has acted without the principal's consent, thereby providing a sufficient basis for the resulting trust, the circumstances validating the transaction provide the recipient with a defence of good faith exchange.

D. MISTAKE

Identifying the types of mistakes which will (or should) give rise to resulting trusts is made difficult by a more general uncertainty over which mistakes will allow for any sort of restitution. Although recovery on the basis of mistake has a long history and is, as Burrows states, 'generally regarded as the central area in the law of restitution',[82] law and equity have responded in different ways to this category and recent developments make it hard to predict whether restitution will be available for certain mistakes. There are two restrictions on the recovery of mistaken payments at common law which have been eroded and are

[74] [1993] 3 All E.R. 717; rev'd [1994] 2 All E.R. 685. [75] At pp. 22–3.
[76] [1993] 3 All E.R. 717, 734.
[77] See *Freeman* v. *Buckhurst Park Properties (Magnal) Ltd.* [1964] 2 Q.B. 480, 503, C.A.
[78] Factors Act 1889, s. 2. [79] Companies Act 1985, ss. 35, 35A, 35B.
[80] *Watteau* v. *Fenwick* [1893] 1 Q.B. 346; *Guinness* v. *Saunders* [1990] 2 A.C. 663, 688–9.
[81] However, the Companies Act 1985, s. 35A(2)(b) states that 'A person shall not be regarded as acting in bad faith by reason only of his knowing that an act is beyond the powers of the directors under the company's constitution'; see Goff and Jones, p. 539.
[82] Burrows (1993a), p. 95.

likely to be swept away. The first, established in *Bilbie* v. *Lumley*,[83] is that payments made with knowledge of the facts, but under mistakes of law, are generally not recoverable. The second derives from *Aiken* v. *Short*, where Bramwell B. suggested that, 'the mistake must be as to a fact which, if true, would make the person paying liable to pay the money'.[84]

The rule barring recovery for mistake of law has been overturned in Australia,[85] Canada,[86] New Zealand[87] and Scotland.[88] In *Woolwich Equitable Building Society* v. *I.R.C.*, Lord Goff noted these developments and the growing criticisms of the rule,[89] while Lord Jauncey stated, 'I very much doubt whether in all cases the distinction between mistakes of fact and of law can be justified much longer'.[90] The Law Commission has recommended its abolition[91] and its future survival is very much in doubt. In any event, the mistake of law bar has never been enforced as vigorously in equity.[92]

The second restriction, that the mistake must be about the liability to pay, was rejected by Robert Goff J., in *Barclays Bank Ltd.* v. *W.J. Simms Son & Cooke (Southern) Ltd.*, where he stated that it was sufficient if 'a person pays money to another under a mistake of fact which causes him to make the payment'.[93] This approach was supported by Dillon L.J. in *Rover International Ltd.* v. *Cannon Film Sales Ltd.*[94] and adopted by the High Court of Australia in *David Securities Pty. Ltd.* v. *Commonwealth Bank of Australia*.[95] This restriction has not prevented equity from rescinding mistaken gifts.[96]

These developments, and many other issues surrounding restitution on the basis of mistake, are admirably dealt with elsewhere.[97] The concern of the present discussion is not so much the extent of restitutionary recovery on the basis of mistake, but whether the resulting trust is a possible response to those mistakes for which restitution is otherwise available. It is suggested that there is no worthwhile distinction to be drawn between the degree of vitiation of intention necessary for the resulting trust and that which will allow mistaken providers of property to obtain restitution by some other means. Three types of mistakes, which have led to the creation of trusts for the providers, are discussed below. However, it

[83] (1802) 2 East. 469; see Burrows (1993a), p. 109 ff.; Goff and Jones, p. 142 ff.
[84] (1856) 1 H.&N. 210, 215.
[85] *David Securities Pty. Ltd.* v. *Commonwealth Bank of Australia* (1992) 175 C.L.R. 353.
[86] *Air Canada* v. *British Columbia* (1989) 59 D.L.R. (4th) 61, S.C.C.
[87] New Zealand Judicature Amendment Act 1958, s. 94A.
[88] *Morgan Guaranty Trust Co. N.Y.* v. *Lothian Regional Council*, 1994 S.C.L.R. 213.
[89] [1993] 1 A.C. 70, 164; see Beatson (1991), p. 163.
[90] Ibid. at p. 192.
[91] Law Commission (1994).
[92] *Gibbon* v. *Mitchell* [1990] 1 W.L.R. 1304; see Burrows (1993a), pp. 112–13.
[93] [1980] Q.B. 677, 695.
[94] [1989] 1 W.L.R. 912, 933.
[95] (1992) 175 C.L.R. 353.
[96] *Lady Hood of Avalon* v. *Mackinnon* [1909] 1 Ch. 476; *Ogilvie* v. *Allen* (1899) 15 T.L.R. 294, H.L.; *Gibbon* v. *Mitchell* [1990] 1 W.L.R. 1304; *University of Canterbury* v. *A.-G.* [1995] 1 N.Z.L.R. 78.
[97] Beatson (1991), pp. 137–76; Birks (1989a), pp. 146–73; Burrows (1993a), pp. 94–138; Goff and Jones, p. 107 ff.

is not suggested that there is any significance in these sub-categories and it is argued further that any mistake, for which the provider of property could obtain restitution in law or equity, will be sufficient to raise a resulting trust.

1. Identity of the Property Transferred

A variety of mistakes, covering a wide range of defective intentions, have been held to create sufficient bases for restitution. The cases in which property has been transferred and recovered, due to a rectifiable misdescription in the transfer documents, belong at the high end of the scale, near ignorance. In *Leuty* v. *Hillas*,[98] the plaintiff and defendant had each purchased adjoining lands from the same vendor. In each transfer, the lands were described incorrectly, causing a portion of the lands purchased by the plaintiff to be conveyed to the defendant. It can be said, without hesitation, that the plaintiff did not intend to benefit the defendant. Until the vendor's mistake was discovered, the plaintiff believed himself to be the owner of the lands in question and was unaware they had been conveyed to the defendant. The facts of *Craddock Brothers* v. *Hunt*[99] are almost identical to those of *Leuty* v. *Hillas* and, in both cases, the defendant was declared to be a trustee of the surplus for the plaintiff. Although not identified as such, these are cases falling squarely within the traditional category of resulting trust in which one person has paid the purchase money for a transfer of land to another.

Blacklocks v. *J.B. Developments (Godalming) Ltd.*[100] is similar, except that the mistake had been made by the plaintiff and not a third party. A misdescription in the transfer had caused him to convey more land than intended to the defendant's predecessor in title. The plaintiff had no intention to transfer the property in question, except perhaps in a notional sense which would prevent him from maintaining a plea of *non est factum*. However, the fact that a conveyance or contract is effective at law is not a bar to a claim for either rectification or a resulting trust. Like *Leuty* v. *Hillas* and *Craddock Brothers* v. *Hunt*, the rectifiable mistake concerned the property transferred and, again, the court declared the defendant to be a trustee of the property in question for the plaintiff. This trust should also be regarded as resulting (as the distinction between gratuitous transfers of land and the payment of the purchase price is relevant only to the presumption of resulting trust and not where the lack of intention to benefit the recipient is proved).[101]

2. Value of the Property Transferred

Further along the scale of defective intention lies *Re Garnett*.[102] In that case, the two plaintiffs each had a quarter interest in a trust of their uncle's estate and

[98] (1858) 2 De G.&J. 110. [99] [1923] 2 Ch. 136, C.A. [100] [1982] Ch. 183.
[101] Above, pp. 18–19. [102] (1885) 31 Ch.D. 1, C.A.

their aunt (the executrix and trustee of the estate) was beneficially entitled to the other half. The plaintiffs released their shares of the estate to their aunt in consideration of £10,550 each, which had been a quarter of the value of the estate at the time when the accounts were passed 4 years earlier. Unknown to all the parties, the quarters were worth more than £15,000 at the time of the release. As a result of this mistake, the plaintiffs were entitled to rescind the release and, in subsequent proceedings, were held to have maintained an equitable interest in the estate notwithstanding the release.[103]

The error was not about which property was released, but the value of that property. From the judgments of Brett M.R. and Fry L.J., it appears that the plaintiffs' lack of knowledge that their shares had been substantially undervalued was sufficient to vitiate their consent to the release. Cotton L.J. took a slightly different tack, treating the release more like a mistaken disposition of a portion of the estate. On either view, the plaintiffs did not intend to give their aunt the benefit of the additional value of their shares in the estate. This vitiation of their intention meant that they retained an equitable interest despite the release, which is best described as arising under a resulting trust.

Melbourne Banking Corp. v. *Brougham* is similar.[104] In that case, the plaintiff alleged that his assignee in bankruptcy had released his equity of redemption in a sheep station under the mistaken belief that the mortgage debt was higher and the value of the station lower than they actually were. The plaintiff failed to prove his case, but the Privy Council was of the opinion that, if the release was voidable, the assignee would have continued to have an equitable interest in the property. As in *Re Garnett*, the mistake concerned the value and not the identity of the property released, but the attendant lack of intention to benefit the mortgagee would have brought about consequences which ought to be described as a resulting trust.

3. Double Payments

At roughly the same point on the scale lies the case of *Lady Hood of Avalon* v. *Mackinnon*.[105] In 1888, the plaintiff and Lord Hood settled half of their marriage settlement on their elder daughter upon her marriage. In 1902 and 1904, after the death of Lord Hood, the plaintiff appointed a total of £8,600 to her younger daughter. Forgetting the 1888 settlement, the plaintiff then settled £8,600 on her elder daughter to equalize the benefits to both daughters. On realising her mistake, the plaintiff brought an action to rescind the second settlement on her eldest daughter. Eve J. held that it had been executed under mistake and granted the relief sought.

The second settlement was intended as a gift to the elder daughter, but that intention was vitiated by the mistake under which it was made. Lady Hood

[103] (1886) 33 Ch.D. 300, C.A.
[104] (1882) 7 App.Cas. 307, P.C.
[105] [1909] 1 Ch. 476.

intended only to give the elder daughter a benefit equal to that given to the younger, forgetting that the benefit had already been given. There was no desire to benefit the elder daughter beyond the amount settled in 1888. The question whether a trust existed did not arise in *Lady Hood of Avalon* v. *Mackinnon*, but the facts were entirely appropriate for a resulting trust. The situation is essentially no different from *Chase Manhattan Bank N.A.* v. *Israel-British Bank (London) Ltd.*, where the plaintiff had mistakenly made the same payment twice and Goulding J. held that the plaintiff had retained an equitable property interest in the second payment.[106] Although Goulding J. did not classify the trust in this situation, he reached this conclusion in reliance on Viscount Haldane L.C.'s speech in *Sinclair* v. *Brougham*, where it was described as 'a resulting trust'.[107] If *El Ajou* v. *Dollar Land Holdings* is any guide, Millett L.J. would also have described that interest as arising under a resulting trust.[108]

4. Other Mistakes

As mentioned above, there is no significance to the preceding three sub-categories. Any mistake, which allows a provider of property to obtain restitution of that property, should vitiate the provider's intention to benefit the recipient to the extent necessary for the resulting trust. In *Chase Manhattan*, Goulding J. said simply that, 'a person who pays money to another under a factual mistake retains an equitable property in it'.[109] There was no suggestion that this resulting trust would not apply in every case in which a mistaken payment could be claimed as money had and received.

Some confusion is created by Goulding J.'s statement that the provider of a mistaken payment 'retains an equitable property in it'.[110] As discussed in Chapter 2,[111] this cannot mean that a pre-existing equitable interest continues unaffected by the mistaken transfer of the legal title. The provider in *Chase Manhattan* did not have an equitable interest in the money prior to the mistaken payment. It began with the legal ownership of the money and obtained a new equitable interest in that money when the legal ownership was transferred. The provider of a mistaken payment 'retains' property only in the sense that the provider continues to have a property interest in the money after the payment. This is not a pre-existing interest which survives the mistaken payment, but a new interest created by it.

Several commentators have treated the proprietary recovery of mistaken payments as an issue which turns upon the passing of property.[112] For example,

[106] [1981] Ch. 105, 119.
[107] *Sinclair* v. *Brougham* [1914] A.C. 398, 421; see pp. 155–7 below.
[108] [1993] 3 All E.R. 717, 734; see p. 125 above.
[109] [1981] Ch. 105, 119.
[110] Ibid.
[111] Above, pp. 51–5.
[112] Birks (1989a), p. 381; Burrows (1993a), p. 107; Birks (1993c) at 197; Swadling (1994a) at 82–3; Swadling (1996) at 127.

Burrows states that, 'the potentially detrimental effect on third parties of giving the plaintiff proprietary rights and remedies suggests that mistake ought to have a narrower scope in relation to whether title passes than in restitution'.[113] Some support for this approach is gleaned from *Barclays Bank* v. *Simms*,[114] where the plaintiff bank had overlooked its customer's instructions to stop payment and was seeking restitution from the payee, Robert Goff J. stated:[115]

> [W]here an action is brought to recover money paid under a mistake of fact, property will almost invariably have passed to the defendant, the effect of the action, if successful, being simply to impose on the defendant a personal obligation to repay the money. Furthermore, the kind of mistake which will ground recovery is . . . far wider than the kind of mistake which will vitiate an intention to transfer property.

With respect, *Barclays Bank* v. *Simms* should not be read as placing a limit on the role of the resulting trust in cases of mistake. Goff J. was simply observing that questions regarding the passing of legal title are normally irrelevant where a plaintiff is seeking restitution of a mistaken payment, because (i) legal ownership of money passes very easily and will normally do so when paid by mistake and (ii) the action for money had and received is a personal claim. The question whether the plaintiff was entitled to a proprietary claim was not tested in that case, because the receiver for the insolvent recipient held the mistaken payment in a separate account and agreed to repay the sum if the personal claim succeeded.[116] Goff and Jones support the view that the mistaken payer should have a proprietary claim against the recipient.[117] Although, like Burrows, they express sympathies for the plight of third parties, their 'admittedly radical'[118] proposals for limiting the provider's proprietary claim are based not on the type of mistake or degree of vitiation, but on the knowledge and solvency of the recipient.[119]

It is suggested, with respect, that the resulting trust and the passing of title are separate issues arising from a mistaken transfer. Their confusion stems from the view of equitable proprietary interests (called 'proprietary arithmetic') which was argued against in Chapter 2. The belief that a beneficial legal owner of property also possesses the equitable ownership of that property leads naturally to the question why a transfer might be effective at law, but not in equity. However, as suggested above,[120] the resulting trust is not caused by a failure to transfer the equitable ownership (which a legal owner does not have), but is equity's response to the unjust enrichment of the recipient. Even in cases where the provider began with an equitable interest,[121] the mistake does not render the

[113] Burrows (1993a), p. 107. [114] [1980] Q.B. 677. [115] Ibid. 689.
[116] Ibid. 685–6. [117] Goff and Jones, pp. 94, 131. [118] Ibid. at p. 96.
[119] Ibid. at pp. 94–8, 130–1. This is discussed further at p. 236 below.
[120] At pp. 102–4.
[121] E.g. *Re Garnett* (1885) 31 Ch.D. 1, C.A.; (1886) 33 Ch.D. 300, C.A.; *Melbourne Banking Corp.* v. *Brougham* (1882) 7 App.Cas. 307, P.C.; see pp. 127–8 above.

transfer of that interest void. A new equitable interest arises from the moment of transfer until the transfer is avoided. This is best understood as a resulting trust responding to the vitiation of the provider's intention to benefit the recipient.

The fact that a resulting trust is a proprietary response is not a reason for supposing that the rules for its creation must accord with those which govern the transfer of legal title. That argument, if valid, would render all resulting trusts suspect. It could also be applied to other restitutionary claims: why have one standard of intention for the passing of property if another standard allows it to be claimed back through rescission, rectification, or as money had and received? The success of this argument would eliminate much of the law of restitution, leaving questions of entitlement to be answered from within the law of property. There are, of course, valid reasons for rules which enable ownership to be determined with certainty and relied upon. However, as argued below in the concluding chapter, the nature of the resulting trust and its susceptibility to defences, such as *bona fide* purchase, adequately protect those concerns.

5. The Way Forward

The trend in the law concerning restitution for mistake, which began in *Barclays Bank* v. *Simms* and derived significant impetus from *David Securities* v. *Commonwealth Bank of Australia*, is towards simpler, more consistent rules for recovery. As the High Court of Australia said in *David Securities*, 'If the payer has made the payment because of a mistake, his or her intention to transfer the money is vitiated and the recipient has been enriched'.[122] The focus is shifting from the question whether the particular mistake is of a kind for which restitution is available to the questions whether the mistake caused the transfer and, if so, whether the recipient has a valid defence to the claim, such as submission to an honest claim, *bona fide* purchase, or change of position.[123] The more traditional approach is not misguided, but merely a different, more complicated method of achieving the same goal of protecting the security of receipts in certain circumstances.

It is still early to predict the extent to which this trend will affect the various sub-categories that can be grouped under the heading 'mistake'. However, it is worth noting that a shift of attention from the categorization of the mistake to an inquiry into causation and defences should allow for greater coherence between this ground for restitution and the resulting trust. The central fact to which all resulting trusts respond is the provider's lack of intention to benefit the recipient. There are situations in which that intention is lacking due to mistake, but restitution is not otherwise available. Recourse to the resulting trust should

[122] (1992) 175 C.L.R. 353, 378.

[123] *Barclays Bank Ltd.* v. *W.J. Simms Son & Cooke (Southern) Ltd.* [1980] Q.B. 677, 695; see Beatson (1991), pp. 137–8, 152, 165, 175, 251; Burrows (1993a), pp. 100–3.

not allow plaintiffs to circumvent carefully worked-out restrictions on recovery for mistake (at least not without proper attention to the reasons for preserving or removing those restrictions).[124]

There are two methods of controlling the application of the resulting trust to achieve consistency with other restitutionary responses to mistake: (i) categorization of the mistake and (ii) defences. The first is to decide that a mistake, which will not otherwise support a claim for restitution, does not vitiate the provider's intention sufficiently to raise a resulting trust. It is certainly legitimate to conclude that the vitiating effect of a mistake depends on the circumstances. As Birks states:[125] '[E]ven if as a matter of impression it looks as though the transfer was not voluntary, you have to go down to the cases to see if it was non-voluntary in the way in which the law counts as calling for restitution. Natural non-voluntariness, the layman's commonsensical version, is only a starting point'.

This approach controls the resulting trust by subordinating it to the same categorization process which has traditionally been used to limit restitution for mistake. Only those mistakes for which the law otherwise allows restitution are deemed capable of vitiating the provider's intention in a legally relevant manner. This approach is not without merit, but it can only partially reconcile the principle of resulting trust with existing restrictions on recovery. For example, where property has been transferred pursuant to contract, the provider's mistake will not normally support a claim to restitution unless it was shared[126] or induced[127] by the recipient or the recipient was aware that the provider was mistaken.[128] The provider's intention is not vitiated to a greater degree where the recipient is aware of that mistake, so why does the resulting trust not apply in any event?

A satisfactory answer to that question is revealed when the focus is shifted from categorization to causation and defence. This is the second method of controlling the resulting trust. Where property is transferred pursuant to contract and the recipient is unaware of the mistake which has vitiated the provider's intention to benefit the recipient, the resulting trust is precluded by the defence of good faith exchange. In *Malden* v. *Menill*,[129] the plaintiffs had participated in a conveyance to the defendant, unaware that they were entitled to a £4,000 charge on the property. Lord Hardwicke C. rejected their claim to recover that money from the innocent recipient:[130] 'Mr. Menill has given very amply for this estate, and shall a mistake of the parties, who knew nothing of the £4,000 at the time, turn to the prejudice of a fair purchaser?' Although this mistake is similar to that which gave the mistaken providers an equitable interest in *Re Garnett* (discussed above),[131] the defence of good faith exchange would preclude a resulting trust, as well as other restitutionary remedies.

[124] Cf. Swadling (1996) at 128.
[125] Birks (1989a), p. 100. See pp. 108–9 above.
[126] *Cooper* v. *Phibbs* (1867) L.R. 2 H.L. 149, 170.
[127] *Newbigging* v. *Adam* (1886) 34 Ch.D. 582, C.A.
[128] *Garrard* v. *Frankel* (1862) 30 Beav. 445, 450–1.
[129] (1737) 2 Atk. 8.
[130] Ibid. at 13.
[131] (1886) 33 Ch.D. 300; see pp. 127–8 above.

E. DURESS

Here begins the discussion of more difficult cases, further along the scale, where the providers intended to benefit the recipients, but their intentions were vitiated by duress, undue influence, etc. They differ from cases of mistake in that the providers had knowledge of all the facts needed to make an informed decision to transfer the property, but were nonetheless entitled to rescind because they did not have the opportunity to freely exercise their judgement.[132] These can be regarded (as they are here) as cases in which the central fact motivating restitution is the vitiation of the providers' intentions. There are other views which concentrate more on the recipient's conduct or other reasons for restitution. For example, Professor Atiyah stated that, 'modern law has come to recognize . . . that a coerced promisor still intends to make his promise. To release him from his promise, therefore, requires some additional justification'.[133] He viewed relief for duress as an illustration of 'the movement . . . towards a greater recognition of collective and paternalistic goals'.[134] In other words (although Atiyah is unlikely to have put it this way), recovery on the basis of duress may be an example of policy-motivated restitution.

A provider is not entitled to recover property just because the decision to provide it was made under duress. Restitution is only available if the pressure was illegitimate, from which it could be inferred that intervention is motivated primarily by public policy.[135] However, the fact that both law and context determine which pressures are legitimate (and therefore a valid motive for a transfer) and which are illegitimate (and therefore an unacceptable vitiation of the intention to transfer) does not detract from the conclusion that vitiation of the provider's intention to benefit the recipient is an essential element in cases of duress. As Birks and Chin stated:[136]

> Pressures are commonplace in society. Freedom of the will or, synonymously, of judgmental capacity is intelligible only within the context of pressures inherent in ordinary social life: freedom is precisely and definitively the freedom to cope with those pressures, and it is impaired only when a pressure alien to that context is introduced.

This vitiation of intention, which is present in every case of duress, should attract the principle of resulting trust if it would otherwise give rise to a right to restitution.

Universe Tankships Inc. of Monrovia v. *I.T.F.*[137] was a case of duress in which the defendants had prevented the plaintiff's ship from leaving port until the plaintiff had paid money to the defendants as union dues and wages for the ship's crew. The plaintiff sought to recover the payment and the case before the House

[132] Birks (1989a), p. 173.
[133] Atiyah (1986), p. 130.
[134] Ibid. at p. 146.
[135] Ibid. at pp. 130–2; cf. Birks (1989a), pp. 173–4.
[136] Birks and Chin at p. 88.
[137] [1983] 1 A.C. 366.

of Lords concerned a small portion of the wages that had been paid to the defendants' welfare fund. The defendants conceded that their actions amounted to economic duress capable of vitiating the plaintiff's consent to make the payments. The main issue was whether the pressure exerted was legitimate. The majority of the law lords held that it was not and the plaintiff was entitled to recover the payment as money had and received. Lord Diplock stated:[138]

> It is not that the party seeking to avoid the contract which he has entered into with another party, or to recover money he has paid to another party in response to a demand, did not know the nature or the precise terms of the contract at the time when he entered into it or did not understand the purpose for which the payment was demanded. The rationale is that his apparent consent was induced by pressure exercised upon him by that other party which the law does not regard as legitimate, with the consequence that the consent is treated in law as revocable unless approbated either expressly or by implication after the illegitimate pressure has ceased to operate on his mind. It is a rationale similar to that which underlies the avoidability of contracts entered into and the recovery of money exacted under colour of office, or undue influence or in consequence of threats of physical duress.

Lord Scarman said that, 'The classic case of duress is . . . not the lack of will to submit but the victim's intentional submission arising from the realisation that there is no other practical choice open to him'.[139] Can the principle of resulting trust apply even though the payment had been made as a rational response to illegitimate pressure? The answer should be 'yes'.[140] As Lord Diplock stated, the common law treats the consent as revocable upon removal of the pressure. Equity must regard the consent as vitiated from the outset.[141] The intention to benefit the recipient was the product of coercion from which the plaintiff was entitled to be free. Once this improperly procured intention has been discounted, there was an absence of intention to benefit the recipient which should attract the principle of resulting trust from the moment the payment was made. Nevertheless, the plaintiff's claim to a resulting trust was rejected by all five law lords. However, as discussed below,[142] the connexion between duress and the resulting trust was not considered.

Goff and Jones state that:[143]

> There is no authority on the question whether a person who pays money or confers some other benefit under duress has, in addition to a personal claim, a restitutionary proprietary claim. In our view the courts should grant the coerced person such a claim and should not be inhibited from doing so by the absence of any fiduciary relationship . . . As the law now stands, a court will deem the equitable title to remain in the plaintiff.

[138] Ibid. at 384. [139] Ibid. at 400 (dissenting on the basis that the pressure was legitimate).
[140] Birks (1992c) at pp. 370–1. [141] See Friedmann (1991) at p. 267.
[142] At p. 140. [143] Goff and Jones, p. 275.

They rely on *Chase Manhattan Bank* v. *Israel British Bank* for this last proposition. If, as suggested above,[144] *Chase Manhattan* is a case of resulting trust, then the law concerning recovery for duress may already be very close to the position advocated in this section.

F. UNDUE INFLUENCE

As Lord Diplock mentioned in *Universe Tankships*, the rationale for recovery for duress is similar to that underlying undue influence. In both situations, the provider is entitled to relief because his or her intention to benefit the recipient was brought about improperly.[145] Lord Browne-Wilkinson explained the operation of undue influence in *C.I.B.C. Mortgages p.l.c.* v. *Pitt*:[146]

> Actual undue influence is a species of fraud. Like any other victim of fraud, a person who has been induced by undue influence to carry out a transaction which he did not freely and knowingly enter into is entitled to have that transaction set aside as of right . . . The effect of the wrongdoer's conduct is to prevent the wronged party from bringing a free will and properly informed mind to bear on the proposed transaction which accordingly must be set aside in equity as a matter of justice.

In *Allcard* v. *Skinner*, Lindley L.J. stated that the purpose of the equitable doctrine of undue influence was not 'to save persons from the consequences of their own folly', but 'to protect people from being forced, tricked or misled in any way by others into parting with their property'.[147] In *Johnson* v. *Buttress*, Dixon J. said:[148] 'The basis of the equitable jurisdiction to set aside an alienation of property on the ground of undue influence is the prevention of an unconscientious use of any special capacity or opportunity that may exist or arise of affecting the alienor's will or freedom of judgment in reference to such a matter'.

A person acting under undue influence, like someone under duress, intends to benefit the other party. However, that intention is improperly produced and therefore defective from the outset. This was pointed out by Lord Eldon C. in *Huguenin* v. *Baseley*, concerning a widow's gift to a distant relation who had taken on the role as her sole advisor:[149] 'Take it, that she intended to give it to him: it is by no means out of the reach of the principle. The question is, not, whether she knew what she was doing, had done, or proposed to do, but how the intention was produced'.

Can an intention to benefit the recipient, which was effective at law but defective in equity, be sufficient to exclude the resulting trust? It would be

[144] At p. 129.
[145] Birks (1992a) pp. 47–9; Burrows (1993a), p. 189; Birks and Chin. Cf. Winder (1939) at 100; Cretney at 11–12.
[146] [1994] 1 A.C. 200, 209.
[147] (1887) 36 Ch.D. 145, 182–3; see Martin (1993a), p. 815.
[148] (1936) 56 C.L.R. 113, 134.
[149] (1807) 14 Ves. 273, 299–300.

inconsistent for a court of equity to set aside a transaction because of defects in the intention to benefit the recipient and yet close its eyes to those same defects when considering the principle of resulting trust. Neither logic nor precedent requires this distinction to be made between the grounds for rescission and the grounds for resulting trust.

In *Allcard* v. *Skinner*,[150] the plaintiff sought to recover large gifts she had made to the superior of her former religious order. All three members of the Court of Appeal thought the gift might be set aside when the plaintiff left the order, but the majority decided that right had been lost through delay and affirmation. Cotton L.J., dissenting on the latter issues, thought that the defendant was a trustee for the plaintiff[151] and that, on leaving the order, 'she was entitled to recover so much of the fund transferred by her as remained in the hands of the Defendant, on the ground that it was property the beneficial interest in which she had never parted with'.[152] Lindley L.J. stated that, 'The equitable title of the donee is imperfect by reason of the influence inevitably resulting from her position, and which influence experience has taught the Courts to regard as undue'.[153]

In *Stump* v. *Gaby*,[154] a man under arrest for debt and in embarrassed circumstances had conveyed property to his attorney. His heir at law sought to set aside the conveyance as having been obtained by fraud and the question arose concerning the heir's standing to bring the action. Lord St. Leonards C. stated:[155]

> I do not deny that a deed may be so fraudulent as to be set aside at law: this, however, is not such a case; but I will assume that the conveyance might have been set aside in equity for fraud: what then is the interest of a party in an estate which he has conveyed to his attorney under circumstances which would give a right in this Court to have the conveyance set aside? In the view of this Court he remains the owner, subject to the repayment of the money which has been advanced by the attorney, and the consequence is that he may devise the estate, not as a legal estate, but as an equitable estate, wholly irrespective of all question as to any rights of entry or action, leaving the conveyance to have its full operation at law, but looking at the equitable right to have it set aside in this Court.

Stump v. *Gaby* was approved by the Lords Justices in *Gresley* v. *Mousley*[156] and the High Court of Australia in *Latec Investments Ltd.* v. *Hotel Terrigal Pty. Ltd.*[157] and there is no reason to doubt that it is good law. As Taylor J. said in the latter case, *Stump* v. *Gaby* and *Gresley* v. *Mousley* provide 'abundant authority for the proposition that the owner of land a transfer of which has been obtained by fraud retains an equitable interest therein'.[158] This interest should be recognized as a resulting trust. There are two potential impediments to this

[150] (1887) 36 Ch.D. 145. [151] Ibid. at 175. [152] Ibid. at 172.
[153] Ibid. at 184. [154] (1852) 2 De G.M.&G. 623. [155] Ibid. at 630.
[156] (1859) 4 De G.&J. 78; see *Dickinson* v. *Burrell* (1866) L.R. 1 Eq. 337.
[157] (1965) 113 C.L.R. 265. [158] Ibid. at 283 (also see at 277, 284, 290).

recognition: (i) the question whether the plaintiff with a right of rectification or rescission has an equitable interest or a mere equity and (ii) the few cases in which the plaintiff recovered property on the basis of vitiated intention, but the resulting trust was rejected. Mere equities are the subject of Chapter 7, while the cases rejecting the resulting trust are dealt with here below, after the remainder of the scale of vitiated intention has been explored.

G. UNCONSCIONABLE CONDUCT

As mentioned near the beginning of this chapter, *Louth* v. *Diprose*[159] may represent the far end of the scale of defective intention. The plaintiff was a solicitor who had become infatuated with the defendant. The relationship was one-sided and the defendant had taken advantage of the plaintiff's infatuation to cause him to purchase a house for her.[160] The plaintiff sought to recover the property on the basis of resulting trust, undue influence, or unconscionable conduct. The courts rejected the resulting trust[161] and the plaintiff was successful on the latter of the two remaining grounds. The trial judge, King C.J., stated:[162] 'There are ample grounds for setting aside the house transaction on the ground of undue influence. Like counsel for the plaintiff, however, I prefer to rest my judgment upon the general principle of unconscionability'.

Deane J. drew the following distinction between the two grounds of relief in *Commercial Bank of Australia Ltd.* v. *Amadio*:[163]

> Undue influence, like common law duress, looks to the quality of the consent or assent of the weaker party . . . Unconscionable dealing looks to the conduct of the stronger party in attempting to enforce, or retain the benefit of, a dealing with a person under a special disability in circumstances where it is not consistent with equity or good conscience that he should do so.

If the unjust factor in cases of unconscionability is the wrongful conduct of the recipient and not the vitiation of the provider's intention to confer the benefit, there would be no basis for applying the principle of resulting trust. We have not only reached the end of the scale of vitiation, but taken a step beyond. The resulting trust would still correspond with the category of non-voluntary transfers of property, but the equitable responses to remarkably similar situations would be different: the resulting trust applying to cases of undue influence (as a response to the vitiation of the provider's intention) and the constructive trust, if any, to cases of unconscionability (as a response to the recipient's wrongful conduct).

There is no need to make this distinction. The basis of unconscionable dealing

[159] (1992) 175 C.L.R. 621. [160] Ibid. at 638. [161] See p. 141 below.
[162] (1990) 54 S.A.S.R. 438, 449. [163] (1983) 151 C.L.R. 447, 474.

is the improper advantage taken of some impairment of the provider's judgement. Although this degree of impairment is not a sufficient ground for relief unless it has been improperly brought about or exploited,[164] relief for unconscionability depends upon some vitiation of the provider's intention to benefit the recipient. This is clear from Mason J.'s description, in *Commercial Bank of Australia Ltd.* v. *Amadio*, of the difference between unconscionable conduct and undue influence:[165]

In the latter the will of the innocent party is not independent and voluntary because it is overborne. In the former the will of the innocent party, even if independent and voluntary, is the result of the disadvantageous position in which he is placed and of the other party unconscientiously taking advantage of that position.

There is no reason for thinking that the two remedies are mutually exclusive in the sense that only one of them is available in a particular situation to the exclusion of the other. Relief on the ground of unconscionable conduct will be granted when unconscientious advantage is taken of an innocent party whose will is overborne so that it is not independent and voluntary, just as it will be granted when such advantage is taken of an innocent party who, though not deprived of an independent and voluntary will, is unable to make a worthwhile judgment as to what is in his best interest.

Brennan J. also made it clear in *Louth* v. *Diprose* that vitiation of intention is a necessary ingredient of unconscionable conduct:[166]

The jurisdiction of equity to set aside gifts procured by unconscionable conduct ordinarily arises from the concatenation of three factors: a relationship between the parties which, to the knowledge of the donee, places the donor at a special disadvantage vis-à-vis the donee; the donee's unconscientious exploitation of the donor's disadvantage; and the consequent overbearing of the will of the donor whereby the donor is unable to make a worthwhile judgment as to what is in his best interest.

In *Louth* v. *Diprose*, the trial judge declared that the recipient held the property on trust for its provider.[167] On appeal, the majority of the full court disapproved of the trust and wanted instead to order the recipient to repay the sum provided for the purchase.[168] Nevertheless, they dismissed the appeal. The declaration of trust was not challenged in the High Court of Australia and left intact, without comment regarding its appropriateness. The members of the full court were rightly sceptical of a declaration of a trust made without articulation of the principles on which the equitable interest was based. As discussed below, the courts in *Louth* v. *Diprose* did not consider the basis on which the trust could be justified: as a resulting trust responding to the vitiation of the provider's intention to benefit the recipient.

[164] *Bridgeman* v. *Green* (1757) Wilm. 58, 61; *Allcard* v. *Skinner* (1887) 36 Ch.D. 145, 182–3; *Tate* v. *Williamson* (1866) L.R. 2 Ch.App. 55; *Blomley* v. *Ryan* (1956) 99 C.L.R. 362.

[165] (1983) 151 C.L.R. 447, 461.

[166] (1992) 175 C.L.R. 621, 626.

[167] (1990) 54 S.A.S.R. 438, 449.

[168] (1990) 54 S.A.S.R. 450, 453–4, 456.

H. FIVE CASES OF VITIATED INTENTION AND RESULTING TRUST

Claims for resulting trusts are only rarely made in cases involving undue influence or duress. Five such cases are considered now: *Hodgson* v. *Marks*,[169] *Universe Tankships Inc.* v. *I.T.F.*,[170] *Simpson* v. *Simpson*,[171] *Louth* v. *Diprose*[172] and *Cheese* v. *Thomas*.[173]

1. *Hodgson* v. *Marks*

The connexion between undue influence and the resulting trust was briefly discussed in *Hodgson* v. *Marks*, in which the plaintiff had been persuaded by her lodger to transfer her house to him. Russell L.J. noted that it was an unchallenged finding of fact that 'the plaintiff did not intend to make any gift to him, and that it was well understood, and indeed orally arranged between them, that the beneficial ownership was to remain in the plaintiff'.[174] His lordship then stated:[175] 'At the outset, to get the point out of the way, let me say that such a finding disposes of any question of undue influence; any such case assumes a transfer of the beneficial interest, but in circumstances which entitles the transferor to recall it'. Although the oral trust was ineffective, the absence of intention to make a gift gave rise to a resulting trust.

The quotation above could be construed as an indication that undue influence and resulting trusts inhabit mutually exclusive spheres, but this should be resisted. Russell L.J.'s conclusion was that the question of undue influence does not arise where the intention to benefit the recipient is wholly absent. He did not address the question whether a resulting trust could arise where that intention existed, but was defective. However, Russell L.J.'s statement that a case of undue influence 'assumes a transfer of the beneficial interest' is difficult.[176] Taken literally and in isolation, this would mean that the question of undue influence could only arise if the resulting trust did not apply, because the resulting trust would return the beneficial interest to the transferor from the outset. Construing Russell L.J.'s remarks in this fashion places them in direct conflict with *Stump* v. *Gaby*, where Lord St. Leonards C. concluded that a transferor, with an equitable right to set aside the conveyance for fraud, 'remains the owner' in equity.[177]

If, instead of saying that a case of undue influence 'assumes a transfer of the beneficial interest', Russell L.J. had said that it 'assumes a *prima facie* transfer of the beneficial interest' or 'assumes an intention to transfer the beneficial interest', there would be no difficulty. As Megarry J. stated in *Re Vandervell's Trusts (No. 2)*, it 'is no small thing notionally to write words into a speech in

[169] [1971] 1 Ch. 892, C.A. [170] [1983] 1 A.C. 366. [171] [1992] 1 F.L.R. 601.
[172] (1992) 175 C.L.R. 621. [173] [1994] 1 All E.R. 35, C.A.
[174] [1971] 1 Ch. 892, 929. [175] Ibid. [176] Ibid.
[177] (1852) 2 De G.M.&G. 623, 630.

the House of Lords'.[178] The same is true of a judgment of the Court of Appeal. However, the suggested re-phrasing of Russell L.J.'s statement brings it into line with what was actually decided. Ms. Hodgson had no intention to benefit her lodger and the question of undue influence did not arise. Russell L.J.'s statement should not be taken to mean that the resulting trust cannot apply where there is an intention to benefit the recipient, however defective. The latter issue did not arise on the facts of the case, nor was it addressed by the Court of Appeal.

2. *Universe Tankships*

In *Universe Tankships Inc.* v. *I.T.F.*,[179] the plaintiff had been forced to pay money to the defendants' welfare fund before the defendants would allow the plaintiff's ship to leave port. The plaintiff made two alternative claims to recover the money paid: (i) that the fund was an invalid purpose trust and the payment made to the invalid trust was held on resulting trust for the plaintiff as settlor and (ii) that the payment was made under duress and recoverable at common law as money had and received. All five law lords agreed that the payment was not made in trust, but as an accretion to the defendants' wealth and, therefore, the resulting trust claim failed.

The question of resulting trust was decided solely on the basis of whether there had been a failed attempt to create an express trust. The plaintiff's case consisted of two entirely separate claims to the same fund and they were treated separately from each other by all five law lords, as indicated in Lord Diplock's speech:[180]

> [T]here is a certain air of artificiality about treating the shipowners as donors of money for trust purposes, when the only object that they had in mind in paying any money to I.T.F. was to get the blacking of the *Universe Sentinel* lifted, and thereafter to get the money back from I.T.F. if they could; but for the purposes of determining what is convenient to refer to as the trust point, one must treat the payment as having been 'voluntary' in the sense that the shipowners' consent to making in was not vitiated by duress.

Although the claim for a resulting trust was rejected, this cannot be taken as authority that the resulting trust cannot apply to property transferred under duress.[181] The proposition that a payment made under duress is, like other payments imperfectly intended, held on resulting trust was never argued or considered in *Universe Tankships*.

3. *Simpson* v. *Simpson*

The resulting trust and rescission for undue influence were both considered in *Simpson* v. *Simpson*,[182] in which a husband suffering from a brain tumour transferred bank accounts and shares into joint names with his wife shortly before his death. Morritt J. held that several of the transfers occurred after the husband had

[178] [1974] Ch. 269, 291. [179] [1983] 1 A.C. 366. [180] Ibid. at 382–3.
[181] See Birks (1989a), pp. 370–1. [182] [1992] 1 F.L.R. 601.

lost capacity and were void. His lordship went on to consider the position if the husband had retained sufficient capacity to make those transfers. Morritt J. stated that 'there is no evidence at all as to the [husband's] intention, assuming he was capable of forming one'[183] and, therefore, the presumption of advancement would have operated in favour of his wife. However, his weakened condition and dependence on his wife meant that the transfers could have been rescinded because of an unrebutted presumption of undue influence.

This *obiter dictum* demonstrates the tension created by treating resulting trusts and rescission as discrete compartments of equity. Morritt J. approached the problem in two stages: 'if these dispositions were made with capacity and an intention to confer a beneficial joint interest on [the wife], then it is to be presumed, unless the contrary is shown, that they were procured by the undue influence of [the wife]'.[184] After presuming an intention to give, which precluded the resulting trust, his lordship presumed defects in that intention, without relating them back to the first question of resulting trust. There is a real difficulty in concurrent findings that a transfer was intended and that it was made when the independent volition of the transferor was impaired. A better approach was taken in *Re Pauling's Settlement Trusts* (concerning apparent gifts from children to their parents), where the presumptions of advancement and undue influence were treated as opposing inferences of fact.[185]

4. *Louth* v. *Diprose*

The possibility of a resulting trust was raised and rejected in *Louth* v. *Diprose*, but this does not create a large obstacle for the present argument. As in *Universe Tankships*, the claim to a resulting trust was made in the alternative to the claim based on undue influence or unconscionability. The plaintiff had sought to establish a resulting trust on the basis of either a common intention to create the trust or the presumption of resulting trust arising from the plaintiff's provision of the purchase money. King C.J. found that the plaintiff had intended to make a gift of the house to the defendant.[186] This negated the possibility of an intention to create a trust and rebutted the presumption of resulting trust, but whether it necessarily prevented the operation of the principle of resulting trust was not considered at trial or on either appeal. The plaintiff's alternative claims based on undue influence and unconscionability were never related back to the claim for a resulting trust.

5. *Cheese* v. *Thomas*

In *Cheese* v. *Thomas*,[187] the plaintiff had contributed more than half the cost of purchasing a house in his great-nephew's name. The case is similar to *Louth* v.

[183] Ibid. at 618. [184] Ibid. at 622. [185] [1964] Ch. 303, 336, C.A.
[186] (1990) 54 S.A.S.R. 438, 445. [187] [1994] 1 All E.R. 35. See pp. 191–2 below.

Diprose, in that the plaintiff made alternative claims to a resulting trust based on common intention and to rescission based on undue influence. The allegation that the parties 'had agreed that the house should be jointly owned'[188] was rejected by the trial judge and not dealt with in the Court of Appeal, where the claim based on undue influence was upheld. Again, the possible connexion between undue influence and resulting trusts was not considered.

In *Cheese* v. *Thomas*, as in *Universe Tankships, Simpson* v. *Simpson* and *Louth* v. *Diprose*, the courts proceeded with a two-stage inquiry: could a resulting trust be established in the traditional manner and, if not, could the plaintiff obtain some other relief on another basis? In *Hodgson* v. *Marks*, the court used the same approach, but never reached the second stage. In consequence, they did not address the question whether the resulting trust does not apply whenever a transfer is imperfectly intended. This is not intended as a criticism of the judgments in any of those cases. They were made in response to the pleadings which, in turn, were based on common conceptions about the traditional categories of resulting trust.

I. SUMMARY

There is a scale of defective intention which gives rise to restitution, ranging from cases of ignorance down to cases of unconscionable conduct. Although the traditional categories of resulting trust belong at the higher end of the scale, as cases where the provider has no intention to benefit the recipient, the resulting trust should apply whenever the provider's intention is vitiated to any degree which is sufficient for restitution on another basis. In some cases of mistake and undue influence, the courts have declared that the provider has an equitable interest in the property transferred to the recipient. This should be recognized as a resulting trust. The proper integration of the resulting trust as one of equity's responses to vitiated intention will depend on a proper understanding of the role of the defences to claims of this nature.

[188] Ibid. at 38.

6
Qualified Intention

This is the second of three chapters exploring the extent to which resulting trusts respond to non-voluntary transfers. It concerns cases in which property has been transferred and the provider of that property did not intend to benefit the recipient in the particular circumstances which have occurred. Unlike the cases of vitiated intention discussed in the previous chapter, the lack of intention to benefit the recipient is not caused by any impairment of the provider's decision-making ability. Instead, the provider has a properly formed, but qualified intention to benefit the recipient; i.e. that intention is conditional upon the happening of certain events. When those events fail to occur or continue as expected, the transfer becomes non-voluntary and restitution is possible on the basis of what is commonly known as 'failure of consideration'.

Care must be taken not to be confused by the narrow meaning which the term 'consideration' has acquired in relation to contracts. It is used here in the broader sense explained by Professor Birks:[1]

> A 'consideration' was once no more than a 'matter considered', and the consideration for doing something was the matter considered in forming the decision to do it. In short, the reason for the act, the state of affairs contemplated as its basis. Failure of consideration for a payment should be understood in that sense. It means that the state of affairs contemplated as the basis or reason for the payment has failed to materialise or, if it did exist, has failed to sustain itself.

The consideration for a payment is commonly the expected counter-performance under a contract, but it may be or include other matters. The *Quistclose* trust (discussed in Chapter 3) provides a good example. The consideration for a loan of money to be used for a specific purpose is twofold: that the loan will be repaid and that the money will be used as specified. If the payment cannot be used in that manner, the latter consideration fails. Restitution by way of resulting trust is possible because the lender's intention to benefit the borrower was conditional upon the happening of an event which failed to occur and the payment became non-voluntary.

The *Quistclose* trust is the main situation in which resulting trusts respond to the lack of intention to benefit the recipient brought about by a failure of consideration. However, it is not the only situation. The resulting trust can and does respond to the failure of purposes other than the intended use of the money paid.

[1] Birks (1989a), p. 223. See Burrows (1993a), pp. 251–3; Goff and Jones, pp. 40–1; *David Securities Pty. Ltd.* v. *Commonwealth Bank of Australia* (1992) 175 C.L.R. 353, 382.

Unfortunately, it is not clear when a failure of another type of consideration will give rise to a resulting trust. Prior to the judgment of the House of Lords in *Westdeutsche Landesbank Girozentrale* v. *Islington London Borough Council*,[2] the payment of money under a void contract might have counted as one of the accepted situations in which resulting trusts arise. The Court of Appeal[3] had reached that conclusion in reliance on the well-known but difficult case, *Sinclair* v. *Brougham*.[4] However, the House of Lords departed from *Sinclair* v. *Brougham* and held that a resulting trust does not arise in response to a failure of consideration in these circumstances.

The primary issues explored in this and the previous chapters are similar: can the vitiation or qualification of the provider's intention to benefit the recipient, which makes the enrichment of the recipient unjust and gives rise to a right of restitution, also give rise to a resulting trust? However, the inquiries lead in somewhat different directions. In the previous chapter, the question was whether the resulting trust could respond to every degree of vitiation which would otherwise give rise to a right to restitution. Here, there is no difficulty with the level of non-voluntariness. In all cases of restitution on the basis of failure of consideration, it is clear that the provider did not intend to benefit the recipient in the circumstances. Naturally, there has been some difficulty working out precisely why the resulting trust responds to some cases of qualified intention and not others. As Birks states:[5]

> It is difficult to see how a difference could be drawn between one failure of consideration and another. It would, for example, be impossible to argue that in some cases the proprietary base is preserved by reason of an especially clear or intense qualification of the transferor's intent to enrich the recipient. For the truth is that failure of consideration always depends on a clear manifestation of that qualified intent.

This chapter is divided into three parts. The first addresses the difficult question why resulting trusts will respond to some, but not all failures of consideration. The second is focused on the particular problems created by void contracts. The third concerns a minor question which affects all restitutionary responses to failure of consideration, including resulting trusts: is restitution possible if the recipient is unaware of the qualification of the provider's intention to confer the benefit?

A. REQUIREMENTS FOR A RESULTING TRUST

In previous chapters, two requirements for a resulting trust have been identified: (i) a transfer of property and (ii) the provider's lack of intention to benefit the recipient. As discussed in this chapter, there are many cases of failure of consideration where those two requirements are met and yet a resulting trust does

[2] [1996] 2 All E.R. 961. [3] [1994] 4 All E.R. 890, 962. [4] [1914] A.C. 398.
[5] Birks (1989a), p. 387.

not arise: the claim for restitution is merely personal for money had and received. Since the degree of non-voluntariness is the same in all cases of failure of consideration, there must be some additional requirement for a resulting trust.

It is helpful to consider this problem in light of the distinctions between the more general categories of trust and debt, which are identified in *Jacobs' Law of Trusts in Australia*:[6]

> A debtor is not a trustee for his creditor since there is no identifiable fund which the latter is entitled to compel the debtor to apply for his benefit . . . If the payee was entitled to use the money as his own, being under an obligation merely to repay the same amount of money at a future time, then he is merely a debtor.

This quotation reveals two necessary requirements for the existence of any trust: (i) the assets must be identifiable and (ii) the recipient must not have been free to use them for his or her own benefit. These can be restated in possibly more familiar language as the requirements of (i) certainty of subject matter[7] and (ii) enforceable obligations with respect to that subject matter.[8] The absence of either will destroy a trust or prevent it from arising.

These two requirements apply to all resulting trusts. They are only now being discussed in detail because they do not create impediments to the creation of resulting trusts in the traditional categories or in cases of vitiated intention to benefit the recipient. In most of those situations, the events giving rise to the resulting trust are present at the outset and the resulting trust arises at the moment the property is transferred to the recipient.[9] Therefore, the recipient is never free to use the property for his or her own benefit. The same is true in cases where a resulting trust arises upon the failure of an express trust: the recipient is either an express or resulting trustee of the property continuously from the moment of receipt. Of course, the resulting trust will cease to exist if the property is destroyed or otherwise ceases to be identifiable.[10]

A difficulty is created in most cases of failure of consideration by the delay between the transfer of property and the failure of the consideration. The resulting trust is not possible until the transfer becomes non-voluntary, which does not occur until the consideration fails. In most cases, the recipient will be free to deal with the property as he or she chooses before that happens. This is demonstrated by *Chillingworth* v. *Esche*,[11] where the plaintiffs had paid £240 to the

[6] Meagher and Gummow, *Jacobs' Law of Trusts*, p. 15. See *Henry* v. *Hammond* [1913] 2 K.B. 515, 521.

[7] *Knight* v. *Knight* (1840) 3 Beav. 148; see *Re Goldcorp Exchange Ltd.* [1995] 1 A.C. 74, 91, P.C.

[8] *Morice* v. *Bishop of Durham* (1804) 9 Ves. 399, 404; *Re Heberley* [1971] N.Z.L.R. 325, 333, C.A.

[9] *D.K.L.R. Holding Co. (No. 2) Pty. Ltd.* v. *Commissioner of Stamp Duties* (1982) 40 A.L.R. 1, 27, H.C.A.; see Friedmann (1991) at p. 267.

[10] See pp. 106–7 above; *Westdeutsche* v. *Islington* [1996] 2 All E.R. 961, 990, H.L.

[11] [1924] 1 Ch. 97, C.A.

defendant as a deposit for a purchase of real property. Their agreement was 'subject to a proper contract being prepared by the vendor's solicitors'.[12] The plaintiffs refused to proceed and were entitled to the repayment of their deposit. Important for present purposes is Warrington L.J.'s view of the deposit in these circumstances:[13] '[T]he purchaser by payment of a deposit shows that he means business. The purchaser has not bound himself, but in order to show a definite intention he is willing to part with money, and run the risk of the vendor spending the money and being unable to return it if negotiations are broken off'. Absent an agreement to the contrary, the vendor's use of the money is unrestricted and the failure of consideration leads to only a personal claim for money had and received.

1. Identifiable Assets

As stated above, a resulting trust cannot exist unless the property subject to the trust is identifiable. However, a resulting trust will not respond to a failure of consideration just because the property (or its substitute) can be identified in the hands of the recipient when the consideration for the transfer fails. If the recipient had previously obtained the unfettered beneficial ownership of the property, there is no convincing reason why a resulting trust should arise. The recipient was perfectly entitled to expend or destroy the property prior to the failure of consideration and the continued existence of identifiable property is a mere fortuity which should not attract a resulting trust.

Eldan Services Ltd. v. *Chandag Motors Ltd.*[14] provides a useful example. The plaintiff had purchased a garage business from the defendant and had paid for a portion of the stock with a post-dated cheque. Before the date at which the cheque became payable, the plaintiff sought an interim injunction, restraining the defendant from presenting the cheque, on the basis that the stock in question was worth much less than the plaintiff had been led to believe. Millett J. dismissed the plaintiff's motion, stating that 'the mere fact that the moneys are still identifiable and are, as it were, in transit between the payer and recipient does not of itself form a basis for any proprietary claim'.[15]

Although this case was a contractual dispute, rather than a claim for restitution following the termination or invalidity of a contract, it does illustrate that mere identifiability of assets is insufficient for proprietary relief. If the plaintiff had been entitled to terminate the contract and recover the money paid on the basis of failure of consideration, the claim would still have been personal. There would be nothing restricting the defendant's ownership of the cheque between receipt and a subsequent failure of consideration.[16]

[12] Ibid. 97. [13] Ibid. 112. [14] [1990] 3 All E.R. 459.
[15] Ibid. 461. [16] Friedmann (1991) at p. 271.

2. Proprietary Base

The view put forward here, that the identifiability of the assets transferred is a necessary but insufficient condition for a proprietary claim to restitution of those assets, finds support in the writings of Professors Birks and Goode. It is implicit in their notion of a 'proprietary base', which they see as an essential requirement for a restitutionary proprietary claim in this context.[17]

Birks describes 'the requirement of an undestroyed proprietary base' as follows: 'a plaintiff who wants to assert an equitable proprietary interest in the surviving enrichment must show facts such that the property in the original receipt did not pass at law *and* equity to the recipient'.[18] Where property is transferred in consideration of expected contractual performance, 'the property passes and . . . does not pass back' if the consideration later fails.[19] According to Birks, the proprietary base is lost and the plaintiff cannot advance 'from claimant *in personam* to claimant *in rem*' by proving that the defendant still holds the property provided by the plaintiff (or its substitute).[20]

Goode said that a sufficient proprietary base exists where property is 'transferred by P to D in circumstances such that D never had, or has lost, the right to it'.[21] This inclusion of the case in which the recipient has lost the right to the property does not set Goode apart, because he later shows that he is contemplating cases where the recipient 'had an interest which was always defeasible and has been defeated'.[22] The example he uses is the *Quistclose* trust[23] and elsewhere he 'distinguishes the buyer's right to recover the price on a total failure of consideration, a right which is purely personal, from the lender's right to recover the money lent on terms that it is to be applied for a particular purpose, the failure of which causes ownership to revest in the lender in equity'.[24]

A proprietary base is more than just the continued existence of identifiable assets provided by the person claiming restitution. Birks suggests that it also requires the continuation of the provider's proprietary interest in those assets. However, this overstates the minimum requirements for proprietary restitution, which is possible so long as the recipient has not obtained the unrestricted ownership of the assets. The provider's continuing interest in the assets is the most common restriction on the recipient's ownership of the assets, but there are others (discussed below). For this reason, Goode's formulation of the proprietary base, which focuses on the lack or defeasiblity of the recipient's interest in the property,[25] is preferable to Birks', which looks only to the provider's interest in the property.[26]

[17] Goode (1987) at 443; Birks (1989a), pp. 378–9; Goode (1991) at p. 219. Also see Burrows (1993a), pp. 43, 372–3.
[18] Birks (1989a), p. 381. See Birks (1995b) at 84, 88, 92.
[19] Birks (1989a), p. 386.
[20] Birks (1989a), pp. 386–7
[21] Goode (1991) at p. 225.
[22] Ibid. 245.
[23] Ibid. 221–2.
[24] Goode (1987) at 440.
[25] Goode (1991) at pp. 225, 245.
[26] Birks (1989a), pp. 378–9; Birks (1995b) at 84, 88.

3. Restrictions on Ownership

As discussed above, the resulting trust will not arise in every case in which (i) property has been transferred to another, (ii) the provider did not intend to benefit the recipient in the circumstances, and (iii) the property or its substitute remains identifiable in the hands of the recipient. If the recipient obtains the unrestricted beneficial ownership of the property before those three conditions are met, restitution is still possible, but a resulting trust is not. Explored here are three circumstances which can operate to restrict the recipient's ownership between receipt of the property and a failure of consideration: (i) where the property is transferred to be used only for specific purposes (i.e. a *Quistclose* trust), (ii) where there is some incidental fetter on the recipient's beneficial ownership and (iii) where the consideration fails at the outset.

Quistclose trusts

As discussed in Chapter 3, when money is paid to be used for a specific purpose, the provider acquires an equitable right to restrain the recipient from misusing the money. Although the recipient is not normally a bare trustee of that money while the purpose remains possible, he or she is never free to use it for any other purpose. If that purpose cannot be fulfilled, the provider's equitable right is not lost, but becomes complete equitable ownership under a resulting trust because there is no permitted use to which the recipient can put that money. The failure of a *Quistclose* trust leads to a resulting trust because there is a non-voluntary transfer of property on the failure of the purpose and because the arrangement creates an enforceable restriction on the recipient's use of the property between receipt and failure.

It is important to appreciate the distinction between a payment for a purpose and a payment *to be used* for a purpose. Although the failure of the purpose in either situation can lead to restitution, a *Quistclose* trust is only possible in the latter. As Lord Mustill stated in *Re Goldcorp Exchange Ltd.*, the *Quistclose* trust requires 'a mutual intention that the moneys should not fall within the general fund of the [recipient's] assets but should be applied for a special designated purpose'.[27] That requirement is not met where the purpose is unrelated to the recipient's use of the payment: the recipient is free to spend the money before the consideration fails.

This important distinction between payments for purposes and payments to be used for purposes is sometimes overlooked.[28] In *Guardian Ocean Cargoes Ltd. v. Banco do Brasil S.A.*,[29] the plaintiffs wanted to purchase a ship they had chartered. The owner was in financial difficulties and the plaintiffs began negotiating with the owner's bankers to refinance the ship. The plaintiffs paid $600,000

[27] [1995] 1 A.C. 74, 100.
[28] e.g. Klinck at 59, 71. See Rickett (1991) at 630–1.
[29] [1991] 2 Lloyd's L.R. 68; [1992] 2 Lloyd's L.R. 193; varied [1994] 2 Lloyd's L.R. 152, C.A.

to the bank on account of the owner's promissory notes and, when negotiations broke down 5 years later, the plaintiffs claimed the return of their payments. Following *Chillingworth* v. *Esche*,[30] Hirst J. ordered repayment of the money. However, his lordship also decided that the arrangement was a *Quistclose* trust and, therefore, the plaintiffs were entitled to compound interest.[31] This latter aspect of the judgment was overturned on appeal.[32]

Hirst J. did not examine the nature of the purpose of the payment. Although the money was paid on account of the owner's indebtedness for the purpose of refinancing the vessel, this did not restrict the bank's use of the funds. As Saville L.J. stated in the Court of Appeal:[33]

> [T]he plaintiffs simply transferred the money to the bank and remained wholly uninterested in how the particular fund was applied or used. What the plaintiffs were interested in was, of course, that the *amounts* of the payments (not the fund itself) was to be taken into account if a refinancing deal was made but was otherwise to be repaid. Given, as I consider was the case, that the payments were made on this basis, they are of course recoverable as a matter of law. To my mind there is neither room nor need for a trust in this case.

Other fetters on ownership

The failure of a *Quistclose* trust is but one species of failure of consideration. It routinely leads to a resulting trust because the purpose for the transfer creates an enforceable restriction on the recipient's use of the property. When property is transferred for another type of purpose (not involving the use of the property transferred), the subsequent failure of that purpose does not normally lead to a resulting trust because the recipient will have been free to deal with the property as he or she chooses before the purpose fails. However, it may happen that the recipient's use of the property has been restricted from receipt until failure, in which case the resulting trust should be possible.

Moseley v. *Cressey's Co.*[34] and *Re Nanwa Goldmines Ltd.*[35] provide good examples. In both cases, a company had circulated a prospectus for the subscription of shares and received deposits for shares before going into receivership. The subscribers claimed that the receiver held their deposits in trust for them. In *Moseley* v. *Cressey's Co.*, the prospectus contained the statement: 'Deposit returned if no allotment made'.[36] Page Wood V.C. stated:[37]

> The contract was—'You are to pay so much per share when you apply for shares, and your deposits will be returned if no allotment is made'—not that the actual thing so deposited was to be paid back; for payment to the company's bankers to the account of the company made the monies *ipso facto* part of the company's assets.

[30] [1924] 1 Ch. 97, C.A.; see n. 11 above.
[31] [1991] 2 Lloyd's L.R. 68, 87; [1992] 2 Lloyd's L.R. 193, 198–9.
[32] [1994] 2 Lloyd's L.R. 152, C.A. [33] Ibid. 159. [34] (1865) L.R. 1 Eq. 405.
[35] [1955] 1 W.L.R. 1080. [36] (1865) L.R. 1 Eq. 405, 408. [37] Ibid. 409.

It was argued that 'these monies were not the monies of the company until the plaintiffs got their shares'.[38] This was rejected by Page Wood V.C., who said: 'What was intended to have been done seems to have been done; and there was no trust created, it was merely a debt'.[39]

In *Re Nanwa Goldmines Ltd.*, the application form stated that the deposits would 'be retained in a separate account'[40] until the conditions for the issue of shares were met. It was conceded that the fact that deposits were held in a separate account did not itself create a trust. However, Harman J. held that the promise to do so distinguished this case from *Moseley* v. *Cressey's Co.*:[41]

> Is the relationship of the subscribers to the company that of creditor and debtor, or had they a lien on this fund or an equity against it so as to be able to attach it for the payment of their debt without allowing other creditors of the company to share with them? That depends on whether the relationship be that of debtor and creditor or of bailor and bailee; and the question turns, in effect, on the words in the form of application, 'and meanwhile will be retained in a separate account.' . . .
>
> What is the point of making such a promise? It seems to me quite clearly to be a representation that the money will be set apart; not in the company's ordinary coffers, but in a separate account . . . I cannot but think that the whole object of making such a promise was to indicate that it would be kept apart and separate, not mixed with the company's monies, until the board saw whether the conditions were fulfilled.

In both cases, there was a failure of a consideration which was unrelated to the use of the money by the company. Although the providers in both cases were entitled to the repayment of their subscriptions, a proprietary response was justified in *Re Nanwa Goldmines Ltd.* because the recipient never obtained the unrestricted beneficial ownership of the money before the consideration failed, as happened in *Moseley* v. *Cressey's Co.* There was no *Quistclose* trust in *Nanwa Goldmines*, but the promise to retain the money in a separate account created an enforceable restriction on the recipient's use of the money which should suffice for the operation of a resulting trust upon the failure of consideration.

It is important to note that the resulting trust does not depend on whether the provider maintained an interest in (or rights concerning) the property between transfer and failure, but on whether the recipient obtained the unfettered beneficial ownership of that property. This is illustrated by *Re Ames' Settlement*,[42] where a father had, on his son's marriage, settled £10,000 in trust for his son for life, with the remainder to his son's wife and their children. The annulment of that marriage 18 years later led to a resulting trust of the remainder for the father's estate. The resulting trust arose, not because the express trust had failed to dispose of the trust property, but because the purpose for creating that express trust had failed. As Vaisey J. said, 'the case is, having regard to the wording of

[38] Ibid. 410. [39] Ibid. [40] [1955] 1 W.L.R. 1080, 1081–2.
[41] Ibid. 1083–4. [42] [1946] Ch. 217.

the settlement, a single case of money paid on a consideration which failed'.[43] The father, as settlor, had retained no interest in the settled property. However, because the property had been placed in trust, none of the recipients obtained the unfettered beneficial ownership of the remainder before the consideration failed.

Similar circumstances exist in many cases of resulting trust upon the failure of an express trust. The resulting trust arises at the moment of failure because the trustees were not intended to enjoy the benefit of their legal ownership.[44] Where the trust fails due to subsequent events, the trustee's use of the trust property prior to the failure is not restricted by any continuation of the settlor's interest (which is usually completely disposed of when the express trust is created),[45] but by the existence of express trust obligations arising at the outset.

This is not intended to diminish the importance of the provider's contribution. The resulting trust is always primarily dependent on the facts that the claimant (i) provided the property in question and (ii) did not intend the recipient to have the benefit of that property in the circumstances. An additional requirement (in all cases of resulting trust) is that the recipient has not obtained the unfettered beneficial ownership of the property before the right to restitution arises. In many cases, the provider will have an interest in, or rights to, the property throughout, e.g. where the resulting trust arises at the outset or where the transfer gives rise to a *Quistclose* trust. However, where there is a delay between a transfer and the moment at which that transfer becomes non-voluntary, the resulting trust depends not on the provider's entitlement to the property during that gap, but on whether that entitlement or some other circumstance has limited the recipient's ownership of the property.

Failure at the outset

Where the consideration for a transfer of property fails at the outset, the provider has a right to restitution from the moment of transfer. The transfer is always 'non-voluntary' and the recipient never obtains the unrestricted beneficial ownership of the property. There is no significant difference between this situation and one in which the provider of the property had a vitiated intention at the outset. A resulting trust should be possible in both.

The difference between initial and subsequent failures of consideration is revealed in *Neste Oy* v. *Lloyds Bank p.l.c.*[46] A shipping company had an agreement whereby they paid their agent in advance for expenses to be incurred by their ships entering ports in the United Kingdom. For each ship due to arrive, the agent would obtain payment of the estimated port costs and its agency fee for that ship. The agent became insolvent and the company sought a declaration that the funds which the agent had received from them, but not applied to port

[43] Ibid. 223. Approved but not applied in *Burgess* v. *Rawnsley* [1975] Ch. 429, C.A.
[44] See pp. 47–9 above. [45] See p. 73 above. [46] [1983] 2 Lloyd's L.R. 658.

costs, were held in trust. Bingham J. said that:[47] 'There was nothing in the payment or the receipt of these funds to show that they were paid or received on terms that they would be applied to the specified purpose and no other, and, if not so applied, would be returned'.

This disposed of the possibility of a *Quistclose* trust and Bingham J. held that five of the six payments in question were not held on trust for the company. However, the sixth payment was received after the agent had decided to stop trading and his lordship declared that this was held on constructive trust for the company:[48]

> It would have seemed little short of sharp practice for [the agent] to take any benefit from the payment, and it would have seemed contrary to any ordinary notion of fairness that the general body of creditors should profit from the accident of a payment made at a time when there was bound to be a failure of consideration.

Bingham J. quoted Cardozo J.'s statement in *Beatty* v. *Guggenheim Exploration Co.* that, 'When property has been acquired in such circumstances that the holder of the legal title may not in good conscience retain the beneficial interest, equity converts him into a trustee'.[49] This and similar authorities supported the declaration of a trust of the sixth payment. It would appear, then, that the agent could in good conscience retain the unused portions of the first five payments and owe only a personal obligation to make restitution of an equivalent sum. Failure of consideration does not itself justify the trust, but a failure at the outset does. This was recognized by the Privy Council in *Re Goldcorp Exchange Ltd.*,[50] where the providers had paid in advance for gold which they had not received when the vendor became insolvent. Their claim that the vendor held their payments on trust was rejected by Lord Mustill:[51]

> It is, of course, obvious that in the end the consideration did fail, when delivery was demanded and not made. But until that time the claimants had the benefit of what they had bargained for, a contract for the sale of unascertained goods. Quite plainly a customer could not on the day after a sale have claimed to recover the price for a total failure of consideration, and this at once puts paid to any question of a residuary proprietary interest and distinguishes the case from those such as *Sinclair* v. *Brougham*, where the transactions under which the moneys were paid were from the start ineffectual; and *Neste Oy* v. *Lloyds Bank Plc.*, where to the knowledge of the payee no performance at all could take place under the contract for which the payment formed the consideration.

It is noteworthy that Lord Mustill treats *Sinclair* v. *Brougham*,[52] which concerned the payment of money under a void contract, as a case in which the consideration failed at the outset. This was the best way to understand why the failure of consideration in that case gave rise to a resulting trust. However, the subsequent overruling of *Sinclair* v. *Brougham* by the House of Lords, in

[47] Ibid. 665. [48] Ibid. 666. [49] (1919) 225 N.Y. 380, 386.
[50] [1995] 1 A.C. 74. [51] Ibid. 103–4. [52] [1914] A.C. 398.

Westdeutsche v. *Islington*,[53] has cast doubt on that conclusion. This is discussed below in the section on void contracts.

Nature of the consideration

In his essay, 'Restitution and Resulting Trusts', Professor Birks explored the possibility that the application of resulting trusts to failures of consideration might depend on the nature of the consideration. For this purpose, he divided considerations into three categories: (i) 'a state of affairs agreed to be the basis of the transfer', other than 'performance undertaken by the other party', (ii) an undertaking to apply 'the money to a particular purpose' and (iii) an undertaking 'to be performed in response to but not with the money or other assets transferred'.[54] Birks admitted that this approach is not entirely satisfactory: the distinction between the categories is 'artificial' because '[t]he degree of conditionality is the same in every case'.[55]

Although the failure of a consideration in the second category (*Quistclose* trusts) will lead to a resulting trust because the nature of the purpose restricts the recipient's ownership of the property, the placement of a consideration in either of the other two categories does not indicate whether a resulting trust will be possible. Recovery in the first category may be proprietary[56] or merely personal[57] and the same is true of the third category.[58] It is suggested, with respect, that the partial success of this classification is coincidental and therefore detrimental, because it masks the true reasons why resulting trusts do or do not respond to failures of consideration. The circumstances of each case must be examined to see if the recipient became entitled to the unfettered beneficial ownership of the property before the consideration failed.[59] As Grant M.R. stated in *Morice* v. *Bishop of Durham*, 'an uncontrollable power of disposition would be ownership, and not a trust'.[60]

B. VOID CONTRACTS

The law relating to the recovery of money paid under a void contract is surprisingly difficult. There is some confusion over the proper application of the principles governing restitution on the ground of failure of consideration. This is exacerbated by a greater uncertainty concerning the role of the resulting trust as a response to failure of consideration. The root of the difficulty may be that insufficient attention has been paid to the distinction between the invalidity of the contract and the failure of consideration. As Professor Burrows states:[61]

[53] [1996] 2 All E.R. 961. [54] Birks (1992c) at p. 357. [55] Ibid.
[56] *Re Ames' Settlement* [1946] Ch. 217.
[57] *Guardian Ocean Cargoes* v. *Banco do Brasil* [1994] 2 Lloyd's L.R. 152.
[58] Cf. *Re Nanwa Goldmines Ltd.* [1955] 1 W.L.R. 1080; *Re Goldcorp Exchange Ltd.* [1995] 1 A.C. 74. [59] See Priestley at p. 234.
[60] (1804) 9 Ves. 399, 404. [61] Burrows (1993a), p. 304.

The law of restitution of money paid under a void contract is sometimes presented as if restitution follows automatically simply because the contract is void. This is inaccurate because it does not isolate the ground of restitution in play. In most void contracts the only possible ground is total failure of consideration, the primary exception being where the plaintiff can base his claim on a mistake of fact.

Examined below are three possible grounds for restitution of property transferred under an invalid contract: (i) failure of consideration, (ii) no consideration, and (iii) mistake.

1. Failure of Consideration

It is often assumed that the consideration for a payment made under a void contract fails merely because that contract is invalid. This assumption makes it difficult to understand why a resulting trust does not arise whenever money is paid under a void contract. The consideration would fail at the outset and a lack of intention to benefit the recipient would be present at the moment of transfer. The recipient would not obtain the unfettered beneficial ownership of the money before the right to restitution arises and there would be no impediment to a resulting trust (so long as the money or its substitute remained identifiable). As discussed below, this view is consistent with *Sinclair* v. *Brougham*,[62] but needs to be re-examined in light of *Westdeutsche* v. *Islington*.[63]

It is important to bear in mind the distinction between the narrow meaning of 'consideration' used in the law of contract and its broader meaning in the law of restitution. As Viscount Simon L.C. stated in *Fibrosa Spolka Akcyjna* v. *Fairbairn Lawson Combe Barbour Ltd.*:[64]

> [I]n the law relating to the formation of contract, the promise to do a thing may often be the consideration, but when one is considering the law of failure of consideration and of the quasi-contractual right to recover money on that ground, it is, generally speaking, not the promise which is referred to as the consideration, but the performance of the promise. The money was paid to secure performance and, if the performance fails the inducement which brought about the payment is not fulfilled.

His lordship was making the point that the previous existence of an obligation to make counter-performance will not preclude restitution if the counter-performance itself fails.[65] However, the converse is also true: the non-existence of the obligation to make counter-performance does not justify restitution on the basis of failure of consideration if the counter-performance is in fact received.[66]

[62] [1914] A.C. 398. [63] [1996] 2 All E.R. 961, H.L.

[64] [1943] A.C. 32, 48. Also see *Baltic Shipping Co.* v. *Dillon* (1993) 176 C.L.R. 344, 350–1; Birks (1993c) at 209–10.

[65] See Birks (1989a), p. 222; Burrows (1993a), pp. 251–2; Goff and Jones, pp. 407–9.

[66] Birks (1993c); Burrows (1995) at 17–18.

This is demonstrated by *Davis* v. *Bryan*, where the Court of King's Bench rejected a claim for restitution after a void annuity had run its full course:[67] 'The testator received the whole of that which he bargained for, and now his representative says that the contract was void from the beginning. Is there any thing like good conscience in the claim?'

The invalidity of the contract is not itself a failure of consideration. It is an event, like frustration or termination, which can lead to restitution on the basis of failure of consideration if the expected counter-performance is not received. This explains why a payment made under a void contract does not normally lead to a resulting trust. The consideration does not fail at the outset unless it is, at that time, impossible to achieve. As *Davis* v. *Bryan*[68] and *Neste Oy* v. *Lloyds Bank p.l.c.*[69] demonstrate, there is no necessary correlation between the invalidity of a contract and the impossibility of obtaining the anticipated counter-performance for which the payment was made. It is noteworthy that the American *Restatement of Restitution* treats 'payment upon a void agreement' and 'failure of purpose' as separate grounds of recovery (albeit both under the heading, 'mistake of law', discussed below).[70]

The view put forward here concerning the relationship between void contracts and failure of consideration is not easily reconciled with *Sinclair* v. *Brougham*, in which Viscount Haldane L.C. held that payments made under a void contract were held on resulting trust.[71] The House of Lords' decision in *Westdeutsche* v. *Islington*,[72] that a resulting trust does not arise in this situation, opens the door to a solution to the problems in this area of the law. However, the House of Lords did not explain why some failures of consideration lead to proprietary restitution but not others. It will be helpful to examine these two cases in some detail.

Sinclair v. *Brougham*

Sinclair v. *Brougham* concerned the winding up of a building society that had improperly carried on a banking business for many years. Borrowing for the business of banking was *ultra vires* the society and the contracts with its depositors, who had paid in over £10m., were void. The depositors and the society's 15,402 class 'A' shareholders agreed to pay the outside creditors and expenses and share the remaining assets of the society *pro rata*. The 28 holders of class 'B' shares, worth £13,300, did not agree to the compromise and an appeal was taken with respect to the fund set aside to pay their claims.

The House of Lords held that the policy which invalidated the borrowing contracts also prevented the depositors from claiming their deposits as money

[67] (1827) 6 B.&C. 651, 655, per Bayley J. [68] Ibid.
[69] [1983] 2 Lloyd's L.R. 658; see n. 46 above. [70] *Restatement of Restitution*, §47, §48.
[71] [1914] A.C. 398, 421. [72] [1996] 2 All E.R. 961.

had and received. However, the depositors were allowed to trace the deposits into the remaining assets of the society and assert an equitable right *in rem*, which ranked equally with the shareholders' claim to distribution of those assets on winding-up. This was a practical solution to the problem concerning the recovery of benefits conferred under void contracts: the contractual promise could not be enforced, directly or indirectly, but the depositors could recover any benefits still surviving in the hands of the society.

The basis of the depositors' equitable proprietary interests was not entirely clear due to the variety of speeches given by the law lords. Lord Parker held that the directors of the society had breached their fiduciary duties to the depositors and that the building society was 'in the position of a person who had innocently received from a fiduciary agent money belonging to another and invested it with money of his own'.[73] Although this view was accepted by the Court of Appeal in *Re Diplock*,[74] it is not easily reconciled with the facts of *Sinclair* v. *Brougham*, as Lord Goff and others have recognized.[75] It is difficult to understand why the directors were in a fiduciary relationship with the depositors and, if so, why they were in breach of their duties when the depositors had consented to the investment of their money.[76] It is also difficult to accept the classification of shareholders as innocent recipients and directors as fiduciaries in breach, when the 28 class 'B' shareholders included all of the directors of the society.[77]

Sinclair v. *Brougham* eventually came to be viewed as a resulting trust responding to a failure of consideration.[78] Viscount Haldane L.C., with whom Lord Atkinson agreed, said that the depositors had 'a claim to follow and recover property with which, in equity at all events, they never really parted'.[79] Following *Re Hallett's Estate*,[80] the remedy granted was an equitable charge over the mixed assets into which the depositors' money had been paid. As Viscount Haldane L.C. recognized, *Re Hallett* involved a breach of a fiduciary duty. However, his lordship did not think the remedy was limited to that situation:[81]

> It was, I think, merely an additional right, which could be enforced by the Court of Chancery in the exercise of its auxiliary jurisdiction, wherever money was held to belong in equity to the plaintiff. If so, . . . I see no reason why the remedy explained by Jessel M.R. in *Hallett's Case* . . . should not apply in the case of a transaction that is ultra vires. The property was never converted into a debt, in equity at all events, and there has been throughout a resulting trust, not of an active character, but sufficient, in my opinion, to bring the transaction within the general principle.

[73] [1914] A.C. 398, 445–6.
[74] [1948] Ch. 465; aff'd *Ministry of Health* v. *Simpson* [1951] A.C. 251.
[75] *Westdeutsche* v. *Islington* [1996] 2 All E.R. 961, 972; Gummow at p. 83; Evans, S., at 400.
[76] [1914] A.C. 398, 422–3, 458.
[77] [1912] 2 Ch. 183, 222–3, C.A.
[78] *Westdeutsche* v. *Islington* [1994] 4 All E.R. 890, 962, C.A.; [1996] 2 All E.R. 961, 968, 971–2, 994–5, H.L.; Birks (1989a), pp. 380–3, 387; Birks (1992c) at pp. 353–5; Butler (1990a) at p. 112; Gummow at pp. 82–3, 85.
[79] [1914] A.C. 398, 418.
[80] (1880) 13 Ch.D. 696, C.A.
[81] [1914] A.C. 398, 421.

For Viscount Haldane L.C., the depositors' equitable proprietary interest was a resulting trust created by a failure of consideration and not by a breach of a fiduciary obligation:[82]

> In the present case the investment was not made in breach of a fiduciary duty on the part of the society, and it was actually made with the authority of the depositors. What was a material point in *Hallett's Case*, therefore, does not occur here. No doubt it was ultra vires of the society to undertake to repay the money. But it was none the less intended that in consideration of giving such an undertaking the society should be entitled to deal with it freely as its own. The consideration failed and the depositors had the right to follow the money so far as invalidly borrowed into the assets in which it had been invested.

The resulting trust arose in *Sinclair* v. *Brougham* because the consideration for the payments by the depositors failed at the outset and that failure removed the society's right to use the money. It appears that Viscount Haldane L.C. viewed the failure of consideration as the failure of the obligation to render counter-performance and not the failure of the counter-performance itself. It might be possible to argue that there is no contradiction with *Fibrosa*[83] in this particular context. The payments in *Sinclair* v. *Brougham* were intended to be bank deposits and their immediate repayment would have rendered that arrangement nugatory. Bank deposits are commonly made for the purpose of creating an assignable chose-in-action, and, therefore, the undertaking to repay the money was an essential part of the intended counter-performance. This is not entirely satisfactory and the conclusion of the House of Lords in *Westdeutsche* v. *Islington*, that a payment under a void contract does not normally give rise to a resulting trust, saves us from having to rely on such fine distinctions.

Westdeutsche v. *Islington*

Westdeutsche Landesbank Girozentrale v. *Islington London Borough Council* involved an interest-rate swap agreement in which the parties made reciprocal loans to each other of £25m., one at a fixed rate of interest and the other at a floating rate. After it was discovered that the agreement was *ultra vires* the council,[84] the bank brought an action against the council to recover the difference between the £2.5m. paid by the bank and the £1.35m. paid by the council during the supposed validity of the agreement. Hobhouse J. and the Court of Appeal held that the council was personally liable at common law for that sum as money had and received, plus simple interest under the Supreme Court Act 1981, section 35A.[85] They also held, relying on *Sinclair* v. *Brougham*, that the bank had an equitable proprietary claim to the money, which entitled it to compound interest in equity. Dillon L.J. stated:[86]

[82] Ibid. 422–3.
[83] [1943] A.C. 32; see n. 64 above.
[84] *Hazell* v. *Hammersmith and Fulham L.B.C.* [1992] 2 A.C. 1.
[85] [1994] 4 All E.R. 890.
[86] Ibid. 962.

Since, contrary to the expectation of the parties, the swap transaction and contract are, and were from the outset, ultra vires and void, the purpose for which the £2.5m. was paid by Westdeutsche to Islington has wholly failed, and the £2.5m. has, from the time Islington received it, been held on a resulting trust for Westdeutsche: see the speech of Viscount Haldane L.C. in *Sinclair* v. *Brougham* . . .

Leave to appeal to the House of Lords was granted with respect only to the amount of interest payable, but the argument revolved around the proprietary claim on which the award of compound interest was based. All five members of the Appellate Committee decided that *Sinclair* v. *Brougham* was either incorrect or inapplicable and that the bank did not have a proprietary claim to the money paid. The majority held that the bank was entitled to statutory simple interest only. Lords Goff and Woolf dissented on the basis that compound interest would be payable on the bank's personal claim for restitution.

Lord Goff and Lord Browne-Wilkinson delivered speeches which considered and rejected the possibility of resulting trust (with Lords Lloyd and Slynn agreeing with the latter speech). Lord Woolf said of both speeches:[87]

That reasoning convinces me that the bank is not entitled to proceed by way of an equitable proprietary claim and that the recipient of a sum of money paid under an ultra vires contract should not be regarded as owing either the duties of a trustee or fiduciary to the payer of that sum. Further than that it is not necessary for me to go.

Reasons for rejecting the resulting trust

Various reasons were given by Lords Goff and Browne-Wilkinson for rejecting the resulting trust of a payment under a void contract: (i) it was not one of the traditional situations in which resulting trusts arise, (ii) there was no identifiable fund to which the trust could attach, (iii) the conscience of the recipient would not be affected until the invalidity of the contract was discovered and (iv) the recipient should not be subject to the onerous consequences of trusteeship.[88] Additionally, Lord Browne-Wilkinson suggested that resulting trusts arise in response to the common intention of the parties to create a trust.[89] None of these reasons directly concerns failure of consideration as an event to which the resulting trust responds. The issues raised by their lordships are examined elsewhere in this book and are discussed only briefly here.

As previous chapters reveal, the first reason is not convincing. The events which give rise to resulting trusts occur in a variety of situations and only an artificial restriction can confine them to the traditional categories. As Lord Goff said (in relation to the issue of compound interest):[90] 'Where the jurisdiction is founded on a principle of justice, I would expect that the categories of case where it is exercised should be regarded not as occupying the whole field but

[87] [1996] 2 All E.R. 961, 1002. [88] Ibid. 973–4, 986–91. [89] Ibid. 990–1.
[90] Ibid. 976.

rather as emanations of the principle, so that the possibility of the jurisdiction being extended to other categories of case is not foreclosed'. The *Quistclose* trust shows that resulting trusts already arise outside the traditional categories in response to failures of consideration. What is needed is an explanation why they do not respond to failures of consideration in cases like *Westdeutsche* v. *Islington.*

The second reason for rejecting the resulting trust, that there was no identifiable subject matter, is better than the first. As Dillon L.J. noted, 'the money initially received by Islington from Westdeutsche was spent by Islington on its ordinary purposes'.[91] The resulting trust cannot exist once the fund or its substitute ceased to be identifiable. However, this does not explain why a resulting trust would not arise at the moment of receipt when the fund was still identifiable. Another explanation is required.

The third reason, that the conscience of the council could not be affected until it became aware that the contract was void, suffers from the same inadequacy as Lord Browne-Wilkinson's additional suggestion that resulting trusts depend on the common intention of the parties to create a trust: neither can be reconciled with a large number of existing cases. As discussed above in Chapter 1, the resulting trust will arise even though the provider of the property or the recipient is unaware of the events to which it responds.[92] There is often no communication between the parties, let alone common intention, and the resulting trust can arise where the parties have not addressed their minds to the question of beneficial ownership[93] or the resulting trust was clearly not intended.[94] The suggestion that a trust cannot arise unless the trustee's conscience is affected, if acted upon, would not only change the law relating to resulting trusts, but have a drastic effect on the law relating to the creation and enforcement of equitable proprietary interests. This is discussed further in Chapter 9.

Lord Browne-Wilkinson first suggested that resulting trusts depended on the common intention of the parties in *Tinsley* v. *Milligan.*[95] In that case, both parties had contributed to the purchase of a home in the plaintiff's name. The intentions of both parties were relevant to the issue of resulting trust because they had both provided consideration for the purchase.[96] However, Lord Browne-Wilkinson relied on cases of constructive trust to conclude that a common intention was required.[97] His lordship's *obiter dictum* in *Westdeutsche* v. *Islington* mingles the requirements for resulting and constructive trusts, possibly because

[91] [1994] 4 All E.R. 890, 966.

[92] e.g. *Ryall* v. *Ryall* (1739) 1 Atk. 59; *Birch* v. *Blagrave* (1755) Amb. 265; *Childers* v. *Childers* (1857) 1 De G.&J. 482; *Williams* v. *Williams* (1863) 32 Beav. 370; *Goodfellow* v. *Robertson* (1871) 18 Gr. 572; *In re Vinogradoff* [1935] W.N. 68; *In re Muller* [1953] N.Z.L.R. 879.

[93] *Brown* v. *Brown* (1993) 31 N.S.W.L.R. 582, C.A.

[94] *Vandervell* v. *I.R.C.* [1967] 2 A.C. 291.

[95] [1994] 1 A.C. 340, 371.

[96] See *Cowcher* v. *Cowcher* [1972] 1 WLR 425, 431; *Calverley* v. *Green* (1984) 155 C.L.R. 242, 251; *Muschinski* v. *Dodds* (1985) A.L.J.R. 52, 54; pp. 36–7 above.

[97] *Grant* v. *Edwards* [1986] Ch. 638, C.A.; *Lloyds Bank p.l.c.* v. *Rosset* [1991] 1 A.C. 107.

of the confusion generated by the variety of speeches in *Pettitt* v. *Pettitt*[98] and *Gissing* v. *Gissing*[99] (and Lord Diplock's statement in the latter case that it was unnecessary to distinguish between resulting, implied, and constructive trusts because they were all exempt from the requirement of writing).[100]

The final reason for rejecting the resulting trust, that an innocent recipient should not be subject to the onerous consequences of trusteeship, is the most cogent of those offered. However, it rests on the unexplored assumption that the duties of a resulting trustee and the consequences of that trust are the same as those associated with an express trust. As discussed at length below in Chapter 9 and the Conclusion, this assumption is incorrect and the fear of extending the resulting trust further into commercial situations is exaggerated.

None of the reasons given for rejecting the resulting trust in *Westdeutsche* v. *Islington* is satisfactory. This should not be too surprising since its true nature was not fully argued or considered.[101] Leave to appeal had been granted with respect only to the award of interest and the law lords themselves raised the possibility that *Sinclair* v. *Brougham* was incorrect or inapplicable. As Lord Goff stated:[102]

> In these circumstances I regard it as particularly desirable that your Lordships should, as far as possible, restrict the inquiry to the actual questions at issue in this appeal, and not be tempted into formulating general principles of a broader nature. If restitution lawyers are hoping to find in your Lordships' speeches broad statements of principle which may definitively establish the future shape of this part of the law, I fear that they may be disappointed.

When did the consideration fail?

Westdeutsche v. *Islington* clearly established that the resulting trust does not arise in response to a payment under a void contract, but failed to explain why some failures of consideration do give rise to resulting trusts while others do not. Due to the limited scope of the appeal, the basis of the bank's entitlement to repayment was not explored. As Lord Goff stated:[103]

> The most serious problem which has remained in this connection is the theoretical question whether recovery can here be said to rest upon the ground of *failure* of consideration. Hobhouse J. thought not. He considered that the true ground in these cases, where the contract is void, is to be found in the absence, rather that the failure of consideration; and in this he was followed by the Court of Appeal. This had the effect that the courts below were not troubled by the question whether there had been a *total* failure of consideration . . . However, since there is before your Lordships no appeal from the decision that the bank was entitled to recover the balance of the payments so made in a personal claim in restitution, the precise identification of the ground of recovery was not explored in

[98] [1970] A.C. 777. [99] [1971] A.C. 886. [100] Ibid. 905. See p. 38 above.
[101] [1996] 2 All E.R. 961, 985–6, 1002, 1018. [102] Ibid. 970. [103] Ibid. 967–8.

argument before the Appellate Committee. It would therefore be inappropriate to express any concluded view upon it.

With no clear indication of the basis of the bank's entitlement to restitution, it is difficult to know why the resulting trust does not arise. Hobhouse J. was right to be concerned about the problems associated with the recovery of payments under void contracts on the basis of failure of consideration. He said that 'total failure of consideration does not suffice to give any right to recover the sums paid' because 'there has been partial performance by both sides and both sides have received benefits under the "contract"'.[104] He avoided the requirement of total failure by basing recovery on the absence of consideration (discussed below) rather than its failure. Lord Goff noted, but did not explore the problem:[105]

There has long been a desire among restitution lawyers to escape from the unfortunate effects of the so-called rule that money is only recoverable at common law on the ground of failure of consideration where the failure is total, by reformulating the rule upon a more principled basis; and signs that this will in due course be done are appearing in judgments throughout the common law world, as appropriate cases arise for decision.

Lord Browne-Wilkinson suggested that the failure of consideration in *Westdeutsche* v. *Islington* was total. Referring to *Sinclair* v. *Brougham*, his lordship stated:[106]

The failure of consideration was *not* partial: the depositors had paid over their money in consideration of a promise to repay. That promise was ultra vires and void; therefore the consideration for the payment of the money wholly failed. So in the present swaps case (though the point is not one under appeal) I think the Court of Appeal were right to hold that the swap moneys were paid on a consideration that wholly failed.

This is difficult to reconcile with *Fibrosa*, where Viscount Simon L.C. said of failure of consideration that 'it is, generally speaking, not the promise which is referred to as the consideration, but the performance of the promise'.[107] It also encounters two other serious difficulties. First, why is someone, who has received everything promised under a void contract, not entitled to restitution on the ground of total failure of consideration?[108] Secondly and more importantly for the resulting trust, why is the recipient, who is obliged to make restitution of the payment from the moment of receipt, entitled to the unfettered beneficial ownership of that money? Lord Browne-Wilkinson's suggestion should lead to the conclusion reached by Viscount Haldane L.C., in *Sinclair* v. *Brougham*, that the failure of the promise to repay the money prevents the recipient from being 'entitled to deal with it freely as its own'.[109]

[104] [1994] 4 All E.R. 890, 925.
[105] [1996] 2 All E.R. 961, 967.
[106] Ibid. 993.
[107] [1943] A.C. 32, 48; see n. 64 above.
[108] See Birks (1993c); Burrows (1995).
[109] [1914] A.C. 398, 423.

Lord Goff believed that Islington had obtained the beneficial ownership of the money paid by Westdeutsche:[110]

> [T]here is no general rule that the property in money paid under a void contract does not pass to the payee; and it is difficult to escape the conclusion that, as a general rule, the beneficial interest to the money likewise passes to the payee. This must certainly be the case where the consideration for the payment fails after the payment is made, as in cases of frustration or breach of contract; and there appears to be no good reason why the same should not apply in cases where, as in the present case, the contract under which the payment is made is void ab initio and the consideration for the payment therefore fails at the time of the payment.

Except for the unexplored assumption that the consideration for a payment under a void contract fails at the outset, this statement is undoubtedly correct and explains why the resulting trust does not arise in this situation. As Lord Mustill recognized in *Re Goldcorp Exchange Ltd.*,[111] the difference between initial and subsequent failures of consideration is fundamentally important to the issue of proprietary restitution. In the latter situation, the proprietary base is lost and the claim is necessarily personal.

Westdeutsche v. *Islington* is best understood as a case in which the consideration for the payment failed subsequently when the parties discovered the invalidity of the contract and performance came to a halt. The only difficulty with this view is 'the so-called rule that money is only recoverable at common law on the ground of failure of consideration where the failure is total'.[112] It is better to confront and modify that rule rather than distort the concept of failure of consideration to avoid it. The restriction no longer applies to cases of frustration,[113] has been subject to a great deal of criticism[114] and is unlikely to survive intact much longer. As the majority of the High Court of Australia stated in *David Securities Pty. Ltd.* v. *Commonwealth Bank of Australia*:[115] 'In cases where consideration can be apportioned or where counter-restitution is relatively simple, insistence on total failure of consideration can be misleading or confusing . . . [A]ny rationale for adhering to the traditional rule requiring *total* failure of consideration disappears'.

Contractual invalidity does have two significant effects not found in other cases of failure of consideration. First, there is no consideration (in the narrow sense) for payments made under a void contract. This eliminates a possible defence based on either bona fide purchase for value or good faith exchange.[116] However, as discussed below, the absence of contractual consideration is not

[110] [1996] 2 All E.R. 961, 973–4. [111] [1995] 1 A.C. 74. 103–4; see n. 51 above.

[112] *Westdeutsche* v. *Islington* [1996] 2 All E.R. 961, 967, per Lord Goff.

[113] Law Reform (Frustrated Contracts) Act 1943; see Goff and Jones, p. 450.

[114] Beatson (1991), pp. 3–4, 63–4, 70–5; Goff and Jones, pp. 402–3, 412–13; Maddaugh and McCamus, pp. 309–10, 338, 424–5, 439; Mason and Carter, §926.

[115] (1992) 175 C.L.R. 353, 383; approved in *Goss* v. *Chilcott* [1996] 3 W.L.R. 180, 188, P.C.

[116] *Lipkin Gorman* v. *Karpnale Ltd.* [1991] 2 A.C. 548.

itself a ground for restitution. Secondly, the invalidity of the contract may give rise to restitution on the basis of mistake as well as failure of consideration.[117] This is also discussed below.

2. No Consideration

The possiblity of restitution on the basis that money has been paid for 'no consideration' cropped up recently in two important cases: *Woolwich Equitable Building Society* v. *I.R.C.*[118] and *Westdeutsche* v. *Islington.*[119] In *Woolwich*, Lord Browne-Wilkinson stated that, 'money was demanded and paid for tax, yet no tax was due: there was a payment for no consideration'.[120] However, his lordship did not suggest that 'no consideration' is a general-purpose unjust factor, but only where 'money paid under an ultra vires demand for a tax or other impost has been paid without consideration'.[121] He was in favour of 'establishing the law in the sense which Lord Goff proposes',[122] which included a clear rejection of 'no consideration' as a sufficient unjust factor.

Lord Goff stated that, 'Where a sum has been paid which is not due, but it has not been paid under a mistake of fact or under compulsion . . . it is generally not recoverable'.[123] The recovery of 'money paid to a public authority pursuant to an ultra vires demand'[124] is a limited exception to that principle:[125]

> [O]ur law of restitution . . . might have developed so as to recognise a condictio indebiti—an action for the recovery of money on the ground that it was not due. But it did not do so. Instead . . . there developed common law actions for the recovery of money paid under mistake of fact, and under certain forms of compulsion. What is now being sought is, in a sense, a reversal of that development, in a particular type of case.

Lord Goff held that policy reasons justified the exceptional recovery of taxes 'levied without the authority of Parliament',[126] not the mere absence of consideration.

Despite Lord Goff's comments on 'no consideration' as an unjust factor, Hobhouse J. used it for that purpose in *Westdeutsche* v. *Islington*. His Lordship did not refer to *Woolwich* v. *I.R.C.* in that part of his judgment, but relied on a series of cases involving void annuities to conclude that:[127] 'The right to restitution arises from the fact that the payment made by the plaintiff to the defendant was made under a purported contract which, unknown to the plaintiff and the defendant, was ultra vires the defendant and wholly void. There was no consideration for the making the payment'.

Hobhouse J. rejected failure of consideration as an unjust factor, because there had never been a valid contract and the failure of consideration had not

[117] *Rover Int. Ltd.* v. *Cannon Film Sales Ltd.* [1989] 1 W.L.R. 912, C.A.
[118] [1993] 1 A.C. 70. [119] [1994] 4 All E.R. 890. [120] [1993] 1 A.C. 70, 198.
[121] Ibid. 197. [122] Ibid. 198. [123] Ibid. 165. [124] Ibid. 166.
[125] Ibid. 172. [126] Ibid. [127] [1994] 4 All E.R. 890, 955–6.

been total. Additionally, in one of the interest-rate swap transactions, 'the contemplated contract was in fact fully performed and neither party can, on the contractual approach, say that there was any failure of consideration, let alone any total failure'.[128]

The Court of Appeal affirmed the judgment of Hobhouse J., subject to a variation of the date when interest began to accrue. Leggatt L.J. agreed with Hobhouse J. that the basis for recovery was 'no consideration' rather than failure of consideration. His lordship noted that the decision in *Woolwich* v. *I.R.C.* 'could be treated as confined to cases of money paid pursuant to an unlawful demand by a public authority', but still thought that the principle was generally applicable to void contracts.[129] The basis of Dillon L.J.'s judgment is not as clear. His lordship seemed to say that there was both a failure of consideration and no consideration for the payment. However, when discussing the annuity cases on which the 'no consideration' approach is based, Dillon L.J. stated:[130] 'The payments were not to be considered as purely voluntary because they had been intended to be made for the consideration expressed in the annuity deed. That is equally the case with the payments each way in the present case. Neither party intended to make a gift to the other'.

As discussed above,[131] the appeal to the House of Lords was restricted to the amount of interest awarded. Therefore, the basis of the bank's entitlement to restitution was not explored. Several commentators have argued strongly and persuasively against the use of 'no consideration' as a ground of restitution.[132] As Burrows stated:[133]

> [A]cceptance of such an idea would radically transform the law of restitution. On the face of it all gifts would now be recoverable. And the existing approach to mistake of fact and duress would be side-stepped if a payer could simply recover (subject to defences) were there has been no consideration. Moreover, the mistake of law bar would be emasculated at a stroke.
>
> Even if one somehow confined 'absence of consideration' to void contracts, it would contradict authority. In the leading cases on restitution of money paid under void contracts, *Sinclair* v. *Brougham* [1914] A.C. 398 and *Rover International Ltd.* v. *Cannon Film Sales Ltd. (No. 3)* [1989] 1 W.L.R. 912, the claims for money had and received were formulated and discussed entirely in terms of failure of consideration and mistake of fact.

All of the cases in which the provider is entitled to restitution of benefits conferred under an invalid contract can be explained on the basis of 'failure of consideration', except one: where the transaction has been completed and both parties have received all they had bargained for. This difference creates an

[128] Ibid. 925, per Hobhouse J. [129] [1994] 4 All E.R. 890, 968. See Swadling (1994a) at 79.
[130] Ibid. 962. See Swadling (1994a) at 75–8. [131] See n. 103 above.
[132] Birks (1993c); Burrows (1993c); Evans, S.; Swadling (1994a); Swadling (1994c); Burrows (1995). [133] Burrows (1993c).

additional argument against restitution on the basis of 'no consideration'. As Birks stated, 'The plaintiff who has received all that he expected under the contract has no substantial ground for restitution' and, therefore, 'his only hope of restitution in respect of his own performance is the technical appeal to "absence of consideration" since, substantially, the consideration has not failed'.[134] For this reason and those set out above, lack of consideration does not provide an adequate justification for restitution.

The presumption of resulting trust is as close as the common law (outside Canada)[135] comes to restitution on the basis of no consideration.[136] It arises where the recipient of property has not provided all of the consideration for the transfer (subject to the presumption of advancement and section 60(3) of the Law of Property Act 1925).[137] However, as discussed above,[138] the lack of consideration is not the basis of the resulting trust, but merely a fact from which the court will infer a lack of intention to benefit the recipient, i.e. a non-voluntary transfer. It is this lack of voluntariness which motivates restitution. Lack of consideration is neither a sufficient basis for the resulting trust (where evidence of an intention to give or lend is available) nor a necessary one.

A transfer of property for 'no consideration' should have the same effect in commercial settings as it does in other situations. In all cases, it should be treated as a circumstance from which the court will infer an absence of intention to benefit the recipient. The presumption of resulting trust does not normally arise where a deed of transfer recites that valuable consideration has been paid or is payable by the recipient. However, where the recital is proven to be false, the presumption will arise in favour of the persons who have provided the consideration for the transfer.[139] Similarly, the presumption should apply where money is paid under a contract which turns out to be void. In both cases, an apparent consideration has turned out not to be due and, if in fact it has not been provided, the presumption of resulting trust should arise. 'No consideration' will not directly motivate restitution, but should (in the absence of evidence to the contrary) provide an inference of non-voluntary transfer, which is capable of doing so.

In most cases, a presumption of resulting trust will not give rise to a resulting trust of money paid under a void contract, because the recipient would obtain the unfettered beneficial ownership of the money at the moment of receipt. However, there may be exceptional cases where that does not occur. In any event, it might be argued that absence of consideration should play the same role for both personal and proprietary claims for restitution by raising an inference

[134] Birks (1993c) at 214, 222. See *Davis* v. *Bryan* (1827) 6 B.&C. 651, n. 67 above.

[135] In *Rathwell* v. *Rathwell* [1978] 2 S.C.R. 436, 455, 'absence of any juristic reason' was accepted as a general unjust factor, possibly through the influence of Québec civil law: L.D. Smith (1992) at 677. See Challies, p. 58; Maddaugh and McCamus, p. 2; Birks (1993c) at 231–2.

[136] See Birks (1989a), p. 9, fn. 1; Burrows (1995) at 26.

[137] Above, pp. 18–19.

[138] At pp. 32, 115.

[139] Above, p. 13.

that the payment was non-voluntary in the circumstances which have occurred. The label 'presumption of resulting trust' is somewhat misleading and unduly restrictive. However, the underlying principle, that a transfer of property for no consideration gives rise to an inference that the provider did not intend to benefit the recipient, ought to be capable of wider application.

3. Mistake

A proper understanding of the relationship between contractual invalidity and failure of consideration would go a long way towards solving the problems associated with the recovery of benefits conferred under void contracts. However, it will not provide a final solution on its own. Plaintiffs with only a personal claim based on failure of consideration will seek to argue that they also have a proprietary claim based on mistake. As recognized in *Rover International Ltd.* v. *Cannon Film Sales Ltd.*,[140] money paid under a void contract is paid for both a consideration which fails and by mistake. In *Westdeutsche* v. *Islington*, the bank claimed restitution on both grounds, but failed on the latter because the mistake was not of fact, but of law.[141]

As discussed in the previous chapter,[142] the rule barring recovery for mistake of law is much criticized, has been overturned in other jurisdictions and is unlikely to survive much longer. The rule does not apply in the USA and it is instructive to note that, according to section 47 of the *Restatement of Restitution*, a person who transfers property to another under a void agreement 'is entitled to restitution from the other if the transferor, because of a mistake of law, (a) erroneously believed the promise to be binding upon him and (b) did not obtain the benefit expected by him in return'.

In *Nuveen* v. *Board of Public Instruction*,[143] the plaintiff had purchased municipal bonds, which turned out to be void, having been issued *ultra vires* of the city. He was able to trace the purchase-money into a school house and claim an equitable proprietary interest in it. Remarkably, the mistake of law produced the same consequences as did the failure of consideration in *Sinclair* v. *Brougham*:[144]

> All having been honestly mistaken, there is no reason why one should lose its contribution rather than the others. The indivisible thing that was produced ought equitably to be shared in proportion to their several contributions toward it . . . Equity will declare a constructive trust in proportion to the contributions of purchase money.

If restitution does become available for mistakes of law, the questions raised in *Westdeutsche* v. *Islington* will need to be re-examined. The intention of a person who pays money under a void contract will be vitiated from the outset

[140] [1989] 1 W.L.R. 912, C.A. [141] [1994] 4 All E.R. 890, 906, 929, 933.
[142] Above, pp. 125–6. [143] (1937) 88 F.2d 175, C.A., 5th Circ.
[144] Ibid. 179, per Sibley J.

and the conditions for a resulting trust will be met. It may turn out that the solution provided by *Sinclair* v. *Brougham* is satisfactory if grounded on mistake rather than failure of consideration. Recovery on the basis of mistake will not be trouble free, but it may prove to be a surer foundation on which to build.[145]

C. RECIPIENT'S KNOWLEDGE

It has been suggested that restitution on the basis of the provider's qualified intention to benefit the recipient is not possible unless the provider has communicated that qualification to the recipient or knows that the recipient is aware of it.[146] However, the resulting trust contradicts this suggestion. It is clear that a resulting trust is possible even though the recipient is unaware of the transfer,[147] let alone the conditions on which it was made. In *Re Vinogradoff* and *Re Muller*,[148] property was transferred to very young children who were unaware of the transfer. In both cases, there was no evidence of the provider's intentions and the presumption of resulting trust was applied. It would certainly be anomalous if that presumption could have been rebutted by proof of a failed, but uncommunicated, purpose for the transfer.

In *Birch* v. *Blagrave*,[149] a father conveyed property to his daughter for the purpose of reducing his estate below a certain value in order to disqualify himself from becoming the Sheriff of London. He intended to retain the beneficial interest in the property conveyed to his daughter and did not inform her of the conveyance. On discovering that this arrangement would not permit him to swear the required oath for disqualification, he paid the usual fine for not accepting the office. The father and daughter died and the father's devisees recovered the property from the daughter's heirs. Lord Hardwicke C. decreed,[150] 'that the deeds . . . proceeded from and were founded on a mistake in the said testator, and were made for a particular purpose which never took effect, and that therefore the trust and beneficial interest thereof ought to be deemed in this court to remain in himself, and to be subject to his disposition by his will'. Even though the daughter never learned of the conveyance, the purpose had failed and there was a resulting trust for the father.[151]

Childers v. *Childers* was similar.[152] A father conveyed land to his son for the purpose of qualifying the son to be a bailiff of Bedford Level. 'The son died

[145] See Birks (1993c) at 228–31; Evans, S.; Mason and Carter, §1016; Carter at pp. 150–2.

[146] Birks (1991a) at pp. 115–6; Burrows (1993a), pp. 320–1.

[147] See *Standing* v. *Bowring* (1885) 16 Ch.D. 282, C.A.; *Dreger* v. *Dreger* [1994] 10 W.W.R. 293, Man.C.A.

[148] [1935] W.N. 68; [1953] N.Z.L.R. 879.

[149] (1755) Amb. 264.

[150] Ibid. 266.

[151] Mowbray, *Lewin on Trusts*, p. 117, treats *Birch* v. *Blagrave* as a resulting trust based on mistake.

[152] (1857) 1 De G.&J. 482.

soon after without having ever heard of the transaction'.[153] It was declared that the son's heiress was a trustee of the land for the father in spite of the argument that 'there was no understanding between the grantor and the grantee; nothing to raise an equity against the latter'.[154]

In *Rose* v. *Rose*,[155] a husband and wife separated and the husband paid the wife for her share of their jointly owned home. The husband's solicitors concocted an elaborate scheme to save stamp duty on the conveyance, which required the husband to declare a trust of the property for the wife. The scheme failed because most of the documents were unregisterable. However, the husband's declaration of trust was valid and the wife claimed an interest in the home when she learned of that declaration 7 years later. Hodgson J. held that the failure of the purpose of the declaration gave rise to a *Quistclose* trust and stated:[156]

> [I]f the declaration of trust is made for a particular purpose, to be effected without the co-operation of the beneficiary, then it does not matter for the purpose of the *Barclays Bank Ltd.* v. *Quistclose Investments Ltd.* doctrine if the beneficiary who has not even heard of the declaration of trust itself does not know and accept the purpose for which the declaration was made.

These cases show that a qualified intention to benefit the recipient can give rise to a resulting trust even though the qualification has not been communicated to the recipient. This does not place the resulting trust out of step with other responses to failure of consideration, but falsifies the assumption that the recipient must be aware of the qualification, thereby bringing failure of consideration into line with other cases of non-voluntary transfer. The recipient of a mistaken payment need not be aware of the provider's mistake[157] and there was never a convincing reason why a qualified intention should be treated any differently. The real relevance of the recipient's knowledge is for the defences of *bona fide* purchase and good faith exchange. Recipients who have given value for a transfer are not affected by qualifications of which they were unaware,[158] but volunteers are liable to restitution regardless of their knowledge or innocence. The same rules apply when the provider is mistaken.[159]

In *Burgess* v. *Rawnsley*,[160] a man and a woman had purchased a house in trust for themselves as joint tenants. Each had a separate, uncommunicated purpose for doing so and the Court of Appeal held (with Lord Denning M.R. disagreeing on this point) that there could be no failure of consideration 'where a trust is created by two people and where there is a failure of purpose for which one of them created the trust but which he did not communicate to the other party and

[153] Ibid. [154] Ibid. 487. [155] (1986) 7 N.S.W.L.R. 679.
[156] Ibid. 686.
[157] *Re Diplock* [1948] Ch. 465; aff'd *Ministry of Health* v. *Simpson* [1951] A.C. 251.
[158] See *Barclays Bank Ltd.* v. *Quistclose Investments Ltd.* [1970] A.C. 567, 582; Oditah at 475.
[159] See pp. 131–2 above. [160] [1975] Ch. 429.

the other did not share'.[161] This can be explained by the fact that there were two contributors to the purchase. As parties to a contract, neither was bound by any secret reservations or qualifications the other might have had. The validity of their contract was preserved by their good faith and absence of notice of the other's qualified intention.[162]

Birks suggests that, unless the provider and recipient have a shared understanding of the purpose of the transfer, the provider has taken the risk that the purpose will not be met and, therefore, is not entitled to restitution on the basis of non-voluntary transfer.[163] It is certainly true that the purpose may be merely a motive for, rather than a condition of, the transfer. The lack of communication of the purpose is a good indication that the purpose was only a motive, but it does not conclusively prove that fact. Communication may serve an important evidentiary function which prevents a disappointed risk-taker from claiming restitution on the basis of an alleged secret qualification of intention to benefit the recipient. In the USA, that problem is avoided by relying on the intentions that providers have 'manifested', without regard to any they might secretly hold.[164]

D. SUMMARY

Where the provider of property to another had only a qualified intention to benefit the recipient in circumstances which have failed to arise or continue as expected, the transfer becomes non-voluntary on that failure and a resulting trust may arise, so long as the property remains identifiable and the recipient has not obtained the unfettered beneficial ownership of the property. If the recipient does obtain the unrestricted use of the property before the right to restitution arises, the 'proprietary base' is lost and the provider will only be entitled to a personal claim for restitution, if any. The proprietary base may be preserved if (i) the consideration fails at the outset, (ii) the property is provided to be used for specific purposes only (i.e. a *Quistclose* trust) or (iii) there is some incidental fetter on the recipient's beneficial ownership between receipt and the failure of consideration.

Where property is transferred under a void contract, the consideration does not fail at the outset, but only subsequently when the invalidity is discovered and the expected counter-performance is not obtained. Therefore, the resulting trust

[161] Ibid. 442, per Browne L.J.

[162] Barker (1995a) at pp. 198–201; Burrows (1993a), pp. 472–3; pp. 36–7 above.

[163] Birks (1991a) at pp. 115–18; Birks (1992a), p. 57. Also see Burrows (1993a), pp. 320–1.

[164] See *Restatement of Restitution*, §57, §58. See *Springette* v. *Defoe* (1992) 24 H.L.R. 552, C.A., where an intention regarding the ownership of a family home did not give rise to a constructive trust because it had not been manifested by words or conduct. Also see *Bosse* v. *Lecke* (1979) 26 N.B.R. (2d) 1, 13, and Hovius and Youdan, pp. 36–8, regarding manifestation of intention required for express trusts.

does not arise because the recipient obtains the unfettered beneficial ownership of the property at the moment of receipt. Absence of consideration is not itself a sufficient reason for restitution, but merely gives rise to an inference of non-voluntary transfer, i.e. a presumption of resulting trust. If restitution becomes possible on the basis of mistake of law, a payment made under a void contract may give rise to a resulting trust because the provider's intention to benefit the recipient will be vitiated from the outset.

Where the recipient is unaware that the provider has only a qualified intention to transfer the benefit of the property, the resulting trust is still possible, unless the recipient is entitled to the defence of *bona fide* purchase or good faith exchange.

7
Mere Equities

There are a variety of ways to reverse unjust enrichment. Three traditional equitable responses to non-voluntary transfer are rectification (correcting mistakes in written documents), rescission (setting aside transactions entered by mistake, undue influence, etc.), and resulting trusts. All three can lead to the recovery of property. Although rectification and rescission can arise in the same case as alternative responses to the same mistake,[1] it has been commonly assumed that these responses do not overlap with the resulting trust (i.e. that the facts which give rise to rectification or rescission will not also give rise to a resulting trust). However, this assumption is no longer valid. As argued in Chapter 5, the resulting trust can apply whenever the provider's intention to benefit the recipient is absent or vitiated, even though the provider is otherwise entitled to recover the property through rectification or rescission.

It is argued in this chapter that, whenever a provider of property to another is entitled to rescind a transaction or recity an instrument and thereby recover any portion of that property, the recipient holds the recoverable property on a resulting trust for the provider from the moment the right of rescission or rectification first arises. In this situation, the order for rectification or rescission restores title to the provider, while the resulting trust means that the provider retains the beneficial ownership of the property until that occurs. As discussed above,[2] the few cases in which courts have considered both rescission and the resulting trust (and rejected one or the other) do not present an obstacle to the present argument. The remaining objection is derived from *Phillips* v. *Phillips*,[3] where Lord Westbury C. said that a person with a right to rescind or rectify a transaction has a mere equity and no equitable interest in the property involved. This chapter is devoted to removing that objection.

A. *PHILLIPS* V. *PHILLIPS*

In *Phillips* v. *Phillips*, an equitable estate, over which the plaintiff had a charge, was conveyed to the defendants as part of a marriage settlement. Lord Westbury C. explained why the defence of *bona fide* purchase was not available to the defendants, who were purchasers for value of the equitable estate:[4]

[1] See *Riverlate Properties Ltd.* v. *Paul* [1975] Ch. 133, C.A. [2] At pp. 139–42.
[3] (1862) 4 De G.F.&J. 208. [4] Ibid. at 215.

I take it to be a clear proposition that every conveyance of an equitable interest is an innocent conveyance, that is to say, the grant of a person entitled merely in equity passes only that which he is justly entitled to and no more. If, therefore, a person seised of an equitable estate (the legal estate being outstanding), makes an assurance by way of mortgage or grants an annuity, and afterwards conveys the whole estate to a purchaser, he can grant to the purchaser that which he has, viz., the estate subject to the mortgage or annuity, and no more. The subsequent grantee takes only that which is left in the grantor.

The difficulty is not with this well-established principle, but with Lord Westbury C.'s further explanation of a situation to which the principle does not apply:[5]

[W]here there are circumstances that give rise to an equity as distinguished from an equitable estate—as for example, an equity to set aside a deed for fraud, or to correct it for mistake—and the purchaser under the instrument maintains the plea of purchase for valuable consideration without notice, the Court will not interfere.

This *obiter dictum* is not only a potential impediment to the present argument, but has proved difficult to reconcile with many other cases on the subject.

Mere equities are considered to be of a lesser nature than equitable proprietary interests. So, for example, a mere equity relating to land is incapable of being an overriding interest under subsection 70(1)(g) of the Land Registration Act 1925.[6] This is also the reason why a mere equity may be defeated by a subsequent purchaser of an equitable interest for value without notice of that equity. The present difficulty lies not with the nature of a mere equity, but with the classification of rights to rescission or rectification as mere equities. It is submitted that these rights are mere equities only when they do not lead to the recovery of property.

B. EQUITABLE INTERESTS IN RECOVERABLE PROPERTY

1. Established Principle

There are many cases establishing that a person with the right to recover property through rectification or rescission has an equitable proprietary interest in the recoverable property and can transfer that interest to third parties. In *Stump* v. *Gaby*,[7] Lord St. Leonards C. held that the grantor of a voidable conveyance continued to be the equitable owner of the property conveyed and could devise his interest in the property, even though no steps had been taken to avoid the conveyance. This was approved in *Gresley* v. *Mousley*,[8] where a testator had sold property at an undervalue to his solicitor and then devised all his real estate to the plaintiff. Knight Bruce and Turner L.JJ. held that the testator had been entitled to set aside the sale and therefore had 'a devisable interest in the property

[5] Ibid. at 218. [6] *National Provincial Bank Ltd.* v. *Ainsworth* [1965] A.C. 1175.
[7] (1852) 2 De G.M.&G. 623; see p. 136 above. [8] (1859) 4 De G.&J. 78.

sold'.[9] It is remarkable that, in *Phillips* v. *Phillips*, no reference was made to either of these cases, which were decided in the previous decade.[10]

In *Dickinson* v. *Burrell*,[11] James Dickinson had conveyed his interest in an estate and, believing the conveyance to have been fraudulently obtained, settled the same interest in trust for his children. The children were entitled to bring an action to set aside the conveyance, but only because their father had an interest in the property he had conveyed. As Romilly M.R. stated:[12]

> [I]f James Dickinson had sold or conveyed the right to sue to set aside the indenture . . . without conveying the property, or his interest in the property, which is the subject of that indenture, that would not have entitled the grantee, A.B., to maintain this bill, but if A.B. had bought the whole of the interest of James Dickinson in the property, then it would. The right of suit is a right incidental to the property conveyed.

It was essential that James Dickinson had an equitable interest and not a mere equity, because the conveyance of his right of rescission, without his equitable interest, would not have entitled his children to sue.[13]

In *Melbourne Banking Corp.* v. *Brougham*,[14] the plaintiff's official assignee in bankruptcy had released his equity of redemption in a sheep station. The plaintiff took a transfer by deed of all the property that had vested in his assignee and sued to rescind the release. The Privy Council advised that the plaintiff (respondent) had standing to bring the action:[15]

> It was contended at the bar that this conveyance was not sufficient to enable the respondent to institute a suit to set aside the release of May, 1870 . . . but if that release was voidable in equity, it is clear, both on principle and on authority, that there was an equitable interest in the Alma station, which, in 1877, continued to be part of the estate vested in the official assignee, and that the deed . . . was sufficient to pass that interest.

Gross v. *Lewis Hillman Ltd.*[16] is a more difficult case that has been subject to some criticism,[17] but it does indicate that it is the equitable interest in recoverable property, and not the mere right of rescission, which is transferable. The plaintiff had purchased some property from the defendant in reliance on misrepresentations made by the defendant. However, the misrepresentations were made to a third party corporation, which had contracted to purchase the property and then authorized the defendant to convey to the plaintiff. The Court of Appeal rejected the plaintiff's argument that the third party's 'right to rescind the contract was attached to the equitable interest in the property which it acquired under the contract and passed to the plaintiff'.[18] Cross L.J. stated:[19]

[9] Ibid. at 89, per Knight Bruce L.J.
[10] See *Latec Investments Ltd.* v. *Hotel Terrigal Pty. Ltd.* (1965) 113 C.L.R. 265, 277.
[11] (1866) L.R. 1 Eq. 337.
[12] Ibid. at 342.
[13] Cf. Neave and Weinberg at 136.
[14] (1882) 7 App.Cas. 307. See p. 128 above.
[15] Ibid. at 311, per Selborne L.C.
[16] [1970] Ch. 445.
[17] Meagher, Gummow and Lehane, §429, p. 121; Neave and Weinberg at 136.
[18] [1970] Ch. 445, 460, per Cross L.J.
[19] Ibid. at 460–1.

Counsel sought to support his contention that a right to rescind for misrepresentation runs with the land taken by the original representee by reference to *Dickinson* v. *Burrell*... But that was a different sort of case. There, property had been assigned by A. to B., in circumstances which, so it was claimed, gave A. an equitable right to recover it and so an equitable interest in it. A. assigned that equitable interest to C., and it was held that C. could sue B. to recover the legal estate. That case does not appear to support the proposition advanced by counsel in the present case. Here, the assignee is not claiming to recover an equitable interest in the property previously conveyed away by his assignor, but is claiming to throw back the property assigned to him not on his immediate assignor but on the party who sold it to his assignor. So that point, in my judgment, fails.

The third party could have rescinded the transaction and recovered the purchase price if it had completed the purchase for itself. In that event, it would have had an equitable interest in the purchase money in the hands of the defendant. However, when the contract was assigned to the plaintiff, the third party had not completed the transaction and rescission would not have led to the recovery of property from the defendant. The third party assigned only its right to complete the purchase and not any equitable interest in recoverable property (which it did not have). The Court of Appeal concluded that the assignment of the right to purchase did not include the assignor's right to reject the purchased property for misrepresentation. This must be correct, for otherwise it should have been possible for the plaintiff to rescind even if she had been unaware of misrepresentations. The real difficulty in the case is the plaintiff's lack of a direct right of rescission against the defendant, whose misrepresentation she had relied on.

In each of the cases described above, the plaintiff was claiming the right of rescission as a transferee from the original victim of the fraud. The success of that claim depended on whether the plaintiff had acquired an equitable interest in property recoverable by rescission. In *Blacklocks* v. *J.B. Developments (Godalming) Ltd.*,[20] the defendant was the transferee from the man to whom the plaintiff had mistakenly conveyed too much land. The plaintiff was able to rectify the original conveyance and recover the additional land because he had an equitable interest in the recoverable portion. He was in occupation of that portion and his equitable interest was enforceable against the defendant as an overriding interest.[21] A mere equity would have been insufficient.[22]

2. Comparison with Constructive Trusts

As disussed above, it is well established that a person who can rectify or rescind a transaction has an equitable interest in any property recoverable thereby. Instructive parallels can be drawn between this and another well established principle

[20] [1982] Ch. 183; see p. 127 above. [21] Land Registration Act 1925, s. 70(1)(g).

[22] *National Provincial Bank Ltd.* v. *Ainsworth* [1965] A.C. 1175; *Williams & Glynn's Bank Ltd.* v. *Boland* [1981] A.C. 487.

that a constructive trust arises in favour of a purchaser under a specifically enforceable contract of sale. As Jessel M.R. said in *Lysaght* v. *Edwards*:[23]

> It appears to me that the effect of a contract for sale has been settled for more than two centuries . . . [T]he moment you have a valid contract for sale the vendor becomes in equity a trustee for the purchaser of the estate sold, and the beneficial ownership passes to the purchaser . . .

The constructive trust in this situation exists 'only if and so far as a Court of Equity would in all the circumstances of the case grant specific performance of the contract'.[24]

The equitable interest that arises in favour of someone who can recover property through rectification or rescission bears some important similarities to the equitable interest that arises in favour of a purchaser under a specifically enforceable contract of sale. They both arise (at least superficially) because a person can compel the transfer of property to himself or herself through the use of what is commonly regarded as a discretionary equitable remedy.[25] Both interests arise at the outset when the facts which give rise to a right to seek rectification, rescission, or specific performance occur.

A further comparison can be made with the constructive trust which arises when someone receives a bribe in breach of fiduciary duty. According to the Privy Council's advice in *Attorney-General for Hong Kong* v. *Reid*:[26]

> The false fiduciary who received the bribe in breach of duty must pay and account for the bribe to the person to whom that duty was owed . . . As soon as the bribe was received it should have been paid or transferred instanter to the person who suffered from the breach of duty. Equity considers done that which ought to have been done. As soon as the bribe was received, whether in cash or in kind, the false fiduciary held the bribe on a constructive trust for the person injured.

The approach used with regard to contracts of sale was applied to bribes: someone with an equitable right to compel the transfer of property to himself or herself has an equitable interest in that property. The advice in *Reid* has been criticized for its application of this principle, because the right to an account of profits does not compel the accounting party to transfer those profits *in specie*.[27] However, this controversy can be ignored for present purposes of comparison. If a purchaser under a contract of sale and a person to whom a fiduciary must pay a bribe have an equitable interest in property because they can compel the transfer of that property to themselves, it would certainly be anomalous if an equitable interest did not arise in favour of a former owner of property who became entitled to rectify or rescind a transaction and compel the re-transfer of

[23] (1876) 2 Ch.D. 499, 506.
[24] *Bunny Industries Ltd.* v. *F.S.W. Enterprises Pty. Ltd.* [1982] Qd.R. 712, 715, per Connolly J.
[25] See Megarry and Wade, pp. 115–16, 624–7.
[26] [1994] 1 A.C. 324, 331, per Lord Templeman.
[27] Birks (1994d) at 12; Crilley at 65–6.

the property to himself or herself. Fortunately, there is no such difficulty because it is well established that the former owner does have an equitable interest in the property from the outset.

It is interesting to note that English and American courts seem to have arrived at a similar position on this issue. The American *Restatement of Restitution* contains the general principle that:[28] 'Where a person holding title to property is subject to an equitable duty to convey it to another on the ground that he would be unjustly enriched if he were permitted to retain it, a constructive trust arises'. The application of that principle to cases where property may be recovered through rescission or rectification leads to the conclusion that the recipient is a trustee of that property from the outset:[29]

> Thus, where a person by fraud or mistake is induced to transfer to another more land than he intended to transfer, or land different from that which he intended to transfer, the transferor is entitled to reformation by requiring a reconveyance of the land which he did not intend to transfer, or a decree vesting the title to such land in him . . . In such a case the transferee while he holds title to the land which he obtained as result of the fraud or mistake holds it upon a constructive trust for the transferor.

It has been suggested that rescission and rectification can lead to the recovery of land or unique chattels, but not other forms of personal property for which monetary compensation would provide an adequate substitute.[30] If true, this would indicate an even greater similarity between this situation and the constructive trust which depends upon the specific enforceability of a contract of sale. However, this suggestion is contradicted by numerous cases which clearly establish that a person with a right to rescind a disposition of goods or other personal property can recover the ownership of that property.[31]

There is a degree of superficiality in saying that an equitable interest in property arises because of the right to obtain that property. The event which gives rise to both that right and the corresponding equitable interest needs to be identified and understood. This is undertaken in more detail in the concluding chapter of this book. The source of the constructive trust of a bribe is easily identified, because that rule was established only recently in *Att.-Gen. Hong Kong* v. *Reid*. The event which creates the obligation to disgorge a bribe and the corresponding equitable interest in that bribe is the acquisition of property in breach of fiduciary duty. The constructive trust can be understood as a response to profit from wrongdoing and compared to other legal and equitable responses to similar events.

This task is not as easy in relation to the constructive trust arising on a

[28] *Restatement of Restitution*, §160. [29] Ibid. p. 650.

[30] Cope (1992) p. 487; also see *Restatement of Restitution*, pp. 664–5.

[31] *Clough* v. *London & N.W. Rail. Co.* (1871) L.R. 7 Exch. 26; *In re Garnett* (1885) 31 Ch.D. 1, C.A.; (1886) 33 Ch.D. 300, C.A.; *Lady Hood of Avalon* v. *Mackinnon* [1909] 1 Ch. 476; *Newtons of Wembley Ltd.* v. *Williams* [1964] 2 All E.R. 135; aff'd [1964] 3 All E.R. 532, C.A.; *Gibbon* v. *Mitchell* [1990] 1 W.L.R. 1304.

contract of sale. The origins of that principle fall within the purview of the legal historian[32] and it is often listed as an accepted category of constructive trust with no attempt to explain or relate it to trusts arising in other situations. Dr. Elias' *Explaining Constructive Trusts* is a notable exception, which attempts to understand this as one of a number of situations in which constructive trusts arise to perfect a choice to dispose of one's options in favour of another.[33] As Lord O'Hagan stated in *Shaw* v. *Foster*, 'By the contract of sale the vendor in the view of a Court of Equity disposes of his right over the estate, and on the execution of the contract becomes constructively a trustee for the vendee'.[34] Although the constructive trust in this situation and the remedy of specific performance are inextricably linked, they are both derived from the same source: a promise to transfer property which the promisor is bound to perform (i.e. damages will not adequately compensate for its breach).

The event which gives rise to a right of rectification is mistake. Rights to rescission arise in response to mistake and several other events, such as incapacity, duress, and undue influence. As discussed in Chapter 5, these are transactions in which one party's intention to benefit another was vitiated from the outset. The event which gives rise to the right to rectify or rescind a transaction, and the corresponding equitable interest in any recoverable property, is the lack of intention to benefit the recipient. When this underlying event is understood and compared with other responses to similar events, it becomes clear that the equitable interest which arises in conjunction with a right to recover property through rectification or rescission is a resulting trust. Working back from those remedies or out from the traditional categories of resulting trust leads to the same conclusion.

C. RECONCILIATION WITH *PHILLIPS* V. *PHILLIPS*

The cases discussed above, which clearly establish that a person with a right of rescission or rectification has an equitable interest in any property recoverable thereby, need to be reconciled with Lord Westbury C.'s classification of both rights as mere equities.[35] It has been suggested that these rights should be treated as proprietary for some purposes, such as whether they may be transferred or be overriding interests, but not for others and, in particular, not in a competition with other equitable interests.[36] However, it is submitted that the best course is to recognize, as the Court of Appeal did in *Gross* v. *Lewis Hillman Ltd.*,[37] that

[32] See Milsom, pp. 223–4; Megarry and Wade, p. 1170.
[33] Elias, pp. 9–16 (discussed further in the conclusion to this book).
[34] (1872) L.R. 5 H.L. 321, 349.
[35] *Phillips* v. *Phillips* (1862) 4 De G.F.&J. 208, 218.
[36] *Blacklocks* v. *J.B. Developments (Godalming) Ltd.* [1982] Ch. 183, 196.
[37] [1970] Ch. 445, 460–1.

an equitable interest exists in property recoverable by rescission or rectification. Where those rights do not lead to the recovery of property, they are mere equities. This solution requires a close examination of *Latec Investments Ltd.* v. *Hotel Terrigal Pty. Ltd.*, because it was considered in that case and did not find favour with Kitto J.[38]

1. *Latec Investments* v. *Hotel Terrigal*

In *Latec*, the plaintiff had mortgaged its hotel under a Torrens land-title system (which meant that the plaintiff remained the legal owner and the mortgagee obtained a registered legal charge on the land). When the plaintiff defaulted on the mortgage, the mortgagee fraudulently exercised its power of sale by selling the hotel to its subsidiary. The subsidiary granted a floating charge over the hotel to a trustee and the beneficial interest in the trust property was sold to *bona fide* purchasers. The floating charge over the hotel crystallized and the plaintiff brought this action to rescind the mortgagee's sale to its subsidiary. All three members of the High Court of Australia agreed that the plaintiff had an equitable interest in the hotel. However, they also agreed that the subsequent *bona fide* purchasers of the equitable estate had priority over the plaintiff's equitable interest.

Two different strategies were used to deal with the contradiction of classifying the plaintiff's right to rescission as an equitable interest, while subjecting that right to subsequent equitable interests. The main strategy, employed by Kitto, Menzies and (to a lesser extent) Taylor JJ., was to treat the plaintiff as having both a mere equity to set aside the fraudulent sale and an equitable interest in the recoverable property. The defence of *bona fide* purchase applied to prevent the plaintiff from asserting its mere equity, thereby disabling it from proving the existence of the equitable interest.[39] Taylor J. adopted an additional strategy. In his view, the defence of *bona fide* purchase had been available to the purchaser of an equitable estate until *Phillips* v. *Phillips*, which changed the law. Lord Westbury C.'s separate treatment of mere equities meant that the change did not extend to cases of rectification or rescission.[40]

Neither approach is inconsistent with the argument presented here. If one accepts that the plaintiff's equitable interest was a resulting trust, it is still possible, in accordance with the reasoning of Kitto and Menzies JJ., that the plaintiff was unable to assert that trust against the *bona fide* purchasers without first establishing its right to rescind the transaction. Taylor J.'s approach can be adopted if it is accepted, on the basis of precedent, that a resulting trust is subject to the defence of *bona fide* purchase of an equitable estate when it arises in a case of rectification or rescission.

Even as it stands, *Latec* does not inhibit the application of the resulting trust to cases of rescission or rectification, but lends support thanks to the High Court

[38] (1965) 113 C.L.R. 265, 277. [39] Ibid. at 278, 286, 290–1. [40] Ibid. at 285–6.

of Australia's unanimous finding that a plaintiff in those circumstances has an equitable interest in the recoverable property (which Menzies J. identified as a trust).[41] However, the treatment of *Phillips* v. *Phillips* is less than satisfactory for several reasons. First, Kitto and Menzies JJ.'s conclusion, that the plaintiff's 'equitable interest is unprovable'[42] where the defence of *bona fide* purchase bars the right to rescind, is not easily reconciled with the well-established principle that the plaintiff's equitable interest arises from the outset, independently of any actions taken to rescind the transaction.[43]

No less difficult is Taylor J.'s suggestion that we treat the application of the defence of *bona fide* purchase to cases of rescission and rectification as historically anomalous. The distinction was justified on the basis that the plaintiff with either of these rights 'required the assistance of a court of equity to remove an impediment to his title as a preliminary to asserting his interest'.[44] This is open to the same objection taken to Kitto and Menzies JJ.'s approach. Additionally, there is no significant difference between this situation and the traditional case of resulting trust in favour of a contributor to the purchase price, whose interest is equally dependent on the assistance of a court of equity. They are the same from the perspective of the *bona fide* purchaser who, in either case, has dealt with the apparent owner of the property in question.

The more fundamental objection to *Latec* is that it only achieves a reconciliation with Lord Westbury C.'s *obiter dictum* in *Phillips* v. *Phillips* by rejecting the real basis of his judgment. The principle established in *Phillips* v. *Phillips* is that the defence of *bona fide* purchase cannot give a later equitable estate priority over an earlier one. The application of the defence to a mere equity is not an exception to the principle, but simply a circumstance to which it does not apply. As Lord Westbury C. stated, 'the defence of a purchaser for valuable consideration is the creature of a Court of Equity, and it can never be used in a manner at variance with the elementary rules which have already been stated'.[45] It applies 'where there are circumstances that give rise to an equity as distinguished from an equitable estate',[46] precisely because there is no prior equitable estate.[47]

The difficulty is caused by Lord Westbury C.'s use of rescission and rectification as examples of mere equities. There are cases where these remedies do not lead to the recovery of property and the plaintiff does not have any equitable interest in property belonging to the defendant. However, once it is recognized that the plaintiff does have such an equitable interest, the case is no longer an example of a mere equity and the defence of *bona fide* purchase of an equitable interest is no longer available.

[41] Ibid. at 291. See Gummow at p. 73.
[42] *Latec Investments* v. *Hotel Terrigal* (n. 38 above) at 278, per Kitto J.
[43] Above, pp. 172–4.
[44] (1965) 113 C.L.R. 265, 286, per Taylor J.
[45] (1862) 4 De G.F.&J. 208, 216.
[46] Ibid. at 218, per Westbury L.C.
[47] Megarry (1955) at 481.

The normal rule for determining the priority of conflicting equitable interests is *qui prior est tempore potior est jure* (he who is first in time is preferred in law), but this is not absolute. The conduct or neglect of the person with the prior interest may be a reason for postponing that interest to a subsequent equitable interest acquired for value and without notice of the first.[48] This occurred in *Abigail* v. *Lapin*, where Lord Wright stated:[49] '[I]t is now clearly established that prima facie priority in time will decide the matter unless . . . that which is relied on to take away the pre-existing equitable title can be shown to be something tangible and distinct having grave and strong effect to accomplish the purpose'.

Although 'the equitable interest of a beneficiary is not in general to be postponed to that of a subsequent incumbrancer who has taken for value under the trustee without notice',[50] Lord Wright noted that this 'rule is one which has been applied to trusts, and not to equitable estates or interests, such as those of unpaid vendors and equitable mortgagees, or to equities like an equity to set aside a conveyance for fraud'.[51] It may well be that resulting trusts arising in certain circumstances should be postponed to subsequent purchasers of conflicting equitable interests for value without notice; e.g. where a rescindable transfer was caused by the transferor's careless mistake. However, the question of priority ought to be confronted directly and not decided by resort to a fictional classification of the resulting trust as a mere equity.

2. Other Cases

In *Latec*, Kitto J. rejected the argument that the classification of mere equity only applies where 'there is an assertion of an equity unaccompanied by an equitable interest'.[52] His lordship chose *Malden* v. *Menill*,[53] *Garrard* v. *Frankel*[54] and *Bainbrigge* v. *Browne*[55] as examples where the defence of *bona fide* purchase of an equitable interest was successful against a prior right of rectification or rescission.[56] However, *Malden* v. *Menill* and *Bainbrigge* v. *Browne* are unhelpful because the defendants in both cases had acquired their interests directly from the plaintiffs. These were not cases like *Phillips* v. *Phillips*, where the *bona fide* purchasers acquired their interests from an intermediary, who was not the owner of the plaintiff's equitable interest and therefore unable to pass it to the purchaser.[57] Where there is no intermediary, the plaintiff is the owner of the entire beneficial interest in question and able to pass it to the defendant. The plaintiff's right to rescind or rectify the transaction and his or her equitable interest in the property in the hands of the defendant are not first in time, but

[48] *Rice* v. *Rice* (1854) 2 Drew. 73; *Shropshire Union Railways and Canal Co.* v. *The Queen* (1875) L.R. 7 H.L. 496; *Breskvar* v. *Wall* (1971) 126 C.L.R. 376.

[49] [1934] A.C. 491, 504, P.C.

[50] Ibid. 505, per Lord Wright.

[51] Ibid.

[52] (1965) 113 C.L.R. 265, 277.

[53] (1737) 2 Atk. 8.

[54] (1862) 30 Beav. 445.

[55] (1881) 18 Ch.D. 188.

[56] (1965) 113 C.L.R. 265, 278.

[57] See Megarry (1955) at 481.

arise (if at all) at the moment of transfer. Both are subject to the defence of good faith exchange, which is analogous to, but distinct from, the defence of *bona fide* purchase.[58]

In *Garrard* v. *Frankel*,[59] the plaintiff landlord wanted to rectify the rent payable in a lease from £130 to £230 per annum, but the tenant had granted an equitable mortgage of the lease to a *bona fide* purchaser, who took priority over the plaintff's right to rectification. This might best be regarded as a case in which the plaintiff had a mere equity unaccompanied by an equitable interest. The right to receive rent is a proprietary right in the hands of the landlord.[60] However, the mistaken reduction of the tenant's obligation to pay rent is not an assignment of the landlord's proprietary right to the tenant.[61] Rectification of the lease did not result in the recovery of property from the defendant, but in the imposition of an additional burden upon her.

There is an *obiter dictum* in *Ernest* v. *Vivian*[62] which is contrary to the present argument. The plaintiff brought an action to set aside a lease, as a fraudulent exercise of the life-tenant's power, against *bona fide* purchasers of the equitable ownership of the lease. Kindersley V.C. held that, if the lease was voidable, the plaintiff's claim was barred by laches. He also thought that *bona fide* purchase of an equitable estate was a good defence to the fraud, but did not explore it any further because of the successful laches defence.[63] The question whether the plaintiff had an equitable interest or a mere equity was not mentioned.

Millett J. has twice expressed an opinion contradicting the present argument. In *Lonrho p.l.c.* v. *Fayed (No. 2)*,[64] the plaintiffs were seeking rescission of a sale of shares and argued that the purchasers were constructive trustees of those shares. Millett J. held that the plaintiffs were not entitled to rescission and struck out their statement of claim. His lordship also said that:[65]

> A contract obtained by fraudulent misrepresentation is voidable, not void, even in equity. The representee may elect to avoid it, but until he does so the representor is not a constructive trustee of the property transferred pursuant to the contract . . . It may well be that if the representee elects to avoid the contract and set aside a transfer of property made pursuant to it the beneficial interest in the property will be treated as having remained vested in him throughout, at least to the extent necessary to support any tracing claim.

Millett J. repeated this observation in *El Ajou* v. *Dollar Land Holdings p.l.c.*, where he stated *obiter* that:[66]

[58] See *Babcock* v. *Lawson* (1880) 5 Q.B.D. 284, 286, C.A.; Barker (1995a) at p. 191; p. 121 above; pp. 237–8 below.

[59] (1862) 30 Beav. 445.

[60] Megarry and Wade, p. 706; see *Boots the Chemist Ltd.* v. *Street* (1983) 268 E.G. 817.

[61] In any event, an assignment of rents is not an interest in land at common law: *Canada Trustco Mortgage Co.* v. *Skoretz* (1983) 147 D.L.R. (3d) 130 (Alta.Q.B.); changed by amendment to the Law of Property Act, R.S.A. 1980, c. L-8, s. 59(1)(b).

[62] (1863) 33 L.J.Ch. 513.

[63] Ibid. at 519.

[64] [1992] 1 W.L.R. 1; discussed at p. 196 below.

[65] Ibid. at 11–12. Also see Millett (1995) at 518.

[66] [1993] 3 All E.R. 717, 734; rev'd on other grounds [1994] 2 All E.R. 685; see pp. 22–3 above.

[I]f the other victims of the fraud can trace their money in equity it must be because, having been induced to purchase the shares by false and fraudulent misrepresentations, they are entitled to rescind the transaction and revest the equitable title to the purchase money in themselves, at least to the extent necessary to support an equitable tracing claim.

Brennan J. took a similar approach in *Daly* v. *Sydney Stock Exchange Ltd.*[67] The plaintiff was the assignee of deposits of money loaned to a firm of stock-brokers. The firm became insolvent and the plaintiff's claim for compensation from the defendant's 'fidelity fund' depended on whether the firm was a trustee of the money.[68] The plaintiff argued that the firm had breached its fiduciary duty by not disclosing the risks of the loan and therefore held the money on constructive trust. Gibbs C.J. stated that 'the only relevant relationship between the firm and the [plaintiff] was that of debtor and creditor'.[69] Brennan J. thought that the firm's breach of its fiduciary obligations would give rise to a right to rescission and stated:[70]

It may be said that a party who elects to avoid a contract and set aside a transfer of property made pursuant to the contract had an equitable interest in the property from the beginning, that the equitable remedies available to him are incidental to that interest and that his equitable interest arose before, and does not depend upon the court's decree.

However, his lordship then went on to follow *Latec* and conclude that the recipient was not a trustee at the outset 'if he received the moneys under a contract which gave him a beneficial title recognized in equity, albeit a beneficial title that is imperfect and liable to be divested by relation back in the event of avoidance of the contract of loan'.[71]

With great respect, these opinions are difficult to reconcile with the well-established principle that the equitable interest in recoverable property arises before, and independently of, the rescission of the transaction that gave rise to that interest. In *El Ajou*, Millett J. made it clear that 'the trust which is operating in these cases is not some new model remedial constructive trust, but an old-fashioned institutional resulting trust'.[72] Therefore, his lordship was not thinking of the trust as a remedy granted with the order of rescisssion and given retroactive effect (which might have been inferred from his *dictum* in *Lonrho* v. *Fayed*). The resulting trust is an equitable response to the existence of certain facts: a transfer of property in circumstances in which the provider did not intend to benefit the recipient. In cases of vitiated intention leading to rectification or rescission, those facts are present at the moment of transfer, which is when the resulting trust arises.

The fact that the resulting trust arises at the outset does not make the transaction void in equity. Instead, equity recognizes the voidable transaction, but makes the recipient a trustee of the recoverable property. There could be significant

[67] (1986) 160 C.L.R. 371.
[68] Securities Industry Act 1975, N.S.W., s. 97.
[69] (1986) 160 C.L.R. 371, 381.
[70] Ibid. at 388.
[71] Ibid. at 390. Also see Sealy (1963) at 127.
[72] Ibid.

differences between these two positions, relating to defences based on delay or affirmation or to aspects of the voidable transaction other than the transfer of recoverable property.

3. Discretionary Remedies

Professor Wade suggested another basis for distinguishing between equitable interests and mere equities:[73]

> The dividing line between equitable interests and mere equities is perhaps the discretionary character of the latter. Equitable claims to set aside deeds, or to secure their rectification, or to reopen a foreclosure, are at the discretion of the court in a way which does not apply to equitable titles such as those of beneficiaries under a trust or a mortgagor's equity of redemption. It is natural that the court should be unwilling to exercise its discretion to the detriment of an innocent purchaser even though he lacks the armour of a legal estate.

Neave and Weinberg adopted a somewhat similar approach, distinguishing between the two depending on whether the plaintiff's right is sufficiently 'defined'.[74] It is interesting that Wade, writing before *Latec*, classified rights to rescission and rectification as mere equities, whereas Neave and Weinberg, writing after, treated them as equitable interests.

Wade classified rescission and rectification as mere equities for much the same reason *Latec* subjected them to the defence of *bona fide* purchase of an equitable interest: their special dependence on the assistance of a court of equity. This might support the objection that there cannot be a resulting trust from the outset if it is uncertain whether rescission and rectification will be ordered at the end of the day. Precedent, establishing that the plaintiff in such a case is the equitable owner of any recoverable property, is a sufficient answer to this objection, but there is at least one other.

The dependence of the plaintiff's claim on the discretion of the court does not mean that the resulting trust is unavailable until it is known which way that discretion will be exercised.[75] The better view is that the trust arises at the outset, but may be determined by subsequent events which cause a court to refuse to exercise its discretion in the plaintiff's favour. As discussed above, this is consistent with the constructive trust which arises on the execution of a contract of sale even though it is not certain that specific performance of that contract will be available in the end.[76] Additional support for this approach can be gleaned from *Guinness p.l.c.* v. *Saunders*.[77] In that case, Mr. Ward, a director of the plaintiff, had received £5.2 million from the plaintiff under a contract made without the approval of the board of directors. Both the Court of Appeal and the House of

[73] Wade at 160. [74] Neave and Weinberg at 26–27.
[75] Cf. Goode (1991a) at pp. 222–3, 232–5, 245.
[76] *Bunny Industries Ltd.* v. *F.S.W. Enterprises Pty. Ltd.* [1982] Qd.R. 712.
[77] [1988] 1 W.L.R. 863; aff'd [1990] 2 W.L.R. 324, H.L.

Lords upheld Browne-Wilkinson V.C.'s declaration that Ward was, upon receipt, a constructive trustee of the money for the plaintiff.[78] Lord Goff doubted whether the constructive trust could apply to a voidable agreement because Ward had acted in good faith, but upheld the trust on the basis that the agreement was void.[79] The Court of Appeal held that the constructive trust was possible even though the agreement was only voidable.

Important for the present discussion is Fox L.J.'s view that the trust arises from the outset, but subsequent events may diminish or extinguish the plaintiff's right to rescission:[80]

> No doubt the constructive trust would have determined if Guinness had ratified the agreement or had delayed for too long in avoiding it. But those circumstances apart, it seems to me that, from the first, Mr. Ward held the money as a constructive trustee for Guinness. The existence of some cross-claim for a quantum meruit or allowance did not impeach or determine that trust. It continues to subsist.

The same reasoning ought to apply to the objection based on the discretionary nature of the remedies of rescission and rectification. Whether the plaintiff's intention has been sufficiently vitiated is a difficult question, but one concerning the state of affairs at the time the transaction was entered into. The answer to that question will, in cases involving the transfer of property, also determine whether a resulting trust arose at the moment of transfer. Issues such as laches or affirmation (or even the exercise of a statutory discretion to 'declare the contract subsisting')[81] do not affect the grounds giving rise to the resulting trust, but what has become of that trust in the interim.

D. SUMMARY

Despite the common assumption that rights to rectification or rescission are mere equities, it turns out to be well established that a person who is entitled to recover property through the exercise of either right has an equitable interest in that property. That interest arises from the outset and, as Millett J. recognized, is a resulting trust. This recognition has been impeded by the *obiter dictum* of Lord Westbury C. in *Phillips* v. *Phillips*. The difficulty is not his lordship's suggestion that mere equities can be defeated by subsequent purchasers of conflicting equitable interests, but his classification of rights to rescission or rectification as mere equities. Although *Latec Investments* v. *Hotel Terrigal* suggests otherwise, there is a valid and important distinction between those cases in which equitable rights lead to the recovery of property and those in which they do not. In the former situation, the recipient holds the recoverable property on resulting trust from the moment of receipt.

[78] [1988] 1 W.L.R. 863, 865.
[79] [1990] 2 W.L.R. 324, 339–40.
[80] [1988] 1 W.L.R. 863, 870.
[81] Misrepresentation Act 1967, s. 2(2).

8
First-Measure Liability

This chapter concerns claims against resulting trustees for restitution in the first measure. As mentioned above,[1] these are personal claims for the value received by the trustee, which are 'determined without reference to whether he still retains' any of that value.[2] Two potential sources of personal liability are considered in this book: (i) the receipt of property belonging in equity to another and (ii) breach of trust. The latter is discussed separately (in Chapter 9) because liability for breach of a resulting trust is not confined to restitution in the first measure. A first-measure claim based on receipt is (arguably) distinct from a claim based on breach of trust.

Where the subject of the resulting trust no longer survives in the hands of the recipient, the resulting trust ceases to exist. However, the provider of the property will often have another valid claim for restitution in the first measure, which exists independently of the resulting trust. For example, in *Chase Manhattan Bank N.A.* v. *Israel-British Bank (London) Ltd.*,[3] the plaintiff had paid the defendant by mistake and had a continuing equitable property interest in any of its money which was still identifiable in the hands of the defendant,[4] i.e. a second-measure claim *in rem*, in addition to a first-measure claim for money had and received.[5] The co-existence of separate first and second-measure claims in relation to the same enrichment does not pose any difficulty.[6] Double recovery is avoided because the first-measure claim is reduced by the value of any recovery in the second measure.[7]

An important question is whether the receipt of property on resulting trust can itself give rise to a claim for restitution in the first measure. In other words, can the resulting trust beneficiary require the resulting trustee to account and pay for the value received, regardless of what becomes of the trust property? In *Westdeutsche Landesbank Girozentrale* v. *Islington London Borough Council*,[8] the Court of Appeal assumed that the answer to this question was 'yes', while the House of Lords did not address this question (having decided that a resulting trust did not arise). As discussed in the previous chapter the bank had paid £2.5 million to the council as part of an *ultra vires* interest-rate swap transaction.

[1] At pp. 105–6. [2] Birks (1989a), p. 6. [3] [1981] Ch. 105.
[4] Ibid. at 119, 128. [5] Ibid. at 115.
[6] See *Barclays Bank Ltd.* v. *Quistclose Investments Ltd.* [1970] A.C. 567, 581; *Australia and New Zealand Banking Group Ltd.* v. *Westpac Banking Corp.* (1988) 164 C.L.R. 662, 673.
[7] *Re Diplock* [1948] Ch. 465, 517; *Re Goldcorp Exchange Ltd.* [1995] 1 A.C. 74, 91, 96–7, P.C.
[8] [1994] 4 All E.R. 890; varied [1996] 2 All E.R. 961, H.L.

Dillon L.J. held that the council was a resulting trustee of that money and, therefore, 'became accountable in equity for the £2.5 million which it received for purposes which were by law incapable of fulfilment'.[9] Even though 'the money initially received by the council from the bank was spent by the council on its ordinary purposes',[10] his lordship held:[11] 'Since it is beyond doubt that the council is solvent, that personal liability in equity subsists whether or not tracing to establish some particular or general charge is possible'.

This conclusion is surprising for two reasons. First, Dillon L.J. relied on *Re Diplock* as authority for this proposition, but (as discussed below) the Court of Appeal said in *Re Diplock* that the equitable claim *in rem* (identified in *Sinclair* v. *Brougham* and *Westdeutsche* v. *Islington* as a resulting trust)[12] would not give rise to personal liability if the recipient was unaware of the provider's claim.[13] The second reason relates to the first. There is a great deal of controversy over whether an innocent recipient can be personally liable in equity to pay for the value of property received. In *Westdeutsche* v. *Islington*, there was no mention of this controversy or the question whether the council was an innocent or knowing recipient.

A. KNOWING RECEIPT

When discussing a recipient's personal liability in equity to pay for the value of property received, the courts usually (but not invariably) use the language of constructive trust. For example, in *International Sales and Agencies Ltd.* v. *Marcus*, Lawson J. said of the personal claim that:[14]

> [T]he knowing recipient of trust property for his own purposes will become a constructive trustee of what he receives if either he was in fact aware at the time that his receipt was affected by a breach of trust, or if he deliberately shut his eyes to the real nature of the transfer to him (this could be called 'imputed notice'), or if an ordinary reasonable man in his position and with his attributes ought to have known of the relevant breach. This I equate with constructive notice.

As Birks points out, the label 'knowing recipient' contains a *petitio principii*: whether knowledge is required for personal liability in equity is the very controversial question at issue in this situation.[15] He argues that all recipients should be strictly liable in equity to make restitution in the first measure (subject to defences such as *bona fide* purchase, change of position, etc.)[16] and is not alone on this

[9] [1994] 4 All E.R. 890, 966 per Dillon L.J. (citing *Re Diplock* [1948] Ch. 465).
[10] Ibid., per Dillon L.J. [11] Ibid. [12] See pp. 156–8 above.
[13] *Re Diplock* [1948] Ch. 465. See pp. 188, 202–3 below. [14] [1982] 3 All E.R. 551, 558.
[15] Birks (1989d) at 298; Birks (1992a), p. 26.
[16] Ibid.; Birks (1992e); Birks (1993e) at 225–9; Birks (1994b).

issue. Millett L.J. has taken this view (writing extra-judicially),[17] as has Professor Martin, who stated:[18]

> In the case of liability for 'knowing receipt', the weight of authority supports the view that constructive knowledge suffices, although the point is not settled. This is an area where the courts should strive to achieve a coherent doctrine by reflecting on the position at common law, where a volunteer is liable for money had and received without regard to his state of knowledge, subject to the defence of change of position . . . The personal action in equity, being restitutionary, should be based not on fault but on the fact of receipt . . . Now that the defence of change of position has been recognised, there is no reason why an innocent volunteer should not be liable in equity to an equitable owner, without regard to his state of knowledge. Any other view leads to the unjust enrichment of the volunteer.

It is well settled that an innocent recipient is, subject to defences, strictly liable in the second measure to restore property still in his or her possession. However, many commentators favour the view that an equitable first-measure claim does and should require some degree of notice, knowledge, or fault on the part of the recipient.[19] The cases are inconsistent: some require a level of knowledge amounting to a lack of probity,[20] others indicate that notice may be sufficient,[21] and a few incline to the view of strict liability, subject to defences.[22]

In *Ministry of Health* v. *Simpson* (*Re Diplock*),[23] the House of Lords held that charities which had innocently received gifts pursuant to an invalid bequest were liable in the first measure to the residual beneficiaries of the estate. It is usually argued that this principle is confined to the administration of estates[24] and, indeed, Lord Simonds made it clear that he was dealing with the assets of a deceased person and not trust property.[25] His lordship stated, 'I do not find in history or in logic any justification for an argument which denies the possibility

[17] Millett (1991) at 80–3.

[18] Martin (1994) at 27. Also see Scott and Fratcher, §292–§292.2; Martin (1993a), pp. 304–7; Swadling (1994b); Barker (1995a) at p. 209; Gardner (1996) at 86.

[19] Harpum (1986); Harpum (1987); Burrows (1990); Baker and Langan, *Snell's Equity*, pp. 193–4; Burrows (1993a), pp. 150–8; Finn (1993); Harpum (1994) at p. 9 (but see p. 24).

[20] *Carl Zeiss Stiftung* v. *Herbert Smith & Co. (No. 2)* [1969] 2 Ch. 276, C.A.; *Baden* v. *Société Générale pour Favoriser le Développement du Commerce et de L'Industrie en France S.A.* [1983] B.C.L.C. 325, [1993] 1 W.L.R. 509, 575; *In re Montagu's Settlement Trusts* [1987] Ch. 264; *Eagle Trust p.l.c.* v. *S.B.C. Securities Ltd.* [1993] 1 W.L.R. 484, 506 (in a commercial context).

[21] *Belmont Finance Corp.* v. *Williams Furniture Ltd. (No. 2)* [1980] 1 All E.R. 393, C.A.; *International Sales and Agencies* v. *Marcus* [1982] 3 All E.R. 551; *Westpac Banking Corp.* v. *Savin* [1985] 2 N.Z.L.R. 41, C.A.; *Agip (Africa) Ltd.* v. *Jackson* [1989] 3 W.L.R. 1367; aff'd [1991] 3 W.L.R. 116, C.A.; *Eagle Trust* v. *S.B.C. Securities* [1993] 1 W.L.R. 484, 496–504 (outside commercial context).

[22] *In re Robinson* [1911] 1 Ch. 502; *Nelson* v. *Larholt* [1948] 1 K.B. 339; *Ministry of Health* v. *Simpson* [1951] A.C. 251; *G.L. Baker Ltd.* v. *Medway Building and Supplies Ltd.* [1982] 2 All E.R. 532; rev'd [1958] 3 All E.R. 540, C.A.

[23] [1951] A.C. 251; aff'g *Re Diplock* [1948] Ch. 465.

[24] See Burrows (1993a), pp. 156–8; Harpum (1994) at pp. 22–4.

[25] [1951] A.C. 251, 265–6.

of an equitable right in the administration of assets because, it is alleged, no comparable right existed in the execution of trusts'.[26] Nevertheless, it is difficult to understand why a wrongly or over-paid legatee should be strictly liable in the first measure, but not a person in receipt of property belonging in equity to another.[27]

In the Court of Appeal, the estate beneficiaries had been successful on both their first-measure claims for value received and their second-measure claims to an equitable proprietary interest. However, those two claims were unrelated: the former was based on a line of authority in connexion with the administration of estates and the latter on *Sinclair* v. *Brougham*. The Court of Appeal stated that the claim *in rem* could not be used as a basis for making the innocent recipient 'personally liable to repay the amount claimed to have belonged to the claimant. The equitable remedies pre-suppose the continued existence of the money either as a separate fund or as part of a mixed fund or as latent in property acquired by means of such a fund'.[28] Although both were equitable, they were independent claims in relation to the same enrichment, in the same way that the mistaken payment by Chase Manhattan Bank gave rise to both a first-measure claim at common law for money had and received to the plaintiff's use and a second-measure equitable proprietary interest.[29]

B. THE WAY FORWARD

The way out of this confusion may be to adopt a general principle that all recipients of property belonging in equity to another will be liable to equitable restitutionary claims in the first measure, regardless of fault, but subject to defences. Whichever path is chosen for the first-measure claim in equity (strict or fault-based), there will need to be some adjustment, or at least thought taken, regarding its application to resulting trustees. Personal liability for the receipt of trust property does not require the prior existence of an express trust of that property.[30] In many cases, the recipient has become a 'constructive trustee' of previously non-trust property which has been misdirected to him or her by the plaintiff's fiduciary. Leaving aside the proper classification of the trust in this situation, liability for receiving property which belongs in equity to another cannot justifiably depend on the event which gives rise to that equitable interest. The personal liability of the resulting trustee ought not to differ from that of the constructive trustee without sufficient reason.

[26] Ibid. at 266. The *Diplock* personal claim was applied by Dankwerts J., in *G.L. Baker* v. *Medway Building and Supplies* [1982] 2 All E.R. 532, to an innocent recipient of misdirected corporate funds, but has not otherwise found favour outside the administration of estates: see *Butler* v. *Broadhead* [1975] Ch. 97; *In re J. Leslie Engineers Co. Ltd.* [1976] 1 W.L.R. 292.

[27] Cf. Burrows (1993a), pp. 156–8.

[28] *Re Diplock* [1948] Ch. 465, 521.

[29] *Chase Manhattan Bank* v. *Israel-British Bank* [1981] Ch. 105.

[30] *Belmont Finance* v. *Williams Furniture (No. 2)* [1980] 1 All E.R. 393, 405.

There have been at least two significant impediments to the logical and consistent development of restitutionary first-measure claims in equity: (i) the use of the term 'constructive trustee' and (ii) the lack of a defence of change of position.

1. Constructive Trustees

The label 'constructive trustee' has been applied to those who assist others to commit breaches of trust, as well as those who receive for their own benefit property belonging in equity to others. Consequently, the courts have often failed to distinguish between the degrees of fault necessary for the two types of liability. It is now recognized that liability for 'knowing assistance' is to compensate for loss caused by the breach of trust and that it requires dishonesty (though not on the part of the trustees themselves),[31] whereas 'knowing receipt' is a liability to make restitution, which ought to arise regardless of fault[32] (and possibly even in the absence of notice).

The 'constructive trustee' label creates even greater confusion when applied to resulting trustees. It needs to be discarded if these (hitherto) discrete branches of equity are to be reconciled. To say that the recipient 'is liable as a constructive trustee'[33] adds a layer of abstraction between the obligation to make restitution in the first measure and the facts giving rise to that obligation.[34] This is not only unnecessary, but entirely inappropriate for resulting trusts. The person who receives property on resulting trust *is* a trustee and it is nonsensical to speak of a personal liability which arises because the resulting trustee will be treated as though he or she were a trustee. Also, to say that the resulting trustee is 'liable' as a trustee merely begs the question regarding the nature and extent of that liability. It is clear that the resulting trustee is liable to account to the beneficiary for the trust property received,[35] but that does not necessarily make him or her liable to pay the amount by which the value received exceeded that which survives. This depends on the allowances to made in taking the account.

2. Change of Position

The imposition of strict, first-measure liability on an innocent donee may have seemed unduly harsh before the recognition of the defence of change of position in *Lipkin Gorman* v. *Karpnale Ltd.*[36] The defence alleviates this concern because

[31] *Royal Brunei Airlines* v. *Tan* [1995] 2 A.C. 378, 392, P.C.; Harpum (1995).

[32] *Belmont Finance* v. *Williams Furniture (No. 2)* [1980] 1 All E.R. 393, 410.

[33] Ibid. at 405, per Buckley L.J.

[34] Birks (1992e) at pp. 153–7; Burrows (1993a), p. 151; Millett (1995b) at 39.

[35] See Waters (1984), pp. 871–2; Baker and Langan, *Snell's Equity*, pp. 231–2.

[36] [1991] 2 A.C. 548. The defence has been accepted in Australia (*David Securities Pty. Ltd.* v. *Commonwealth Bank of Australia* (1992) 175 C.L.R. 353); Canada (*Storthoaks (R.M.)* v. *Mobil Oil Canada Ltd.* (1975) 55 D.L.R. (3d) 1, S.C.C.) and the USA (*Restatement of Restitution*, §69).

it reduces the claim against the innocent recipient by the sum of (i) any unusual expenses or liabilities incurred in reliance on the receipt[37] and (ii) any decrease in the value surviving without benefit to the recipient.[38]

C. CHANGES IN THE VALUE OF TRUST PROPERTY

A largely unexplored issue is the resulting trustee's liability for any decrease in value or loss of the trust property without benefit to the trustee. The normal principle of trust law is that the beneficiaries bear any loss which occurs without the trustee's fault, i.e. risk follows the beneficial ownership.[39] The application of this principle may vary according to the situation in which the resulting trust arises. The two important variables are the degrees of knowledge of the provider and of the recipient. In typical cases (such as a contribution to the purchase in the name of another or the failure of an express trust), both parties are aware of and have consented to the provision of property by one to the other. This can be contrasted with situations where either the provider did not intend to transfer property to the recipient[40] or the recipient was unaware of the provider's entitlement.[41]

Where the provider did not intend to transfer property to the recipient, the latter's personal liability is (or ought to be) indistinguishable from that of a 'constructive trustee' who has received property in breach of trust. The arguments in favour of either strict or fault-based liability are equally applicable to both situations. The innocent recipient will be protected from liability for loss of the property through the defence of change of position. However, there is no reason to allow the defence to a recipient who is aware of the circumstances and ought to have been aware of the provider's claim. The provider should not have to bear the risk of loss where he or she has not consented to the transfer and the recipient was aware of the facts giving rise to the obligation to re-convey.[42]

The situation changes if the provider has consented to the recipient's legal (but not beneficial) ownership. That consent should protect the recipient from liability for any decrease in the value surviving, unless he or she was at fault or received a benefit therefrom.[43] It probably makes no difference to the recipient

[37] Birks (1989a), p. 410; Goff and Jones, p. 741. See p. 192 below.

[38] *Restatement of Restitution*, §142; Burrows (1993a), p. 427; Nolan (1995) at pp. 150–1; cf. Birks (1996a) at pp. 61–2.

[39] *Morley* v. *Morley* (1678) 2 Ch.Cas. 2; *Speight* v. *Gaunt* (1883) 9 App.Cas. 1; Scott and Fratcher, §204.

[40] e.g. *Lane* v. *Dighton* (1762) Amb. 409 (provider unaware of transfer); *Goodfellow* v. *Robertson* (1871) 18 Gr. 572 (provider suffering from mental infirmity). See pp. 21–3 above.

[41] e.g. *In re Vinogradoff* [1935] W.N. 68 (recipient unaware of transfer); *Sinclair* v. *Brougham* [1914] A.C. 398 (recipient unaware that consideration for transfer had failed).

[42] *Restatement of Restitution*, §69(3)(b), §178, comment b.

[43] *Lockhart* v. *Reilly* (1856) 25 L.J.Eq. 697, 701; *Re Pauling's Settlement Trusts* [1964] Ch. 303; Scott and Fratcher, §216; Baker and Langan, *Snell's Equity,* p. 294.

who was unaware of the provider's entitlement and able to rely on the defence of change of position. However, the recipient who was aware would not be able to rely on the defence (according to the current understanding of this emergent concept).[44]

Matusewich v. *Matusewich*[45] and *Cheese* v. *Thomas*[46] provide useful examples for the discussion of this issue. In both cases, the plaintiff had contributed to the purchase of a house in the defendant's name, the house was sold and the proceeds were used for the defendant's benefit. Each defendant was personally liable to repay the amount of the plaintiff's share of the sale proceeds which had been appropriated to his own benefit. The defendant in *Matusewich* was personally liable as a defaulting resulting trustee. Although the defendant in *Cheese* v. *Thomas* was liable on the basis of undue influence, the Court of Appeal stated that he would have been liable for the same amount as a resulting trustee.[47]

The important point for present purposes is that the plaintiffs did not recover either the value the defendant initially received or the value surviving. Their personal claims were based on a proportionate share of the sale proceeds. In *Matusewich*, the value of the house had risen: the plaintiff paid $1,000, but was entitled to almost $3,000 of the sale proceeds. In *Cheese* v. *Thomas*, the value of the house had fallen: the plaintiff had contributed £43,000, but was entitled to less than £30,000. There are (at least) three possible explanations of the measure of the resulting trustee's personal liability in this situation: (i) compensation for breach of trust, independent of the two measures of restitution, (ii) restitution in the first-measure of the value of the property initially received, subject to the defence of change of position, or (iii) restitution in the first-measure of the value of the property converted to the resulting trustee's own use. Although each explanation has merit, the second is inferior to the other two.

1. Breach of Trust

Breach of trust was the source of the personal liability in *Matusewich* and it could also explain *Cheese* v. *Thomas*, if that had been a case of resulting trust. All or a portion of the provider's beneficial interest was used for the benefit of the recipient, in breach of his obligation to restore it to the provider. As discussed in the next chapter, compensation for a breach of trust arises independently of the two measures of restitution. However, it does not satisfactorily explain the liability of a recipient who is unaware of the provider's entitlement. Where the recipient has received a benefit from the resulting trust, his or her personal liability can also be explained as restitution of that benefit apart from the breach of duty.

[44] *Restatement of Restitution*, §142(3)(b). [45] (1978) 4 Fam.L.R. 258 (W.A.).
[46] [1994] 1 All E.R. 35, C.A. [47] Ibid. at 41.

2. Change of Position

The second possible explanation is that the recipient is liable in the first measure for the value of the provider's initial contribution, subject to the defence of change of position.[48] Notwithstanding the recipient's awareness of the facts giving rise to the resulting trust, the provider's consent to the transfer of legal title means that the recipient is innocent and entitled to the defence until he or she acts inconsistently with the provider's interest. This is compatible with the Court of Appeal's approach to rescission in *Cheese* v. *Thomas*, where Nicholls V.C. said:[49]

> If, for this purpose, the transaction in this case is analysed simply as a payment of £43,000 by Mr. Cheese to Mr. Thomas in return for the right to live in Mr. Thomas's house, there is a strong case for ordering repayment of £43,000, the benefit received by Mr. Thomas, regardless of the subsequent fall in the value of the house . . . In my view the present case stands differently. Mr. Cheese paid Mr. Thomas £43,000, not outright, but as part of the purchase price of a house in which both would have rights.

The Court of Appeal thought it would be harsh 'to require Mr. Thomas to shoulder the whole of the loss', given the nature of the transaction and the fact that he was 'an innocent fiduciary'.[50] If this is true where the plaintiff entered into the transaction under undue influence, it must apply *a fortiori* to the typical case of resulting trust in which one party contributes to the acquisition of property in the name of another. The difficulty with this analysis of the personal liability in *Cheese* v. *Thomas* is that it cannot account for cases, like *Matusewich*, where the property increases in value. Change of position is a defence to a restitutionary claim and cannot be used as a means of increasing the measure of that claim.

3. Beneficial Receipt

The third explanation is that the value received is not the initial payment used to acquire the beneficial interest, but the value of that interest at the time it is taken by the resulting trustee for his or her own benefit. Support for this approach can be gleaned from *Agip (Africa) Ltd.* v. *Jackson*.[51] In that case, over $500,000 had been fraudulently diverted by the plaintiff's chief accountant to the defendants, who had paid all but $45,000 away as part of a money-laundering scheme. The plaintiff was entitled to recover the value surviving and the defendants were liable to repay the balance because they had 'dishonestly assisted in the misapplication'.[52] Notwithstanding their dishonesty, they were not liable 'on the basis of knowing receipt' of the money because they 'did not receive or apply it for their own use and benefit'.[53]

[48] See Chen-Wishart, at 177–8; Birks and Chin, at p. 74.
[49] [1994] 1 All E.R. 35, 40.
[50] Ibid. at 43, per Nicholls V.C.
[51] [1989] 3 W.L.R. 1367; aff'd [1991] 3 W.L.R. 116, C.A.
[52] Ibid. at 1392, per Millett J.
[53] Ibid. at 1388, per Millett J.

According to Millett J., the essential feature of receipt-based liability 'is that the recipient must have received the property for his own use and benefit'.[54] In cases of resulting trust where legal title to the property has passed to the recipient with the consent of its provider, there is nothing to indicate that the recipient has taken it for his or her own use and benefit until he or she does some act inconsistent with the resulting trust. The provider's consent protects the recipient from receipt-based liability without the need to resort to the defence of change of position. In *Matusewich*, the husband had not received the wife's $1,000 for his own use and benefit because she had consented to its investment in the house and he had done nothing inconsistent with her beneficial interest until he converted her share of the sale proceeds to his own use and benefit. His receipt occurred at that moment and the first measure was not $1,000, but her share of the proceeds.[55]

This last explanation is perhaps the best and most consistently useful of the three. It has several advantages. First, it builds on (or is consistent with) the familiar concept of breach of trust, while providing an explanation of personal liability apart from any wrongdoing. Secondly, it is consistent with what appears to be the direction of receipt-based liability in equity. Thirdly, it provides for the consistent treatment of increases and decreases in the value of the trust property. Fourthly, it explains why the resulting trustee is not normally personally liable for any loss or decrease in the value of property in his or her hands with the beneficiary's consent, without amending the concept of change of position to cover situations where the recipient was aware of the provider's entitlement.

D. SUMMARY

Resulting trustees are normally liable in the second measure to restore the trust property still surviving in their hands. First-measure claims against resulting trustees for restitution of the value received should be possible, subject to the defence of change of position. It is not clear whether an innocent recipient can be liable to an equitable first-measure claim, but the provider may have other co-existing personal claims (e.g. money had and received). A first-measure claim against a resulting trustee should be based on the value of the property when it is converted to his or her own use and benefit, rather than its value on initial receipt.

[54] Ibid.

[55] This is not contradicted by Burrows (1993a), p. 258, when he states that the first measure is the value initially received and not the value surviving at the time of a subsequent failure of consideration. Whether and when defendants receive for their own benefit is a separate issue.

9
Fiduciary Obligations

Fiduciary obligations provide a potential source of personal liability for the resulting trustee in addition to the first-measure claim based on the receipt of property belonging in equity to another. Unlike the first-measure claim discussed in the previous chapter, fiduciary obligations create liabilities which are not necessarily restitutionary. However, if the resulting trust is capable of a greater role as a response to unjust enrichment, it is important to consider the potential consequences of that response. The nature and extent of the resulting trustee's fiduciary obligations are considered first, followed by an examination of three potential consequences of those obligations: liability for breach of trust, presumptions against a wrongdoer, and liability for compound interest.

A. NATURE AND EXTENT OF THE OBLIGATIONS

1. Variety of Fiduciary Relations

Fiduciary obligations usually arise because of the relationship between the parties. The trust is the central example of a fiduciary relationship and it was by analogy to it that fiduciary duties were extended to people in other relationships, such as agents, partners, solicitors, and corporate directors.[1] The Law Commission refers to them as 'status-based fiduciaries', meaning 'people who by virtue of their involvement in certain relationships are considered, without further inquiry, to be fiduciaries.'[2] People may also become fiduciaries in relationships which do not normally involve fiduciary obligations. The Law Commission calls them 'fact-based fiduciaries' to indicate that 'the fiduciary duties are incurred because of the factual situation of the particular relationship'.[3] It may also be possible for fiduciary obligations to arise, not from the nature of the relationship between the parties, but from a particular event, such as a mistaken payment.[4]

[1] Waters (1984), pp. 712–15; Goff and Jones, pp. 643–7; Glover, p. 32 ff.

[2] Law Commission (1992) §2.4.3. See *Hospital Products Ltd.* v. *U.S. Surgical Corp.* (1984) 156 C.L.R. 41, 68, 96, 141.

[3] Ibid. See Flannigan at 301; Maddaugh and McCamus, pp. 576–87; *Lac Minerals Ltd.* v. *International Corona Resources Ltd.* (1989) 61 D.L.R. (4th) 14, 29, S.C.C.; noted by Davies (1990a); *Commonwealth Bank of Australia* v. *Smith* (1991) 102 A.L.R. 453.

[4] *Chase Manhattan Bank N.A.* v. *Israel-British Bank (London) Ltd.* [1981] Ch. 105, 119.

As Lord Mustill said in *Re Goldcorp Exchange Ltd.*, 'To describe someone as a fiduciary, without more, is meaningless'.[5] In the words of Frankfurter J., it 'only begins analysis'.[6] There is no standard set of fiduciary obligations applicable to all fiduciaries. As Fletcher Moulton L.J. said in *Re Coomber*, there are many types of fiduciary relationships, ranging from 'the relation of myself to an errand boy who is bound to bring me back my change' to relations of 'infinite trust'.[7] Courts of equity will interfere in each relationship to enforce the fiduciary obligations appropriate to that relationship. However, as Fletcher Moulton L.J. also stated, it would be 'absurd' to 'conclude that every kind of fiduciary relation justifies every kind of interference . . . The nature of the fiduciary relation must be such that it justifies the interference'.[8]

2. Trustees

As the premier fiduciary, the trustee is normally subject to obligations of the highest degree. The express trustee's duty of loyalty prohibits any conflict of interest or profit from the position, unless authorized by the trust instrument, statute, or the court.[9] In addition, the express trustee is normally expected to exercise a high standard of care in relation to the investment and preservation of the trust property.[10] Not all trustees are subject to the same standard of care, depending on the nature of the trust to be performed and the character of the trustee. It has been said 'that a higher duty of care is plainly due from someone like a trust corporation which carries on a specialised business of trust management',[11] whereas infant trustees were not liable for losses caused by their failure to perform their trust duties.[12]

The nature and extent of fiduciary obligations are also variable according to the type of trust. For example, the vendor under a specifically enforceable contract for the sale of land is a constructive trustee of that property for the purchaser.[13] 'However', as the Law Commission stated, 'it is a most unusual trusteeship: the vendor remains entitled to possession of, and to the rents and profits from, the property, contrary to the normal principle that a trustee cannot profit from his trust'.[14] Professor Martin has observed that, 'each party is continuing to guard

[5] [1995] 1 A.C. 74, 98, P.C.
[6] *Securities & Exchange Comm'n* v. *Chenery Corp.* (1943) 318 U.S. 80, 86.
[7] [1911] 1 Ch. 723, 728.
[8] Ibid. at 729. See A.W. Scott (1949) at 541; Goff and Jones, p. 646.
[9] *Boardman* v. *Phipps* [1967] 2 A.C. 46; *Re Duke of Norfolk's Settlement Trusts* [1982] Ch. 61, C.A.; Baker and Langan, *Snell's Equity*, pp. 245–57; Martin (1993a), pp. 575–84.
[10] *Learoyd* v. *Whiteley* (1887) 12 A.C. 727, 733; *Baker* v. *Langan, Snell's Equity*, p. 213; Martin (1993a), p. 499 ff.
[11] *Bartlett* v. *Barclays Bank Trust Co. Ltd.* [1980] Ch. 515, 534, per Brightman J.
[12] *Hindmarsh* v. *Southgate* (1827) 3 Russ. 324; Scott and Fratcher, §215.
[13] *Shaw* v. *Foster* (1872) L.R. 5 H.L. 321. See Law Commission (1988); Waters (1964), pp. 74–141.
[14] Law Commission (1990), §2.6, p. 4. See Hackney, p. 37.

his own interests against the other in a way which is quite inconsistent with the existence of the relationship of trustee and beneficiary'.[15]

Lonrho p.l.c. v. *Fayed (No. 2)*[16] provides another example of the lesser degree of fiduciary obligations applicable to some trusts. The plaintiffs were seeking rescission of a sale of shares on the basis of fraudulent misrepresentation. They also argued that the purchasers (i) held those shares on constructive trust, (ii) had acquired further shares in breach of their duties as trustees not to have conflicting interests or profit from the trust and, therefore, (iii) were constructive trustees of the additional shares. Millett J. rejected this argument:[17]

> It is a mistake to suppose that in every situation in which the constructive trust arises the legal owner is necessarily subject to all the fiduciary obligations and disabilities of an express trustee. Even after the representee has elected to avoid the contract and reclaim the property, the obligations of the representor would in my judgment be analogous to those of a vendor of property contracted to be sold, and would not extend beyond the property actually obtained by the contract and liable to be returned.

3. Resulting Trustees

Although constructive trustees are in some circumstances subject to less onerous duties than express trustees, the situation regarding resulting trustees is far from clear. In most cases of resulting trust, the plaintiff is only seeking recovery in the second-measure of the surviving trust property and, therefore, the nature and extent of the resulting trustee's personal liability are rarely discussed. In some cases (discussed below), the fiduciary nature of the resulting trust has given rise to liability for breach of trust,[18] evidentiary presumptions being made against the trustee,[19] and awards of compound interest.[20]

It appears that the resulting trust is regarded as a fiduciary relationship in the USA,[21] whereas the constructive trust is not.[22] There are two important things to note about the American position: (i) the purposes for which the resulting trustee has been classified as a fiduciary and (ii) their classification of trusts as either constructive or resulting. First, the fiduciary nature of the resulting trust tends to be used for purposes other than enforcing personal liabilities for breach of fiduciary duties. Professor Scott refers to it in a section on laches and limitation periods.[23]

[15] Martin (1993a), p. 319. [16] [1992] 1 W.L.R. 1.

[17] Ibid. at 11. [18] *Matusewich* v. *Matusewich* (1978) 4 Fam.L.R. 258 (W.A.).

[19] *Westdeutsche Landesbank Girozentrale* v. *Islington L.B.C.* [1994] 4 All E.R. 890; varied [1996] 2 All E.R. 961, H.L.

[20] Ibid. at 954; *Matusewich* v. *Matusewich* (1978) 4 Fam.L.R. 258; *Guardian Ocean Cargoes Ltd.* v. *Banco do Brasil S.A. (No. 3)* [1992] 2 Lloyd's L.R. 193; rev'd [1994] 2 Lloyd's L.R. 152, C.A.

[21] *Tricentrol Oil* v. *Annesley* (1991) 809 S.W.2d 218; *Restatement of Restitution*, §160, p. 642; *Restatement of Trusts*, vol. 2, p. 326; Scott and Fratcher, §409.

[22] *Salisbury* v. *Tibbetts* (1958) 259 F.2d 59, 64; *Restatement of Restitution*, §160, p. 641; Scott and Fratcher, §462. See Frankel, at pp. 180–2.

[23] Scott and Fratcher, §409.

This was followed in *Ross* v. *USA*,[24] where the beneficiary of a resulting trust was re-assessed in 1955 for taxes on the profits of the sale of the trust property in 1944. The court held that the claim was not barred by the statute of limitations because of an exception in the statute regarding fiduciary relationships. Although the claim was personal, it had nothing to do with the trustee's fiduciary obligations (being a claim against the beneficiary), but was made in respect of a normal incidence of beneficial ownership.

In *Tricentrol Oil Trading Inc.* v. *Annesley*,[25] the plaintiff had purchased two seats on the New York Mercantile Exchange in the name of its president, Mr. Touchstone. When Touchstone was removed from corporate office, the parties released each other from all claims. Two months later, the plaintiff sought recovery of the seats (worth $546,000) on the basis of resulting trust. Touchstone argued that the plaintiff's claim was barred by its release. The Texas Supreme Court stated:[26]

> The trustee of a resulting trust stands in a fiduciary relationship with the beneficiaries insofar as the trust property is concerned . . . the release is ineffective as to the trust property, i.e. the seats, because Touchstone, in his capacity as trustee, failed to make a full and frank disclosure of his claim to the same. Although a resulting trust does not carry with it all of the duties of a trustee acting under an express trust, such a trustee has a duty to hold and convey the property according to the beneficiary's demands.

The characterization of Touchstone as a fiduciary was relevant to the availability of the plaintiff's second-measure claim for the property held on resulting trust. As in *Ross* v. *USA*, it was not used as a source of additional personal liability.

The second thing to note about the American view of the respective fiduciary obligations of resulting and constructive trustees is their classification of these two trusts. As discussed below,[27] the constructive trust is more commonly used in America than in England, while the resulting trust is restricted by statute and equity to a far greater extent there than it is here. Many of the trusts which are identified as constructive (and not involving a fiduciary relationship) in America would probably be classified as resulting under English law.

As discussed in Chapter 6, one of the reasons the House of Lords rejected the resulting trust in *Westdeutsche* v. *Islington* was the concern that an innocent recipient of money should not be subjected to the onerous consequences of trusteeship.[28] Both Lord Goff and Lord Browne-Wilkinson referred to a comment on the judgment of the Court of Appeal, in which Professor Burrows said:[29]

> [I]f this analysis is correct, and Islington were, as Dillon L.J. insisted, resulting trustees of the £2.5 million paid by Westdeutsche, the consequences are dramatic. For, unless one somehow cuts back the normal incidents of trusteeship, it ought to follow that the trustee

[24] (1957) 148 F.Supp. 330, U.S.Dist.Ct., Mass. [25] (1991) 809 S.W.2d 218, Tex.S.C.
[26] Ibid. at 220. [27] At p. 226. [28] [1996] 2 All E.R. 961, 974, 986.
[29] [1995] R.L.R. 15, 27.

is personally strictly liable to account as a fiduciary for profits made from the trust property . . . Again, applying the normal trust rules, . . . if the payee fails to return the money when the payee demands it, on the ground that he has changed his position, this will still constitute a breach of fiduciary duty for which the payer can claim an account of loss or gain . . . Similarly, the application of normal trust rules would mean that there would be no limitation period applicable to the equitable action . . . In summary, the startling conclusion is that . . . the recipient of a mistaken payment is always a wrongdoer and the Birksian divide between unjust enrichment by subtraction and unjust enrichment by wrongdoing is shattered.

All of these concerns rest on the unexplored assumption that a resulting trust involves all the duties and consequences of an express trust. As noted above, it is recognized that constructive trustees are not necessarily subject to the same fiduciary standards and there does not appear to be any basis for this assumption regarding resulting trustees. Indeed, *Lonrho p.l.c.* v. *Fayed (No. 2)*, in which Millett J. said it would be 'a mistake to suppose that in every situation in which the constructive trust arises the legal owner is necessarily subject to all the fiduciary obligations and disabilities of an express trustee',[30] might best be viewed as a case of potential resulting (rather than constructive) trust.

Resulting (and constructive) trusts create a problem for the imposition of fiduciary obligations. The recipient of the property is a trustee and therefore a fiduciary for its provider, but that trust arises by operation of law as a response to an event, rather than from a voluntary undertaking of that relationship. Although the resulting trust is accepted as a fiduciary relationship, it often appears to be more like a case of fiduciary obligations arising from an event rather than a relationship. Whether the resulting trustee is regarded as a 'status-based' or 'fact-based' fiduciary[31] should depend on the situation giving rise to the resulting trust, as should the nature and degree of the obligations associated with it.

4. Scale of Resulting Trust Obligations

At the lower end of the scale are cases where the resulting trust arises in the absence of any pre-existing fiduciary relationship and without the knowledge of the resulting trustee. *Sinclair* v. *Brougham*[32] was just such a case and, although it has been overruled with respect to whether a payment under a void contract gives rise to a resulting trust,[33] it contains valuable insights into the consequences of resulting trusts in situations involving innocent recipients. In *Chase Manhattan Bank N.A.* v. *Israel-British Bank (London) Ltd.*, Goulding J. used *Sinclair* v. *Brougham* to support his conclusion that 'a person who pays money to another under a factual mistake retains an equitable property in it and the

[30] [1992] 1 W.L.R. 1, 11. See n. 16 above.
[31] Law Commission (1992).
[32] [1914] A.C. 398.
[33] *Westdeutsche* v. *Islington L.B.C.* [1996] 2 All E.R. 961. See pp. 157–8 above.

conscience of the other is subject to a fiduciary duty to respect his proprietary right'.[34] In other words, an event gives rise to the recipient's fiduciary obligation to respect the provider's proprietary right. As the Texas Supreme Court stated, the resulting trust is 'a fiduciary relationship . . . *insofar as the trust property is concerned*'.[35] The fiduciary obligations need not extend beyond those necessary to protect the provider's interest in that property. There is no reason to involve the strict duties of loyalty applicable to an express trustee. In *Sinclair* v. *Brougham*, Viscount Haldane L.C. held that there had 'been no breach of fiduciary duty on the part of the society'[36] even though the society had received the depositors' money on resulting trust and used it for its own benefit.

At the higher end of the scale are cases where the resulting trust arises on the failure of an express trust. The resulting trustee has agreed to obey strict rules of fidelity and exercise a certain standard of care as an express trustee and there is no reason for those obligations to cease when the express trust fails (unless the resulting trustee reasonably believes himself or herself to be entitled to the surplus). The trustee is already in a fiduciary relationship when the resulting trust arises (albeit with the beneficiaries of the express trust and not the settlor). Although the resulting trustee is a fiduciary only 'insofar as the trust property is concerned', that must involve the same duties of loyalty and care he or she has previously consented to observe with respect to that same property. As Ford and Lee state:[37] 'Where the resulting trust arises in relation to an express trust the trustee's duties of administration under the express trust will be owed as much for the benefit of the person entitled under the resulting trust as for the benefit of any beneficiaries under the express trust'.

The resulting trust which arises when one person has contributed to the purchase of property in the name another, with the knowledge of both parties, occupies the middle ground between fact-based and status-based fiduciaries. *Tricentrol Oil Trading Inc.* v. *Annesley* was just such a case and the Texas Supreme Court accepted that the 'resulting trust does not carry with it all of the duties of a trustee acting under an express trust'.[38] The recipient's knowing acceptance of a contribution does not mean that he or she has consented to undertake the office of express trustee and all its duties of loyalty and care. Nevertheless, the provider of the property is vulnerable to the actions of the recipient as legal owner and is therefore placing some degree of trust and confidence in the latter. The willing acceptance of a contribution in that situation ought to lead to greater fiduciary obligations than those applied to the unwitting recipient.[39]

Where one person has contributed to a purchase in the name of another, the arrangement is often intended for the mutual benefit of both parties. Therefore,

[34] [1981] Ch. 105, 119.

[35] *Tricentrol Oil* v. *Annesley* (1991) 809 S.W.2d 218, 220 (emphasis added).

[36] [1914] A.C. 398, 424. [37] Ford and Lee, §21180.

[38] *Tricentrol Oil* v. *Annesley* (1991) 809 S.W.2d 218, 220.

[39] See *Taddeo* v. *Taddeo* (1978) 19 S.A.S.R. 347, 368.

the normal rules that trustees are not allowed to profit from their position or engage in conflicts of interest are somewhat inappropriate. A lesser degree of fiduciary obligations may be inherent in the relationship, which is somewhat akin to a partnership.[40] However, it may be that the recipient is relieved of higher duties by the provider's consent to the arrangement.[41] Although the distinction is fine and unlikely to have any practical effect, the 'partnership' analysis directs attention to the objective nature of the relationship between the parties, whereas the 'consent' analysis looks more to the subjective state of mind of the provider. It is therefore possible that the level of fiduciary obligations will not always be the same on each analysis.

Just as there is no uniform set of obligations applicable to all fiduciaries, there is no one set for all trustees or even all resulting trustees. The principle of resulting trust applies in such a wide variety of situations that it is impossible to deduce, solely from the classification of resulting trust, that any particular set of fiduciary obligations applies. If it is remembered that a finding of resulting trust 'only begins analysis'[42] into the level of fiduciary obligations involved, many concerns about the greater role of the resulting trust, and its extension into commercial activities,[43] will be alleviated.

B. LIABILITY FOR BREACH OF TRUST

The liability for breach of trust can be restitutionary. For example, trustees who secretly profit from their office may be liable to account for and pay that profit to the beneficiaries of the trust.[44] This is restitution in the first measure of the benefit the trustees acquired in breach of the duties they owed to those beneficiaries.[45] However, liability for breach of trust is more typically compensatory than restitutionary. Trustees are liable for any loss to the value of the trust property caused by a breach of their duties of care or loyalty, regardless of whether they have derived a benefit thereby.[46] The liability tends to be strict, so that even honest trustees may be liable for an unintended breach. As stated in *Modern Equity*:[47] 'This liability is independent of fraud, intent or personal incompetence; it exists where the breach is innocent or merely technical. The object of the rule is not to punish the trustee, but to compensate the beneficiaries'.

[40] See *Aas* v. *Benham* [1891] 2 Ch. 244, C.A.

[41] See *Regal (Hastings) Ltd.* v. *Gulliver* (1942) [1967] 2 A.C. 134; Scott and Fratcher, §216.

[42] *S.E.C.* v. *Chenery Corp.* (1943) 318 U.S. 80, 86, per Frankfurter J.

[43] See Mason at 245.

[44] e.g. *Boardman* v. *Phipps* [1967] 2 A.C. 46.

[45] Goff and Jones, pp. 643–70; Birks (1989a), pp. 332–3.

[46] *In re Pauling's Settlement Trusts* [1964] Ch. 303, 338, C.A.; Scott and Fratcher, §205, §206; Baker and Langan, *Snell's Equity*, p. 287.

[47] Martin (1993a), p. 619.

1. Innocent Recipients

Resulting trustees are sometimes unaware of the existence of the trust or even their receipt of trust property.[48] This raises the question whether they can be liable for breach of trust in spite of their innocence. Express trustees may be liable even though they have acted honestly and reasonably,[49] but the strict application of the standard of care (like the duty of loyalty) is justified by their consent to undertake that onerous office. It would be quite remarkable if recipients of property on resulting trust could be required to compensate the trust beneficiaries for the failure to perform duties which were not voluntarily undertaken and of which they were not aware. As Mr. Hackney states:[50]

> [I]n what sense is it right to call the unknowing infant resulting trustee, into whose name property has been secretly and voluntarily transferred, a fiduciary? Such a person can have none of the duties or powers of the express trustee and ought to have only an obligation to restore the property on demand, if still in possession of it. Even reckless disregard of property one does not know one has (the infant, grown old, but still unknowing, negligently loses the property) should not produce liability. No more should innocent transfer on.

The resulting trustee, who was unaware of any fetter on his or her beneficial ownership of the property, should not be liable in these circumstances. To hold otherwise would create an unwarranted interference with the enjoyment of apparently beneficial legal ownership. The Law Commission has reached the same conclusion in relation to the defence of change of position. They 'believe that, in principle, a person ought to be able to spend money to which he appears entitled as he chooses' and have therefore recommended that the defence be available for losses caused by a careless recipient, provided he or she acted honestly.[51] One counter-argument might be that equity already interferes with apparently beneficial legal ownership by enforcing prior equitable claims to property against innocent donees. However, the equitable owner is only entitled to recover the value surviving or, possibly, the value received, subject to the defence of change of position. Either way, the innocent recipient is not liable to compensate the owner for losses to the property and the label 'resulting trustee' should not itself produce additional personal liabilities.

A resulting trustee's liability to pay compensation for losses caused by a breach of trust should not be affected by whether he or she has obtained a benefit thereby. The arguments set out here apply with equal force in either situation and the trustee's receipt of a benefit is irrelevant to the issue of compensation.

[48] e.g. *In re Vinogradoff* [1935] W.N. 68.
[49] e.g. *Davis* v. *Hutchings* [1907] 1 Ch. 356; see Scott and Fratcher, §201.
[50] Hackney, p. 167.
[51] Law Commission (1994) §2.23, p. 19; see Nolan (1995).

In *Sinclair* v. *Brougham*, the society had used the money received on resulting trust for its own purposes and was not in breach of its fiduciary obligations. Lord Parker said:[52] 'If the [recipient] had notice that the money was held in a fiduciary capacity, he would be in exactly the same position as the fiduciary agent . . . But if he had not such notice this would not be the case. There would on his part be no misconduct at all'. The innocent recipient's liability for using the trust property for his or her own benefit is not explicable as a breach of trust, but as restitution of the enrichment regardless of fault. Although the knowing recipient would be liable for breach of trust, this liability is concurrent with the obligation to make restitution in the first-measure.

This brings the discussion full circle to first-measure claims for restitution (discussed in the previous chapter). Although equity may be moving in the direction of strict, receipt-based liability, the imposition of strict liability for breach of trust is not consistent with (and may run counter to) the two principal factors motivating that trend. The first factor is the availability of the defence of change of position.[53] It has developed as a defence to restitutionary claims and, so far, there has been no suggestion that it is a defence to claims for compensation for loss arising from breach of trust. Since every owner of property which belongs in equity to another is, by definition, a trustee of that property,[54] strict liability to compensate for breach of trust would effectively nullify the defence of change of position for most first-measure restitutionary claims based on the receipt of such property.[55]

The second factor which has encouraged the trend towards strict liability for the receipt of property belonging in equity to another has been the recognition that this liability is based on receipt and not fault. Requiring a recipient to pay compensation for the breach of a duty, of which he or she was unaware, flies in the face of the very concern which has impeded the development of receipt-based liability. In *Re Diplock*,[56] the beneficiaries of the estate had advanced two personal claims in equity against the wrongly-paid charities: (i) constructive trusteeship based on notice of the invalidity of the bequest under which they were paid and (ii) strict liability for the receipt of the property of a deceased person to which they were not entitled. The second was successful (along with the equitable proprietary claim to the value surviving), but the Court of Appeal rejected the claim that the charities had notice of the invalidity and said, 'if, as admitted in this case, they took the money bona fide believing themselves to be entitled to it, they should not have imposed upon them the heavy obligations of trusteeship'.[57]

Although the recipient of property belonging in equity to another will be a trustee of that property for that other, there is no justification for imposing any personal liability for breach of the obligations associated with that trust until

[52] [1914] A.C. 398, 442–3.
[53] Above, pp. 189–90.
[54] See Birks (1996b) at 11–12.
[55] Burrows (1995) at 27.
[56] [1948] Ch. 465, C.A.
[57] Ibid. at 478.

the recipient has or ought to have become cognisant of those obligations. The imposition of this type of liability on innocent recipients was precisely what the Court of Appeal rejected in *Re Diplock*.

2. Exoneration from Liability

There are compelling reasons for not imposing personal liability for breach of trust on innocent recipients, but on what basis should they be exonerated from the liability that knowing recipients would bear in otherwise similar circumstances? Four possibilities are that, until they are (or ought to be) aware of the trust, innocent recipients (i) are not trustees, (ii) do not have any personal trust obligations, (iii) are not in breach of their trust obligations, or (iv) are in breach of trust, but can be excused from liability.

No trust

One possibility is that innocent recipients of property can never be liable for breach of trust simply because there is no trust so long as they remain innocent. This was suggested by Lord Browne-Wilkinson in *Westdeutsche* v. *Islington L.B.C.*:[58]

> Since the equitable jurisdiction to enforce trusts depends upon the conscience of the holder of the legal interest being affected, he cannot be a trustee of the property if and so long as he is ignorant of the facts alleged to affect his conscience, i.e. until he is aware that he is intended to hold the property for the benefit of others in the case of an express or implied trust, or, in the case of a constructive trust, of the factors which are alleged to affect his conscience.

This possibility needs to be examined in some detail, because it concerns the fundamental nature of the trust. It offers a deceptively simple way of eliminating the dilemma of the innocent trustee, but turns out to produce several more serious problems.

Lord Browne-Wilkinson's statement was probably true at more than one stage in the development of the trust, but is difficult to reconcile with the modern law of trusts. The origins of the use are not clearly known, but it seems likely that uses were first enforced in ecclesiastical courts (which had jurisdiction over wills) and later in chancery because the consciences of feoffees *que uses* were affected.[59] The rules for the enforcement of uses developed into a settled body of law and, after the Statute of Uses 1536, the creation and execution of uses gave rise to several sophisticated conveyancing devices.[60] The use no longer depended on its effect on the conscience of the feoffee *que use*. For example,

[58] [1996] 2 All E.R. 961, 988.
[59] See Barton (1965); Milsom pp. 200–15; Simpson (1986) pp. 176–81; Baker (1990) p. 286.
[60] See Megarry and Wade, pp. 1170–2; Simpson (1986) pp. 188–90.

a conveyance 'unto and to the use of B and his heirs',[61] ensured that B received legal title through the creation and execution of a use in favour of himself. This cannot be explained on the basis that B was bound in conscience to hold the property for his own use. The use arose simply because the conditions for its creation had been met.

When the modern trust began to develop as a use upon a use, chancery again appealed to conscience to justify the enforcement of the second use.[62] However, the law continued to develop and now most trusts arise because the conditions for their creation are met and not directly because the conscience of the trustee is affected in any particular way. Professor Maitland gives an example which is useful for present purposes:[63] 'I declare myself a trustee of this watch for my son who is in India. If afterwards I sell that watch, although my son has never heard of the benefit that I intended for him, I commit a breach of trust and my son has an equitable cause of action against me'.

The only satisfactory explanation why my conscience is affected in this example is that all the conditions for the creation of an express trust have been met and I am a trustee of the watch. This breaks down if the existence of that trust is made to depend on my conscience being affected.

In most cases of trust, the trustee will be aware of the trust or the facts giving rise to it. This coincidence may lead to the erroneous assumption that such knowledge or notice is one of the conditions for the creation of a trust. Trusts respond to a variety of events. Only some of these include wrongdoing on the part of the trustee; e.g. profit from a breach of fiduciary duty.[64] In other situations, the facts which give rise to the trust necessarily involve the trustee's knowledge of those facts; e.g. a specifically enforceable contract of sale[65] or a common intention to share a family home.[66] However, express and resulting trusts can come into existence in response to facts which occur without the trustee's knowledge.

The express trust depends upon the effective expression of the settlor's intention to create a trust of identifiable subject matter in favour of certain permissible objects, together with vesting of the title to the subject matter in the trustee.[67] All this can occur without the trustee's knowledge. This is demonstrated by *Smith* v. *Wheeler*,[68] where Sir Simon Mayne had, in 1643, assigned leasehold property to two trustees in trust for himself for life, with the remainder going to the defendant in the events which occurred. Mayne was later attained for treason for the murder of King Charles I and his property was forfeit to King Charles II, who assigned the lease to the plaintiff. The trustees were unaware of the trust

[61] Megarry and Wade, p. 1173.
[62] See Megarry and Wade, pp. 1172–3; Simpson (1986) pp. 199–207.
[63] Maitland, p. 54.
[64] e.g. *A.-G. Hong Kong* v. *Reid* [1994] 1 A.C. 324, P.C.
[65] e.g. *Bunny Industries Ltd.* v. *F.S.W. Enterprises Pty. Ltd.* [1982] Qd.R. 712.
[66] e.g. *Grant* v. *Edwards* [1986] Ch. 638, C.A.
[67] *Knight* v. *Knight* (1840) 3 Beav. 148; *Milroy* v. *Lord* (1862) 4 De G.F.&J. 264.
[68] (1671) 1 Lev. 279, 2 Keb. 565, 609 & 643, 1 Vent. 128, 1 Mod. 17 & 38.

until after Mayne's death in 1661. The whole Court of King's Bench held that the trust was valid and that only Mayne's equitable life estate was forfeit.

This was followed in *Siggers* v. *Evans*,[69] where a settlor executed a deed assigning property to a trustee in trust for the trustee and others. The settlor wrote to the trustee to inform him of the deed, but a writ of *fieri facias* was delivered to the sheriff the next day before the trustee acknowledged and accepted the trust. The case turned on whether the trust came into existence before the delivery of the writ and the court held that the trust was created when the deed was executed without the trustee's knowledge. Campbell C.J. said, 'we think it much safer that one general rule should prevail, than . . . that doubts should be raised as to the particular moment at which the deed operates by the assent of the grantee'.[70]

In *Mallott* v. *Wilson*,[71] a settlor made a voluntary settlement of property to a trustee in trust. The trustee disclaimed the trust in the following year and the settlor made a different voluntary settlement of the same property 22 years later. After the settlor's death, the question arose whether the beneficiaries of the first or second settlement were entitled to the property. Byrne J. held that the first trust was effectively created when the settlement was executed and that the trustee's disclaimer revested the property in the settlor subject to that trust. As Professor Scott said:[72]

> Acceptance by the trustee is necessary in order to subject him to a duty to the beneficiaries to perform the trust and to subject him to liabilities to third persons as legal owner of the trust property, but it is not a condition precedent to the creation of the trust. Disclaimer by the trustee relieves him from such duties and liabilities, but does not terminate the interest of the beneficiaries in the trust property.

As discussed in previous chapters, there are several cases in which resulting trusts have arisen without the trustee's knowledge, such as *Re Vinogradoff*[73] and *Re Muller*,[74] where the resulting trustees were children under the age of 7, and *Birch* v. *Blagrave*[75] and *Childers* v. *Childers*,[76] where the resulting trustees died without learning of the transfers of the trust property. In the latter case, it was unsuccessfully argued on behalf of the infant heiress of the resulting trustee that 'there was no understanding between the grantor and the grantee; nothing to raise an equity against the latter'.[77] A resulting trust arose in each of these cases even though the trustee had no notice of the facts giving rise to the trust and there was nothing to affect the conscience of the trustee in any particular way. This is not surprising because the resulting trust responds to events which can occur wholly without the trustee's knowledge.

In *Westdeutsche* v. *Islington*, Lord Browne-Wilkinson explained *Birch* v. *Blagrave*, *Childers* v. *Childers*, *Re Vinogradoff*, and *Re Muller* as cases where,

[69] (1855) 5 E.&B. 367. [70] Ibid. 383. [71] [1903] 2 Ch. 494.
[72] Scott and Fratcher, §35. Cf. Maitland, pp. 55–6; Matthews (1981).
[73] [1935] W.N. 68. [74] [1953] N.Z.L.R. 879. [75] (1755) Amb. 264.
[76] (1857) 1 De G.&J. 482. [77] Ibid. 487.

'by the time action was brought, [the original recipient] or his successors in title have become aware of the facts which give rise to a resulting trust; his conscience was affected as from the time of such discovery and *thereafter* he held on a resulting trust under which the property was recovered from him'.[78] This explanation is hard to accept for at least two reasons. First, it is not easily reconciled with the cases themselves. Secondly, delaying the creation of the trust until the trustees have sufficient notice to affect their consciences may have a drastic effect on a number of important matters which depend on the timing of the creation of the resulting trust, such as entitlement to income, liability for taxation, risk and insurance, commencement of limitation periods, transfer and transmission of property interests, and priority of competing claims.[79]

In *Birch* v. *Blagrave*, a father conveyed several estates to his daughter and continued to cut timber on the estates and receive the rents of them. Both father and daughter died while the daughter was unaware of the conveyance. If the resulting trust did not arise until after their deaths, there ought to have been an account of those profits for the daughter's estate. Instead, Lord Hardwicke C. declared that, notwithstanding the conveyance by the father, 'the trust and beneficial interest thereof ought to be deemed in this court to remain in himself, and to be subject to the disposition by his will'.[80] It is difficult to understand why the father was able to devise those estates if he had no beneficial interest in them at the time of his death. It is also difficult to understand why the consciences of the daughter's heirs at law ought to be affected in favour of the father's devisees unless the daughter held the property on resulting trust for the father or his devisees at the time of her death. The events giving rise to the resulting trust happened many years earlier at the time of the initial conveyance, which was when the resulting trust arose.

In *Re Vinogradoff*,[81] a grandmother transferred stock into joint names with her grand-daughter, who was 4 years old. The grandmother received the income from the stock until her death and her estate was not required to account for that income. Instead, Farwell J. said that, 'the stock was not the property of the infant, but formed part of the estate of the testatrix'.[82] The same situation occurred in *Re Muller*,[83] where an aunt deposited money in the names of her niece and nephew (then aged 2 and 6). The infants and their parents were unaware of the deposits and the aunt collected the interest during her life. These cases were decided on the basis that a resulting trust arose at the outset when the events giving rise to that trust occurred.

Making the creation of trusts depend on the affected conscience of the trustee would mean that many cases were wrongly decided. It would also lead to difficulties due to the potential uncertainty over when a trust arises. *Re Garnett*[84]

[78] [1996] 2 All E.R. 961, 988. [79] Birks (1996b) at 19–20. [80] (1755) Amb. 264, 266.
[81] [1935] W.N. 68. [82] Ibid. [83] [1953] N.Z.L.R. 879.
[84] (1885) 31 Ch.D. 1, C.A.; (1886) 33 Ch.D. 300, C.A.; see pp. 127–8 above.

provides a useful example. The plaintiff had released her share in a trust estate in consideration of £10,500 under the mistaken belief that this represented the true value of her share. Unknown to everyone involved, including the trustee, her share was worth more than £15,000 at the time. After the trustee's death 20 years later, the mistake was discovered and the plaintiff was entitled to rescind her release. In a marriage settlement executed shortly after the release, the plaintiff had covenanted to settle any after-acquired property worth more than £300. The Court of Appeal held that this did not include her share in the trust because it was 'then existing property of the intended wife, even though its existence was not known'.[85] The outcome would have been different if the plaintiff's equitable property interest depended on the conscience of the trustee, who was never aware of the mistake.

The creation of a resulting trust in this situation depends on the transfer of property and the provider's lack of intention to benefit the recipient. The question of intention can be difficult, but it concerns the state of affairs at the moment of transfer. Therefore, if there is a resulting trust, one can at least say with certainty when it arises. Introducing the affected conscience of the trustee as an additional requirement for the creation of a trust has alarming consequences. The inquiry would no longer be restricted to the events taking place at the moment of transfer, but could, in a case like *Re Garnett*, span the remaining years of the trustee's life. This is an enormous task, which could well leave the identity of the beneficial owner of the trust property in doubt for a long period of time. *Re Garnett* illustrates just one of many problems which can only be solved by knowing with certainty when a resulting trust arises.

Vandervell v. *I.R.C.*[86] (discussed at length in Chapter 2 above) concerns another matter which depends on the timing of the creation of a resulting trust: liability for taxation. It demonstrates convincingly that resulting trusts arise without regard to the conscience of the resulting trustee. As part of a scheme to make a gift to the Royal College of Surgeons and to avoid taxation, Mr. Vandervell caused shares to be transferred to the College and an option to purchase those shares to be granted to a trust company. The House of Lords held that the trust company was not intended to have the benefit of the option to purchase and therefore held it on resulting trust for Mr. Vandervell from the moment of receipt. No one involved foresaw this possibility. Mr. Vandervell did not want the shares and had tried to rid himself of any interest in them. It cannot be said that the conscience of the trust company was affected in any way and yet Mr. Vandervell incurred a substantial tax liability precisely because a resulting trust arose at the outset.[87]

In *Westdeutsche* v. *Islington L.B.C.*, Lord Browne-Wilkinson suggested that there is a distinction between the creation of a trust (which depends on the

[85] (1886) 33 Ch.D. 300, 305, per Cotton L.J.
[86] [1967] 2 A.C. 291.
[87] See Birks (1996b) at 19–20.

conscience of the owner of the trust property being affected through notice of the trust) and the continued existence of the trust in the hands of subsequent owners of that property (which does not):[88]

Once a trust is established, as from the date of its establishment the beneficiary has, in equity, a proprietary interest in the trust property, which proprietary interest will be enforceable in equity against any subsequent holder of the property (whether the original property or substituted property into which it can be traced) other than a purchaser for value of the legal interest without notice.

It is difficult to understand how this can be reconciled with his lordship's view that the 'equitable jurisdiction to enforce trusts depends upon the conscience of the holder of the legal interest being affected'.[89] What affects the conscience of an innocent subsequent recipient of trust property or distinguishes that person from the innocent original recipient? Why would equity ignore the original volunteer recipient, but not subsequent recipients, who are equally innocent and may even have given value for the property (though without acquiring the legal estate)?

Consider an example in which A pays money by mistake to B, who makes a gift of that money to C, who has no notice of the mistake. If, as Lord Browne-Wilkinson suggests,[90] the trust of a mistaken payment depends on the recipient's notice, C's beneficial entitlement to that money will depend on whether B had notice of the mistake before the gift to C was made. It is difficult to understand why B's notice should matter or why the outcome should be any different if C had received the mistaken payment directly from A. The trust is responding to the transfer of property and A's lack of intention to benefit the recipient. Although the recipient's knowledge or notice is relevant to the defences of *bona fide* purchase or good faith exchange (where the recipient has given value) or change of position,[91] it is not a relevant fact to which the trust responds.

To link the creation of equitable property interests directly to the affected conscience of the legal title holder, as Lord Browne-Wilkinson suggested, would be a difficult and dangerous departure from existing law. There is little to be gained by such a move and much to be lost. The modern law of trusts is the unfinished product of years of evolution which allows most of the events which give rise to trusts to be identified with some degree of certainty. Re-introducing the requirement of an affected conscience would undo much of this work and lead to the difficulties described above. As Professor Birks stated:[92]

The only way to overcome these problems would be to repeat the process which some may think that centuries of history have already achieved, namely to reduce 'affected conscience' to a list, no doubt a long and sophisticated list, of discoverable situations deemed by law to affect conscience . . . But once conscience is 'deemed to be affected' in this way it becomes a fifth wheel on the coach.

[88] [1996] 2 All E.R. 961, 988. [89] Ibid. [90] Ibid. 997.
[91] See pp. 189–90, 192 above. [92] Birks (1996b) at 20. See Milson (1981), p. 95.

It is helpful to recall a passage in the Court of Appeal's judgment in *Re Diplock*, concerning the equitable personal liability of charitable organizations to refund legacies paid to them by mistake:[93]

> It is no doubt true that an equitable claim predicates that the consciences of the defendant must be affected. But we have failed to observe any justification, in the judgments cited, for the suggestion that the state of the defendant's conscience depends upon his knowledge or assumed knowledge that his title to the money paid to him may or may not be defeasible in favour of other interested persons. The test as regards conscience seems rather to be whether at the time when the payment was made the legatee received anything more than, at the time, he was properly entitled to receive.

This was affirmed by the House of Lords, where Lord Simonds stated:[94]

> The Court of Chancery, it was said, acted on the conscience, and, unless the defendant had behaved in an unconscientious manner, would make no decree against him. The appellant, or those through whom he claimed, having received a legacy in good faith and having spent it without knowledge of any flaw in their title, ought not in conscience to be ordered to refund. My Lords, I find little help in such generalities. On the propriety of a legatee refusing to repay to the true owner the money that he has wrongly received I do not think it necessary to express any judgment. It is a matter on which opinions may well differ. The broad fact remains that the Court of Chancery, in order to mitigate the rigour of the common law or to supply its deficiencies, established the rule of equity which I have described, and this rule did not excuse the wrongly paid legatee from repayment because he had spent what he had been wrongly paid.

Similar comments could be made about the resulting trust. Whatever its origins, the resulting trust has evolved into a response to non-voluntary transfer and arises when that event occurs, regardless of the resulting trustee's notice of that event. The personal liability of the innocent resulting trustee is a separate issue, but one which cannot be resolved by denying the existence of the trust.

No duties

As suggested above, there is a scale of fiduciary obligations applicable to resulting trusts, according to the circumstances in which they arise. It may be that the innocence of the resulting trustee is a circumstance which takes that trust to (or off) the lower end of the scale. If this is true, then actions, which would constitute a breach of trust by a knowing recipient, are not wrongful for the innocent recipient because both persons are not subject to the same trust obligations.

However, the innocent resulting trustee cannot be entirely free of personal obligations with respect to the trust property. The trust evolved from the enforcement in Chancery of personal obligations against the feoffee *que use*.[95] Although

[93] [1948] Ch. 465, 488.
[94] *Ministry of Health* v. *Simpson* [1951] A.C. 251, 276; aff'g *Re Diplock*, ibid.
[95] Megarry and Wade, pp. 110–15; Maitland, pp. 28–30.

we are past the debate over whether beneficiaries have rights *in rem* as well as rights *in personam*,[96] it is inconceivable that the former could exist without the latter. Every trust necessarily 'involves the existence of equitable duties imposed upon the holder of the title to the property to deal with it for the benefit of another'.[97]

Since resulting trusts can arise without the knowledge of the recipients, from the moment of their receipt, even innocent recipients must be under some form of personal obligation with respect to the trust property. Hackney provides the best solution: such persons 'have only an obligation to restore the property on demand, if still in possession of it'.[98] The minimum duty, applicable to all resulting trustees, is to convey the property at the request of the trust beneficiary. With the request comes a degree of knowledge which moves the trust up the scale of fiduciary obligations to include a duty to preserve the trust property and possibly other duties, depending on the circumstances.

No breach

Another possible approach would be to apply the same duties to innocent and knowing recipients (in otherwise similar circumstances), but decide that there can be no breach of trust unless the recipient was at least aware of the circumstances giving rise to the resulting trust. It is interesting to compare the position taken in the American *Restatement of Restitution* concerning the common law obligation to make restitution following the receipt of property by mistake:[99] 'There is no breach of duty to make restitution because of a transfer made by mistake until the transferee or beneficiary has notice of the facts upon which the transferor's right depends and has had a reasonable opportunity for making restitution'.

There may be an important distinction between the primary liability to make restitution and the secondary liability for the wrong of knowingly breaching that primary liability.[100] However, this is somewhat difficult to apply to trusts because honest and well-meaning express trustees and other fiduciaries can be liable for the unintended breach of their duties.[101] Liability for breach of trust does not require a guilty mind.

As Lord King C. stated in *Keech* v. *Sandford*, strict liability for breach of trust 'may seem hard',[102] but it can be justified by the express trustee's consent to that

[96] See Cook; A.W. Scott (1917); Maitland, pp. 29–32, 106–7; Hackney, pp. 21–7; Scott and Fratcher, §130; Baker and Langan, *Snell's Equity*, pp. 23–4; Hovius and Youdan, pp. 28–30; Gray, pp. 47–50.

[97] Meagher and Gummow, *Jacobs' Law of Trusts*, p. 9; Scott and Fratcher, §2.3; Baker and Langan, *Snell's Equity*, p. 89.

[98] Hackney, p. 167. See Burrows (1995) at 28.

[99] *Restatement of Restitution*, §63; cf. *Baker* v. *Courage & Co.* [1910] 1 K.B. 56, 65; Lightwood (1909), p. 239.

[100] See Birks (1989a), p. 39; Birks (1996c).

[101] *Keech* v. *Sandford* (1726) Sel.Cas.T.King 61; *Bray* v. *Ford* [1896] A.C. 44, 51; *Regal (Hastings)* v. *Gulliver* (1942) [1967] 2 A.C. 134; *Boardman* v. *Phipps* [1967] 2 A.C. 46.

[102] (1726) Sel.Cas.T.King 61, 62.

task. There is a legitimate distinction to be drawn between someone who fails to appreciate the duties associated with an office voluntarily undertaken and someone who is unaware of that office. Knowing recipients can at least take steps to restore the property to their beneficiaries and rid themselves of the fiduciary obligations arising on receipt. A hard rule would become oppressive if it imposed liability on innocent recipients, who have undertaken no fiduciary duties and are unaware of their possible existence. However, these are arguments in support of the (preferable) view that innocent recipients should not be subject to the same duties as those who are aware of the circumstances giving rise to the resulting trust.

Statutory relief

Dr. Elias suggests that section 61 of the Trustee Act 1925 'offers a viable but as yet unexplored base for a change of position defence which is general to trustees'.[103] That section states that:[104]

> If it appears to the court that a trustee, whether appointed by the court or otherwise, is or may be personally liable for any breach of trust . . . but has acted honestly and reasonably, and ought fairly to be excused for the breach of trust . . . then the court may relieve him either wholly or partly from personal liability for the same.

The onus of proof is on the trustee to demonstrate that he or she has acted honesty and reasonably.[105] Honesty alone is not sufficient: in *Williams* v. *Byron*, trustees were not excused for leaving trust money with a solicitor who stole it.[106] Trustees may be acting 'reasonably' if they observe the same standard of conduct that persons of ordinary intelligence and diligence exercise over their own affairs.[107] However, Farwell J. stated in *Re Lord De Clifford's Estate*:[108]

> I am not prepared to say that a trustee has acted honestly and reasonably and ought fairly to be excused as a trustee merely on the ground that he has acted in exactly the same way with respect to his own money. The fact that he has acted with equal foolishness in both cases will not justify relief under this statute.

Elias suggests that section 61 applies to resulting (and constructive) trustees,[109] but its application to innocent recipients of property belonging in equity to others does not appear to have been considered.[110] As suggested above,[111] innocent recipients ought to be able to deal with property they believe to be their own in any manner they choose, however foolish. Although this would not be

[103] Elias, p. 20.
[104] Trustee Act 1925, s. 61. Also see Waters (1984), pp. 1025–31.
[105] *Re Stuart* [1897] 2 Ch. 583, 590.
[106] *Williams* v. *Byron* (1901) 18 T.L.R. 172.
[107] *Re Turner* [1897] 1 Ch. 536, 542.
[108] [1900] 2 Ch. 707, 716.
[109] Elias, p. 20; see Trustee Act 1925, s. 68(17); cf. Law Commission (1995) §15.7.
[110] This issue was raised, but avoided, in *Baden* v. *Société Générale pour Favoriser le Développement du Commerce et de L'Industrie en France S.A.* [1983] B.C.L.C. 325, [1993] 1 W.L.R. 509, 609.
[111] At pp. 201–3.

acting reasonably according to *Re Lord De Clifford's Estate*, there is a significant difference between one who has undertaken the office of trustee, or at least been aware of its existence, and one who has not. It may be that innocent recipients will always have 'acted honestly and reasonably and ought fairly to be excused' until they become (or ought to have become) aware of the obligation to restore the trust property.

In any event, innocent recipients should not have to rely on section 61. It would be a reproach to our system of law to require wholly innocent recipients to obtain forgiveness for disregarding unsuspected equitable interests. Instead, they should be considered not to be in breach of trust obligations of which they had no reason to be aware.[112] Although section 61 is designed to save trustees from liability for the unwitting breach of their trust obligations, it should left for those trustees who have undertaken that office or are at least aware of the circumstances giving rise to it.

C. PRESUMPTIONS AGAINST WRONGDOERS

Another potential consequence of a fiduciary relationship is that, in a dispute between the fiduciary and the beneficiary, the court will sometimes resolve evidential difficulties adversely to the fiduciary.[113] This occurred in *Re Hallett's Estate*,[114] where an agent, in breach of his fiduciary obligations, received the proceeds from the sale of his principal's property and mixed them with his own funds. The agent was presumed to have expended his own money in the account and not that which belonged in equity to his principal.[115] This presumption was applied by Hobhouse J. in *Westdeutsche* v. *Islington*.[116]

As discussed above, the Court of Appeal held in *Westdeutsche* v. *Islington* that the council was personally liable in equity to repay the money received from the bank on resulting trust. At trial, Hobhouse J. had reached the conclusion that the council was liable in equity for that same sum, but on the basis that the value continued to survive in the hands of the council. The Court of Appeal declined to comment on the correctness of this approach, even though it was clear that the money had been 'spent by the council on its ordinary purposes'.[117] It is respectfully suggested that the use of presumptions against a fiduciary to establish the existence of surviving value was incorrect in the circumstances and that a second-measure claim should not have been possible.

Hobhouse J., like the Court of Appeal, relied on *Sinclair* v. *Brougham* to find that the bank had an equitable proprietary interest in the money paid to the

[112] Hackney, p. 167. [113] See Birks (1989a), pp. 368–70.
[114] (1879) 13 Ch.D. 696, C.A. [115] Ibid. at 743. Also see *In re Oatway* [1903] 2 Ch. 356.
[116] [1994] 4 All E.R. 890, 938–40; varied, [1996] 2 All E.R. 961, H.L.
[117] [1994] 4 All E.R. 890, 966, per Dillon L.J.

council, which gave rise to a fiduciary relationship between the parties. However, contrary to *Sinclair* v. *Brougham* and *Re Diplock* (where the recipients were not required to subordinate their interests to those of the equitable owners), Hobhouse J. went on to conclude that:[118] 'Once the equity has been held to exist the burden of proof is upon the holder of the fund to prove what has happened to it . . . If the fiduciary wants to say that the relevant monies have been dissipated, he must prove that that is the only possible conclusion on the evidence'. His lordship conceded that any attempt by the council to prove that the value no longer survived 'would almost certainly be an impossible and fruitless exercise'.[119] Therefore, the presumption against the council led to the conclusion that all of its assets were subject to an equitable charge in favour of the bank.

All the cases Hobhouse J. cited in support of this adverse presumption involved express trustees acting in breach of trust.[120] The presumption had not previously been applied against an innocent recipient and *Sinclair* v. *Brougham* and *Re Diplock* suggest that it should not be done. As the Court of Appeal stated in *Re Diplock*, it would be 'inequitable for the true owner of the money to claim priority over the volunteer for the reason that the volunteer is innocent and cannot be said to act unconscionably if he claims equal treatment for himself'.[121]

In *Re Tilley's Will Trusts*, Ungoed-Thomas J. stated that, 'If a trustee mixes trust assets with his own, the onus is on the trustee to distinguish the separate assets, and to the extent that he fails to do so they belong to the trust'.[122] This principle was applied in that case to an express trustee and was stated correctly for that purpose. However, by not making any exception for resulting (and constructive) trustees, it has been put too broadly. Ungoed-Thomas J. derived the principle from *Lupton* v. *White*, where Lord Eldon C. set it out in narrower terms as,[123]

> the great principle, familiar both at law and in equity, that, if a man, *having undertaken to keep the property of another distinct*, mixes it with his own, the whole must both at law and in equity be taken to be the property of the other, until the former puts the subject under such circumstances, that it may be distinguished satisfactorily, as it might have been before that unauthorised mixture upon his part.

Innocent recipients, who become resulting trustees by operation of law, have not 'undertaken to keep the property of another distinct' and, therefore, the principle in *Lupton* v. *White* should have no application before they become aware of the obligation to restore the property to its provider.

In *Lupton* v. *White*, the plaintiff had obtained an injunction preventing the defendants, who operated neighbouring lead mines, from working mines under his property. The injunction was lifted on the defendants undertaking to account

[118] [1994] 4 All E.R. 890, 938, 939. [119] Ibid. at 188.
[120] *Cook* v. *Addison* (1869) L.R. 7 Eq. 466; *Re Oatway* [1903] 2 Ch. 356; *In re Tilley's Will Trusts* [1967] Ch. 1179. [121] *Re Diplock* [1948] Ch. 465, 539.
[122] [1967] Ch. 1179, 1183. [123] (1808) 15 Ves. 432, 436 (emphasis added).

for the lead ore removed from under the plaintiff's property. They failed to keep a separate account of the lead so removed and had made it impossible for the amount to be determined by inspection of the mines. Although there had been 'a case of violation of property, previous to the injunction', that only gave rise to the 'right to an account upon ordinary principles'.[124] Evidentiary presumptions were not made against the defendants until after the injunction, when they were in violation of their undertaking to keep the property separate. Lord Eldon C. explained:[125]

> If the parties have been permitted for a long course of years to deal with property as their own, considering themselves under no obligation to keep accounts, as if there was any adverse interest, having no reason to believe the property belonged to another, though it would not follow, that, being unable to give an accurate account, they should keep the property, yet the account would be directed, not according to the strict course, but in such a manner as under all the circumstances would be fit.

With respect, Hobhouse J. should not have applied any evidentiary presumptions against Islington, which had no reason to suspect that the money was not beneficially its own. However, even where that presumption is applicable, it should not be applied to the Draconian extent that inevitably produces a charge over all of the resulting trustee's assets.[126] As Joyce J. stated in *Re Oatway* (where an express trustee had improperly mixed the trust assets with his own funds), 'this rule is carried no further than necessity requires, and is applied only to cases where the compound is such as to render it impossible to apportion the respective shares of the parties'.[127] The rule is used solely to resolve evidential impossibilities adversely to the wrongdoer whose breach of duty has created those impossibilities. It should not allow the plaintiff to claim other assets of the recipient in the absence of any evidence connecting them to the plaintiff's input. In the words of Lord Mustill in *Re Goldcorp Exchange Ltd.*:[128] 'Such a trust or interest would differ fundamentally from those so far discussed, in that it would not arise directly from the transaction . . . but would be created by the court as a measure of justice after the event'.

Although his lordship was speaking of the imposition of a remedial constructive trust over unrelated assets of the recipient, his observations can be applied to the use of fictitious presumptions for the same purpose, as can his criticism that it would give the plaintiff 'an adventitious benefit devoid of the foundation in logic and justice which underlies this important new branch of the law'.[129]

[124] Ibid. at 441, per Eldon L.C. [125] Ibid. at 443.
[126] Goode (1987) at 446; Burrows (1993c) at 482.
[127] [1903] 2 Ch. 356, 359. [128] [1995] 1 A.C. 74, 99 (and see 104–5).
[129] Ibid. Also see *Re Diplock* [1948] Ch. 465, 521; *Indian Oil Corp. Ltd.* v. *Greenstone Shipping Co. S.A.* [1988] Q.B. 345; *Barlow Clowes Int. Ltd.* v. *Vaughan* [1992] 4 All E.R. 22, C.A.; Goode (1987) at 445–7; Birks (1989a), pp. 472–3; cf. *Space Investments Ltd.* v. *C.I.B.C. Trust Co. (Bahamas) Ltd.* [1987] 1 W.L.R. 1072, P.C.

D. INTEREST

This final part of the discussion of the potential consequences of the resulting trust concerns the court's equitable jurisdiction to order resulting trustees to pay compound interest on the money subject to the trust. At common law, debts did not carry interest unless the parties otherwise agreed.[130] This was amended by statute so that courts could order simple interest to be paid on debts,[131] including restitutionary first-measure claims for money had and received.[132] Courts of equity are not limited by the statute to awards of simple interest, but have an independent jurisdiction to award compound interest.[133]

In *Westdeutsche* v. *Islington*, Hobhouse J. and the Court of Appeal held that the plaintiff bank had an equitable proprietary claim to money paid under a void agreement, which entitled it to compound interest in equity.[134] The House of Lords held that the bank did not have a proprietary claim and was therefore entitled to statutory simple interest only.[135] Lords Goff and Woolf dissented on the basis that compound interest should be payable on the bank's personal restitutionary claim. This meant that none of the law lords had occasion to consider whether the existence of a resulting trust is a sufficient justification for an award of compound interest. It is suggested here that it is not.

Trustees who receive interest on trust property are always chargeable with that interest regardless of fault.[136] There is normally no liability to pay more interest than they have received unless they are in breach of trust for failing to invest the trust property, in which case they are liable for the interest that should have been earned.[137] Trustees who become liable to pay compensation for breach of trust are usually required to pay simple interest on that sum.[138] However, trustees who misappropriate trust property and use it in business may be liable to pay compound interest on the assumption that they have made at least that much profit.[139]

The purpose of an award of compound interest in equity is (i) to ensure that a fiduciary does not make a profit from a breach of his or her obligations and (ii) to compensate the beneficiary for the loss caused by the breach.[140] It is not

[130] *London, Chatham and Dover Railway Co.* v. *South Eastern Railway Co.* [1893] A.C. 429.

[131] Civil Procedure Act 1833, s. 28; Law Reform (Miscellaneous Provisions) Act 1934, s. 3; Supreme Court Act 1981, s. 35A (created by the Adminsitration of Justice Act 1982, s. 15). See Law Commission (1978) §11, p. 3; *President of India* v. *La Pintada Compania Navigacion S.A.* [1985] A.C. 104.

[132] *Woolwich Equitable Building Society* v. *I.R.C.* [1993] A.C. 70; Burrows (1993a), pp. 30–1.

[133] See *President of India* v. *La Pintada* [1985] A.C. 104, 116.

[134] [1994] 4 All E.R. 890.

[135] [1996] 2 All E.R. 961.

[136] *A.-G.* v. *Alford* (1855) 4 De G.M.&G. 843, 851–2; *In re Emmet's Estate* (1881) 17 Ch.D. 142, 149–50; Scott and Fratcher, §207.1; Baker and Langan, *Snell's Equity*, pp. 288–9.

[137] See n. 136 above.

[138] Scott and Fratcher, §207, §207.2; Baker and Langan, *Snell's Equity*, p. 288; Sheridan, pp. 437–8; Ford and Lee, §17140.

[139] Scott and Fratcher, §207.2; Baker and Langan, *Snell's Equity*, p. 289.

[140] *Wallersteiner* v. *Moir (No. 2)* [1975] Q.B. 373, 388, C.A.

awarded in every case involving a fiduciary, but used only sparingly. As Dunn L.J. stated in *O'Sullivan* v. *Management Agency & Music Ltd.*:[141] 'It is only in cases of breaches of fiduciary duty that compound interest can be awarded, since at common law . . . interest cannot be charged on interest. But in equity compound interest can be charged where the profits made in breach of fiduciary duty have been used in trade'. In *Wallersteiner* v. *Moir*, Buckley L.J. stated that, 'The defaulting trustee is normally charged with simple interest only, but if it is established that he has used the money in trade he may be charged compound interest'.[142]

1. Innocent Recipients

In *Westdeutsche* v. *Islington*, Hobhouse J. chose not to award interest for the period before the defendant council should have been aware of its obligation to make restitution.[143] The Court of Appeal overturned this aspect of Hobhouse J.'s judgment and awarded compound interest from the date of receipt. Even if the council had been a resulting trustee of the money received from the bank, there are good reasons why compound interest should not have been awarded in *Westdeutsche* v. *Islington*, or at least not before the council was aware of the facts giving rise to the resulting trust. First, for the reasons stated above regarding liability for breach of trust,[144] neither of the two purposes of an award of compound interest (profit stripping and compensation for loss) are applicable to innocent resulting trustees. In the absence of wrongdoing, the award of interest should do no more than effect restitution of the value actually provided to the innocent recipient by the claimant. The 'fiduciary' label is by itself an insufficient basis for any other measure of recovery.

The second reason for not awarding compound interest is related to the first. Awards of compound interest are based on a presumption that wrongdoing fiduciaries engaged in trade have used the misappropriated funds to earn the equivalent of compound interest.[145] As Lord Denning M.R. pointed out, this presumption against the wrongdoer is twofold:[146] 'On general principles I think it should be presumed that the company (had it not been deprived of the money) would have made the most beneficial use open to it . . . Alternatively, it should be presumed that the wrongdoer made the most beneficial use of it'.

As discussed in the previous section, it is improper to apply to innocent resulting trustees adverse presumptions based on misconduct. In *Re Diplock*, the Court of Appeal held that the plaintiffs' personal claims to recover the value of

[141] [1985] Q.B. 428, 461 (also see at 473–4); *Polish Steam Ship Co.* v. *Atlantic Maritime Co.* [1985] Q.B. 41, 61, C.A.

[142] [1975] Q.B. 373, 397.

[143] [1994] 4 All E.R. 890, 954.

[144] Above, pp. 195, 200.

[145] *A.-G.* v. *Alford* (1855) 4 De G.M.&G. 843, 851–2; *Burdick* v. *Garrick* (1870) 5 Ch.App. 233, 241, 243; *Wallersteiner* v. *Moir* [1975] Q.B. 373, 388, 397; *O'Sullivan* v. *Management Agency & Music Ltd.* [1985] Q.B. 428, 473.

[146] *Wallersteiner* v. *Moir* [1975] Q.B. 373, 388.

the improperly distributed estate assets did not include interest.[147] The court went on to say that, 'The same may not however be true as regards the claims in rem, at least where the appellants are able to "trace" their proprietary interest into some specific investment'.[148] In other words, a proprietary second-measure claim against an innocent recipient may include interest where it can be proven (and not merely presumed) that interest was actually earned with the recoverable property.

2. Changing the Law

The last issue to be considered here is whether equity's discretion to award compound interest should be extended to cases involving innocent resulting trustees as well as wrongdoing fiduciaries. It has been recognized that simple interest does not provide adequate compensation for the loss of the use of money in modern times.[149] It may be desirable to routinely allow compound interest on restitutionary claims where it is an accurate measure of the enrichment obtained at the expense of its provider. This was the approach taken by Lords Goff and Woolf, dissenting in *Westdeutsche* v. *Islington*. Lord Goff noted that equitable compound interest is awarded in 'cases of breach of duty by trustees and other fiduciaries'[150] and concluded that it 'is therefore available to achieve justice in a limited area of what is now seen as the law of restitution, viz where the defendant has acquired a benefit through his wrongful act'.[151] In Lord Goff's opinion, the principle could be applied more generally to cases involving restitution, regardless of whether the benefits were acquired by a wrongful act.

Lords Goff and Woolf believed that compound interest should be available in equity whenever the plaintiff is entitled to restitution. The important question is not whether the claim is proprietary or personal or whether the defendant is innocent or a wrongdoer, but whether compound interest is needed to achieve full restitution of the benefit received by the defendant.[152] The value of the benefit includes the cost of borrowing where it is proven that the recipient would have borrowed the money in any event. However, that is not necessarily true in other cases. Recipients may prefer not to have the money at that rate of interest or may have used it differently had they known of the liability to pay such interest. They should be permitted to subjectively devalue the benefit provided by the use of the money,[153] in which case their enrichment would include only the money received and any interest they have actually earned or saved.

The change advocated by Lords Goff and Woolf is based on the purpose of an award of compound interest on a restitutionary claim. Lord Goff stated, 'I

[147] [1948] Ch. 465, 507; citing *Gittins* v. *Steele* (1818) 1 Swanst. 199. [148] Ibid. at 517.

[149] *Bartlett* v. *Barclays Bank Trust Co. Ltd* [1980] Ch. 515, 546–7; *Techno-Impex* v. *Gebr. Van Weelde Scheepvaartkantoor B.V.* [1981] Q.B. 648, 665; Bowles and Whelan.

[150] [1996] 2 All E.R. 961, 976. [151] Ibid. 977. [152] Ibid. 978–81, 1010.

[153] See Birks (1989a), pp. 109–14. See p. 95 above.

find the reasoning which would restrict the equitable jurisdiction to award compound interest to cases where the claim is proprietary in nature to be both technical and unrealistic'.[154] A difficulty with the Court of Appeal's approach in *Westdeusche* v. *Islington* is that it also advocates a change in the law, but without proper consideration of the reasons for doing so. Awards of compound interest had been exceptional in equity (even among claims against wrongdoing fiduciaries), but the Court of Appeal would permit them in all cases involving the receipt of property belonging in equity to another, regardless of the recipient's fault. Using the proprietary nature of the claim as a justification for an award of compound interest is no less artificial than using it as a restriction on such an award.

Compound interest was awarded against a resulting trustee in two other cases, but there were other circumstances justifying those awards. In *Matusewich* v. *Matusewich*,[155] the Family Court of Western Australia ordered a husband to pay compound interest on the proceeds from the sale of the matrimonial home, which he held on resulting trust for his wife, but had used to purchase a commercial fishing boat. He was aware of his wife's interest in the home and this was an ordinary exercise of the equitable jurisdiction to award compound interest against a fiduciary who knowingly misappropriates trust funds for use in trade.

In *Guardian Ocean Cargoes Ltd.* v. *Banco do Brasil S.A. (No. 3)*,[156] the plaintiffs had paid $600,000 to the bank to be used in a possible refinancing arrangement the parties were negotiating. The negotiations failed after several years and the plaintiffs were entitled to a refund of their payments as money had and received on the basis of failure of consideration. Hirst J. also held that the failure gave rise to a *Quistclose* trust and, as trustee, the bank was liable to pay compound interest. The Court of Appeal overturned that aspect of the judgment and, therefore, the plaintiffs were only entitled to simple interest under the Supreme Court Act 1981.

Hirst J. rejected the bank's 'submission that compound interest is only to be awarded in exceptional cases where the defendant is guilty of serious misconduct'.[157] His lordship decided that the bank's culpability was irrelevant and held that an award of compound interest was appropriate because the bank was 'essentially engaged in investment business, and must be presumed to have used the money for normal banking purposes as part of its working capital, and thus to have been in a position to earn compound interest'.[158]

It is important to note that the presumption was not justified by any wrongdoing, but was the proper conclusion to be drawn from the facts. The bank was aware that the payment was conditional and invested the money in a New York bank account. It had lost all records of the interest it had earned with the money and Hirst J. accepted expert evidence of the interest the bank would have received

[154] [1996] 2 All E.R. 961, 978. [155] (1978) 4 Fam.L.R. 258.
[156] [1992] 2 Lloyd's L.R. 193; rev'd in part [1994] 2 Lloyd's L.R. 152, C.A.
[157] Ibid. at 198. [158] Ibid. at 199.

in New York, including the fact that interest would have been compounded quarterly. Nevertheless, his lordship awarded interest compounded annually, i.e. less than the interest actually received by the bank. The award was no greater than the income earned with the trust property and therefore entirely appropriate against an innocent recipient.

The Law Reform (Miscellaneous Provisions) Act 1934, which was enacted following a report of the Law Revision Committee,[159] expressly excluded 'the giving of interest upon interest'.[160] In 1978, the Law Commission recommended changes to the 1934 Act, but rejected a statutory discretion to award compound interest.[161] This resulted in an addition to the Supreme Court Act 1981 authorising awards of 'simple interest' only.[162] Although the Law Commission recommended the preservation of the equitable jurisdiction to award compound interest, this was on the understanding that it was only possible in 'the case in which a person, acting in breach of a fiduciary duty, makes a profit for himself out of the misuse of funds'.[163] The expansion of this equitable jurisdiction, as advocated in *Westdeutsche* v. *Islington*, would neatly side-step the recommendations of the Law Reform Commission and Parliament's interventions in this area. There are arguments for and against such a move, but, at the very least, the change should not be made without due consideration of what is involved. The approach taken by Lords Goff and Woolf has much to commend it, but the same cannot be said of the strategic use of the resulting trust for that purpose.

E. SUMMARY

The fiduciary obligations associated with a resulting trust depend on the situation in which the trust arises. The resulting trust on the failure of a prior express trust normally attracts the same duties that applied to the failed trust. The innocent recipient of property belonging in equity to another should only be subject to a duty to convey it at the beneficiary's request. There should be no liability for breach of the fiduciary obligations associated with the resulting trust before the trustee becomes aware of the circumstances giving rise to that trust.

Courts should not use the existence of the resulting trust as a basis for drawing adverse evidentiary presumptions against the trustee. These are only justifiable in cases of wrongdoing, i.e. where the resulting trustee has knowingly breached the trust obligations. Resulting trustees should not be liable to pay any more interest than is actually earned or saved with the trust property, unless they use the trust property in trade with knowledge of the circumstances giving rise to the trust.

[159] *Second Interim Report* (1934, Cmnd. 4546); see Law Commission (1978) §§142–4, pp. 42–3
[160] Law Reform (Miscellaneous Provisions) Act 1934, s. 3(1)(a).
[161] Law Commission (1978) §85, §§150–6. [162] Supreme Court Act 1981, s. 35A.
[163] Law Commission (1978) §154, p. 46.

Conclusion

The resulting trust and its place in the law of restitution have been explored and the conclusions can be briefly summarized. There are two requirements for every resulting trust: (i) a transfer of property (ii) in circumstances in which the provider of that property did not intend to benefit the recipient. The property may be any interest in any type of property or asset, so long as it is capable of being the subject of a trust. The provider may be a previous owner of the property in question or someone who has contributed to the recipient's acquisition of that property.

The fact that the provider did not intend to benefit the recipient is presumed (i.e. there is a presumption of resulting trust) where the recipient has not provided all of the consideration for the acquisition of the property, except in two situations. First, equity presumes that a gift was intended if the provider was the recipient's husband or father (or possibly mother) or stood *in loco parentis* to the recipient (i.e. there is a presumption of advancement). Secondly, the Law of Property Act 1925 may prevent the presumption of resulting trust from arising where the property is land and the provider was its previous owner. In cases where the presumption does not apply, the resulting trust is still possible if it is proven that the provider did not intend to benefit the recipient.

All resulting trusts effect restitution of what would otherwise be the unjust enrichment of the recipient. They are created neither by the consent of the recipient nor by the intention of the provider to create a trust. The resulting trust is not merely the passive preservation of the provider's pre-existing property interest, but is one of equity's active responses to non-voluntary transfer. Non-voluntariness is a difficult issue, but any defect in or qualification of the intention to benefit the recipient, which gives the provider a right to restitution, should also give rise to a resulting trust, so long as the property remains identifiable and the recipient has not obtained the unfettered beneficial ownership of that property before the right to restitution arises.

This final chapter considers three aspects of the law of trusts and law of restitution which are affected by these conclusions: (i) the classification of trusts, (ii) proprietary restitution, and (iii) defences to restitutionary claims. It then looks at the way forward.

A. CLASSIFICATION OF TRUSTS

Classification is not merely an academic process carried on for instructional purposes.[1] It allows us to see the similarities which connect apparently different

[1] Cf. Birks (1989a), pp. 1–6; Atiyah (1986), pp. 48, 52.

situations, thereby enabling the consistent application of rules to persons who are, in essence, similarly situated. Conversely, it exposes important distinctions between apparently similar situations, thereby providing a logical basis on which the application of the rules can diverge where appropriate. As suggested at the beginning of this book,[2] it is possible to classify trusts in a number of different ways, but the most useful would be to relate them to the events which are the primary causes of other legal responses. Confusion over the events which give rise to resulting and constructive trusts has made that task difficult, if not impossible. In *Explaining Constructive Trusts*, Dr. Elias went a long way towards achieving that goal, by identifying the primary aims which motivate constructive trusts. A proper understanding of resulting trusts would place the goal within reach. The purpose of this section is not to justify the divisions we find in other areas of the law (which are, and are likely to remain, controversial)[3] nor to provide a comprehensive framework for the law of trusts. It is primarily intended to locate the resulting trust within the law of trusts according to the events which give rise to them.

1. Intention and Consent

The most common method of dividing the law of trusts is according to whether they are created by the intention of the parties or by operation of law.[4] It is generally accepted that express trusts are the product of intention and constructive trusts are not. However, uncertainty over the resulting trust has made it difficult to locate that trust on one side or the other and, in *Re Vandervell's Trusts (No. 2)*,[5] that difficulty was met by dividing the trust according to the judgment of Solomon.[6]

The division between express trusts, on one hand, and resulting or constructive trusts, on the other, has been preserved over the years by the statutory provisions which require express trusts of land to be made in writing and exempt resulting and constructive trusts from that requirement.[7] This has led to the suggestion that there are no further meaningful divisions to be made.[8] However, with respect, it would be a remarkable jurisprudential failure if the only conclusion we could reach about the events which give rise to trusts is that some trusts are created by the intentional acts of the parties and the remainder are not. As discussed below, even this division is not entirely secure and we would be left with a pragmatic classification that merely hives off trusts of land which require writing.

[2] At pp. 2–5. [3] See Birks (1983); Burrows (1983); Atiyah (1986), pp. 10–56.

[4] See Costigan; Mowbray, *Lewin on Trusts*, p. 6; Waters (1984), p. 17; Scott and Fratcher §462.1; Gardner (1990), p. 225; Baker and Langan, *Snell's Equity*, p. 101; Martin (1993a), p. 71; Oakley (1994), p. 27. [5] [1974] Ch. 269; see Chapter 2 above.

[6] 1 Kings 3: 16–28.

[7] Statute of Frauds 1677, ss. 7, 8; replaced by Law of Property Act 1925, s. 53; see Megarry and Wade, pp. 478–9; Hackney, pp. 146–7.

[8] See *Gissing* v. *Gissing* [1971] A.C. 886, 905; Hackney, p. 147.

There is utility in classifications which relate trusts not just to intentional acts, but to other causative events as well.

Express trusts

All express trusts are fundamentally dependent on the intentions of the parties. The settlor defines the beneficial interests and controls the nature and extent of the trustee's obligations, while the trustee must consent to that office. Although express trusts occupy the central position within the law of trusts, a comparison with the law of obligations reveals that its closest counterpart (a bare promise) occupies a relatively minor part of contract law. Apart from deeds under seal, a promise is not normally enforceable without some consideration flowing from, or detrimental reliance by, the promisee.[9] Turning back to the law of trusts to see which trusts respond to the combination of the provider's intention and the recipient's consideration, reliance, or expectation, reveals that this role is filled by the constructive trust (see below).

Resulting trusts

The role of intention in resulting trusts is a negative one. The primary question is always whether the provider intended to benefit the recipient and not whether he or she intended to create a trust. The latter question is relevant, of course, to whether the provider has succeeded in creating an express trust, but its relevance to the resulting trust is only as an indication of a lack of intention to benefit the recipient.[10] Although a resulting trust may be identical to an express trust which the provider intended, but failed, to create, this is fortuitous because the facts which give rise to a resulting trust and define its content (the unjust enrichment of the recipient) are different from those which create and define an express trust (the intentional actions of the settlor).[11]

There is an interesting similarity (but no apparent historical connexion)[12] between the resulting trust and the action for money had and received. The latter is a species of action upon the case in which the plaintiff would allege that the defendant was indebted and had promised to pay (*indebitatus assumpsit*) for money received to the plaintiff's use.[13] It once depended on a real promise, but was extended to actions based on fictional promises, thereby allowing its use as a response to unjust enrichment.[14] Unfortunately, this led to confusion over the role of the 'implied' promise in such an action[15] and, in *Sinclair* v. *Brougham*, Viscount Haldane L.C. stated:[16]

[9] See Hackney, pp. 116–17; Atiyah (1986), pp. 10 ff., 179 ff.; Baker (1990), pp. 360–400.
[10] *Hodgson* v. *Marks* [1971] 1 Ch. 892, C.A.
[11] Above, pp. 99–102.
[12] See Baker (1990), pp. 409, 425.
[13] Birks (1984) at 4–5.
[14] *Moses* v. *Macferlan* (1760) 2 Burr. 1005; Jackson, pp. 39–41; Birks (1984); Birks (1989a), pp. 29–39; Baker (1990), pp. 413–26; Goff and Jones, pp. 5–11.
[15] Birks (1989a), pp. 24–39; Goff and Jones, pp. 10–11.
[16] [1914] A.C. 398, 415.

[S]o far as proceedings in personam are concerned, the common law of England really recognizes (unlike Roman law) only actions of two classes, those founded on contract and those founded on tort. When it speaks of actions arising quasi ex contractu it refers merely to a class of action in theory based on a contract which is imputed to the defendant by a fiction of law. The fiction can only be set up with effect if such a contract would be valid if it really existed.

The development of the resulting trust followed a similar pattern.[17] The resulting use began as an implication that a feoffment made with neither consideration (in a broad sense) nor declaration of use was intended to be to the feoffor's use. However, it developed to become a direct response to the lack of consideration and declared use, i.e. whenever a feoffment was made without apparent reason, such as kinship or bargain and sale. When the resulting trust evolved, it did not depend on the implied intention to create a trust and could respond in cases where the implication of that intention would be impossible.

As Professor Maitland remarked, the terms 'implied contract' and 'implied trust' are similar in their potential for confusion:[18]

When studying the law of contract your attention will have been drawn to a very similar, a parallel, ambiguity—sometimes 'Implied Contract' stands for a true contract constituted rather by acts than by words, sometimes it stands for a 'Contract implied by law', or '*Quasi* Contract', an obligation which is no true contract but which is treated for many purposes as though it was a contract. Turning now to trusts 'created by operation of law', we might similarly call them '*Quasi* trusts'; but that term is not in use.

The risk of confusion can be alleviated by (i) the abandonment of terms like 'implied contract' and 'implied trust' and (ii) the recognition of unjust enrichment as the generic event to which the common law obligation and the resulting trust each respond.[19] It is perhaps ironic that the 'implied contract' theory, which interfered with the proper development of the action for money had and received in *Sinclair* v. *Brougham*, led Viscount Haldane L.C. to recognize the resulting trust as an alternative response to unjust enrichment.[20] The irony is stronger in *Westdeutsche* v. *Islington*, where the converse took place: the 'implied contract' theory of restitution was finally laid to rest, but not without an attempt to resurrect the 'implied trust' theory of resulting trusts.[21]

Constructive trusts

Constructive trusts are often treated as a breed apart because (it is said) they are the only trusts for which intention is irrelevant.[22] On closer inspection, however, this turns out to be a comparison of apples and oranges. When speaking of the role of intention in the creation of express and resulting trusts, commentators

[17] See pp. 16–17 above. [18] Maitland, p. 74. [19] Birks (1984) at 22–4.
[20] [1914] A.C. 398, 421. [21] [1996] 2 All E.R. 961, 990–1, 993.
[22] Costigan at 448–50; Oakley (1987), pp. 1, 15 (but see p. 1, fn. 1); Scott and Fratcher, §462.1; Baker and Langan, *Snell's Equity*, p. 101; Oakley (1994), p. 27. Cf. Litman at 450.

focus on the intention of the settlor or provider of the property but, when considering the constructive trust, look instead to the intention of the trustee. It is true that express trusts require the consent of the trustees, but they do not fail for lack of a trustee and the intention which creates and defines the express trust is the settlor's. The intention of the resulting trustee, like that of the constructive trustee, is normally irrelevant.[23]

As Elias points out, many constructive trusts further the aim of perfecting a 'choice to dispose of one's options in favour of another person'.[24] For example, the content of constructive trusts imposed to enforce secret trusts,[25] mutual wills,[26] or common intentions regarding the ownership of family homes[27] is primarily dependent on the intentions of the parties. It is not suggested that these trusts are intentionally created. Nevertheless, the facts to which they respond are (i) an intention to dispose of property in favour of another and (ii) the inducement of or reliance on that intention.[28] This reveals that these constructive trusts have more in common with contractual obligations than do resulting trusts. A further example is provided by the constructive trust of land which is subject to a specifically enforceable contract of sale.[29] Again, the trust depends upon the intentions of the parties: in this case, a promise to dispose of property, for which the recipient has provided valuable consideration.

Even where a constructive trust responds to a breach of fiduciary duty and removes the improper gains the fiduciary has made thereby,[30] intention is not entirely irrelevant. As discussed below, the trust transfers the wrongfully obtained profits to the victim of that wrong, even though none of the parties involved intended to create a trust. However, the victim's consent to the wrongdoer's conduct would normally provide a defence to the claim, unless there was some vitiation or qualification of that consent or a policy reason for ignoring it.[31] The various roles played by intention in cases of constructive trusts are clearly different from the role it plays for the resulting trust. Rational distinctions based on intention can be drawn between these two categories of trust, but it cannot be done on the basis that intention is relevant in one category, but not the other.

2. Unjust Enrichment (by Subtraction)

The trusts in this category are responding not to the intention or consent of the parties, but to the unjust enrichment of one person at the expense of another.

[23] Above, pp. 36–7, 99–100. [24] Elias, p. 9.

[25] e.g. *In re Boyes* (1884) 26 Ch.D. 531; *Blackwell* v. *Blackwell* [1929] A.C. 318.

[26] e.g. *In re Dale* [1993] 3 W.L.R. 652; see Waters (1984), pp. 412–25.

[27] e.g. *Grant* v. *Ewards* [1986] Ch. 638, C.A.

[28] Elias, pp. 56–66; Gardner (1990), pp. 225–8, 231–2; see Ford and Lee, §22260 ff.

[29] e.g. *Shaw* v. *Foster* (1872) L.R. 5 H.L. 321; see Elias, pp. 50–6; Gardner (1990), pp. 230–2.

[30] e.g. *Regal (Hastings) Ltd.* v. *Gulliver* (1942) [1967] 2 A.C. 134.

[31] *Lockhart* v. *Reilly* (1856) 25 L.J.Eq. 697; *In re Pauling's Settlement Trusts* [1964] Ch. 303, 335–8, C.A.; *Boardman* v. *Phipps* [1967] 2 A.C. 46, 117; Baker and Langan, *Snell's Equity*, p. 294; Ford and Lee, §22150.

They cause that enrichment to be given up to that other and are, by definition, restitutionary. There are two ways in which an enrichment may be at the expense of another: (i) because it was subtracted from or provided by that other or (ii) because it was acquired by doing a wrong to that other. In the latter category (discussed below under the heading 'Wrongs'), the wrongful conduct is an essential part of the events giving rise to the trust. In the former category (discussed here) the events which give rise to the trust are (i) an enrichment of the trustee, (ii) which was subtracted from or provided by the trust beneficiary, (iii) in circumstances which render that enrichment unjust. In most cases, the enrichment is unjust because the beneficiary did not intend to benefit the trustee in the circumstances (i.e. the main 'unjust factor' is non-voluntary transfer), but there may be cases where restitution is available on another basis, such as unconscientious receipt or public policy.[32]

All resulting trusts belong in this category of (subtractive) unjust enrichment. Is the converse true: are all the trusts which respond to this category of events resulting? The express trust has no role to play because it is always created and defined by the settlor's intention. Can the constructive trust apply? These questions may surprise, even now, because it has been so commonly assumed that the trusts operating in this category are constructive. However, the majority (if not all) of the events which give rise to trusts in this category are non-voluntary transfers. It turns out that these are the events which give rise to resulting trusts. This realization leads to two main questions. First, should all trusts responding to non-voluntary transfer be classified as resulting (i.e. is the primary trust in this category resulting)? Secondly, are there events in this category, other than non-voluntary transfers of property, which give rise to trusts and, if so, are those trusts resulting (i.e. is the only trust in this category resulting)?

The primary trust

It is suggested that any trust which responds to non-voluntary transfer is resulting and should be recognized as such. The classification 'resulting' is far more precise, descriptive, and useful than the amorphous 'constructive', in much the same way that 'dolphin' compares to 'marine animal'. The 'resulting' classification tells us that the trust property was provided to the resulting trustee by the trust beneficiary and is being returned because the beneficiary did not intend the trustee to receive it beneficially. In contrast, the 'constructive' label tells us only that the trust in question was not expressly created.[33] Sadly, it does not even indicate whether the trustee ever held property in trust or is merely under a personal liability to account as if he or she had.[34]

It is commonly assumed in North America that the trust operating in this

[32] Birks (1990b) at 21; Birks and Chambers, p. vii.
[33] See Birks (1994c).
[34] See pp. 2, 189 above; Gardner (1994) at pp. 186–7.

category is constructive. That position is secure in the USA for two main reasons: (i) the relatively long history and wide acceptance of the constructive trust as a proprietary remedy for unjust enrichment[35] and (ii) the restricted role of the resulting trust (caused by the statutory abolition of resulting trusts in several states[36] and the fact that the presumption of resulting trust has never been applied to gratuitous transfers).[37] Notwithstanding the American preference for constructive over resulting trusts, the logical distinction between the two is not entirely clear in the USA. According to the *Restatement of the Law of Restitution*:[38]

> A resulting trust arises where a transfer of property is made under circumstances which raise an inference that the person making the transfer or causing it to be made did not intend the transferee to have the beneficial interest in the property transferred. A constructive trust is imposed not because of the intention of the parties but because the person holding the title to property would profit by a wrong or would be unjustly enriched if he were permitted to keep the property.

This does not provide a basis for distinction where the enrichment in question is unjust precisely because the provider did not intend to benefit the recipient (i.e. most of the category under discussion).[39]

Canada made its conversion to the American approach in a series of family property cases decided by the Supreme Court of Canada[40] in the wake of *Pettitt* v. *Pettitt* and *Gissing* v. *Gissing*.[41] The issues were presented as a conflict between the English 'common intention' resulting trust and the American 'remedial' constructive trust. However, this juxtaposition turns out to be false. It is recognized (outside Canada, at least) that a 'common intention' in this context leads more often to constructive than resulting trusts[42] and, in many family property cases, the court is not reversing unjust enrichments subtracted from the plaintiff, but fulfilling relied-upon expectations.[43] Nevertheless, the Supreme Court said it was rejecting the resulting trust in favour of a constructive trust based on unjust enrichment, thereby leaving the restitutionary role of the Canadian resulting trust in doubt. Though doubtful, it remains possible. The forgotten Canadian cases which are cited above in support of that role[44] have not been overruled or

[35] See Seavey and Scott at 40–5.

[36] See Scott and Fratcher, §440.2–§440.4; Bogert and Bogert, §467.

[37] Scott and Fratcher, §405; Bogert and Bogert, §453. See pp. 14–15 above.

[38] *Restatement of Restitution*, §160, p. 642.

[39] Palmer notes the potential for confusion: *The Law of Restitution*, vol. 2 (1978) §6.7, p. 61; see Bogert and Bogert, §451, §458.

[40] *Murdoch* v. *Murdoch* (1973) 41 D.L.R. (3d) 367; *Rathwell* v. *Rathwell* (1978) 83 D.L.R. (3d) 289; *Pettkus* v. *Becker* (1980) 117 D.L.R. (3d) 257. See Waters (1984), pp. 346–57; Waters (1992) at pp. 467–73.

[41] [1970] A.C. 777; [1971] A.C. 886.

[42] Above, pp. 37–8.

[43] See *Baumgartner* v. *Baumgartner* (1987) 164 C.L.R. 137; *Gillies* v. *Keogh* [1989] 2 N.Z.L.R. 327, C.A.; Waters (1984), pp. 357–61; Elias, p. 157; Scane; Gardner (1993); Parkinson; Eekelaar; Matthews (1994).

[44] See pp. 22–3 above.

re-classified and several Canadian commentators have noticed the connexion between resulting trusts and restitution.[45]

Prior to 1996, the resulting trust had been treated more favourably on this side of the Atlantic. Trusts are often declared in cases of unjust enrichment (by subtraction), but seldom classified, and, despite the efforts of Professor Waters,[46] the North American approach is still viewed here with scepticism.[47] In *Sinclair* v. *Brougham*,[48] *El Ajou* v. *Dollar Land Holdings p.l.c.*[49] and *Westdeutsche Bank* v. *Islington L.B.C.*,[50] the resulting trust was recognized as a response to what can be described as 'unjust enrichment by subtraction'.

In 1996, Mr. Swadling published an essay which cast doubts on the proper role of the resulting trust.[51] Those doubts were shared by Lord Browne-Wilkinson in *Westdeutsche* v. *Islington*.[52] However, their scepticism is based on the view that resulting trusts arise only in defined traditional categories in response to a presumed intention to create a trust. As this book has endeavoured to show, that view can explain the origins of the resulting use, but (with respect) cannot be reconciled with the modern law of resulting trusts.[53] It would mean that a host of cases, going back at least as far as *Ryall* v. *Ryall*,[54] are wrongly decided. Resulting trusts arise because the provider of property to another did not intend to benefit the recipient. As Chapter 4 demonstrates, the resulting trust is a restitutionary response to unjust enrichment, even if one looks no further than its traditional categories. However, the events which give rise to resulting trusts occur in other contexts and only an artificial restriction can prevent them from arising in those contexts.

These developments have not been matched in Australia and New Zealand. However, the resulting trust has not been adversely treated down under and Gummow J. (of the High Court of Australia) has recognized extra-judicially the restitutionary role of the resulting trust.[55]

There is still a tendency to classify as constructive those trusts which reverse unjust enrichment, even though the courts did not make that classification themselves. The treatment of *Chase Manhattan Bank N.A.* v. *Israel-British Bank (London) Ltd.*[56] is a glaring example. Goulding J. declared that the recipient of a mistaken payment was a trustee for its provider and many commentators have classified or treated it with constructive trusts.[57] However, an important question

[45] Tory at 59–60; Waters (1984), pp. 374–5; Litman at 469; Hovius and Youdan, p. 106; Scane at 264–5.
[46] Waters (1964).
[47] See the three essays by Waters, Gardner, and Birks, all in Birks (1994a), vol. 2 at pp. 165, 186 and 214, respectively; cf. *Westdeutsche Landesbank* v. *Islington* [1996] 2 All E.R. 961, 999.
[48] [1914] A.C. 398.
[49] [1993] 3 All E.R. 717; rev'd [1994] 2 All E.R. 685, C.A.
[50] [1994] 4 All E.R. 890.
[51] Swadling (1996).
[52] [1996] 2 All E.R. 961, 986.
[53] Birks (1996b) at 18.
[54] (1739) 1 Atk. 59.
[55] Gummow (1990) at pp. 82–5.
[56] [1981] Ch. 105.
[57] Waters (1984), pp. 387–97; Elias, p. 2 (but see p. 68, fn. 89); Maddaugh and McCamus, p. 95; Cope (1992), pp. 488–92; Burrows (1993a), p. 36; Goff and Jones, p. 130; Birks and Chambers, p. 48; Swadling (1996).

in that case was whether there was any conflict between English and New York law on the subject. His lordship recognized that the facts would give rise to a constructive trust under New York law, but refused to classify the English response as such. Instead, Goulding J. relied on Viscount Haldane L.C.'s speech in *Sinclair* v. *Brougham* to conclude that 'a person who pays money to another under a factual mistake retains an equitable property in it'.[58] Viscount Haldane L.C. classified that interest as a resulting trust and, since Goulding J. refused to call it constructive when invited to do so, there is no reason to assume otherwise.

The only trust?

It is suggested above that all trusts which respond to non-voluntary transfer are resulting and, therefore, the resulting trust is the primary proprietary response to unjust enrichment (by subtraction). The issue here is whether the resulting trust is the only trust responding to this category of events. There are two situations which belong in this category of unjust enrichment, but do not involve non-voluntary transfers of property: (i) where the enrichment is something other than property or assets capable of being the subject matter of a trust (e.g. services) and (ii) where the reason for restitution is something other than non-voluntariness (e.g. unconscientious receipt). Can these events give rise to trusts and, if so, are those trusts resulting or constructive?

Other enrichments

In all cases of resulting trust, the enrichment to the recipient is the acquisition of property and it is that property (or its substitute) which is held in trust for the provider. This is not to be confused with the provider's contribution to the purchase price, which can be any consideration (including farm animals, promises to pay, or the performance of services)[59] provided to a third party in exchange for the property provided to the recipient. However, the provision of that same consideration directly to the recipient will not give rise to a resulting trust over other property owned by that recipient. In that case, any trust of the other property is responding to the parties intentions or expectations regarding its ownership and is therefore either express or constructive (and not restitutionary).

Other enrichments can give rise to other restitutionary responses (e.g. *quantum meruit*), but they do not give rise to trusts in the absence of relied-upon intentions or expectations. In family property cases, courts often impose trusts over family homes and other family assets for the benefit of a party to the relationship who has detrimentally relied on expectations or intentions that he or she would acquire a share in that property. It is not essential that the detriment corresponds to the trust property, thus revealing that the intentions or expectations of the parties are the primary events which give rise to the constructive trust in this context and define its content.[60]

[58] [1981] Ch. 105, 119. [59] Above, pp. 13–14. [60] Birks (1994c) at pp. 221–2.

Some confusion over this issue is caused by the persistent Canadian treatment of family property cases under the guise of unjust enrichment. However, even where the value of the property subject to the trust is equivalent to the value of the services provided by the trust beneficiary,[61] that trust cannot be explained solely as a response to that unjust enrichment. In other words, the court may choose the quantum of the response by reference to the unjust enrichment (usually on a rough-and-ready basis), but neither the proprietary nature of the response nor the selection of the property subject to the trust are referable to the 'unjust enrichment by subtraction'. Despite the stated Canadian preference for an unjust enrichment analysis, the events giving rise to those trusts necessarily include detrimental reliance on expectations or intentions regarding the ownership of the property in question.[62]

Other unjust factors

Whether (and how) trusts might respond to subtractive enrichments, which are unjust for some reason other than non-voluntariness, is a difficult issue, made worse by a more general uncertainty over the existence and operation of these other unjust factors. Some of the controversies, such as the debate over free acceptance,[63] are irrelevant to the present discussion, because the unjust factor, if it does exist, gives rise to only personal responses. However, other unjust factors can be involved in cases where the provider of property is seeking its restitution. Unconscientious receipt provides a useful example. In *Louth* v. *Diprose*,[64] a man had purchased a house for a woman with whom he was infatuated. She had caused him to make that gift by unconscientiously manipulating his emotions and he was entitled to recover it. As suggested above,[65] an essential part of a claim of this nature is a degree of non-voluntariness, which should be sufficient to attract the resulting trust. If, however, this is incorrect and non-voluntariness is not required, then the trust response is brought into doubt.[66]

It is difficult to understand why a provider of property should be entitled to restitution (let alone a trust) if he or she intentionally, with neither impairment of judgement nor qualification, caused the beneficial ownership of that property to be transferred to another. Even in cases of restitution for wrongs, the victim's consent to the enrichment is a complete defence to the claim.[67] If restitution is available in such circumstances, then the courts will have to work out whether it should be personal or by way of trust and, if the latter, then whether the trust is (i) a resulting trust extended to respond to unjust factors other than non-voluntary transfer, (ii) a constructive trust responding to subtractive unjust

[61] e.g. *Peter* v. *Beblow* [1993] 1 S.C.R. 980, 101 D.L.R. (4th) 140; noted Farquhar; Birks (1994c) at p. 219.

[62] e.g. *Pettkus* v. *Becker* (1980) 117 D.L.R. (3d) 257, 274; see Gardner (1993).

[63] See Burrows (1988); Birks (1991a).

[64] (1992) 175 C.L.R. 621.

[65] At pp. 137–8.

[66] As discussed above at p. 138, members of the Full Court of South Australia were concerned whether a trust was an appropriate response.

[67] See pp. 195, 200 above.

enrichment or (iii) a constructive trust responding to the recipient's wrongful conduct (as discussed below). It is suggested that such a trust would be best understood as a response to a wrong (but much better would be the recognition that non-voluntariness is a key factor in these circumstances).

3. Wrongs

In this category, the primary event to which the trust responds is the wrongful conduct of the trustee. The central example here is the unauthorized profit by fiduciaries in breach of their duties.[68] The trust imposed in this situation effects restitution of that profit to the persons to whom the fiduciary duties were owed (i.e. the victims of the wrong). There is an important division between this and the previous category.[69] Although restitution is a response in both categories, the causative events are different. In the previous category, the trust is generated by the unjust enrichment (subtracted from the trust beneficiary) and, like all responses to unjust enrichment, is necessarily restitutionary. Here, the primary event is the wrong. Although the trust is also restitutionary, because it requires the trustee to give up an unjust enrichment (a gain made by wrongdoing), there are other responses to wrongdoing, such as the liability to make compensation for losses.

Express and resulting trusts have no role to play in this category. This is the central and exclusive domain of the constructive trust. Although resulting trusts can arise in cases where the trustee has acted wrongly, they never arise in response to that wrong. In such a case, the resulting trust is possible because the facts present two causes of action: a gain made by wrongful conduct (generating a constructive trust) and a subtractive unjust enrichment (generating a resulting trust).[70]

4. Elias' Thesis

In *Explaining Constructive Trusts*, Dr. Elias proposes what he calls 'the third thesis'. He rejects both 'the radical thesis', which seeks to explain all constructive trusts as responses to unjust enrichment, and 'the sceptical thesis', 'that there is no coherent general scheme for resolving the problems of classification and justification which the rules on constructive trusts raise'.[71] In its place, Elias suggests that all constructive trusts further one or more of three aims: (i) perfection of one's 'choice to dispose of one's options in favour of another',[72] (ii) restitution of surviving gains made through another's loss, or (iii) reparation of

[68] *Keech* v. *Sandford* (1726) Sel.Cas.T.King 61; *Boardman* v. *Phipps* [1967] 2 A.C. 46.

[69] Birks (1990b); L.D. Smith (1992); Burrows (1993a), p. 376 ff.; Jaffey at 32. Cf. Barker (1995b) at 473.

[70] See p. 108 above.

[71] Elias, p. 150.

[72] Ibid. at p. 9.

losses inflicted on a trust estate. His organization, according to the aims which constructive trusts further, is similar to, but distinct from, the approach used here of relating trusts to the events to which they respond. This shift of focus (from response to event) produces a different alignment of the subject matter. Another major difference is produced by the different scope of the two inquiries. Elias' task was the rationalization of the rules governing constructive trusts and it is understandable that he treats, as part of that task, the work ascribed here to resulting trusts.[73]

The perfection aim

The perfection aim can be matched to the causative events of intention and consent, but not to unjust enrichment or wrongs. Secret trusts provide a good example. Where a testator disposes of property, in the belief that the recipient will hold that property for the benefit of a third party, the court will often enforce a trust for that third party, even though the formal requirements for testamentary dispositions are not met.[74] In contrast, the failure to meet the formal requirements for an *inter vivos* trust for a third party will usually produce a resulting trust. In both cases, the intention to benefit the third party reveals a lack of intention to benefit the recipient and, therefore, the recipient would be unjustly enriched if allowed to retain the property. However, the secret trust, which carries the property on to the third party, cannot be explained solely by reference to the unjust enrichment.[75] The events giving rise to that trust necessarily include the positive intention to benefit that third party. There are no convincing reasons to give effect to similar intentions where the disposition is *inter vivos* and the restitution of the unjust enrichment would allow the provider to perfect the intended disposition of so desired.[76]

The restitution aim

It is here that Elias' thesis produces a different organization from the approach based on causative events. This is to be expected because restitution is a response to two distinct events: unjust enrichment (by subtraction) and profit from wrongdoing. Both events are treated by Elias (under the respective labels of 'pecuniary losses' and 'non-pecuniary losses') as giving rise to constructive trusts furthering the restitution aim. As suggested above, there are valid reasons for treating these trusts separately according to the events producing them. When

[73] Elias does note the possible role of the resulting trust at pp. 17, 72, 107, 111, 162–3.

[74] See Gardner (1990), pp. 80–7; Clark and Ross Martyn, *Theobald on Wills*, pp. 106–12.

[75] But cf. Birks (1989a), pp. 64–5, 135–6, where secret trusts are treated as examples of 'interceptive subtraction' from the intended third party. Unless the third party is otherwise entitled to the property, the trust in his or her favour can only be explained as perfection of the testator's choice; see Gardner (1990), pp. 225–8; L.D. Smith (1991); Burrows (1993a), pp. 45–54; Ford and Lee, §6350.

[76] Cf. Youdan (1984); Feltham; Youdan (1988); Scott and Fratcher, §55.1; Gardner (1990), p. 81.

that is done, it turns out that the trusts responding to (subtractive) unjust enrichment are primarily (if not always) resulting. Constructive trusts still further the restitution aim, but in response to wrongdoing.

The reparation aim

It might be assumed that a re-organization of trusts based on causative events would bring together, as responses to wrongdoing, those constructive trusts which further either the restitution aim or the reparation aim. However, on closer inspection, it turns out that there are no actual trusts which further the reparation aim, but only those cases where someone is personally liable to account 'as a constructive trustee'. The cases Elias places here are also commonly known by the names 'knowing assistance' and 'knowing receipt'.[77] When organized by causative events, the liability for assisting a breach of trust belongs with constructive trusts as a response to wrongdoing, while the liability for receiving trust property belongs with resulting trusts as a response to unjust enrichment. Elias treats them together, under the reparation aim, because he views the imposition of first-measure liabilities, without reference to surviving enrichment, as compensation for loss.[78]

5. The Importance of Classifying Trusts

The importance of the proper classification of trusts was discussed near the beginning of this book[79] and, hopefully, is now apparent. Nevertheless, it may be worthwhile to state (or re-affirm) three reasons why we need to understand and organize trusts according to the events to which they respond. First, it allows us to avoid false conflicts. For example, it was argued in *Hodgson* v. *Marks*[80] that a resulting trust could not arise if the provider attempted, but failed, to create an express trust with the same content. The Court of Appeal recognized that those trusts respond to different events and that the absence of the requirements for one trust does not prevent the other from arising. This is not intended to suggest that the inquiries are completely independent. In *Hodgson* v. *Marks*, the resulting trust was only possible because the express trust had failed. The event to which the resulting trust responded (the unjust enrichment of the recipient) would have been absent if a valid express trust had disposed of the equitable ownership of the property in favour of the provider (or anyone else).[81]

Secondly, a single case may present facts falling into more than one category of causative event (i.e. more than one type of trust is possible). For example, two people may contribute to the purchase of a home by one of the parties. The events may be capable of giving rise to both a resulting trust in proportion to their contributions and a constructive trust in accordance with relied-upon

[77] See p. 189 above. [78] Elias, pp. 29, 78–83. [79] At pp. 2–5.
[80] [1971] 1 Ch. 892; see pp. 25, 101 above. [81] Cf. Ford and Lee, §21060.

expectations of beneficial ownership.[82] There may be valid reasons for preferring one over the other. For example, the trusts may give rise to different proportions of beneficial ownership or one may be more deserving of recognition in insolvency.[83] A Canadian judge suggested that a claim against a bankrupt for a constructive trust of a family home needed leave of the bankruptcy court, whereas claims for express or resulting trusts could proceed independently.[84] Goff and Jones suggest that, 'if the claim is *not* based on an existing equitable title', the availability of the trust itself should be linked to the trustee's solvency.[85] Both the subject matter of a trust and its treatment may depend on the category of events to which it responded and, therefore, courts need to make open and informed decisions when such choices are presented.

This leads to the third reason for the identification and classification of the events to which each trust responds: the proper development and consistent application of the law depends upon it. Witness the confusion which followed the avoidance of that question in *Gissing* v. *Gissing* (and still persists in Canada).[86] This is not intended to suggest that rigid rules of classification should ever prevent courts from finding proper solutions to the problems before them. As Mr. Eekelaar said of the legal controversies surrounding family property disputes:[87]

> Some of the debate has drifted into doctrinal disputations about the nature of constructive or resulting trusts . . . I think this is unfortunate because in such debates it is easy to lose sight of the true nature of the problems which litigants have brought to the courts for a solution . . . these are not problems *of* legal doctrine . . . there is a common set of issues which pose problems *for* legal doctrine. It is the task of legal doctrine to find a solution, not to bury itself within introspective analyses about itself.

The problems in this area, like all others involving the creation of trusts, can only be made easier by the clear articulation of the events which give rise to those trusts. This guidance is essential for future courts and for potential litigants, who are better able to avoid the expenses and traumas of litigation if they can make reasonable predictions about its outcome.

B. PROPRIETARY RESTITUTION

A great achievement of the modern law of restitution has been the recognition of unjust enrichment as a separate category of events giving rise to legal and equitable responses. This has revealed the similarities between those events (e.g.

[82] e.g. *Ulrich* v. *Ulrich* [1968] 1 W.L.R. 180, C.A.

[83] Hayton (1990) in Goldstein, at p. 610; Matthews (1994) at 43–4.

[84] *Bedard* v. *Schell* [1987] 4 W.W.R. 699 (Sask.); see Litman at 463–5; Hovius and Youdan, pp. 155–6.

[85] Goff and Jones, p. 101.

[86] [1971] A.C. 886, 905; see pp. 37–8, 159–60 above.

[87] Eekelaar at p. 204.

mistake, duress, failure of consideration) and between the responses to those events (e.g. actions for money had and received, rescission, resulting trusts). This revelation has led naturally to the difficult questions why certain events in this category should give rise to certain responses, but not others, and, more particularly, which events should lead to proprietary responses. There are justifiable fears regarding the adverse effects of proprietary restitution on the legitimate interests of other claimants to the recipient's property. These difficulties are more pronounced in North America, where the constructive trust has become a potential response to most events belonging in the category of unjust enrichment.[88]

Three main strategies have been proposed to control the spread of proprietary restitution. Each links the availability of a proprietary response to events which are additional or incidental to those which give rise to the right to restitution: (i) a proprietary base, (ii) the provider's willingness to risk the recipient's insolvency, or (iii) the recipient's solvency itself. It is suggested that the first strategy, as embodied by the resulting trust, provides the most meaningful basis for distinction.

1. A Proprietary Base

As discussed in Chapter 6,[89] the resulting trust is a response which fulfils Professor Goode's requirements for a 'proprietary base'. Every resulting trust requires that the claimant (i) has provided the property and (ii) did not intend to benefit the recipient in the circumstances and, further, that the property (iii) is identifiable in the hands of the recipient and (iv) has never been a freely available part of his or her general assets before the right to restitution arose. A claim for restitution of unjust enrichment which does not meet all four of these requirements (i.e. to which the resulting trust does not apply) should be only personal. This is not to say that trusts should not respond to other events, such as perfectionary constructive trusts responding to detrimentally relied-upon expectations. However, where the causative event is unjust enrichment (by subtraction), if the resulting trust does not apply, there is no convincing justification for a trust on another basis.

Claims for restitution for wrongs pose other difficulties. There is no requirement that the claimant has provided the property in question and, hence, often no possibility of a proprietary base (or resulting trust). Although both (subtractive) unjust enrichments and wrongs give rise to restitutionary responses, the aims of those responses are not the same. For example, the courts will need to work out whether the aim which requires restitution of profits earned in breach of fiduciary duties (to preserve the loyalty of all fiduciaries) can be achieved by a personal response, as the Court of Appeal assumed in *Lister* v. *Stubbs*,[90] or requires

[88] *Restatement of Restitution*, §160; Maddaugh and McCamus, p. 78 ff.
[89] Above, p. 147. [90] (1890) 45 Ch.D. 1.

proprietary intervention, as the Privy Council advised in *Attorney-General for Hong Kong* v. *Reid*.[91]

2. The Risk of Insolvency

Some commentators favour a distinction based on whether the provider willingly took the risk of the recipient's insolvency. This strategy distinguishes the provider, who had a vitiated intention to benefit the recipient and is therefore 'an involuntary creditor',[92] from the provider with a qualified intention, who belongs to the class of 'merely voluntary and unsecured creditors of the bankrupt'.[93] With respect, this draws the line in the wrong place. In both cases, restitution (including the resulting trust) is responding to the lack of intention to benefit the recipient. The enrichment is no more 'voluntary' in one case than another. Much better is the distinction between different cases of failure of consideration, based on whether the recipient obtained the unfettered beneficial ownership of the property before the right to restitution arose.[94]

It is also suggested here that a line based on the risk of insolvency would not be bright enough. It is not obvious why a provider who believes 'that the recipient will perform his part of the bargain' is any more of a risk-taker than a mistaken payer.[95] In an important American essay, Professor Sherwin suggested that, although 'the claimant's position as an involuntary creditor' is not a sufficient basis for proprietary restitution from an insolvent recipient,[96] it is a necessary condition which justifies proprietary relief when two other factors are present: (i) the claim is based on unjust enrichment by subtraction of property from the claimant and (ii) that property (or its substitute) remains identifiable among the recipient's assets.[97] A proprietary base assumes the presence of those additional factors and one is left wondering why risk should become the deciding factor, rather than the preservation of that proprietary base. Sherwin is driven to argue that 'the constructive trust claimant's position as a voluntary creditor is a question of degree'[98] and that providers with a vitiated intention to benefit the recipient might be treated as risk-takers, depending on the degree or nature of the recipient's fraud or undue influence.[99] This reveals the inadequacy of the 'risk' test: whenever the provider is entitled to restitution on the basis of non-voluntary transfer, it is difficult to then make the nature of the response depend upon the degree of voluntariness.

[91] [1994] 1 A.C. 324; see p. 108 above; Birks (1993d); Millett (1993); Crilley; J.C. Smith; McKendrick (1994); Jaffey at 44.

[92] Maddaugh and McCamus, p. 96. Cf. Oakley (1995) at 397–402.

[93] Ibid. at 327.

[94] Above, p. 148 ff.

[95] Goode (1987) at 439; Burrows (1993a), p. 42.

[96] Sherwin at 336.

[97] Ibid. at 329–40. Also see Youdan (1992) at pp. 585–6.

[98] Sherwin at 352.

[99] Ibid. at 350–5.

3. The Recipient's Solvency

Goff and Jones argue that the nature of the provider's claim should 'be dependent upon whether the defendant knew or did not know the facts which ground the claim' and 'upon whether he is insolvent or solvent'.[100] It is appreciated that the recipient's knowledge will affect his or her entitlement to defences, such as *bona fide* purchase, change of position, and good faith exchange,[101] and the evidentiary presumptions to be made in the process of identifying the property subject to the claim.[102] However, with respect, it is difficult to understand why an event like a bankruptcy petition, which is unconnected with the provider's claim or the property he or she is claiming, should alter the nature of that claim.[103] As Birks stated, 'The sanctity of property and its immunity to discretionary "adjustment" is deeply rooted in legal thought. It is dictated by respect for the individual and individual preferences and by the fear of prejudicing third parties'.[104] Although there may be arguments favouring the use of judicial discretion in certain contexts, such as family property disputes, linking the provider's claim to the recipient's solvency is essentially, as Mr. Gardner stated,[105]

> an inclination to exercise the discretion inter parties in such a way as not to prejudice the third party. Is this the best approach? It could be said to be the worst of both worlds. The remedy which is otherwise appropriate inter parties is cut back; indeed, proprietary effect is denied just when it would be valuable. Yet the third party is still not told exactly where she stands, ahead of time, as she wants to be.

The fairest treatment of all concerned is not through the discretionary adjustment of property rights on insolvency, but by ensuring that proprietary responses to unjust enrichment are never 'lightly conceded' and can 'be known with certainty and precision'.[106] This is best achieved through the resulting trust.

C. DEFENCES

A better understanding of the true nature of the resulting trust will make it possible in many situations which were previously thought to give the provider only a personal claim to restitution. This may raise fears that the trust will upset the balance between the restitutionary rights of providers and the legitimate interests of recipients in the security of their receipts.[107] On closer inspection, those fears

[100] Goff and Jones, p. 95. [101] See pp. 121, 132, 168–9 above.
[102] See pp. 212–14 above.
[103] Oditah said 'it would give unsecured creditors a perverse incentive to make "strategic" use of insolvency proceedings and encourage opportunistic behaviour' if insolvency were allowed to derogate from existing property rights: Oditah at 472.
[104] Birks (1994c) at p. 223. See Birks (1989a) p. 378; Birks (1995b) at 84–5.
[105] Gardner (1994) at p. 200. [106] Birks (1989a), p. 378.
[107] Burrows (1995) at 27; Swadling (1996) at 126; *Westdeutsche Landesbank* v. *Islington* [1996] 2 All E.R. 961, 974, 986.

are greatly alleviated by the available defences. Resulting trusts are subject to destruction by *bona fide* purchase[108] and to claims for counter-restitution.[109] Their equitable nature allows for a fine tuning of the balance between the interests of the parties. The successful integration of resulting trusts with other restitutionary responses will depend, in part, on the proper application of the defences available to claims based on unjust enrichment.

1. Change of Position and Bona Fide Purchase

The recognition of the defence of 'change of position', in *Lipkin Gorman* v. *Karpnale Ltd.*,[110] should allow for a more consistent development of the law of restitution, by protecting those recipients who would be detrimentally affected by a restitutionary claim, rather than by artificially limiting the events which give rise to such a claim.[111] However, the apple cart could be upset if the defence did not apply to resulting trusts. Innocent recipients may incur liabilities and make expenditures in reliance on their apparent beneficial ownership of other property subject to a resulting trust. The trust, which would otherwise continue intact, should be partially determined by the amount to which the recipient's overall enrichment is reduced.[112] Similarly, as Mr. Barker has convincingly demonstrated, the defence of *bona fide* purchase, which developed in response to proprietary claims, will be undermined if it is not permitted to operate against first-measure claims based on the receipt of property belonging in equity to another.[113] This cross-fertilization of defences to claims *in rem* and *in personam* should allow the resulting trust to extend beyond its traditional categories with only minimal disruption.

2. Good Faith Exchange

More attention needs to be paid, in both personal and proprietary contexts, to the defence of 'good faith exchange'. There will be many cases in which the provider of property had only a vitiated or qualified intention to benefit the recipient and yet the resulting trust will not be possible, because the recipient acquired the property for valuable consideration and in good faith, unaware of that vitiation or qualification. It is clear that neither the transfer of property for valuable consideration[114] nor the innocence of the recipient[115] is sufficient on its own to

[108] Above, p. 35. [109] See *Gross* v. *French* (1975) 238 E.G. 39, C.A.

[110] [1991] 2 A.C. 548.

[111] See Birks (1992a) pp. 123–5; McKendrick (1992b); Burrows (1993a), pp. 421–31; Goff and Jones, pp. 133–4, 739–45; ppp. 131–2 above.

[112] *Restatement of Restitution*, §178; See Burrows (1993a), p. 431; Goff and Jones, p. 745; Nolan (1995) at pp. 178–9; Birks (1996a) at pp. 55–6.

[113] Barker (1995a) at p. 194; Birks (1996a) at p. 65.

[114] e.g. *Barclays Bank Ltd.* v. *Quistclose Investments Ltd.* [1970] A.C. 567; *Re EVTR* [1987] B.C.L.C. 646, C.A.

[115] e.g. *Re Vinogradoff* [1935] W.N. 68; *In re Muller* [1953] N.Z.L.R. 879.

prevent a resulting trust from arising. Together, they form the defence of good faith exchange, which is similar to, but distinct from, the defence of *bona fide* purchase. As Barker stated, 'the objective principle of contract law and the restitutionary defence of bona fide purchase pursue the same aim (security for those engaged in exchange-transactions), but in different contexts'.[116]

The difference in context (two parties instead of three) produces a few differences. First, the defence of good faith exchange should prevent the resulting trust from arising, while a *bona fide* purchase defeats an existing trust. Whether this has any practical significance remains to be seen. Secondly, the defence of *bona fide* purchase does not apply to purchasers of equitable interests,[117] whereas the defence of good faith exchange is not so limited.[118] Thirdly, when land is registered, the question whether a *bona fide* purchaser has notice of the resulting trust depends on whether the beneficiary has an over-riding interest.[119] This does not affect the defence of good faith exchange, where the recipient has dealt directly with the provider and the question of notice is directed to defects in the provider's intention to confer the benefit.[120] However, this distinction is sometimes overlooked.[121]

3. Limitation of Actions

Professor Burrows argued against the creation of resulting trusts in response to mistaken payments because 'the application of normal trust rules would mean that there would be no limitation period applicable to the equitable action; for under the Limitation Act 1980, s. 21(1) there is no statutory limitation period for actions to recover trust property or its proceeds'.[122] However, with respect, the application of limitation periods to claims against resulting trustees is not settled and there are indications that some claims would be subject to the same limitation period as the common law action for money had and received.

Subsection 21(3) of the Limitation Act 1980 imposes a 6-year limitation period on 'an action by a beneficiary to recover trust property or in respect of any breach of trust', subject to two broad exceptions in subsection 21(1), which states that:

> No period of limitation prescribed by this Act shall apply to an action by a beneficiary under a trust, being an action—(a) in respect of any fraud or fraudulent breach of trust to which the trustee was a party or privy; or (b) to recover from the trustee trust property

[116] Barker (1995a) at p. 201.

[117] *Phillips* v. *Phillips* (1862) 4 De G.F.&J. 208; see pp. 171–2, 178–80 above.

[118] *Bainbrigge* v. *Browne* (1881) 18 Ch.D. 188, 196.

[119] Land Registration Act 1925, s. 70(1); see *Hodgson* v. *Marks* [1971] 1 Ch. 892, C.A.; *Blacklocks* v. *J.B. Developments (Godalming) Ltd.* [1982] Ch. 183.

[120] See *Barclays Bank p.l.c.* v. *O'Brien* [1994] 1 A.C. 180; *C.I.B.C. Mortgages p.l.c.* v. *Pitt* [1994] 1 A.C. 200; Mee (1995).

[121] See Lawson at 284–5.

[122] Burrows (1995) at 27.

or the proceeds of trust property in the possession of the trustee, or previously received by the trustee and converted to his use.

If the exception in subsection 21(1)(b) is interpreted to include all claims against resulting trustees, then an innocent recipient of a mistaken payment would not be protected by a limitation period as Burrows feared. However, the courts have interpreted that exception narrowly and it does not apply to every trust arising by operation of law. A closer inspection reveals that the limitation of an action to recover a mistaken payment is treated much the same way in equity as it is at common law. There is no express limitation of actions for money had and received and yet that gap has been filled through judicial interpretation. The claim for money had and received used to be limited by statute as an action upon the case,[123] but fell between the cracks after 1939 amendments translated that into what is now an 'action founded on simple contract'.[124] In *Re Diplock*, the Court of Appeal stated:[125]

We assume in [the defendant's] favour that the words 'action founded on simple contract' must be taken to cover actions for money had and received, formerly actions on the case, and, as such, covered in express terms by the Statute of James I. The assumption must we think be made though the words used cannot be regarded as felicitous.

Although the Statute of James I (Limitation Act 1623) applied only to actions at common law, equitable claims would be limited by analogy to the statute.[126] The first statutes to deal with limitation of actions against trustees merely provided exemptions for claims against express trustees.[127] These did not change the established equitable principle that claims against express trustees and some (but not all) constructive and resulting trustees were not subject to limitation periods.[128] The Trustee Act 1888 introduced limitation periods for claims against trustees, which are similar to those now in effect. The trustee could 'plead the lapse of time as a bar to such action . . . as if the claim had been against him in an action of debt for money had and received',[129] subject to the two exceptions quoted above from subsection 21(1) of the Limitation Act 1980.

The Trustee Act 1888 was the first limitation statute to expressly provide for trusts arising by operation of law: 'the expression "trustee" shall be deemed to include . . . a trustee whose trust arises by construction or implication of law as well as an express trustee'.[130] The current statute is similar, stating that 'the

[123] Limitation Act 1623, 21 Jac. 1, c. 16, s. 3. [124] Limitation Act 1980, s. 5.

[125] [1948] Ch. 465, 514; aff'd *Ministry of Health* v. *Simpson* [1951] A.C. 251; see *Westdeutsche* v. *Islington* [1994] 4 All E.R. 890, 942–3; McLean (1989) at 475–6; Goff and Jones, pp. 755–6.

[126] See *Knox* v. *Gye* (1872) L.R. 5 H.L. 656, 674; Lightwood, pp. 251–2; Brunyate, p. 4 ff.

[127] Real Property Limitation Act 1833, s. 25; Judicature Act 1873, s. 25(2); see Lightwood, p. 68; Brunyate, pp. 53–8; Franks, p. 64.

[128] *Beckford* v. *Wade* (1805) 17 Ves. 87; *Burdick* v. *Garrick* (1870) L.R. 5 Ch. 233; *Soar* v. *Ashwell* [1893] 2 Q.B. 390 C.A.; *Patrick* v. *Simpson* (1889) 24 Q.B.D. 128; Lightwood, pp. 68–9.

[129] Trustee Act 1888, s. 8(1)(b). [130] Trustee Act 1888, s. 1(3).

expressions "trust" and "trustee" extend to implied and constructive trusts'.[131] Notwithstanding this definition, courts have interpreted the exemption narrowly and it does not include every trust arising by operation of law.[132]

In *Taylor* v. *Davies*,[133] the defendant was an inspector of the estate of an insolvent Ontario firm and, in breach of his fiduciary duty, had purchased land from the firm at a tenth of its true value. The firm's creditors brought an action to recover the property from the defendant more than 12 years later. The Ontario Limitations Act provided a ten-year limit on claims to recover land, but also exempted claims against trustees in the same manner as the Trustee Act 1888 and Limitation Act 1980. The Privy Council advised that the exemption did not apply even though the defendant was a constructive trustee of the property as a result of his breach of fiduciary duty:[134]

> The expressions 'trust property' and 'retained by the trustee' properly apply not to a case where a person having taken possession of property on his own behalf, is liable to be declared a trustee by the Court; but rather to a case where he originally took possession upon trust for or on behalf of others. In other words, they refer to cases where a trust arose before the occurrence of the transaction impeached and not to cases where it arises only by reason of that transaction.

The Privy Council relied on cases which had decided that some constructive trusts are treated as express trusts while others are subject to the limitation statutes by analogy.[135] It then considered and rejected the argument that the law had been changed by provisions in the Ontario Limitations Act which are equivalent to those now found in the Limitation Act 1980:[136]

> Sect. 47, sub-s. 1, it is said, defines a trustee as including 'a trustee whose trust arises by construction or implication of law', and, accordingly, the exclusion from s. 47, sub-s. 2, of a claim to recover 'trust property or the proceeds thereof still retained by the trustee' must apply to property in the hands of a constructive trustee or of any person claiming under him otherwise than by purchase for value without notice. If this contention be correct, then the section, which was presumably passed for the relief of trustees, has seriously altered for the worse the position of a constructive trustee, and . . . a doctrine has been introduced which may be 'fatal to the security of property'.

Taylor v. *Davies* has been applied to bar claims by companies to recover misappropriated assets by way of constructive trust in *Clarkson* v. *Davies*,[137]

[131] Trustee Act 1925, s. 68(17); Limitation Act 1980, s. 38(1).

[132] See Lightwood, pp. 282–3; but cf. 28 *Halsbury's Laws* (4th edn, 1979) §833; McLean (1989) at 497–8; McGee, p. 250; and *Nelson* v. *Rye* [1996] 2 All E.R. 186, 199; which do not consider the cases discussed below.

[133] [1920] A.C. 636.

[134] Ibid. 653, per Viscount Cave.

[135] e.g. *Beckford* v. *Wade* (1805) 17 Ves. 87, P.C.; *Burdick* v. *Garrick* (1870) L.R. 5 Ch. 233; *Soar* v. *Ashwell* [1893] 2 Q.B. 390, C.A.

[136] [1920] A.C. 636, 652, per Viscount Cave quoting from the Limitation Act, R.S.O. 1914, and *Beckford* v. *Wade* (1805) 17 Ves. 87, 97.

[137] [1923] A.C. 100, P.C. Also see *Metropolitan Bank* v. *Heiron* (1880) 5 Ex.D. 319, C.A.

where the company's money had been paid as a bribe, and *J.L.O. Ranch Ltd.* v. *Logan*,[138] where the company's land had been improperly purchased by its director. Although it does not seem to have been considered in connexion with a resulting trust, it ought to apply *a fortiori* to a claim to recover property mistakenly transferred to an innocent recipient.

In *Re Blake*,[139] the personal estate of an intestate was paid to the Crown in 1883 and claimed as trust property by the next of kin many years later. Maugham J. thought it was similar to an action to recover money paid to an innocent recipient by mistake and that, in the absence of any express statutory limitation period, 'a lapse of 6 years from the date of discovery of the mistake, would . . . be a complete answer to the claim'.[140] His lordship's comments on the application of limitation periods to constructive trusts are relevant to resulting trusts:[141]

> Constructive trusts are of various kinds, and without attempting a classification I may point out that there is a wide difference from the point of view of lapse of time between cases where the constructive trustee must be taken to have knowingly assumed the obligations of a trustee and those where the relationship is due merely to equitable principles . . . [W]here the constructive trust is one in which an equitable obligation arises from the circumstances of the case, and there has been no intention to create a trust and no improper conduct in reference to trust property from which the court will infer a direct trust, there is in general no objection to the defendant appealing to the lapse of time.

It has been suggested that resulting trusts should be exempt from limitation periods.[142] However, this suggestion was made without regard to the possible application of resulting trusts outside their traditional categories. Resulting trusts arise in a variety of situations and they cannot be treated alike when considering the limitation of actions. On one hand are resulting trusts which arise on the failure of an express trust. Resulting trustees who were intended to be express trustees have been treated as such for the purpose of limitation periods.[143] On the other hand are resulting trusts of mistaken payments to innocent recipients, who ought to be entitled to the normal 6-year limitation period. The situations in between will need to be worked out on a principled basis.

Where a contribution to the purchase of property has been made with the consent of all concerned, the resulting trust which arises should be exempt from limitation periods under the Limitation Act 1980, s. 21(1).[144] Like the resulting trust arising on the failure of an express trust, there is a sufficient fiduciary relationship created by the arrangement to justify its placement with express trusts for limitation purposes. As Bowen L.J. stated in *Soar* v. *Ashwell*:[145]

[138] (1987) 54 Alta.L.R. (2d) 130 (Trussler J.); cf. *G.L. Baker Ltd.* v. *Medway Building and Supplies Ltd.* [1958] 2 All E.R. 532 (Danckwerts J.); rev'd [1958] 3 All E.R. 540, C.A.

[139] [1932] 1 Ch. 54. [140] Ibid. 63. [141] Ibid. 62–3.

[142] Brunyate, pp. 60–1; Franks, pp. 66–7, 71–2; Scott and Fratcher, §409.

[143] *Patrick* v. *Simpson* (1889) 24 Q.B.D. 128; cf. *In re Lacy* [1899] 2 Ch. 149.

[144] Cf. Lightwood, p. 74. Also see *Re Landi* [1939] Ch. 828, C.A., where a claim between co-tenants was exempt from limitations because they held the property on trust for sale under the Law of Property Act 1925, s. 35.

[145] [1893] 2 Q.B. 390, 397.

[A] person occupying a fiduciary relation, who has property deposited with him on the strength of such relation, is to be dealt with as an express, and not merely a constructive, trustee of such property. His possession of such property is never in virtue of any right of his own, but is coloured from the first by the trust and confidence in virtue of which he received it.

4. Laches and Acquiescence

Even if no limitation period applies, a trustee who suffers serious prejudice through the plaintiff's delay in bringing the action should be entitled to a defence based on laches or acquiescence.[146] One form of prejudice relates to the proof of the creation or continued existence of the trust. As Lord Cottenham C. stated in *Att.-Gen.* v. *Fishmongers' Company*:[147]

If there be no doubt as to the origin and existence of a trust, the principles of justice and the interests of mankind require that the lapse of time should not enable those who are mere trustees to appropriate to themselves that which is the property of others; but in questions of doubt whether any trust exists, and whether those in possession are not entitled to the property for their own benefit, the principles of justice and the interests of mankind require that the utmost regard should be paid to the length of time during which there has been enjoyment inconsistent with the existence of the supposed trust.

This may be especially relevant to a resulting trust, since its creation depends on the provider's intention at the moment of transfer. Even in cases of resulting trust upon the failure of an express trust, there may be a genuine dispute over whether the trustees were intended to enjoy the surplus property for their own benefit (although this is usually resolved by reference to the settlor's intentions as expressed in the instrument creating the express trust).

Prejudice may also be suffered through the loss of evidence which might establish some other defence to a claim to the trust property or for breach of trust.[148] Delay or acquiescence may also provide a defence if it has caused the trustees to deal with the trust property and arrange their affairs in the belief that they are beneficially entitled to that property.[149]

D. THE WAY FORWARD

To begin an inquiry into the resulting trust in the face of many confident (and learned) opinions that, 'The law with regard to resulting trusts is not in doubt',[150]

[146] *Rochefoucauld* v. *Boustead* [1897] 1 Ch. 196; Lightwood, pp. 272–3; Brunyate, pp. 234–44; Franks, pp. 260–2; Scott and Fratcher, §409; Meagher, Gummow and Lehane, pp. 798–803.

[147] (1841) 5 My.&Cr. 16, 17–18. Also see *Beckford* v. *Wade* (1805) 17 Ves. 87, 97; *Soar* v. *Ashwell* [1893] 2 Q.B. 390, 400; *Orr* v. *Ford* (1989) 167 C.L.R. 316.

[148] See *Orr* v. *Ford* (1989) 167 C.L.R. 316.

[149] See *Re Jarvis* [1958] 2 All E.R. 336; *Hourigan* v. *Trustees Executors & Agency Co. Ltd.* (1934) 51 C.L.R. 619; *Orr* v. *Ford* (1989) 167 C.L.R. 316.

[150] *Vandervell* v. *I.R.C.* [1967] 2 A.C. 291, 307, per Lord Reid; see p. 1 above.

may have seemed nothing more than idle curiosity. However, that confidence, born more of a long familiarity with the resulting trust than a deep understanding of its nature, turned out to be misplaced. We knew what a resulting trust looked like and where it could be found, but were never entirely sure what lay beneath the surface. A closer inspection reveals that the event which gives rise to every resulting trust is unjust enrichment (by subtraction) and that every resulting trust effects restitution of that enrichment to its provider. That proves true even if we stray no further than the traditional categories in which resulting trusts have been known to arise. However, when that discovery is made, it quickly becomes apparent that the event which gives rise to a resulting trust occurs in a much wider variety of circumstances.

Does this understanding change the law? That depends on what we mean by 'change'. It should lead to a more consistent and logical application of the resulting trust within its traditional categories and, more dramatically, to its more regular employment outside those categories. However, this is not change in a law reform sense, but (as Birks says of our modern understanding of the law of restitution) only the change that 'comes from better understanding of what is there already'.[151] Mr. Matthews may disagree:[152] 'When Professor Birks says that reordering legal subjects gives a *better* understanding, we must be clear what he means: he means it gives a *different* understanding, resulting (sooner or later) in different legal rules, which he thinks . . . would be better than the ones we have now'.

It is true that a better (or different) understanding of the resulting trust cannot help but produce change. It may indeed lead to 'different legal rules', depending on what we mean by 'different'. Is the statement, 'a recipient of a mistaken payment is a resulting trustee of that payment for its provider', a different rule of merely another application of the existing rule that 'a transfer of property gives rise to a resulting trust if the provider did not intend to benefit the recipient'?

Matthews has another complaint:[153]

> The non-proprietary part of restitution collects together rules of law that (generally speaking) were not claimed by other 'established' law subjects, i.e., tort, contract, administrative law. But the proprietary part according to Professor Birks does not collect together waifs and strays outside the law of property. On the contrary, it comes in the front door, gathers up a number of important property rules, and tries to walk off with them. On any view, the established order is being interfered with.

It is true that the rules governing resulting trusts are not 'waifs and strays outside the law of' trusts, but this book is certainly not an attempt 'to walk off with them'. Those rules are, and will remain, firmly grounded in the law of trusts. The primary change is the removal of the confusion surrounding the events which give rise to resulting trusts. As with all trusts and property interests, this

[151] Birks (1989a), p. 27. See p. 7 above.
[152] Matthews (1995) at pp. 36–7. [153] Ibid. at p. 69.

can only be beneficial. If it turns out that more events give rise to resulting trusts than previously suspected, the resulting trust is not moving, but getting an addition to its existing home. Complaints about imperialism should be directed, if anywhere, to Chancery.

The recognition of the resulting trust's wider role is likely to lead or contribute to some refinement of certain rules, such as the concept of a mere equity, the 'mistake of law' bar, the requirement of 'total failure of consideration', the first-measure liability and fiduciary duties of resulting trustees, and the various defences to restitutionary claims. Many of these changes are already proposed or under way, but they will be better accomplished with the knowledge that the resulting trust is one of the responses to unjust enrichment which needs to be reckoned with.

We have nearly assembled the puzzle of events which give rise to all trusts. Elias filled in a large portion of that puzzle with his work on constructive trusts. The present work on resulting trusts, which is a continuation of much that has gone before[154] (and has been going on for more than 250 years),[155] will hopefully bring the puzzle nearer to its completion. With most of the picture now revealed, a more fundamental change is possible. It should no longer be necessary or acceptable to declare a trust because it would be inequitable or unconscionable for the trustee to retain the property in question. These are conclusions that a trust exists or should exist, but without revealing why. The owner's conscience can only be affected if the claimant is entitled to some interest in that property. That interest is almost certainly a trust[156] and we are left guessing what events have given rise to it. The tools now exist to identify those events. The courts can and must say whether the trust is perfecting a relied-upon expectation (for example), effecting restitution of unjust enrichment, responding to a wrong (and it is no good saying that it is wrong to keep the property), or responding to some other event.

[154] See p. 7 above. [155] See *Ryall* v. *Ryall* (1739) 1 Atk. 59; pp. 21–2 above.
[156] *Gissing* v. *Gissing* [1971] A.C. 886, 904; *Cowcher* v. *Cowcher* [1972] 1 W.L.R. 425, 429.

Bibliography

AMERICAN LAW INSTITUTE, *Restatement of the Law of Restitution* (St. Paul, Minnesota, 1937)

—— *Restatement of the Law of Trusts, Second* (St. Paul, Minnesota, 1959)

—— *Restatement of the Law of Contracts, Second* (St. Paul, Minnesota, 1981)

ANDREWS, N., 'Payments made under Mistake of Law: a Legal Error Exposed in Scotland' (1995) 54 C.L.J. 246

ARORA, A., 'The Bank's Liability as a Constructive Trustee' [1990] J.B.L. 217

ARROWSMITH, S., 'Mistake and the Role of the "Submission to an Honest Claim"' in Burrows, *Essays on the Law of Restitution* (1991) at p. 17

ATIYAH, P.S. (1982), 'Economic Duress and the "Overborne Will"' (1982) 98 L.Q.R. 197

—— (1986), *Essays on Contract* (Oxford, 1986)

BAKER, J.H. (1977), 'The Use upon a Use in Equity 1558–1625' (1977) 93 L.Q.R. 33

—— (1990), *An Introduction to English Legal History*, 3rd edn. (London, 1990)

BAKER, P.V., and LANGAN, P.St.J., *Snell's Equity*, 29th edn. (London, 1990)

BARKER, K. (1995a), 'After Change of Position: Good Faith Exchange in the Modern Law of Restitution' in Birks, *Laundering and Tracing* (1995) at p. 191

—— (1995b), 'Unjust Enrichment: Containing the Beast' (1995) 15 O.J.L.S. 457

BARTON, J.L. (1965), 'The Medieval Use' (1965) 81 L.Q.R. 564

—— (1966), 'The Statute of Uses and the Trust of Freeholds' (1966) 82 L.Q.R. 215

BEATSON, J. (1975), 'Repudiation of Illegal Purpose as a Ground for Restitution' (1975) 91 L.Q.R. 313

—— (1988), 'Unjust Enrichment in the High Court of Australia' (1988) 104 L.Q.R. 13

—— (1989), 'Restitutionary Remedies for Void and Ineffective Contracts' (1989) 105 L.Q.R. 179

—— (1991), *The Use and Abuse of Unjust Enrichment* (Oxford, 1991)

—— (1993a), 'Public Law, Restitution and the Role of the House of Lords' (1993) 109 L.Q.R. 1

—— (1993b), 'Restitution of Taxes, Levies and Other Imposts: Defining the Extent of the Woolwich Principle' (1993) 109 L.Q.R. 401

—— (1995), 'Restitution of Overpaid Tax, Discretion and Passing-on' (1995) 111 L.Q.R. 375

BEATSON, J., and BIRKS, P., 'Unrequested Payment of Another's Debt' (1976) 92 L.Q.R. 188

BEATSON, J., and BISHOP, W., 'Mistaken Payments in the Law of Restitution' (1986) 36 U.T.L.J. 149

BEATSON, J., and FRIEDMANN, D. (eds.), *Good Faith and Fault in Contract* (Oxford, 1995)

BELL, A., 'Bona Vacantia', in Palmer and McKendrick, *Interests in Goods* (1993) at p. 401

Birks, P. (1983), 'Restitution and Freedom of Contract' (1983) 36 C.L.P. 141
—— (1984), 'English and Roman Learning in *Moses* v. *Macjerlan*' (1984) 37 C.L.P. 1
—— (1988), 'Personal Restitution in Equity' [1988] L.M.C.L.Q. 128
—— (1989a), *An Introduction to the Law of Restitution*, revised edn. (Oxford, 1989)
—— (1989b), 'Misdirected Funds' (1989) 105 L.Q.R. 352
—— (1989c), 'Misdirected Funds Again' (1989) 105 L.Q.R. 528
—— (1989d), 'Misdirected Funds: Restitution from the Recipient' [1989] L.M.C.L.Q. 296
—— (1990a), 'Restitution from the Executive: A Tercentenary Footnote to the Bill of Rights' in Finn, *Essays on Restitution* (1990) at p. 161
—— (1990b), 'The Independence of Restitutionary Causes of Action' (1990) 16 U.Qld.L.J. 1
—— (1990c), 'The Remedies for Abuse of Confidential Information' [1990] L.M.C.L.Q. 460
—— (1991a), 'In Defence of Free Acceptance' in Burrows, *Essays on the Law of Restitution* (1991) at p. 105
—— (1991b), Review of Maddaugh and McCamus, *The Law of Restitution* (1991) 70 C.B.R. 814
—— (1992a), *Restitution—The Future* (Sydney, 1992)
—— (1992b), 'Civil Wrongs: A New World' in *Butterworth Lectures 1990–91* (London, 1992) at p. 55
—— (1992c), 'Restitution and Resulting Trusts' in Goldstein, *Equity and Contemporary Legal Developments* (1992) at p. 335
—— (1992d), '"When Money is Paid in Pursuance of a Void Authority"—A Duty to Repay?' [1992] Public L. 580
—— (1992e), 'Trusts in the Recovery of Misapplied Assets: Tracing, Trusts and Restitution' in McKendrick, *Commercial Aspects of Trusts and Fiduciary Obligations* (1992) at p. 149
—— (1993a), 'Mixtures' in Palmer and McKendrick, *Interests in Goods* (1993) at p. 449
—— (1993b), 'Modernising the Law of Restitution' (1993) 109 L.Q.R. 164
—— (1993c), 'No Consideration: Restitution After Void Contracts' (1993) 23 U.W.A.L.Rev. 195
—— (1993d), 'Obligations and Property in Equity: Lister v. Stubbs in the Limelight' [1993] L.M.C.L.Q. 30
—— (1993e), 'Persistent Problems in Misdirected Money: A Quintet' [1993] L.M.C.L.Q. 218
—— (1994a) (ed.), *The Frontiers of Liability* (Oxford, 1994)
—— (1994b), 'Gifts of Other People's Money' in Birks, *The Frontiers of Liability*, vol. 1 (1994) at p. 31
—— (1994c), 'Proprietary Rights as Remedies' in Birks, *The Frontiers of Liability*, vol. 2 (1994) at p. 214
—— (1994d), 'Property in the Profits of Wrongdoing' (1994) 24 U.W.A.L. Rev. 8
—— (1995a) (ed.), *Laundering and Tracing* (Oxford, 1995)
—— (1995b), 'Establishing a Proprietary Base' [1995] R.L.R. 83
—— (1995c) 'Proprietary Restitution: an Intelligible Approach' (1995) 9 T.L.Int. 43
—— (1996a) 'Change of Position: the Nature of the Defence and its Relationship to other Restitutionary Defences' in McInnes, *Restitution: Developments in Unjust Enrichment* (1996) at p. 49

BIRKS, P. (1996b) 'Trusts Raised to Reverse Unjust Enrichment: the Westdeutsche Case' [1996] R.L.R. 3

—— (1996c) 'Equity in the Modern Law' (1996) 26 U.W.A.L.Rev. 1

BIRKS, P., and CHAMBERS, R., *The Restitution Research Resource 1994* (Oxford, 1994)

BIRKS, P., and CHIN N.Y., 'On the Nature of Undue Influence' in BEATSON and FRIEDMANN, *Good Faith and Fault in Contract* (1995) at p. 57

BIRKS, P., and MCLEOD, G., 'The Implied Contract Theory of Quasi-Contract: Civilian Opinion Current in the Century Before Blackstone' (1986) 6 O.J.L.S. 46

BOGERT, G.G., and BOGERT, G.T., *The Law of Trusts and Trustees*, 2nd revised edn. (St. Paul, Minnesota, 1977–94)

BOWLES, R.A., and WHELAN, C.J., 'Interest on Debts' (1985) 48 M.L.R. 229

BRIDGE, M., 'The Quistclose Trust in a World of Secured Transactions' (1992) 12 O.J.L.S. 333

BRUNYATE, J., *Limitations of Actions in Equity* (London, 1932)

BRYAN, M. (1990), 'Constructive Trusts: a New Zealand Development' (1990) 106 L.Q.R. 213

—— (1993), 'The Meaning of Notice in Tracing Claims' (1993) 109 L.Q.R. 368

—— (1994) 'Constructive Trusts and Unconscionability in Australia: on the Road to Unattainable Perfection' (1994) 8 T.L.Int. 74

BUCKLEY, R.A., 'Social Security Fraud as Illegality' (1994) 110 L.Q.R. 3

BURROWS, A. (1983), 'Contract, Tort and Restitution—A Satisfactory Division or Not?' (1983) 99 L.Q.R. 217

—— (1988), 'Free Acceptance and the Law of Restitution' (1988) 104 L.Q.R. 576

—— (1990), 'Misdirected Funds—A Reply' (1990) 106 L.Q.R. 20

—— (1991a) (ed.), *Essays on the Law of Restitution* (Oxford, 1991)

—— (1991b), 'Public Authorities, Ultra Vires and Restitution' in Burrows, *Essays on the Law of Restitution* (1991) at p. 39

—— (1993a), *The Law of Restitution* (London, 1993)

—— (1993b), 'Restitution for Mistake in Australia' (1993) 13 O.J.L.S. 584

—— (1993c), 'Restitution of Payments made under Swaps Transactions' (1993) 143 N.L.J. 480

—— (1995), 'Swaps and the Friction between Common Law and Equity' [1995] R.L.R. 15

BUTLER, P. (1990a), 'Mistaken Payments, Change of Position and Restitution' in Finn, *Essays on Restitution* (1990) at p. 87

—— (1990b), 'Viewing Restitution at the Level of a Secondary Remedial Obligation' (1990) 16 U.Qld.L.J. 27

CANE, P., 'Do Banks Dare Lend to Local Authorities?' (1994) 110 L.Q.R. 514

CARTER, J.W., 'Restitution and Contract Risk' in McInnes, *Restitution: Developments in Unjust Enrichment* (1996) at p. 137

CHALLIES, G.S., *The Doctrine of Unjustified Enrichment in the Law of the Province of Quebec*, 2nd edn. (Montreal, 1952)

CHAMBERS, R., 'Restitution of Money Paid to Third Persons' (1993) 57 Sask.L.Rev. 325

CHEN-WISHART, M., 'Loss Sharing, Undue Influence and Manifest Disadvantage' (1994) 110 L.Q.R. 173

CHIN N.Y., 'Relieving Against Forfeiture: Windfalls and Conscience' (1995) 25 U.W.A.L.Rev. 110

CLARK, J.B., and ROSS MARTYN, J.G., *Theobald on Wills*, 15th edn. (London, 1993)

CLARKE, P.J., 'Land Law and Trusts' [1994] All E.R.Rev. 241
COOK, W.W., 'The Powers of Courts of Equity' (1915) 15 Col.L.Rev. 37, 106 and 228
COOKE, E., 'Trespass, Mesne Profits and Restitution' (1994) 110 L.Q.R. 420
COOKE, R., 'The Place of Equity and Equitable Doctrines in the Contemporary Common Law World: A New Zealand Perspective' in Waters, *Equity, Fiduciaries and Trusts 1993* (1993) at p. 25
COPE, M. (1986), 'Undue Influence and Alleged Manifestly Disadvantageous Transactions' (1986) 60 A.L.J. 87
—— (1992), *Constructive Trusts* (Sydney, 1992)
CORBIN, A.L., 'Waiver of Tort and Suit in Assumpsit' (1910) 19 Yale L.J. 221
COSTIGAN, G.P., Jr., 'The Classification of Trusts as Express, Resulting, and Constructive' (1914) 27 Harv.L.Rev. 437
CRETNEY, S.M., 'Mere Puppets, Folly and Imprudence: Undue Influence for the Twenty-First Century' [1994] R.L.R. 3
CRILLEY, D., 'A Case of Proprietary Overkill' [1994] R.L.R. 57
DAVIES, J.D. (1979), 'Informal Arrangements Affecting Land' (1979) 8 Syd.L.Rev. 578
—— (1990a), 'Duties of Confidence and Loyalty' [1990] L.M.C.L.Q. 4
—— (1990b), 'Informally Created Trusts of Land and Some Alternatives to Them' (1990) 106 L.Q.R. 539
—— (1993), 'Equitable Compensation: "Causation, Forseeability and Remoteness"' in Waters, *Equity, Fiduciaries and Trusts 1993* (1993) at p. 297
DAWSON, J.P. (1951), *Unjust Enrichment: a Comparative Analysis* (Boston, 1951)
—— (1959), 'Restitution or Damages?' (1959) 20 Ohio State L.J. 175
DICKSON, B., 'Restitution and Illegal Transactions' in Burrows, *Essays on the Law of Restitution* (1991) at p. 171
DIXON, M., 'Looking Up a Remedy for Inequitable Conduct' (1994) 53 C.L.J. 232
EEKELAAR, J., 'Non-Marital Property' in Birks, *The Frontiers of Liability*, vol. 2 (1994) at p. 204
ELIAS, G., *Explaining Constructive Trusts* (Oxford, 1990)
ENONCHONG, N., 'Title Claims and Illegal Transactions' (1995) 111 L.Q.R. 135
EVANS, P.T., 'The Fall and Rise of the Remedial Constructive Trust?' [1989] Conv. 418
EVANS, S., 'Void Swaps Contracts: Restitution at Law and in Equity' [1994] Conv. 395
FARQUHAR, K.B., 'Unjust Enrichment—Special Relationship—Domestic Services—Remedial Constructive Trust: *Peter* v. *Beblow*' (1993) 72 C.B.R. 538
FEHLBERG, B., 'The Husband, the Bank, the Wife and her Signature' (1994) 57 M.L.R. 467
FELTHAM, J.D., 'Informal Trusts and Third Parties' [1987] Conv. 246
FENNELL, S., 'Misdirected Funds: Problems of Inconsistency' (1994) 57 M.L.R. 38
FERGUSON, P., 'Constructive Trusts—A Note of Caution' (1993) 109 L.Q.R. 114
FINN, P.D. (1977) (ed.), *Fiduciary Obligations* (Sydney, 1977)
—— (1985) (ed.), *Essays in Equity* (Sydney, 1985)
—— (1987) (ed.), *Equity and Commercial Relationships* (Sydney, 1987)
—— (1989), 'The Fiduciary Principle' in Youdan, *Equity, Fiduciaries and Trusts* (1989) at p. 1
—— (1990) (ed.), *Essays on Restitution* (Sydney, 1990)
—— (1993), 'The Liability of Third Parties for Knowing Receipt or Assistance' in Waters, *Equity, Fiduciaries and Trusts 1993* (1993) at p. 195
—— (1994), 'Unconscionable Conduct' (1994) 8 J.C.L. 37

FLANNIGAN, R., 'The Fiduciary Obligation' (1989) 9 O.J.L.S. 285

FORD, H.A.J., and LEE, W.A., *Principles of the Law of Trusts*, 3rd edn. (Sydney, 1996)

FRANKEL, T., 'Fiduciary Relationship in the United States Today' in Waters, *Equity, Fiduciaries and Trusts 1993* (1993) at p. 173

FRANKS, M., *Limitation of Actions* (London, 1959)

FRATCHER, W.F., 'New Directions in the Employment of Equitable Doctrines: Home Purchase Developments' in Youdan, *Equity, Fiduciaries and Trusts* (1989) at p. 349

FRIEDMANN, D. (1991), 'Valid, Voidable, Qualified and Non-existing Obligations: An Alternative Perspective on the Law of Restitution' in Burrows, *Essays on the Law of Restitution* (1991) at p. 247

— (1995), 'The Performance Interest in Contract Damages' (1995) 111 L.Q.R. 628

FULLER, L.L., and PERDUE, W.R., 'The Reliance Interest in Contract Damages' (1936) 46 Yale L.J. 52, 373

FURMSTON, M.P., and SIMPSON, A.W.B., *Cheshire, Fifoot & Furmston's Law of Contract*, 12th edn. (London, 1991)

GARDNER, S. (1982), 'The Proprietary Effect of Contractual Obligations under *Tulk* v. *Moxhay* and *De Mattos* v. *Gibson*' (1982) 98 L.Q.R. 279

— (1986), 'Equity, Estate Contracts and the Judicature Acts: *Walsh* v. *Lonsdale* Revisited' (1986) 7 O.J.L.S. 60

— (1990), *An Introduction to the Law of Trusts* (Oxford, 1990)

— (1992), 'New Angles on Unincorporated Associations' [1992] Conv. 41

— (1993), 'Rethinking Family Property' (1993) 109 L.Q.R. 263

— (1994), 'The Element of Discretion' in Birks, *The Frontiers of Liability*, vol. 2 (1994) at p. 186

— (1996), 'Knowing Assistance and Knowing Receipt: Taking Stock' (1996) 112 L.Q.R. 56

GARNER, M., 'The Role of Subjective Benefit in the Law of Unjust Enrichment' (1990) 10 O.J.L.S. 42

GLOVER, J., *Commercial Equity: Fiduciary Relationships* (Melbourne, 1995)

GODDARD, D., 'Equity, Volunteers and Ducks' [1988] Conv. 19

GOFF, R., and JONES, G., *The Law of Restitution*, 4th edn. (London, 1993)

GOLDSTEIN, S.R., *Equity and Contemporary Legal Developments* (Jerusalem, 1992)

GOODE, R. (1976), 'The Right to Trace and its Impact in Commercial Transactions' (1976) 92 L.Q.R. 360 and 528

— (1987), 'Ownership and Obligation in Commercial Transactions' (1987) 103 L.Q.R. 433

— (1991), 'Property and Unjust Enrichment' in Burrows, *Essays on the Law of Restitution* (1991) at p. 215

— (1994), 'Charges Over Book Debts: A Missed Opportunity' (1994) 110 L.Q.R. 592

GOODHART, W., and JONES, G., 'The Infiltration of Equitable Doctrine into English Commercial Law' (1980) 43 M.L.R. 489

GRAY, K., *Elements of Land Law*, 2nd edn. (London, 1993)

GREEN, B., 'The Dissolution of Unincorporated Non-Profit Associations' (1980) 43 M.L.R. 626

GRIGSBY, W.E., *Story's Commentaries on Equity Jurisprudence*, 1st English edn. (London, 1884)

GUMMOW, W.M.C., 'Unjust Enrichment, Restitution and Proprietary Remedies' in Finn, *Essays on Restitution* (1990) at p. 47
HACKNEY, J., *Understanding Equity and Trusts* (London, 1987)
HALLIWELL, M., 'The Stranger as Constructive Trustee Revisited' [1989] Conv. 328
HAMMOND, G., 'Equity and Abortive Commercial Transactions' (1990) 106 L.Q.R. 207
HANBURY, H.G., *Modern Equity* (London, 1935)
HARDCASTLE, I.M., '"Purpose Trusts": How Close to Quistclose?' (1988) 85(36) L.S.Gaz. 14
HARDINGHAM, I.J., 'Unconscionable Dealing' in Finn, *Essays in Equity* (1985) at p. 1
HARDMAN, F.W., 'The Law of Escheat' (1888) 4 L.Q.R. 318
HARPUM, C. (1986), 'The Stranger as Constructive Trustee' (1986) 102 L.Q.R. 114 and 267
—— (1987), 'Liability for Intermeddling with Trusts' (1987) 50 M.L.R. 217
—— (1994), 'The Basis of Equitable Liability' in Birks, *The Frontiers of Liability*, vol. 1 (1994) at p. 9
—— (1995), 'Accessory Liability for Procuring or Assisting a Breach of Trust' (1995) 111 L.Q.R. 545
HAYTON, D.J. (1987), *Underhill & Hayton: Law Relating to Trusts and Trustees*, 14th edn. (London, 1987)
—— (1988), 'Remedial Constructive Trusts of Homes; an Overseas View' [1988] Conv. 259
—— (1989), 'Constructive Trusts: Is the Remedying of Unjust Enrichment a Satisfactory Approach?' in Youdan, *Equity, Fiduciaries and Trusts* (1989) at p. 205
—— (1990) 'Equitable Rights of Cohabitees' [1990] Conv. 370; reprinted in Goldstein, *Equity and Contemporary Legal Developments* (1992) at p. 590
—— (1991), *Cases and Commentary on the Law of Trusts*, 9th edn. (London, 1991)
—— (1993a), *The Law of Trusts*, 2nd edn. (London, 1993)
—— (1993b), 'Constructive Trusts of Homes—a Bold Approach' (1993) 109 L.Q.R. 485
—— (1994), 'Uncertainty of Subject-Matter of Trusts' (1994) 110 L.Q.R. 335
—— (1995), 'Equity's Identification Rules' in Birks, *Laundering and Tracing* (1995) at p. 1
HAZELTINE, H.D., 'Editor's Preface: Quasi-Contractual Obligations' in Jackson, *The History of Quasi-Contract in English Law* (1936) at p. ix
HEYDON, J.D. (1994), 'Causal Relationships between a Fiduciary's Default and the Principal's Loss' (1994) 110 L.Q.R. 328
—— (1995), 'The Negligent Fiduciary' (1995) 111 L.Q.R. 1
HILL, T., 'Restitution from Public Authorities and the Treasury's Position: *Woolwich Equitable Building Society* v. *I.R.C.*' (1993) 56 M.L.R. 856
HOFFMAN, L., 'The Redundancy of Knowing Assistance' in Birks, *The Frontiers of Liability*, vol. 1 (1994) at p. 27
HOLDSWORTH, W.S., *A History of English Law* (London, 1903–72)
HOLMES, O.W., 'Early English Equity' (1885) 1 L.Q.R. 162
HOVIUS, B., and YOUDAN, T.G., *The Law of Family Property* (Toronto, 1991)
HUDSON, A.H. (1984a), 'Is Divesting Abandonment Possible at Common Law?' (1984) 100 L.Q.R. 110
—— (1984b), 'Mental Incapacity in the Law of Contract and Property' [1984] Conv. 32
—— (1986), 'Mental Incapacity Revisited' [1986] Conv. 178

HUDSON, A.H. (1993), 'Abandonment', in Palmer and McKendrick, *Interests in Goods* (1993) at p. 423

HUTCHINSON, R.B., 'The Necessity of Conferring a Benefit for Recovery in Quasi-Contract' (1968) 19 Hastings L.J. 1259

IBBETSON, D., 'Implied Contracts and Restitution: History in the High Court of Australia' (1988) 8 O.J.L.S. 312

ING, N.D., *Bona Vacantia* (London, 1971)

JACKSON, R.M., *The History of Quasi-Contract in English Law* (Cambridge, 1936)

JAFFEY, P., 'Restitutionary Damages and Disgorgement' [1995] R.L.R. 30

JONES, G. (1990), 'A Topography of the Law of Restitution' in Finn, *Essays on Restitution* (1990) at p. 1

—— (1991) 'The Law of Restitution: The Past and the Future' in Burrows, *Essays on the Law of Restitution* (1991) at p. 1

—— (1992), 'Knowing Receipt and Knowing Assistance' in Goldstein, *Equity and Contemporary Legal Developments* (1992) at p. 374

—— (1993), 'Payments of Money Under Mistake of Law: a Comparative View' (1993) 52 C.L.J. 225

JORDON, F., *Chapters on Equity in New South Wales*, 6th edn. (Sydney, 1947)

KIRALFY, A.K.R., *A Source Book of English Law* (London, 1957)

KLINCK, D.R., 'The Quistclose Trust in Canada' (1994) 23 Can.Bus.L.J. 45

KULL, A., 'USA' [1995] R.L.R. 222

LASSON, K., 'Scholarship Amok: Excesses in the Pursuit of Truth and Tenure' (1990) 103 Harv.L.Rev. 926

LAURIE, G.T., 'Error of Law and Unjust Enrichment in Scotland' (1995) 111 L.Q.R. 379

LAW COMMISSION (1975), *Penalty Clauses and Forfeiture of Monies Paid* (1975, W.P. No. 61)

—— (1978), *Law of Contract: Report on Interest* (1978, Law Com. No. 88)

—— (1988), *Transfer of Land: Passing of Risk from Vendor to Purchaser* (1988, W.P. No. 109)

—— (1990), *Transfer of Land: Risk of Damage After Contract for Sale* (1990, Law Com. No. 191)

—— (1992), *Fiduciary Duties and Regulatory Rules* (1992, L.C.C.P. No. 124)

—— (1994), *Restitution: Mistakes of Law and Ultra Vires Public Authority Receipts and Payments* (1994, Law Com. No. 227)

—— (1995), *Fiduciary Duties and Regulatory Rules* (1995, Law Com. No. 236)

LAWSON, A., 'O'Brien and its Legacy: Principle, Equity and Certainty?' (1995) 54 C.L.J. 280

LEHANE, J.R.F., 'Undue Influence, Misrepresentation and Third Parties' (1994) 110 L.Q.R. 167

LIGHTWOOD, J.M., *The Time Limit on Actions* (London, 1909)

LITMAN, M.M., 'The Emergence of Unjust Enrichment as a Cause of Action and the Remedy of Constructive Trust' (1988) 26 Alta.L.Rev. 407

LOUGHLAN, P., 'Liability for Assistance in a Breach of Fiduciary Duty' (1989) 9 O.J.L.S. 260

LOWE, N.V., 'The Advancement of an Intended Wife: a Reply' (1976) 120 Sol.J. 141

MADDAUGH, P.D., and MCCAMUS, J.D., *The Law of Restitution* (Aurora: Ontario, 1990)

MAITLAND, F.W., *Equity*, revised edn. (Cambridge, 1936)

MANITOBA LAW REFORM COMMISSION, *Non-Charitable Purpose Trusts* (Winnipeg, 1992, No. 77)

MANN, F.A., *The Legal Aspect of Money*, 5th edn. (Oxford, 1992)

MARTIN, J.E. (1991a), 'Recent Cases' [1991] Conv. 364

—— (1991b), Review of G. Elias, *Explaining Constructive Trusts* (1991) 107 L.Q.R. 166

—— (1993a), *Hanbury and Martin's Modern Equity*, 14th edn. (London, 1993)

—— (1993b), 'Tracing, Fraud and Ultra Vires' [1993] Conv. 370

—— (1994), 'Fusion, Fallacy and Confusion; A Comparative Study' [1994] Conv. 13

MASON, A., 'The Place of Equity and Equitable Remedies in the Contemporary Common Law World' (1994) 110 L.Q.R. 238

MASON, K., and CARTER, J.W., *Restitution Law in Australia* (Sydney, 1995)

MATTHEWS, P. (1981), 'The Constitution of Disclaimed Trusts Inter Vivos' [1981] Conv. 141

—— (1989), 'The Efficacy of Trustee Exemption Clauses in English Law' [1989] Conv. 42

—— (1994), 'Resulting Trusts and Subsequent Contributions' (1994) 8 T.L.Int. 43

—— (1995), 'The Legal and Moral Limits of Common Law Tracing' in Birks, *Laundering and Tracing* (1995) at p. 23

MAUDSLEY, R.H. (1959), 'Proprietary Remedies for the Recovery of Money' (1959) 75 L.Q.R. 234

—— (1964) 'Incompletely Constituted Trusts' in Pound et al., *Perspectives of Law* (1964) at p. 240

MAXTON, J.K. (1986), 'De Facto Spouses and the Presumption of Advancement' (1986) 12 N.Z.U.L.Rev. 79

—— (1990a), 'Quistclose Developments in New Zealand' (1990) 9 Int.Bank.L. 216

—— (1990b), 'Equity' [1990] N.Z. Recent L. 89

—— (1991), 'Equity' [1991] N.Z. Recent L. 117

—— (1992), 'Equity' [1992] N.Z. Recent L. 123

MCBRIDE, N.J., and MCGRATH, P., 'The Nature of Restitution' (1995) 15 O.J.L.S. 33

MCCAMUS, J.D., 'Unjust Enrichment: Its Role and Its Limits' in Waters, *Equity, Fiduciaries and Trusts 1993* (1993) at p. 129

MCCLEAN, A.J., 'The Theoretical Basis of the Trustee's Duty of Loyalty' (1969) 7 Alta.L.Rev. 218

MCGEE, A., *Limitation Periods*, 2nd edn. (London, 1994)

MCINNES, M.P. (1993), 'Restitutionary Relief for Incontrovertible Benefits' (1993) 109 L.Q.R. 521

—— (1994a), 'Incontrovertible Benefits in the Supreme Court of Canada' (1994) 23 Can. Bus. L.J. 122

—— (1994b), 'Restitution and the Rescue of Life' (1994) 32 Alta.L.Rev. 37

—— (1996a), *Restitution: Developments in Unjust Enrichment* (Sydney, 1996)

—— (1996b), 'The Structure and Challenges of Unjust Enrichment' in McInnes, Restitution: Developments in Unjust Enrichment (1996) at p. 17

MCKENDRICK, E. (1988), 'The Battle of the Forms and the Law of Restitution' (1988) 8 O.J.L.S. 197

—— (1991a), 'Tracing Misdirected Funds' [1991] L.M.C.L.Q. 378

—— (1991b), 'Restitution of Tax Unlawfully Demanded' (1991) 107 L.Q.R. 526

—— (1992a), *Commercial Aspects of Trusts and Fiduciary Obligations* (Oxford, 1992)

McKendrick, E. (1992b), 'Restitution, Misdirected Funds and Change of Position' (1992) 55 M.L.R. 377
—— (1993), 'Restitution of Unlawfully Demanded Tax' [1993] L.M.C.L.Q. 88
—— (1994), 'Unascertained Goods: Ownership and Obligation Distinguished' (1994) 110 L.Q.R. 509
McLachlin, B.M., 'The Place of Equity and Equitable Doctrines in the Contemporary Common Law World: A Canadian Perspective' in Waters, *Equity, Fiduciaries and Trusts 1993* (1993) at p. 37
McLean, H.M., 'Limitation of Actions in Restitution' (1989) 48 C.L.J. 472
Mead, G., 'Free Acceptance: Some Further Considerations' (1989) 105 L.Q.R. 460
Meagher, R.P., and Gummow, W.M.C., *Jacobs' Law of Trusts in Australia*, 5th edn. (Sydney, 1986)
Meagher, R.P., Gummow, W.M.C., and Lehane, J.R.F., *Equity: Doctrines and Remedies*, 3rd edn. (Sydney, 1992)
Mee, J. (1993), 'Trusts of the Family Home: The Irish Experience' [1993] Conv. 359
—— (1995), 'Undue Influence, Misrepresentation and the Doctrine of Notice' (1995) 54 C.L.J. 536
Megarry, R.E. (1941), 'The Statute of Uses and the Power to Devise' (1941) 7 C.L.J. 354
—— (1955), 'Mere Equities, the Bona Fide Purchaser and the Deserted Wife' (1955) 71 L.Q.R. 480
Megarry, R.E., and Wade, H.W.R., *The Law of Real Property*, 5th edn. (London, 1984)
Millett, P.J. (1985), 'The Quistclose Trust: Who Can Enforce It?' (1985) 101 L.Q.R. 269
—— (1991), 'Tracing the Proceeds of Fraud' (1991) 107 L.Q.R. 71; reprinted in Goldstein, *Equity and Contemporary Legal Developments* (1992) at p. 407
—— (1993), 'Bribes and Secret Commissions' [1993] R.L.R. 7
—— (1995a), Review of A. Burrows, *The Law of Restitution* (1995) 111 L.Q.R. 517
—— (1995b), 'Equity—the Road Ahead' (1995) 9 T.L.Int. 35
Milsom, S.F.C., *Historical Foundations of the Common Law*, 2nd edn. (London, 1981)
Morgan, E.M., 'Presumptions' (1937) 12 Wash.L.Rev. 255
Moriarty, S. (1986), Review of P. Birks, *An Introduction to the Law of Restitution* (1986) 45 C.L.J. 128
—— (1995), 'Tracing, Mixing and Laundering' in Birks, *Laundering and Tracing* (1995) at p. 73
Morris, M.L., 'Rediscovering the Resulting Trust: Modern Maneuvers for a Dated Doctrine?' (1983) 17 Akron L.Rev. 43
Mowbray, W.J., *Lewin on Trusts*, 16th edn. (London, 1964)
Neave, M., 'Three Approaches to Family Property Disputes—Intention/Belief, Unjust Enrichment or Unconscionability' in Youdan, *Equity, Fiduciaries and Trusts* (1989) at p. 247
Neave, M., and Weinberg, M., 'The Nature and Function of Equities' (1978–9) 6 U.Tas.L.Rev. 24 and 115
Nolan, R. (1994), 'Targeting Trustees—Liability for Breach of Trust' (1994) 53 C.L.J. 450
—— (1995), 'Change of Position' in Birks, *Laundering and Tracing* (1995) at p. 135
Norman, H., 'Tracing the Proceeds of Crime—an Inequitable Solution?' in Birks, *Laundering and Tracing* (1995) at p. 95

OAKLEY, A.J. (1987), *Constructive Trusts*, 2nd edn. (London, 1987)

—— (1992), 'The Precise Effect of the Imposition of a Constructive Trust' in Goldstein, *Equity and Contemporary Legal Developments* (1992) at p. 427

—— (1994), *Parker and Mellows: The Modern Law of Trusts*, 6th edn. (London, 1994)

—— (1995), 'Proprietary Claims and their Priority in Insolvency' (1995) 54 C.L.J. 377

OCKELTON, M., 'Share and Share Alike?' (1994) 53 C.L.J. 448

O'CONNOR, P., 'Happy Partners or Strange Bedfellows: the Blending of Remedial and Institutional Features in the Evolving Constructive Trust' (1996) 20 Mel.U.L.Rev. 735

ODITAH, F., 'Assets and the Treatment of Claims in Insolvency' (1992) 108 L.Q.R. 459

OOSTERHOFF, A.H., and GILLESE, E.E., *Text, Commentary and Cases on Trusts*, 4th edn. (Toronto, 1992)

PACIOCCO, D.M., 'The Remedial Constructive Trust: A Principled Basis for Priority over Creditors' (1989) 68 C.B.R. 315

PALMER, G.E., *The Law of Restitution* (Boston, 1978–95)

PALMER, N., and MCKENDRICK, E., *Interests in Goods* (London, 1993)

PARKINSON, P. (1993), 'Beyond *Pettkus* v. *Becker*: Quantifying Relief for Unjust Enrichment' (1993) 43 U.T.L.J. 217

—— (ed.) (1996), *The Principles of Equity* (Sydney, 1996)

PETTIT, P.H. (1989), 'Farewell Section 40' [1989] Conv. 431

—— (1993), *Equity and the Law of Trusts*, 7th edn. (London, 1993)

PHANG, A. 'The Uses of Unconscionability' (1995) 111 L.Q.R. 559

POUND, R., GRISWOLD, E.N., and SUTHERLAND, A.E. (eds.) *Perspectives of Law: Essays for Austin Wakeman Scott* (Boston, 1964)

PRIESTLY, L.J., 'The Romalpa Clause and the Quistclose Trust' in Finn, *Equity and Commercial Relationships* (1987) at p. 217

RANDALL, A.E., *Story's Commentaries on Equity Jurisprudence*, 3rd English edn. (London, 1920)

Restatement, see American Law Institute, above

RICKETT, C.E.F. (1980), 'Unincorporated Associations and their Dissolution' (1980) 39 C.L.J. 88

—— (1989), 'Mutual Wills and the Law of Restitution' (1989) 105 L.Q.R. 534

—— (1990), 'Trust or Tort? Tort and Trust? Some Questions about Civil Liability' [1990] N.Z. Recent L. 259

—— (1991), 'Different Views on the Scope of the Quistclose Analysis: English and Antipodean Insights' (1991) 107 L.Q.R. 608

—— (1992), 'Loans for Purposes: Implied Contract, Express Trust or Pure Unjust Enrichment?' [1992] L.M.C.L.Q. 3

—— (1993), 'Trusts and Insolvency: The Nature and Place of the Quistclose Trust' in Waters, *Equity, Fiduciaries and Trusts 1993* (1993) at p. 325

RICKETT, C.E.F., and ZOHRAB, P., 'Trusteeship and Proprietary Remedies—Let the Banker Beware!' [1991] N.Z. Recent L. 202

RIDDALL, J.G., *The Law of Trusts*, 4th edn. (London, 1992)

ROSE, F.D., 'Restitution for the Rescuer' (1989) 9 O.J.L.S. 167

SARMAS, L. (1994a), 'Storytelling and the Law: a Case Study of *Lowth* v. *Diprose*' (1994) 19 Mel.U.L.Rev. 701

—— (1994b), 'A Step in the Wrong Direction: the Emergence of Gender "Neutrality" in the Equitable Presumption of Advancement' (1994) 19 Mel.U.L.Rev. 758

SCANE, R.E., 'Relationships "Tantamount to Spousal", Unjust Enrichment and Constructive Trusts' (1991) 70 C.B.R. 260

SCOTT, A.W. (1917), 'The Nature of the Rights of the Cestui Que Trust' (1917) 17 Col.L.Rev. 269

—— (1949), 'The Fiduciary Principle' (1949) 37 Cal.L.Rev. 539

SCOTT, A.W., and FRATCHER, W.F., *The Law of Trusts*, 4th edn. (Boston, 1989)

SCOTT, S.R., 'The Constructive Trust and the Recovery of Advance Payments' (1991) 14 N.Z.U.L. Rev. 375

SEALY, L.S. (1962), 'Fiduciary Relationships' [1962] C.L.J. 69

—— (1963), 'Some Principles of Fiduciary Obligation' [1963] C.L.J. 119

SEAVEY, W.A., and SCOTT, A.W., 'Restitution' (1938) 54 L.Q.R. 29

SHEPHERD, J.C., 'Towards a Unified Concept of Fiduciary Relationships' (1981) 97 L.Q.R. 51

SHERIDAN, L.A., *Keeton and Sheridan's The Law of Trusts*, 12th edn. (Chichester, 1993)

SHERWIN, E.L., 'Constructive Trusts in Bankruptcy' [1989] U.Ill.L.Rev. 297

SIMPSON, A.W.B. (1986), *A History of the Land Law*, 2nd edn. (Oxford, 1986)

—— (1987), *A History of the Common Law of Contract* (Oxford, 1987)

SMART, P.S.J., 'Holding Property for Non-Charitable Purposes: Mandates, Conditions and Estoppels' [1987] Conv. 415

SMITH, J.C., '*Lister* v. *Stubbs* and the Criminal Law' (1994) 110 L.Q.R. 180

SMITH, L.D. (1991), 'Three-Party Restitution: A Critique of Birks's Theory of Interceptive Subtraction' (1991) 11 O.J.L.S. 481

—— (1992), 'The Province of the Law of Restitution' (1992) 71 C.B.R. 672

—— (1994), *Tracing, Property and Restitution* (Oxford D.Phil. thesis, 1994)

—— (1995), 'Tracing into the Payment of a Debt' (1995) 54 C.L.J. 290

STEVENS, D. (1989), 'Restitution, Property and the Cause of Action in Unjust Enrichment: Getting by with Fewer Things' (1989) 39 U.T.L.J. 258 and 325

—— (1994), 'Restitution—Compulsion: *Peel (RM)* v. *The Queen*' (1994) 73 C.B.R. 84

STEVENS, J., 'Dishonest Assistance' [1995] R.L.R. 105

STOLJAR, S.J. (1987a), *The Law of Quasi-Contract*, 2nd edn. (Sydney, 1987)

—— (1987b), 'Unjust Enrichment and Unjust Sacrifice' (1987) 50 M.L.R. 603

STONE, H.F., 'Resulting Trusts and the Statute of Frauds' (1906) 6 Col.L.Rev. 326

STOWE, H., 'The "Unruly Horse" has Bolted: *Tinsley* v. *Milligan*' (1994) 57 M.L.R. 441

SWADLING, W. (1994a), 'Restitution for No Consideration' [1994] R.L.R. 73

—— (1994b), 'Some Lessons from the Law of Torts' in Birks, *The Frontiers of Liability*, vol. 1 (1994) at p. 41

—— (1994c), 'Restitution' [1994] All E.R.Rev. 349

—— (1996), 'A New Role for Resulting Trusts?' (1996) 16 Leg.St. 110

THOMPSON, M.P., 'Priorities in Registered Land' [1988] Conv. 453

TORY, J.C., 'Informally Created Interests in Land' (1981) 39 U.T.Fac.L.Rev. 55

TYLER, E.L.G., 'The Presumption of Advancement in Relation to Personalty' (1966) 30 Conv. 223

VINTER, E., *A Treatise on the History and Law of Fiduciary Relationships and Resulting Trusts* (Cambridge, 1955)

VIRGO, G., 'Restitution of Overpaid Tax—Justice at the Expense of Certainty' (1993) 52 C.L.J. 31

WADE, H.W.R., 'Husband and Wife—Deserted Wife's Right to Matrimonial Home—Equitable Interests and "Mere Equities"' (1955) 13 C.L.J. 158
WARBURTON, J. (1985), 'The Holding of Property by Unincorporated Associations' [1985] Conv. 318
—— (1988), 'Resulting Trusts—Your Flexible Friend' [1988] Conv. 361
WATERS, D.W.M. (1964), *The Constructive Trust* (London, 1964)
—— (1970), 'The Doctrine of Resulting Trusts in Common Law Canada' (1970) 16 McGill L.J. 187
—— (1984), *Law of Trusts in Canada*, 2nd edn. (Toronto, 1984)
—— (1988), 'Where is Equity Going?' (1988) 18 U.W.A.L.Rev. 3
—— (1992), 'The Constructive Trust in Evolution: Substantive and Remedial' in Goldstein, *Equity and Contemporary Legal Developments* (1992) at p. 457
—— (1993) (ed.), *Equity, Fiduciaries and Trusts 1993* (Toronto, 1993)
—— (1994), 'The Nature of the Remedial Constructive Trust' in Birks, *The Frontiers of Liability*, vol. 2 (1994) at p. 165
WATTS, P. (1990), 'Restitution' [1990] N.Z. Recent L. 330
—— (1994), 'Bribes and Constructive Trusts' (1994) 110 L.Q.R. 178
—— (1995), 'Restitution—a Property Principle and a Services Principle' [1995] R.L.R. 49
WEINRIB, E.J., 'The Fiduciary Obligation' (1975) 25 U.T.L.J. 1
WHITE, P.D., 'The Illusion of the Mere Equity' (1967) 5 Syd.L.Rev. 499
WIGHTMAN, J., 'Reviving Contract' (1989) 52 M.L.R. 115
WINDER, W.H.D. (1939), 'Undue Influence and Coercion' (1939) 3 M.L.R. 97
—— (1940), 'Undue Influence and Fiduciary Relationship' (1940) 4 Conv. (N.S.) 274
WINFIELD, P.H., *The Province of the Law of Tort* (Cambridge, 1931)
WORTHINGTON, S., 'Proprietary Restitution—Void, Voidable and Uncompleted Contracts' (1995) 9 T.L.Int. 113
WRIGHT, LORD, '*Sinclair* v. *Brougham*' (1938) 6 C.L.J. 305
YOUDAN, T.G. (1984), 'Formalities for Trusts of Land and the Doctrine in *Rochefoucauld* v. *Boustead*' (1984) 43 C.L.J. 306
—— (1988), 'Informal Trusts and Third Parties: A Response' [1988] Conv. 267
—— (1989a) (ed.), *Equity, Fiduciaries and Trusts* (Toronto, 1989)
—— (1989b), 'The Fiduciary Principle: The Applicability of Proprietary Remedies' in Youdan, *Equity, Fiduciaries and Trusts* (1989) at p. 93
—— (1992), 'Equitable Transformations of Family Property Law' in Goldstein, *Equity and Contemporary Legal Developments* (1992) at p. 517
—— (1993), 'Resulting and Constructive Trusts' [1993] Lectures L.S.U.C. 169
ZIFF, B.H., *Principles of Property Law*, 2nd edn. (Toronto, 1996)
ZIMMERMANN, R., 'Unjustified Enrichment: the Modern Civilian Approach' (1995) 15 O.J.L.S. 403

Index